PRAISE FOR *AXIS OF R*

"The broader "Middle East" if we include Afghanistan North Africa and Iran has been in a state of war throughout the 21st century. It is a story of imperial war conquest resistance and blowback. And it's not over yet. None of the fires lit in 2001 and after have been extinguished and most are burning more fiercely than ever. A huge monster of bitterness hatred and alienation has been created which will haunt us and our children even yet unborn. Western policy has been worse than a crime it's been a blunder. Tim Anderson's epic study shows what a crime, what a blunder it has been. And how ugly the monster which now stalks the land. My land, your land, the whole of humanity. It is a must read."

—*GEORGE GALLOWAY,*
British politician, writer and broadcaster

"*Axis of Resistance* will take its place alongside the few books worth reading on how and by whom the flickering lights of the imperial twilight of 'the West' in the Middle East were finally extinguished."

—*DR. JEREMY SALT,*
Middle East historian, former professor
Melbourne University and Birkeit University

"An excellent book by an exceptional author and activist who understands well the shakers and makers of the region within the new world order shaped by rising global forces."

—*AMAL WAHDAN,*
Veteran Palestinian activist,
Al Quds / Jerusalem, Occupied Palestine

"For decades now Western understanding of the conflicts in the Middle East has been obfuscated by the effects of both intensive propaganda and ideology. Whether you agree or disagree with Anderson's arguments, *Axis of Resistance* is an important starting point for much needed soul searching, public debate and self-reflection by publics, academics and politicians. Such debate is essential if we are to rein in the West's imperial ambitions, which have caused so much suffering and destruction, and allow genuine independence for all the peoples of the Middle East. "

—DR PIERS ROBINSON
Organisation for Propaganda Studies
Former Professor of Politics, Society and Political Journalism at Sheffield University

"A refreshing analysis of West Asia's regional alliances that was pushed into existence by continuous Western hegemony. Dr. Tim provides a comprehensible flow to accentuate that the alliance amongst the Axis of Resistance nations has less to do with its religious identity and more to do with its principled independence, great capacity and independent political will."

—DR MARWA OSMAN
Lebanese academic, broadcaster and writer

AXIS OF RESISTANCE

Towards an Independent
Middle East

TIM ANDERSON

Clarity Press, Inc

© 2019 Tim Anderson
ISBN: 978-1-949762-16-7
EBOOK ISBN: 978-1-949762-17-4

In-house editor: Diana G. Collier
Cover: R. Jordan P. Santos

Infographics and photos including cover photo by Tim Anderson © 2019, except where noted

Cover photos:
Top: photos of the many Syrian soldier-martyrs from Duella, a southern suburb of Damascus
Bottom: children in the city of Deir Ezzor, after its liberation from DAESH, October 2017

ALL RIGHTS RESERVED: Except for purposes of review, this book may not be copied, or stored in any information retrieval system, in whole or in part, without permission in writing from the publishers.

Library of Congress Control Number:2019944962

Clarity Press, Inc.
2625 Piedmont Rd. NE, Ste. 56
Atlanta, GA. 30324 , USA
http://www.claritypress.com

TABLE OF CONTENTS

Acknowledgements	6

Part 1: Imperialism and Resistance
1. The Axis and the 'New Middle East'	11
2. Empires, Resistance and Self-Determination	19
3. Sanctions as Siege Warfare	34
4. Myth and Method in Studies of War	54

Part 2: Collapse of the Dirty War on Syria
5. The Dirty War Revisited	62
6. The Liberation of Aleppo	89
7. The US-Fighting-ISIS Deception: The Crime at Jabal al Tharda	107
8. WMD Take 2: Chemical Weapons in Syria	135
9. The Human Rights Industry in Humanitarian War	150
10. The Pseudo-Left and the 'Syrian Revolution'	200
11. Refugees as Weapons of War	212

Part 3: The West Asian Alliance
12. The Future of Palestine	232
13. Hezbollah and the Regional Resistance	278
14. Why Iran Matters	316
15. Towards West Asia	350

Part 4: Postscript
16. War, Solidarity and Abuse	355

Index	372

About the Author
Dr Tim Anderson is Director of the Centre for Counter Hegemonic Studies. He was for 20 years an academic in Political Economy at the University of Sydney and before that taught at several other Australian universities. He researches and writes on development, rights and self-determination in Latin America, the Asia-Pacific and the Middle East. He has published many dozens of articles in a range of academic books and journals. His most recent books are: Land and Livelihoods in Papua New Guinea (2015), The Dirty War on Syria (2016, in ten languages) and Countering War Propaganda of the Dirty War on Syria (2017).

Note on Sources and Method
I have used a wide variety of mostly English language sources. This is because I am thinking of other English speakers, to whom this book is mainly directed. I want them to be able to access relevant sources. I am also aware of the widespread western prejudice against Russian, Iranian, Arab and Latin American sources, but I use these as well. On occasion translations were needed, including of interviews in Middle East countries. However, I have used western and English language sources where possible, not because they are more reliable, but to characterise positions and to make use of common ground and admissions.

ACKNOWLEDGEMENTS

Axis of Resistance: towards an independent Middle East follows my 2016 book *The Dirty War on Syria*, and owes much to those who helped me begin studying the aggression against that remarkable country. Both books are written mostly in an academic style, where sources are provided for important facts and ideas. However, behind the academic style are briefings from many people who have helped me understand both detail and the big picture.

I would like to acknowledge and thank my Syrian friends, my teachers, who helped me gain some insight into their astonishing country and culture, as well as into the conflict. I can't mention all but have to at least mention Reme, Elham, Jasmine, Ahmed, Maram, Hanadi, Tania, Fawaz, Maher, Iyad, Samer, Mazen, Rana, Afraa and Mohammed. I also acknowledge the Syrian Islamic scholars, the late Sheikh Mohammed Said Ramadan al Bouti and dear Mufti Ahmad Badreddin Hassoun.

My understanding of the various forms of hybrid warfare in the Middle East also owes much to my study of and friends in Latin America, in recent decades.

I also wish to acknowledge and thank the publishers and translators of various editions of *The Dirty War on Syria*: Global Research (Montreal) and Michel Chossudovsky for the English version; Oktoberförlaget for the Swedish version (Det smutsiga kriget mot Syrien); ΚΟΚΚΙΝΗ ΟΡΧΗΣΤΡΑ and Panagiotis Karystinos for the Greek version (Ο ΒΡΩΜΙΚΟΣ ΠΟΛΕΜΟΣ ΕΝΑΝΤΙΑ ΣΤΗ ΣΥΡΙΑ); the Centre for Hegemonic Studies, Jose Manuel Chala LeBlanch and Marlene Obeid for the Spanish version (La Guerra Sucia contra Siria); Zambon Verlag for the Italian version (La Sporca Guerra contro La Siria); Forlagið Bókabúð for the Icelandic version (Stríðið gegn Sýrlandi); Liepsen Verlag, Herman Ploppa and Jochen Mitschka for the German version (Der Schmutzige Krieg gegen Syrien); Šahinpašić and Osman Softic for the Bosnian version (Nečasni rat protiv Sirije); the Islamic Republic News Agency and Ali

Shamsabadi for the Farsi version; and the Damascus Centre for Research and Studies, Hames Zrek and Nahed T. Hashem for the Arabic version.

For my wider research I also want to thank Amal, Salah, Aysar and Naji in Palestine; Marwa, Fouad, Zeinab, Ali M, Ali T, Aya, Nami, Firas and Hala in Lebanon; Sinan, Ghoufran, Nisreen, Sara, Hayat, Nidal, Nihad, Bouthaina, Tammam, Fares, Camille and Walid in Syria; Yusra, Thana and Ahmed in Iraq; and Fatima, Ali, Sharmine, Asadi, Majid, Gholamreza and Amirmohammad in the Islamic Republic of Iran. My apologies to those I may have inadvertently omitted.

Of course, none of these friends and teachers are to blame for any of my errors; of which there are, hopefully, only a few. As all authors must, I take responsibility for my own words.

Parts of some of these chapters have been published before, often at Global Research, American Herald Tribune and the Centre for Counter Hegemonic Studies. In each case material has been edited and updated for the book, along with the new material.

Tim Anderson
June 2019

Part I

Imperialism and Resistance

Chapter One

THE AXIS AND THE 'NEW MIDDLE EAST'

Iran, Iraq and Syria face common enemies together. Military leaders of Iran, Iraq and Syria meet in Damascus, March 2019. Photo by SANA.

In the series of 21st century wars in West Asia, initiated by Washington in the name of a 'New Middle East', resistance forces are prevailing. Like all imperial gambits before it the plan has been to subjugate the entire region – this one in the name of US-led 'freedom' – to secure privileged access to its tremendous resources and then dictate terms of access to all other players. On various pretexts Afghanistan and Iraq were invaded and Libya was destroyed. Washington made good use of its client states, Israel and Saudi Arabia, to divide and weaken the independent states and peoples. However, Israel's attempts to disarm the Lebanese resistance failed, huge Saudi- and Qatari-backed proxy wars against Syria and Iraq were eventually put down, the indigenous insurrection in Yemen cannot be defeated and the Islamic Republic of Iran, the centre of imperial obsession, remains strong.

The key to a definitive defeat of Washington's ambitions lies in greater regional integration of the resistance forces. That integration is led by Iran, the undisputed leader of an 'Axis of Resistance' to foreign domination and Zionist expansion. Tehran's position has less to do with its religious identity and more to do with its principled independence, great capacity and independent political will. Russia has become an important ally of this Axis but – because of its wider interests and its compromised relationship with Israel – we cannot regard it as a full member of the regional resistance. Yet Iran and the other Axis countries have formed an alliance with Russia, to frustrate Washington's regional ambition and preserve their own security (Naqqash 2019).

Iran's importance is seen through Tel Aviv's fear of Tehran 'at Israel's borders', and through Washington's obsessive jealousy at the Islamic Republic's regional influence. When Zionist analysts and think tanks warn of the danger of a 'widening Iranian corridor' or 'land bridge' from Tehran to Beirut (Debka 2018; Lappin 2018), they tell us that independent Arab and Muslim regional integration remains their great fear. There would be substantial benefits in such integration for the peoples of the region. However, imperialism wants to keep those peoples weak and divided. That reminds us why imperialism is such a great enemy of human society. It is also why, in the final stages of the failed war on Syria, the task of US occupation forces has been to block key border crossings between Iraq and Syria (Mylroie 2018). Such obstruction is unlikely to last.

This book, *Axis of Resistance: towards an independent Middle East*, follows my 2016 book *The Dirty War on Syria*, examining the end of the war on Syria and exploring wider elements of the regional conflict. Behind the particular histories there are three basic propositions.

First, there is a single – and an essentially colonial – war in the Middle East or West Asian region. This hybrid war drives each particular conflict, from Libya to Afghanistan, and has several features: propaganda offensives promoting the heroic role of a US-led coalition improbably delivering 'freedom' from a long line of supposed 'brutal dictators'; economic siege warfare through sanctions and blockades; terrorist proxy wars; direct invasions followed by military occupations; and repression through client state regimes. In 2006 the Bush administration called this project the 'New Middle East' (Condoleezza Rice in Bransten 2006). In 2009 Obama declared that it involved a 'new beginning' with Islam (Obama 2009). That marked a shift from direct invasions to greater use of sectarian, Saudi-style 'Islamist' proxy armies. Yet it seems these were as much mercenary militia as religious zealots.

The strategy of this regional war has been to destroy the independent states of the region, subjugate independent peoples and dominate the entire region. By this logic, resistance forces must be kept fragmented. Regardless of any specific pretext for each conflict, the wave of bloody aggression has a single aim: to secure privileged access to the region's resources and so dictate terms of access to Russia, China and any other outside power. The fact that other powers are subject to this jealous focus does not imply that they are themselves imperial powers, and that we are therefore witnessing inter-imperial rivalry. It simply demonstrates that would-be empires are always obsessed with the fear of the next large, potential rival.

Second, while the extraordinary pretexts for each war must be studied, with independent evidence, they cannot be fully understood separately. Each aggression forms part of a broader strategy. The separate wars can be seen most clearly with regard to the regional plan, and indeed the globalist ambitions of the patron.

Similarly, the resistance in particular countries can and should be studied, but their integration into the regional resistance remains critical to their success. No single independent state or people has the capacity to prevail against this onslaught. As Cuba's national hero Jose Marti said of the independent nations of Latin America in the late 19th century, facing both the Spanish and the rising North American empire: 'The trees must form ranks to keep the giant with seven-league boots from passing! ... we must move in lines as compact as the veins of silver that lie at the roots of the Andes' (Martí 1892). Small states and peoples cannot fight big powers alone; they must form a strong alliance.

Third, the resistance to foreign domination in each country, and regionally, is the historical outcome of particular forces. Resistance has a common character but no idealised personality. It is informed by different cultural and religious principles, historical circumstances and social formations. Yet the common defence is of popular self-determination and maintaining accountable social structures that serve broad social interests. In every circumstance imperial intervention is destructive of that accountability and those interests. So it is that, in the West Asian region, the Resistance combines secular-pluralist, Shi'a and Sunni Muslim, Christian, Druze, socialist, secular and Arab nationalist traditions. Notwithstanding the fact that organised resistance requires strong social structures, the primary contradiction of this struggle is not 'capitalism v socialism' but rather imperialism versus independence. No social gains can be built without an independent and locally accountable body politic; nor can they be defended in face of the sustained onslaught without strong regional coordination and collective action.

As with *The Dirty War on Syria*, this book addresses the myths created to advance the multiple wars and myths about the resistance. It also attempts some provisional history of the conflicts. The focus on resistance, I suggest, can help us understand and anticipate the defeat of great powers, something not really possible for those whose analysis begins and ends with power.

Once again, this book is written, not so much for those who are committed to western myths, as for those honest and curious people who engage with such myths. Once again I use reason, ethical principles and independent evidence, in the hope that this might construct and provide a useful resource.

I hope the book is a contribution to a broader group of independent histories of the US-led 21st century wars against the peoples of the Middle East or West Asia. Many such histories are necessary, in light of the intense propaganda which accompanies

The Axis and the 'New Middle East Policy'

each bloody conflict. Two decades of neo-colonial aggression against the Arab and Muslim peoples of the region have destroyed more than 2 million lives and have shattered many critical social structures. Yet the aggressors are unrepentant and there is, so far, no end in sight.

As a keen observer and student I firmly believe that the aggression can only be defeated by a united resistance bloc, such as has been foreshadowed by the Axis of Resistance. There is no contradiction between documenting the wars and holding such an opinion, as I explain when speaking of the myth of analytical 'neutrality', in chapter four.

The anatomy of this massive regional war and its multiple crimes must be documented and exposed. That it has not yet been well documented, in the western and English-speaking worlds, is due to the collapse of a critical, anti-war culture and a failure of western solidarity and internationalism.

I would put the reasons for that collapse in this way. First, an elite consensus has been forged amongst the imperial and former colonial powers, including both the realist and the liberal wings, that a globalised order must be enforced on the oil rich region. The realist approach presents self-interest in intervention more directly; the liberal approach presents an old-style 'civilising mission' with the contemporary language of human rights and democracy. It has to be admitted that the repeated stories of 'saving' foreign and hardly known peoples from their own states and societies has been a great success within western culture. That offer of a heroic self-image seduced most western liberals. Their vanity deceived them.

Second, and despite the range of popular media options opened up by the internet, there has been tight corporate and state media backing for that elite consensus. That is explained by ongoing control of this media by the same private financial-entrepreneurial groups that dominate western governments. To put it bluntly, and in the words of the late Salvador Allende of Chile, when he spoke of media reporting on Cuba in the early 1960s: 'they lie every minute of every day' (in Timossi 2007).

Well at least they do this while each war is in play. After Iraq and Libya were destroyed, the defence of those false pretexts was thought less important.

Third, such histories are lacking but necessary, because of the failure of western internationalism. With some honourable exceptions, many have found the pseudo revolutions and fabricated humanitarian pretexts for war quite attractive. It seems to appeal to what I have called a 'saviour complex' in the colonial cultures. The disengagement of western left-liberals from anti-war campaigns has weakened the field of critical writing and analysis.

This book is divided into four sections. Part 1 on 'Imperialism and Resistance' begins with this introduction, then turns to some broader reflections on self-determination and empires. There follows a chapter on the role of sanctions as a form of economic siege warfare, then a discussion on the myth of neutrality during war and some necessary elements of method in the study of war.

Part 2 'Collapse of the Dirty War on Syria' comprises a series of thematic essays on the final years of the war on Syria. It begins with some updated themes from my 2016 book, which addressed both the 'humanitarian' and the 'protective' intervention rationales of that dirty war. That includes an update of key evidence which shows that all the internationally proscribed terrorist groups in Syria and Iraq were backed by the US-led coalition, in attempts to destroy the independent Syrian state and to destabilise and weaken the new Iraqi state. There follows an account of the liberation of Aleppo, Syria's second city, which documents the pretexts used in attempts to block the Syrian Army from driving al Qaeda groups out of Syria's second city. 'The US-Fighting-ISIS Deception: DAESH and the Crime at Jabal al Tharda' draws on the author's firsthand investigation of a September 2016 massacre of Syrian soldiers in eastern Syria, in which the US coalition directly coordinated its attacks to assist the internationally banned terrorist group. The method of deciphering contemporary controversies, introduced in the first section, is applied to the protracted scandals over chemical weapon use in Syria in 'WMD take two', drawing parallels with the false pretexts of the 2003 Iraq invasion. A more detailed chapter on 'The Human Rights Industry in Humanitarian War', illustrated with examples from Syria, shows the use in hybrid war of embedded NGOs and other war propagandists. Particular attention is paid to the role of the corporate-NGOs Human Rights Watch and Amnesty International. The section concludes with reflections on left illusions about the so-called Syrian revolution, and the use of refugees as instruments of war propaganda.

Part 3 'The West Asian Alliance' introduces three other nations of the regional resistance: Palestine, Lebanon and Iran. 'The Future of Palestine' reviews the longstanding conflict generated by the Israeli colony which in recent decades has become an apartheid state. This chapter reviews the history, ideology and practice of the Zionist colony, and the achievements of the Palestinian resistance, before moving to an assessment of the prospects for a democratic Palestine, taking into account all obstacles and advantages. 'Hezbollah and the Regional Resistance' examines myths about the leading party of the Lebanese Resistance, in particular the accusations of sectarianism and terrorism, before explaining the rise of Hezbollah in Lebanon and its wider influence, particularly on the popular resistance in Iraq. 'Why Iran Matters' reviews the leading state of the Axis, charting its development from the 1979 Revolution and documenting its human development achievements and challenges. The constant and multi-faceted war against Iran helped drive this nation's emergence as the heart of the regional resistance. The section concludes with 'Towards West Asia', which sums up the prospects for an independent region no longer defined as the 'Middle East' of a Eurocentric world. That transition will require commitment, sacrifice and regional unity.

A final chapter tells the more personal story of this writer's own journey in documenting and defending other peoples. It is a reflection on free and independent expression in an abusive, colonial culture. Nevertheless that struggle is a necessary process for anyone who believes in understanding great conflicts, and in sharing those understandings with others.

Bibliography:

Anderson, Tim (2016) *The Dirty War on Syria,* Global Research, Montreal

Bransten, Jeremy (2006) 'Middle East: Rice Calls For A 'New Middle East'', Radio Free Europe ' Radio Liberty, 25 July, online: https://www.rferl.org/a/1070088.html

Debka (2018) 'Allowing Iran's land bridge to Syria – an Israeli mistake like ignoring Egyptian and Syrian 1973 war preparations', 17 September, online:https://www.debka.com/allowing-irans-land-bridge-to-syria-an-israeli-mistake-like-ignoring-egyptian-and-syrian-1973-incursions/

Lappin, Yaakov (2018) 'The danger of a widening Iranian corridor through Syria', Begin-Sadat Center for Strategic Studies, 24 December, online: https://besacenter.org/perspectives-papers/iranian-corridor-syria/

Martí, José (1892) 'Our America', El Partido Liberal, Mexico City, 5 March, online: http://www.historyofcuba.com/history/marti/America.htm

Mylroie, Laurie (2018) 'Shadowy battle over Iran's 'land bridge' continues', Kurdistan 24, 2 July, online: http://www.kurdistan24.net/en/news/d7ad6c6e-1dca-4ed8-bd80-f4f00503cf3e

Naqqash, Anis al (2019) 'Hezbollah-linked Analyst on reality of Russia's alliance with Iran/Hezbollah', Middle East Observer, 11 March, online: http://middleeastobserver.net/video-senior-analyst-close-to-hezbollah-on-reality-of-russian-alliance-with-iran-resistance-axis-english-subs/

Obama, Barack (2009) 'Text: Obama's Speech in Cairo - The New York Times', *New York Times*, 4 June, online: https://www.nytimes.com/2009/06/04/us/politics/04obama.text.html

Timossi, Jorge (2007) *Fascismos Paralelos : El Golpe de Estado en Chile*, Ocean Sur, La Habana

Chapter Two

EMPIRES, RESISTANCE AND SELF-DETERMINATION

> *"All peoples have the right to self-determination. By virtue of that right they freely determine their political status and freely pursue their economic, social and cultural development."*
>
> Article 1, International Covenant on Civil and Political Rights, 1966

Human beings are extraordinarily social creatures. We raise our children far longer than those of any other species. It takes years for human children to walk, talk and feed themselves. Contemporary systems of formal education require at least ten years and often much more. The social structures for this education, along with those for security, health, housing and other forms of social support, are constructed with regard to physical and cultural circumstances. Even in ancient societies we see much evidence of the sharing of knowledge in areas of engineering, astronomy, agriculture, mathematics, religion and health including surgery. Much of our applied technology, for example types of housing, water use and crop storage, is quite specific to particular circumstances. All of this is to say that social organisation begins for functional reasons, which have to do with support for and reproduction of human society, which later becomes dysfunctional through class formation, feudalism and imperialism.

Non-Aligned Summit in Venezuela, 2016. The Non Aligned Movement of 120 countries has always stressed self-determination and non-intervention. Photo by Telesur

This social character of human society – along with its structures and achievements – is why invasions by outside groups, generally to seize control of resources and land, are so destructive. Apart from bringing conflict, death and destruction, these interventions damage social structures and accountability mechanisms. Yet like colonies of ants or bees, human societies rebuild these structures after the foreign body has been expelled. A foreign occupation, without local accountability, can never do this. We saw this damage in the imperial era, when great powers imposed colonial structures to serve their own interests. There was no such thing, for example, as mass education in British colonial India, until the empire was forced to leave. Empires have long brutalised and degraded entire populations and that is why they have been resisted everywhere.

So what is the character of imperialism and of the resistance? In the simplest of terms, empires are anti-social projects of aggression and domination. A variety of historically contingent resistance movements seek to resist foreign aggression and throw off foreign domination. As a result of those resistance struggles, in particular anti-colonial struggles, international law and norms of the late 20th century moved to reject colonial and neo-colonial interventions, and to recognise the right of peoples to self-determination.

1. Empires and Resistance

As a project which relentlessly seeks domination and the subjugation of entire regions, imperialism threatens the very core of human society. None of this is a mystery, or an esoteric truth. A human consensus rejected imperial domination and enshrined the right to self-determination at the very centre of the 20th century human rights project, 'apart from and before all of the other rights' (OHCHR 1984). That principle gained recognition from historic struggles against past empires.

Yet imperialism survives, indeed thrives, and in contemporary doublespeak is often said to have left a legacy of civilisation, culture and order. Bureaucrats and other imperial devotees have romanticised the achievements of Roman and Napoleonic law, lauding the monumental gifts of the British imperial project while ignoring the dreadful legacy of mass illiteracy, slavery, famine and genocide. These days, along with their projects of conquest and selective disarmament, imperial powers claim to be the guarantors of prosperity and freedom, even at times the champions of popular revolution and emancipation.

Just as the British Raj pretended to be the protector of Indian women, opposing the practice of 'sati' or widow burning, a century later a 'North Atlantic' (NATO) occupation force in Afghanistan presented itself as the defender of Afghan women. Of course, the NATO states did not invade that small country out of any concern for women's rights. Nor were women's rights advanced by the military occupation. In fact, very few women in subjugated societies ever had the chance to go to school, and so start on the path to self-empowerment. The literacy rate for adult women in India, just a few years after independence, in 1951, was only 9% (PIB 2008). Colonisers rarely had an interest in such things.

By the late 20th century, when the ideas of colonisation and imperialism had become unfashionable, new names were given to projects of domination. Imperialism was said to have disappeared while a stabilising and benevolent 'hegemony' aided 'global governance'. Foreign predations came through privatizations, later termed 'partnerships' (Tabb 2007). Humanitarian interventions by an 'international community' were made in response to alleged popular demand. The great protector had re-emerged while it was said that imperialism, in an age of supposed liberty and democracy, had ceased to exist.

How has that claim been justified? The era of European colonies had supposedly ended, and that was often said to be the end of imperialism. Yet there were accusations of ongoing 'economic imperialism' or neo-colonialism through the power of giant corporations. This analysis was developed by critical liberals and neo-Marxists, even though it was countered with 'economic' claims of diffuse 'market forces' (Ould-May 1996: 14). While European historians took the question seriously, liberalism had historically taken two different positions. The first, represented by the English liberal John Stuart Mill, backed the notion of the 'civilising mission' of empire:

> Colonisation ... is the best affair of business in which the capital of an old and wealthy country can engage ... the same rules of international morality do not apply ... between civilised nations and barbarians ... [the British Empire provides] a great advantage to mankind (Mill in Sullivan 1983).

Today's imperialism is also seen as a way of vindicating the earlier empires. This view has been resurrected and conscripted in the service of the 21st century humanitarian interventions.

The second and more radical liberal view, spelt out by John Hobson, was anti-imperial, arguing that it was driven by and benefited some special interest groups but attracted greater costs for British international relations and business interests (Hobson 1902). That critical tradition, if subordinate in British liberalism, persists today.

A distinctly North American view of imperialism was formed in the 1970s, in response to constant criticism of US imperialism, especially of Washington's regular interventions in Latin America (Blum 2008; McPherson 2016). Unlike the Europeans, Washington had always denied having had colonies, or an empire. The notion of a 'benevolent hegemon' was formed to justify the 'exceptional' role claimed for itself by the USA. The world was in need of a unique powerful state, a type of benevolent dictator, to secure the world order and provide 'public goods' to other nations, such as security, a stable currency exchange and mechanisms of 'free trade'. This Hegemonic Stability Theory (Kindleberger 1976; Keohane 1982) was used, after the demise of the bipolar world, to back the claimed need for a 'single superpower', and for a New World Order (Engelhardt 2014). This was a theory of benign imperialism, using another name.

Left traditions took imperialism more seriously. Neo-Marxists in the 20th century pointed to the role of giant corporations in driving imperial interventions in the interests of domination. Lenin observed that competition between the European empires drove war, and that the big banks were engaged in the 'financial strangulation' of the world:

> economically imperialism – or the era of finance capitalism – is the highest stage in the development of [monopoly] capitalism ... [which] has grown into a world system of colonial oppression and financial strangulation of the overwhelming majority of the people of the world by a handful of 'advanced' countries (Lenin 1916).

Imperialism was identified with the export of excess capital. Later neo-Marxists (Karl Marx himself did not write much about imperialism) spoke of 'monopoly power' as a means of siphoning off a surplus generated from labour and resources in the many 'peripheral' countries, into the financial centres of New York and London (Baran and Sweezy 1966; Frank 1967). These were useful contributions. However, because empires as large political projects developed over time, and had existed for millennia, it seems too crude to simply equate the export of capital with imperialism.

The current status of the USA, the greatest capital importer of all time (IMF 2018) yet maintaining 'nearly 800 military bases in more than 70 countries and territories' (Vine 2015), serves to illustrate this point. The world's most highly armed, aggressive and expansionist state became the greatest capital importer. Similarly, the foreign investment power of contemporary China does not automatically make that large nation an empire, in any traditional sense. As imperialism existed well before contemporary capitalism, we cannot begin and end with simple 'economic' definitions. There are common traditional features which we cannot ignore.

The empires themselves acknowledge these common features: the wish to dominate entire regions, subjugate peoples, gain (at the least) privileged access to the resources of those regions (Ahmed 2014; Ward 2019). These projects were rarely in the interest of just one industry or one commercial operation, but rather of large groups, clustered around a powerful state. In Marxist terminology, it is said the dominant state acts in the interest of the ruling class 'as a whole', rather than in any particular or immediate class interest. In other words, these large political projects involve substantial planning and look for a 'return' in the longer term. Necessary imperial strategy includes dividing the peoples of the target region, so that they cannot combine to build a strong resistance. This 'divide and rule' doctrine was borrowed by the British Empire from the Roman Empire (Tharoor 2017). In a similar way, the imperial ambitions of Nazi Germany in the mid-20th century emulated aspects of the British Empire, including its racial theories and 'divide and rule' strategies (Strobl 2000). The domination and control of entire regions necessarily requires the exclusion of other great powers. That is well understood, and forms part of north American 'Hegemonic Stability Theory'.

A common feature of empires has been their efforts to degrade the image of the target populations, often with theories of supposed racial inferiority. Indeed, the root of substantial and material racism can be traced back to imperial and colonial histories (Pieterse 1989; Rex 1973). Contemporary historians who romanticise the contributions of empires pay little attention to the contributions of the colonised cultures (e.g. Ferguson 2004), no matter how long they survived and flourished.

Even into the 21st century many European 'modernisers' maintain the false claim that traditional systems of land tenure and land care (powerful protectors of community food security and cultural integrity) were at the root of the poverty of dispossessed peoples (Hughes 2004). These poor understandings mimic those of the conqueror of ancient Gaul, Julius Caesar. He recognised the Druid religious class of Celtic Europe, and the extent of their studies. However, he focussed mainly on the martial achievements of the Gauls in France, wrongly believing that these people had 'no zeal' for agriculture and that women had low status in Gallic society (Caesar 2006: 102-107). The reverse was the case. Agriculture was often very well developed in traditional societies; and women generally had lower status in militaristic imperial cultures.

Distorted imperial histories should prompt us to rethink the contributions of those subordinate societies, as also the claims made for the contributions of imperial cultures. Of what use were the latter, even to the inhabitants of their own metropolis? Imperial Rome buried the conquered towns, seized resources, and copied, ignored or denied the science and technologies of conquered cultures. The pyramids of Egypt, regarded as symbols of a great civilisation, represented forced labour and crippling taxes to most ordinary Egyptians of that time. Peasant families 'wavered between abject poverty and utter destitution' (Wilkinson 2010: 364-365). Alexander the Great's conquests, built on appalling slaughter, delivered little of human value. While he became 'a benchmark for every conqueror since', the empire he built 'collapsed the moment he was gone ... [and the main] work he wrought was destruction' (Grainger 2007: 102). Yet many contemporary societies lionise Alexander the Great. In each case the simple truth was, the sooner these emperors were dead or disgraced and their armies scattered, the sooner millions of human beings could breathe easy, free of fear and relentless bloodshed.

If empires are projects of domination, how can we characterise the resistance? Comparative studies show a variety of forms but some common features. We could say that resistance has a historically contingent personality but a more universal character.

The Cuban Revolution drew on 19th century humanism and united front anti-imperialism, making central the commitment to public education and public health, while seeking regional alliances with other Latin American states. Venezuela after two centuries carried the mantle of Bolivar, with the aim of unifying the Americas. In Iran, after the social democratic opposition was crushed by a US-backed dictatorship in the 1950s, the principal resistance and central force of the 1979 Revolution came through the mosques. Syria maintained a secular, Pan-Arab current, where 'secular' meant a commitment to community and religious pluralism. Meanwhile the Palestine resistance has drawn on secular, socialist and Islamic traditions.

Despite this diversity of form, resistance to imperialism does share a common character. First, it must develop an organised strategy to resist the particular threat it faces. Second, successful resistance movements must build sufficiently strong social structures both to survive imperial assault and to support the resistance peoples. This requires organisation and unity; it is not a task for an individualistic or consumer driven society. Third, there is the need to encourage social participation, including at the emotional, artistic and material levels. A participatory society is necessary to develop strong social bonds and capabilities. Opposing the oppressive project forges such qualities. As the Mexican socialist Angel Guerra Cabrera wrote:

> The aggression of foreign powers gives revolutionary people the opportunity to raise their political consciousness and self-esteem, increase their willingness and the culture of resistance and test their ability to defeat powerful enemies (Guerra Cabrera 2019).

2. Self Determination

In the post-colonial era, the principle of the self-determination of peoples was finally recognised in international law. This was not the clever idea of some individual or group but rather the result of centuries of common struggle against domination and colonialism.

By the 1960s the United Nations had become increasingly populated by states representing the former colonies. The influence of their voices – reflecting a broader and more inclusive representation of humanity than the those of the former colonial powers – grew in the construction of international human rights agreements. The weight of the former colonies helped forge some crucial shifts in emphasis. The most important of these was the creation of the right to self-determination. That term had been applied before to nations, but not to peoples. It did not form part of the 1948 Universal Declaration of Human Rights.

The turning point came in December 1960, when the General Assembly passed Resolution 1514, the Declaration on Decolonisation (UNGA 1960). A powerful consensus behind this declaration demanded an end to centuries of colonisation. Article one of Resolution 1514 began:

> The subjection of peoples to alien subjugation, domination and exploitation constitutes a denial of fundamental human rights, being contrary to the United Nations Charter and an impediment to the promotion of world peace and cooperation.

The Declaration thus rejected 'alien subjugation', and went on to articulate self-determination as a right of all peoples, rejecting the 'inadequacy of political, economic, social or educational preparedness' as a reason for delaying decolonisation, condemning the armed repression of dependent peoples struggling for independence, opposing attempts to disrupt 'the national unity or territorial integrity of a country' and calling for processes to deliver a free and independent political voice to all peoples. An important force behind this drive was the Non-Aligned Movement, an international coalition made up of former colonies.

Eighty-nine countries voted for the Declaration on Decolonisation, none voted against but nine abstained (Australia, Belgium, Dominican Republic, France, Portugal, Spain, Union of South Africa, United Kingdom, United States of America). This latter group included all the major colonial powers (Emerson 1971: 459). In other words, the declaration was forced on the colonial powers and, while they refused to support it, they felt ashamed to oppose it.

The Declaration on Decolonisation articulated the phrase

that would be adopted, word-for-word, as Article One of each of the twin Covenants of the International Bill of Rights, six years later: 'All peoples have the right to self-determination. By virtue of that right they freely determine their political status and freely pursue their economic, social and cultural development' (OHCHR 2007).

The body interpreting these rights would later call self-determination an 'essential condition' for the guarantee and promotion of all other rights, standing 'apart from and before all the other rights' in the Covenants. One important consequence was that 'states must refrain from interfering in the internal affairs of other states' so as not to compromise this right (OHCHR 1984). This reasoning remains important in an age where imperial culture promotes wars in the name of 'human rights interventions'. In the wealthy countries, non-interference in the sovereign affairs of other countries came to be seen as a barrier to intervention. However, in the developing countries, most of which are former colonies, it is seen as the cornerstone of human rights. The 118 member Non Aligned Movement repeatedly cites sovereignty and non-intervention as key and founding principles (Willetts 1978).

Indigenous peoples – colonised minorities who had had no say in state formation and were unable to assert full independence – also raised their voices and demands around this new principle (Lam 1992). While certain groups had secured some rights from the colonial powers, they also asserted rights from the pre-colonial order, including the right to define their own identity and existence (Daes 2008: 8-13). The principle had thus spread beyond its anticipated bounds, threatening to empower the most marginalised of groups.

Self-determination, which demanded a voice for 'the wretched of the earth' (Fanon 1961), had become the great and dangerous idea of the twentieth century, just as the ideas of Darwin, Ricardo and Marx had endangered privilege in the previous century. This right to self-determination became, in the 20th century, a tool for colonial peoples seeking independence, newly independent nations reaching for political-economic autonomy and indigenous peoples seeking self-governance and redress for dispossession of their lands and cultures.

The process continued, into the new international order. In the wake of the collapse of the Soviet Union into several states, and just as the imperial powers were seizing control of the UN Security Council, the UN General Assembly proclaimed an 'International Decade for the Eradication of Colonialism' (1990-2000). This was immediately followed by a 'Second International Decade for the Eradication of Colonialism' (2001-2010). Decolonisations proceeded into the 21st century (e.g. Timor Leste), along with the maintenance of a decolonisation list.

In some countries new forms of indigenous self-government emerged, while others began to recognise inalienable indigenous rights to land, in an era of otherwise barely restrained commodification. The process was full of contradictions. For example, while the small island states of the South West Pacific gained their independence, a growing recourse to interventionism against them as 'failed' states took place. This was despite their remarkably successful processes of state-building, without the violence and coercion that had characterised European state and empire formation (Wesley-Smith 2007).

Of course, there are limits to human rights protocols and arguments. All new ideas are subject to transformation or capture by powerful interests, even when the ideas are emancipatory. Recognition of the value of such ideas requires social education and conscience building; the more so when imperial newspeak represents bombardment as 'liberation' and corporate privilege as 'economic reform'. A constant struggle is required to distinguish emancipatory processes from the privileged set of property, market and franchise rights demanded by despots and the great powers. Yet this struggle is aided by conflicts between the growing body of accepted and universal formal rights, on the one hand, and the wildly uneven and contradictory local outcomes on the other. Such contradictions bring new life to the notion of self-determination.

This chapter has outlined some themes of relevance to the book. Human beings, I suggest, are highly social and need accountable social structures. Yet those structures and processes are targeted by foreign interventions. Imperialism is a well organised project led by a strong state which aims to dominate entire regions and their peoples, with the aim of assuming privileged control over resources, including the ability to determine the terms of access of all others. In face of this, resistance has a historically contingent personality, which depends on its material and cultural circumstances, but also a common character, which requires strong organisation, social structures of resistance and mutual support, and participatory mechanisms. The act of organised resistance is, in itself, constitutive of this character. The right to self-determination, developed in the post-colonial period of the late 20th century, has effectively outlawed imperialism and colonialism. Yet both persist, through deceptive pretexts which seek to perpetuate aggressive wars for the purpose of domination, and to that end manufacture disinformation and evade international norms.

Bibliography:

Ahmed, Nafeez (2014) 'Iraq invasion was about oil', *The Guardian*, 21 March, online: https://www.theguardian.com/environment/earth-insight/2014/mar/20/iraq-war-oil-resources-energy-peak-scarcity-economy

Baran, Paul and Paul Sweezy (1966) *Monopoly Capital*, Monthly Review Press, New York

Blum, William (2008) *Killing Hope: U.S. Military and C.I.A. Interventions Since World War II*, Common Courage Press, Monroe (Maine)

Caesar, Julius (2006) *The Gallic War*, Dover, New York, Book VI (53BC)

Daes, Erica-Irene A. (2008) 'An overview of the history of indigenous peoples: self-determination and the United Nations', *Cambridge Review of International Affairs*, Vol 21, 13 August, online: https://www.tandfonline.com/doi/abs/10.1080/09575570701828386

Emerson, Rupert (1971) 'Self-Determination', 65 *Am. J. Int'l L.* 459

Engelhardt, Tom (2014) *Shadow Government: Surveillance, Secret Wars, and a Global Security State in a Single-Superpower World*, Haymarket Books, Chicago

Fanon, Franz (1961) *The Wretched of the Earth*, Grove Press, New York

Ferguson, Niall (2004) *Colossus: The Price of America's Empire*, Allen lane, London

Frank, Andre Gunder (1967) *Capitalism and Underdevelopment in Latin America*, Monthly Review Press, New York

Grainger, John D. (2007) *Alexander the Great Failure: the Collapse of the Macedonian Empire*, Hambledon Continuum, London

Guerra Cabrera, Angel (2019) 'Goodbye, Guaidó', Resumen Latinoamericano, 14 march, online: https://www.resumen-english.org/2019/03/goodbye-guaido/ - original in Spanish at *La Jornada* here: https://www.jornada.com.mx/2019/03/14/opinion/024a1mun

Hobson, John (1902) *Imperialism: A Study*, James Pott and Company, New York

Hughes, Helen (2004) 'The Pacific is Viable!' CIS Issue Analysis 53, Centre for Independent Studies, Sydney, online: http://www.cis.org.au/publications/issue-analysis/the-pacific-is-viable/

IMF (2018) 'Tackling Global Imbalances amid Rising Trade Tensions', International Monetary Fund, July, online: https://www.imf.org/en/Publications/ESR/Issues/2018/07/19/2018-external-sector-report

Keohane, Robert (1982) 'The Demand for International Regimes', *International Organization*, Vol. 36, No. 2, International Regimes (Spring, 1982), pp. 325-355

Kindleberger, Charles (1976) 'Systems of International Economic Organization', in David Calleo, (ed) *Money and the Coming World Order*, New York University Press, New York

am, Maivan Clech (1992) "Making Room for Peoples at the United Nations: Thoughts Provoked by Indigenous Claims to Self-Determination," *Cornell International Law Journal:* Vol. 25: Iss. 3, Article 7. online: http://scholarship.law.cornell.edu/cilj/vol25/iss3/7

McPherson, Alan (2013) *A Short History of U.S. Interventions in Latin America and the Caribbean,* Wiley-Blackwell, Hoboken

OHCHR (1984) 'General Comment No. 12: The right to self-determination of peoples' (Art. 1), 13/03/84, The right to self-determination of peoples (Article 1) (Twenty-first session, 1984)

OHCHR (2007) International Covenant on Civil and Political Rights (Adopted and opened for signature, ratification and accession by General Assembly resolution 2200A (XXI) of 16 December 1966, entry into force 23 March 1976)

Ould-May, Mohameden (1996) *Global Restructuring and Peripheral States,* Littlefield Adams, Huber Heights OH (USA)

PIB (2008) 'Efforts to Eradicate Illiteracy in India', Press Information Bureau, Government of India, online: http://pib.nic.in/newsite/erelease.aspx?relid=42161

Pieterse, Jan (1989) *Empire and Emancipation: Power and Liberation on a World Scale,* Praeger, New York

Polanyi, Karl (1944) *The Great Transformation*, Farrar & Rinehart, New York

Rex, John (1973) *Race, Colonialism and the City*, Routledge, Abingdon (Oxfordshire)

Strobl, Gerwin (2000) *The Germanic Isle: Nazi Perceptions of Britain*, Cambridge University Press, Cambridge (UK)

Sullivan, Eileen P (1983) 'Liberalism and Imperialism: J. S. Mill's Defense of the British Empire,' *Journal of the History of Ideas*, Vol. 44, No. 4 (Oct. - Dec.), 599-617

Tabb, William K. (2007) 'Imperialism: In Tribute to Harry Magdoff', *Monthly Review*, 1 March, online: https://monthlyreview.org/2007/03/01/imperialism-in-tribute-to-harry-magdoff/

Tharoor, Shashi (2017) 'The Partition: The British game of 'divide and rule'', Al Jazeera, 10 August, online: https://www.aljazeera.com/indepth/opinion/2017/08/partition-british-game-divide-rule-170808101655163.html

UNGA (1960) 'Declaration on the Granting of Independence to Colonial Countries and Peoples', United Nations General Assembly, Resolution 1514 (XV)

Vine, David (2015) 'Where in the World Is the U.S. Military?', Politico, June/July, online: https://www.politico.com/magazine/story/2015/06/us-military-bases-around-the-world-119321

Ward, Alex (2019) 'Andrew McCabe claims Trump wanted war in Venezuela because "they have all that oil", Vox, 20 February, online: https://www.vox.com/world/2019/2/20/18233394/mccabe-trump-venezuela-war-oil-lawrence

Wesley-Smith, Terence (2007) 'Self-determination in Oceania', *Race and Class*, 48(3)

Wilkinson, Toby (2010) *The Rise and Fall of Ancient Egypt*, Bloomsbury, London

Willetts, Peter (1978) *The non-aligned movement: the origins of a Third World alliance*, F. Pinter, London

Chapter Three

SANCTIONS AS SIEGE WARFARE

WHO: West sanctions on Syria hitting children's cancer treatment, March 15, 2017.

EU claims food and medicines are exempt, but harsh financial sanctions on Syria block procurement. WHO says critical shortages of cancer medication, insulin, anaesthetics, antibiotics for intensive care, serums, intravenous fluids and other blood products and vaccines. Economic sanctions are often acts of aggression.

This chapter studies the persistent use of economic 'sanctions' as a measure of hybrid warfare, and so part of the composite aggression which includes malicious propaganda, economic siege, sabotage, terrorism and at times open warfare.

This discussion largely ignores the debate over whether sanctions achieved the 'foreign policy goals' of the USA. Such goals are almost entirely contrary to the post-1945 international order. As it happens, even though the unilateral US use of sanctions has expanded in recent decades (Carter 1987), studies have found them to be a 'success' in only 12% to 34% of cases (Pape 1998: 66). Washington insiders like Richard Hass admit that 'all too often sanctions ... hurt American economic interests without changing the target's behaviour for the better' (Haas 1998). All this has occurred in a period in which liberal trade and investment has been promoted through agencies such as the GATT/WTO and regional bodies. In these circumstances, the expansion of unilateral sanctions regimes is perhaps surprising, unless sanctions are understood as supplementary weapons of war.

In any case, this discussion keeps its focus on resistance to what is increasingly recognised as illegitimate economic aggression, and even great crimes. For this purpose the first question must be, what are legitimate 'sanctions' or economic reprisals, and where does illegitimate economic aggression begin? Next, what are the parameters of this siege warfare? Several dozen countries have been directly targeted, by the USA and by the European Union. Finally, what resistance strategies have been adopted by key targets such as Cuba, Iran, Syria and North Korea?

1. When do sanctions become warfare?

When does a simple refusal to engage in commercial relations (or 'an embargo') become aggression or siege warfare? There is some law on this question, but it is not strictly a legal matter. Questions of political legitimacy also arise.

In traditional international law there are two principles said to limit a state's retaliation against others: that the response should be 'in proportion' to an alleged action by the other; and that any reprisal only comes after attempts at negotiation (Shneyer and Barta 1981: 465). So for example, it is said that the initial US sanctions against Cuba (before the fuller measures imposed in 1962) could have been argued as justifiable counter-measures during the breakdown in negotiations over compensation for property nationalised in 1960-61 (White 2018: 8). Yet the later, stronger measures, with illegitimate political and coercive goals, breach a range of international laws.

As the US Office of Legal Counsel acknowledged in 1962 with regard to Washington's plan to launch a blockade of Cuba, the term 'blockade' has a special warlike meaning and "there is no such thing as a 'pacific blockade' or a 'blockade during time of peace'". It was, however, argued that a blockade might be justified 'to preserve the peace' (OLC 1962).

The US has maintained the softer term 'embargo' for its various economic measures against Cuba, to draw attention to the less aggressive sounding 'prohibitions on exports between one country and another'. Nevertheless, since 1962 the US measures have comprised an economic blockade, as they attempted to pressure the Cuban people and 'to control actions of third party states' (Shneyer and Barta 1981: 452). The tightening of this blockade in the 1990s has been described as a policy of imposing 'deliberate harm' (White 2018: 14).

Yet international law prohibits the exercise of economic coercion, by the principle of non-intervention and through an implied ban in the UN Charter. This is supplemented by customary and treaty law in areas such as trade, shipping and telecommunications. The illegality is more obvious when there is an 'unlawful intent', such as damaging the economy of another nation or retaliation for the purpose of political coercion (Shneyer and Barta 1981: 468, 471-475). Also illegal are measures which damage the rights of third parties. Unlawful aims, aggressive intent and damage to third parties can be seen throughout much of Washington's unilateral sanctions regimes.

However, given that sanctions against nations affect

entire populations, there is an additional question over their political legitimacy. Does the affected population 'consent' to the measures? This principle was respected in the process of building legitimate sanctions against the apartheid system in South Africa. It has particular force because political legitimacy pretexts (e.g. an alleged lack of democracy in the targeted state) are used for aggressive sanctions. So a fair question is: has there been any attempt to show the demand for sanctions by those most likely to be affected?

The demand for boycott and sanctions on apartheid South Africa was charted very carefully by a broad coalition of popular movements. A consensus was developed for national and then international boycotts in the late 1950s, then the call for sanctions came in the early 1960s, after many mass organisations were banned. Following this, the UN General Assembly adopted resolution 1761 (XVII) which called on members states to impose sanctions on South Africa. As Reddy (1965: 10) points out, 'the initiative for boycott and sanctions came from the national liberation movement of South Africa, and [was] carried forward internationally with the support of African and other states, as well as men and women of conscience in western countries'. Western states eventually joined in with sanctions in the late 1980s. After they made their contribution to the ending of apartheid, Nelson Mandela in 1993 called for an end to sanctions (except for those on arms, until a transitional government was established), as concrete steps were by then being taken to dismantle the apartheid system (Preston 1993).

Unilateral sanctions applied by the EU and the USA do not take such a course. It is not hard to find evidence of unlawful and malign intent against entire populations, in the history of Washington's sanction regimes. Concerning Cuba, in the early 1960s, senior US official Lester Mallory argued for damaging economic attacks on the population as a means of indirectly undermining what they acknowledged was a popular Cuban government:

> The majority of Cubans support Castro (the lowest estimate I have seen is 50 percent) ... The only foreseeable means of alienating internal support is through disenchantment and disaffection based on economic dissatisfaction and hardship ... every possible means should be undertaken promptly to weaken the economic life of Cuba ... to bring about hunger, desperation and overthrow of government (Mallory 1960).

This was a calculated assault on an entire population.

Cuba, in its report for the UN in 2018, said that US blockade laws and regulations (a combination of ten laws and decrees) since 1962 breached the UN Charter and GATT-WTO trade law, while also violating the rights of third party sovereign nations. The sanctions in law are accompanied by 'prohibitions, threats and blackmail' against third parties, by US Government representatives. The measures aimed at 'bringing the Cuban people to its knees by hunger and diseases [and] has resulted in sensitive social sectors such as public health and food being kept among the principal objectives' of the US blockade (MINREX 2018: 51-55).

Similarly, when speaking of measures against the democratically elected government of Salvador Allende in Chile in the early 1970s, US President Nixon expressed the hope of forcing political upheaval and change by measures designed 'to make the economy scream' (Kornbluh 2017). That meant Nixon intended direct damage to public health, food security, well-being and safety. It was effectively a criminal intent.

The reckless, war-linked nature of US sanctions was further illustrated in the economic measures against Iraq, prior to the illegal 2003 invasion. In that case US sanctions were reinforced by UN sanctions, after the First Gulf War of 1990-91. North American columnist Thomas Friedman urged Washington's attacks on its former client state in Baghdad, calling for:

bombing Iraq, over and over and over again ... America will use force, without negotiation, hesitation or UN approval ... Blow up a different power station in Iraq every week, so no-one knows when the lights will go off or who's in charge.

Diplomat Madeleine Albright infamously responded, 'We think the price is worth it', to the question of whether she could justify, as the price of sanctions, the death of 500,000 Iraqi children. She later claimed 'Saddam Hussein ... is the one responsible for starving children, not the United States of America' (Arnove 2000: 14-15, 112). That was a self-serving excuse, intended to deflect attention from a great criminal project.

A similarly illegal threat was heard more recently from US Secretary of State Mike Pompeo, in relation to a new round of US sanctions imposed on Iran. Washington's lead diplomat threatened the Iranian people with imposed hunger if their government persisted with military support for the independent peoples of the region (Palestine, Lebanon, Syria, Iraq and Yemen): 'The leadership has to make a decision that they want their people to eat' (Cole 2018), he said, trying to shift the blame for US aggression onto others. Successive US administrations have 'normalised' sanctions regimes as aggressive practice which forms part of broader war and illegitimate regime change strategy.

In none of these examples of US sanctions regimes against Cuba, Chile, Iraq and Iran, was there any real attempt to seek consent or approval from the affected populations. These sanctions regimes had none of the democratic character of those imposed on apartheid South Africa.

2. The scope of economic war

Concern at the United Nations over the widespread use of 'coercive unilateral measures' led to a UN Human Rights Council statement in 2014, which rejected the use of unilateral coercive measures 'not in accordance with international law, international humanitarian law, the Charter of the United Nations and the norms and principles governing peaceful relations among states' (UNGA 2014: 3). This was a welcome move.

Soon after, Mr Idriss Jazairy was appointed by the Human Rights Council as the first Special Rapporteur on the negative impact of the unilateral coercive measures on the enjoyment of human rights. This move was fairly plainly aimed at the USA and the European Union, which maintain unilateral sanctions on dozens of smaller countries. At the time of writing the European Union maintained measures against 34 countries and the USA had some form of direct sanctions against 25 countries (see Table 1). Those figures do not include countries affected by thematic sanctions regimes (against drugs, terrorism, etc.) and the many countries affected by 'third party' measures. In a number of cases there were parallel (but often differently defined) multilateral measures at the United Nations.

In 1996, the European Union imposed its own sanctions on the USA in response to Washington's strong unilateral 'third party' sanctions on states and companies doing business with Cuba (The Cuban Liberty and Democratic Solidarity (Libertad) Act of 1996, known as the Helms–Burton law). Those EU measures simply managed to secure some temporary exemptions for European companies. However, from 2009 onwards, beginning with the Obama administration, European banks were attacked with huge 'fines' for breaching US sanctions against Cuba, Iran and some other countries (See Table 2). That EU-US conflict escalated further in 2018, when the Trump administration arbitrarily re-imposed sanctions on Iran.

Prior to 2009, most of the fines reported by the US Treasury's Office of Foreign Asset Control (OFAC) were on US citizens and residents, for such things as importing a box of Cuban cigars. Those fines amounted to a few million dollars per year. However, from 2009 onwards, apparently as part of the Democrat Party's 'smart power' doctrine (Barzegar 2008), the scope of Washington's economic penalties expanded rapidly into hundreds of millions of dollars. Individual companies, mostly European banks, were forced to 'settle' with huge individual payments to the

Table 1
Countries 'sanctioned' by the USA and the European Union

Country	USA	European Union	United Nations
Afghanistan		X	X
Balkans (6 countries)	X		
Belarus	X	X	
Bosnia and Herzegovina		X	
Burundi	X	X	
Central African Republic	X	X	X
China		X	
Cuba	X		
Dem Rep Congo	X	X	X
Egypt		X	
Eritrea		X	X
Guinea		X	
Guinea-Bissau		X	X
Haiti		X	
Iran	X	X	X
Iraq	X	X	X
Lebanon	X	X	X
Libya	X	X	X
Maldives		X	
Mali		X	X
Moldova		X	
Montenegro		X	
Myanmar (Burma)		X	
Nicaragua	X		
North Korea (DPRK)	X	X	X
Russia		X	
Serbia		X	
Somalia	X	X	X
South Sudan	X	X	X
Sudan	X	X	
Syria	X	X	X
Tunisia		X	
Ukraine	X	X	
United States		X	
Venezuela	X	X	
Yemen	X	X	X
Zimbabwe	X	X	

Sources: European Union 2019; US Dept of Treasury 2019a

US Treasury, effectively as the price for continuing to do business in the USA (see Table 2). In this way the third-party character of US unilateral sanctions, reinforced by unilateral laws against Cuba (Hoffman 1998), became far more aggressive. At the same time the then Secretary General of Amnesty International, Irene Khan, denounced the fact that 'millions of Cubans were being deprived of 'vital medicines and medical equipment' (Tution 2009)

Table 2: OFAC Major Penalties, 2008-2018

Year	Total USD million	Of which the largest were (USD million)
2008	3.5	--
2009	772.4	Lloyds TSB 217m; Credit Suisse 536m
2010	200.7	Barclays Bank 176m
2011	91.6	J.P. Morgan 88m
2012	1,139.1	ING Bank 619m; HSBC Bank 375m; Standard Chartered 132m
2013	137.1	Weatherford Intl 91m
2014	1,205.2	BNP Paribas 963m; Clearstream Banking 151m; Fokker services 50m
2015	8.9bn + 599.7	BNP Paribas 8.9bn; Credit Agricole 329m; Commerzbank 258m
2016	21.6	--
2017	119.5	Zhongxing Telecom 100m
2018	91	Société Générale SA 53m
Source: US Dept. of Treasury 2019b; Raymond 2015		

These large fines on European banks were for multiple violations of US unilateral sanctions on Iran and Cuba, but also on Sudan, Libya, Sudan, Burma, Liberia and some of the thematic sanctions programs (such as the US program on 'weapons of mass destruction' and US drug programs). For example, the $963m fine on BNP Paribas (in 2014) was for breaches of US sanctions on Sudan, Iran, Cuba and Burma; it seems that the year after this 2014 settlement a US court imposed an additional $8.9 billion fine on the bank (Raymond 2015). The $619m fine on the ING Bank (in 2012) was for breaches of US sanctions on Cuba, Burma, Sudan, Libya and Iran; and the $329m fine on Credit Agricole (in 2015) was for breaches of US sanctions on Sudan, Burma, Cuba and Iran (US Department of Treasury 2019b). The US was acting against its target countries, but also trying to enforce blockades on their targets' commerce with third parties.

Due to the scale of this economic aggression, concern reached the United Nations, where experts began to report on the humanitarian and legal implications. As Washington made a spectacle of trying deliver a small amount of aid to Venezuela – after imposing sanctions, seizing Venezuelan assets and designating an unelected opposition leader as the country's 'interim president' – UN rapporteur Alfred de Zayas pointed out that US sanctions on Venezuela were 'killing ordinary people'. The 'economic warfare' practised by the US, EU and Canada were 'significant factors' that had hurt Venezuela's economy, he said (Selby-Green 2019), adding that US sanctions could amount to 'crimes against humanity', as they were contributing to 'needless deaths' (Webb 2019).

The UN's Special Rapporteur on the use of 'unilateral coercive measures', Idriss Jazairy, was similarly critical of the economic aggression. He said 'sanctions which can lead to starvation and medical shortages are not the answer to the crisis in Venezuela ... I am especially concerned to hear that these sanctions are aimed at changing the government of Venezuela' (UN News 2019). 'Coercion, whether military or economic, must never be used to seek a change in government in a sovereign state' he said (OHCHR 2019). The Trump administration made no effort to disguise its overt political interference. It was widely recognised that sanctions were part of Washington's efforts to overthrow the Venezuelan government 'and install a more business friendly regime' (Selby-Green 2019). 'Business friendly' was a euphemism for a plan for wide-scale privatisation, from which US companies would benefit through seizing control of the resources and productive assets of yet another oil-rich country (Parraga 2019).

US sanctions regimes often comprise a mixture of law and executive decree. The measures against Cuba date from 1962 and draw on older 'trading with the enemy' law. However, these measures have been supplemented by 1992 and 1996 laws and by presidential decrees (US Dept. of Treasury 2019c). The more recent US sanctions imposed on Syria have been by US executive orders in 2004, 2006, 2008, 2011 and 2012. These decrees have created a list of 'prohibited transactions and exempt transactions', with general and specific licenses (OFAC 2013). Decrees and discretionary licensing (e.g. to allow certain business transactions that suit particular US business interests) introduces a fair degree of arbitrariness. Political demands over the form, policies and even the individuals that Washington requires to be removed from foreign governments have been directly addressed in US law, e.g. in the Helms Burton law—1996 (Hoffmann 1998). Such demands have no basis in international law.

However, Washington managed to get UN Security Council support for sanctions on Iran in 2010 over that country's nuclear energy program. This was despite the fact that, as was well recognised, ordinary people would be hurt (Farshneshani 2014) and that any attempt to disarm that large country would be ineffective. The then CIA Director, Leon Panetta, said that 'sanctions could help weaken the regime [and] create serious economic problems' but they would probably not affect Iran's nuclear program (Vira 2010). Unsurprisinglly, the sanctions did limit access to finance and foreign exchange, decreasing investment and creating unemployment. That led to an economic slowdown, but also helped Iranian diversification, reducing its vulnerability to external factors (Majidi and Zaroum 2016).

The eventual nuclear agreement of 2015 (JCPOA) aimed to allow the intervening parties 'to gain confidence in the exclusively peaceful nature of Iran's [nuclear] programme ... [and would in exchange] produce the comprehensive lifting of all UN Security Council sanctions as well as multilateral and national sanctions related to Iran's nuclear programme, including steps on access in areas of trade, technology, finance and energy' (JCPOA 2015). But the JCPOA delivered very few of those benefits to Iran, as the US under President Trump reneged on the deal. While the EU made some moves to bypass US financial enforcement, most European companies were reluctant to risk their US investments by resuming business with Iran.

Parallel to the economic war on Iran were attempts to weaken the most effective resistance forces in the region. Washington imposed sanctions on Hezbollah (which had saved Lebanon from Israeli invasion and occupation) and on some of the Iran-linked Popular Mobilisation Units of Iraq (which had saved Iraq from DAESH). In late 2015 the US Congress passed the Hizbollah International Financing Prevention Act. The US Ambassador to Lebanon, Elizabeth Richard, said soon after that the 'main problem' in Lebanon was Hezbollah. Her government wanted 'to dismantle Hezbollah's international financial network [but also] help the Lebanese institutions and the Lebanese people' (Ayyoub 2016). These were nice sounding but deceptive words. Once again ordinary people were the likely subjects of the aggression. The Great Prophet Hospital in Beirut (owned by Hezbollah) could be targeted, as could Jihad al Bina, the Hezbollah NGO for construction contracting, along with various educational institutions 'with tens of thousands of students' (Aziz 2016). The US uses a variety of pretexts, including the claim that Hezbollah is a 'key player' in global narcotics trafficking and money laundering, so as 'to finance its military operations'. Hezbollah denies this and its Lebanese allies called on Washington to avoid 'collateral damage' (Arbid 2016).

3. Resistance strategies

The countries targeted by this economic warfare are typically relatively independent countries, with governments of one form or another. They have been forced to pay a price for that independence. The countries have responded in different ways, according to their circumstances and cultural traditions. There have been many moves towards self-sufficient strategies, as well as seeking strategic economic relationships with reliable partners. These moves to generate some relative immunity to sanctions can be seen, for example, in the recent histories of Syria and Iran (Maloney and Takeyh 2011).

In Iran the strategy debate has been between liberals, who have pursued normalisation and greater openness with western countries, and 'principalists' ('hardliners', in western terminology) who stress the need for strategic relationships in a 'resistance economy'. The Supreme Leader Ayatollah Khamenei proposed the 'resistance economy' in response to the constant aggression, so as to be able to 'withstand shocks', to boost investment in energy and build a 'knowledge economy', alongside greater links with Russia and China (Toumaj 2014). The greater openness agenda, championed by President Rouhani, seemed to have made an advance with the JCPOA agreement of 2015; indeed, there were some economic gains over 2016-2017 (Bokhari 2017). However, Washington's scrapping of JCPOA commitments helped turn the logic of the debate back towards the resistance economy.

Perhaps the two most interesting contrasts in strategy are long term targets Cuba and North Korea (DPRK). Cuba has pursued a diplomatic path to undermine attempts by Washington to isolate the island. It does this with the understanding that it cannot physically escape its giant neighbour to the north, and so must seek some kind of coexistence, if not normalisation. It also has the advantage of strong historical links with most other Latin American and Caribbean countries, a common language and shared colonial and neo-colonial histories. Cuba has reinforced these bonds with its health cooperation programs, by which it sends doctors and trains thousands of foreign students in medicine.

Little Cuba has become the biggest trainer of foreign doctors in the world (Kirk and Erisman 2009). When the US took advantage of Cuba's economic depression in the 1990s, due to the collapse of trading relations with the Soviet Union (Anderson 2002), Cuba began a diplomatic offensive with yearly motions at the United Nations General Assembly. Over more than two decades the small nation achieved tremendous success. Between 1992 and 2018 the UN General Assembly voted against the US blockade of Cuba 27 times. Since 2015 the Cuban motion has gained the support of 191 states (MINREX 2018: 51-55, 78-79). In 2013 Cuba under President Raul Castro was elected to the Presidency of the 600 million person bloc, the Community of Latin American and Caribbean States (CELAC) (Henao 2013). In 2014, the Obama administration, when reopening diplomatic relations with the island, admitted that its isolation policy was 'outdated' and had 'failed', and that it was the USA which had become isolated (Baker 2014).

North Korea (the DPRK), which has always enjoyed good relations with Cuba, pursued a quite different strategy. After the demise of its strong political relations with China in recent decades, and after its own economic depression following the collapse of trade with the Soviet Union, the country had fewer options. Its official 'Juche' ideology stresses human beings as masters of their own destiny and carries a strong degree of self-reliance (Kurbanov 2019). Circumstances have also conditioned this approach. From the 1990s onwards the DPRK was surrounded by enemies (the former colonial power Japan; and a US military occupation in the south of the peninsula) and two more indifferent giant neighbours. The possibilities for partnerships were few. North Korea's response to aggression has been to reciprocate, at least verbally, to counter-threaten and give signs that it is not to be messed with (Green 2018). Developing nuclear weapons was a logical step for this reciprocal confrontationism.

UN sanctions over the country's deterrent nuclear weapons program were at first said to have had little impact on DPRK trade with its two largest partners, China and South Korea (Noland

2009). The DPRK did have 'extensive trading relationships' with China and Russia and, until recently, with South Korea (Nanto and Chanlett-Avery 2010). However, there is still relatively little impact from sanctions because of its 'very thin and fragile financial links to the rest of the world' (Noland 2010). Even a news site antagonistic to Pyongyang recognised that the hunger of the 1990s has not returned. Despite UN sanctions, trade with China has increased and there has been some internal 'marketisation', bringing some expanded livelihood options (Kang Mi Jin 2016).

In recent times North Korea's relations with Russia and China have improved, with both committed, at the least, to preventing the installation of another US puppet at their borders. Further, a new round of improved relations with South Korea, and the popular prospect of reunification, opens some real options (Power 2018). The greatest obstacle remains the US military presence, and Washington's fears over its own future role on the peninsula, if north and south Korea build closer relations. Those developments, in turn, have required greater diplomacy, at least to build confidence with Seoul and Beijing. Despite the nuclear threats in 2017, the embattled independent nation has launched a new diplomatic offensive. Yet, as is the case elsewhere, sanctions have become established as an everyday part of hybrid and siege warfare by the imperial power.

Bibliography

Anderson, Tim (2002) 'Island Socialism: Cuban crisis and Structural Adjustment', *Journal of Australian Political Economy,* Number 49, June, pp.56-86

Arbid, Jeremy (2016) 'Damage Control: Lebanon braces itself for US anti-Hezbollah law', *Executive magazine,* News Media, Beirut, April, pp.14-18, online: http://www.executive-magazine.com/economics-policy/16297

Arnove, Anthony (Ed) (2000) *Iraq Under Siege: the deadly impact of sanctions and war*, South End Press, Massachusetts

Ayyoub, Sabah (2016) 'New US Ambassador to Lebanon: I came to Paralyse Hezbollah', Al Manar, 19 July, online: http://english.almanar.com.lb/1901

Aziz, Jean (2016) 'Will US Terrorism finance law do more harm than good in Lebanon?', Al Monitor, 11 May, online: https://www.al-monitor.com/pulse/originals/2016/05/us-act-against-hezbollah-impact-lebanon-banks.html

Baker, Peter (2014) 'U.S. to Restore Full Relations With Cuba, Erasing a Last Trace of Cold War Hostility', *New York Times*, 17 December, online: https://www.nytimes.com/2014/12/18/world/americas/us-cuba-relations.html

Barzehar, Kayhan (2008) 'Joseph Nye on Smart Power in Iran-U.S. Relations', Belfer Centre, 11 July, online: https://www.belfercenter.org/publication/joseph-nye-smart-power-iran-us-relations

Bokhari, Kamran (2017) 'Iran's economy is bouncing back', Geopolitical Futures, 2 February, online: https://geopoliticalfutures.com/irans-economy-is-bouncing-back/

Carter, Barry E. (1987) 'International Economic Sanctions: improving the haphazard U.S. Legal Regime', *California Law Review*, Vol 75, No 4, July, online: https://scholarship.law.georgetown.edu/cgi/viewcontent.cgi?article=2598&context=facpub

Cole, Brendan (2018) 'Mike Pompeo says Iran mist listen to U.S. "if they want their people to eat"', *Newsweek*, 9 November, online: https://www.newsweek.com/mike-pompeo-says-iran-must-listen-us-if-they-want-their-people-eat-1208465

European Union (2019) 'EU Sanctions Map', March, online: https://www.sanctionsmap.eu/#/main

Farshneshani, Beheshteh (2014) 'In Iran, Sanctions Hurt the Wrong People', *New York Times*, 22 January, online: https://www.nytimes.com/roomfordebate/2013/11/19/sanctions-successes-and-failures/in-iran-sanctions-hurt-the-wrong-people

Garfield, Richard, Julia Devin and Joy Fausey (1995) 'The Health Impact of Economic Sanctions', Bulletin of the New York Academy of Medicine, Winter, 454-469, online: https://www.ncbi.nlm.nih.gov/pubmed/10101382

Green, Christopher (2018) 'The Modest Diplomatic Promise of North Korea's Charm Offensive', International Crisis Group, 11 March, online: https://www.crisisgroup.org/asia/north-east-asia/korean-peninsula/modest-diplomatic-promise-north-koreas-charm-offensive

Haass, Richard N. (1998) 'Economic Sanctions: too much of a bad thing', Brookings, 1 June, online: https://www.brookings.edu/research/economic-sanctions-too-much-of-a-bad-thing/

Henao, Luis Andres (2013) 'Cuba's Castro assumes CELAC presidency', The San Diego Union-Tribune, 28 January, online: https://www.sandiegouniontribune.com/sdut-cubas-castro-assumes-celac-

presidency-2013jan28-story.html
Hoffman, Bert (1998) 'The Helms-Burton law and its consequences for Cuba, the United States and Europe', paper at the Latin American Institute at the Free University of Berlin, Germany, 24-26 September online: http://lasa.international.pitt.edu/LASA98/Hoffmann.pdf
JCPOA (2015) 'Joint Comprehensive Plan of Action', E3/EU+3 (China, France, Germany, the Russian Federation, the United Kingdom and the United States, with the High Representative of the European Union for Foreign Affairs and Security Policy) and the Islamic Republic of Iran, Vienna, Europarl, 14 July, online: http://www.europarl.europa.eu/cmsdata/122460/full-text-of-the-iran-nuclear-deal.pdf
Kang Mi Jin (2016) 'How sanctions affected North Korea's economy in 2016', Daily NK, 26 December, online: https://www.dailynk.com/english/how-sanctions-affected-north-korea/
Kirk, John M and H. Michael Erisman (2009) Cuban Medical Internationalism, Palgrave MacMillan, New York
Kornbluh, Peter (2017) 'Chile and the United States: Declassified Documents Relating to the Military Coup, September 11, 1973', National Security Archive Electronic Briefing Book No. 8, online: https://nsarchive2.gwu.edu/NSAEBB/NSAEBB8/nsaebb8i.htm
Kurbanov, Sergei O. (2019) 'North Korea's juche ideology: indigenous communism or traditional thought?', Critical Asian Studies, DOI: 10.1080/14672715.2019.1566750
Majidi, Ali Feghe and Zaahra Zaroum (2016) 'The Impact of sanctions on the economy of Iran', International Journal of Resistive Economics, vol. 4, issue 1, pp.84-99, online: https://econpapers.repec.org/article/trdjournl/v_3a4_3ay_3a2016_3ai_3a1_3ap_3a84-99.htm
Mallory, Lester (1960) '499. Memorandum From the Deputy Assistant Secretary of State for Inter-American Affairs (Mallory) to the Assistant Secretary of State for Inter-American Affairs (Rubottom)', FOREIGN RELATIONS OF THE UNITED STATES, 1958–1960, CUBA, VOLUME VI, Washington, 6 April, online: https://history.state.gov/historicaldocuments/frus1958-60v06/d499
Maloney, Suzanne and Ray Takeyh (2011) 'The Self-Limiting Success of Iran Sanctions', Brookings, 29 November, online: https://www.brookings.edu/articles/the-self-limiting-success-of-iran-sanctions/
MINREX (2018) 'Cuba Blockade June 2018', 'On resolution 72/4 of the United Nations General Assembly entitled 'Necessity of ending the economic, commercial and financial blockade imposed by the United States of America against Cuba', 48-83, online: http://www.cubavsbloqueo.cu/sites/default/files/InformeBloqueo2018/informe_bloqueo_2018ingles.pdf

Nanto, Dock and Emma Chanlett-Avery (2010) 'North Korea: Economic Leverage and Policy'. Congressional Research Service, 22 Jan, online: http://www.nkeconwatch.com/nk-uploads/1-2010-Economic-leverage.pdf

Noland, Marcus (2009) 'The (Non) Impact of UN Sanctions on North Korea', East-West Center Working Papers, Economics Series, No. 98, East-West Center, Washington DC, online: https://www.eastwestcenter.org/publications/non-impact-un-sanctions-north-korea

Noland, Marcus (2010) 'Why Sanctions can hurt North Korea', Council on Foreign Relations, 4 August, online: https://www.cfr.org/interview/why-sanctions-can-hurt-north-korea

OFAC (2013) 'Syria Sanctions Program', Department of Treasury, 2 August update, online: https://www.treasury.gov/resource-center/sanctions/programs/documents/syria.pdf

OHCHR (2019) 'Venezuela sanctions harm human rights of innocent people, UN expert warns', Office of the High Commissioner for Human Rights, 31 January, online: https://www.ohchr.org/en/NewsEvents/Pages/DisplayNews.aspx?NewsID=24131&LangID=E

OLC (1962) 'Legal and Practical Consequences of a Blockade of Cuba', Memorandum, Office of Legal Counsel, US Department of Justice, 19 October, online: https://fas.org/irp/agency/doj/olc/cuba.pdf

Pape, Robert A. (1998) 'Why Economic Sanctions Still do not work', International Security, Volume 23, Issue 1, Summer, p.66-77, online: https://www.mitpressjournals.org/doi/10.1162/isec.23.1.66

Parraga, Marianna (2019) 'Venezuela's Guaido readies to open up oil industry after years of nationalization', Reuters, 13 March, online: https://www.reuters.com/article/us-venezuela-politics-energy-law/venezuelas-guaido-readies-to-open-up-oil-industry-after-years-of-nationalization-idUSKBN1QT2HP

Power, John (2018) 'Could Hong Kong's 'one country, two systems' work for Korea?', SCMP, 27 October, online: https://www.scmp.com/week-asia/geopolitics/article/2170456/could-hong-kongs-one-country-two-systems-work-korea

Preston, Julia (1993) 'End sanctions, Mandela says', Washington Post, 25 September, online: www.washingtonpost.com/archive/politics/1993/09/25/end-sanctions-mandela-says/0d6536b1-86bf-4526-9665-50a591178c7c

Raymond, Nate (2015) 'BNP Paribas sentenced in $8.9 billion accord over sanctions violations', Reuters, 2 May, online: https://www.reuters.com/article/us-bnp-paribas-settlement-sentencing/bnp-paribas-sentenced-in-8-9-billion-accord-over-sanctions-violations-idUSKBN0NM41K20150501

Reddy, E.S. (1965) 'Notes on the Origins of the Movement for Sanctions against South Africa', Paper for the UN Special Committee against Apartheid, South African History Online, February, online: https://www.sahistory.org.za/archive/notes-origins-movement-sanctions-against-south-africa-es-reddy

Selby-Green, Michael (2019) 'Venezuela crisis: former UN rapporteur says US sanctions are killing citizens', The Independent, 26 January, online: https://www.independent.co.uk/news/world/americas/venezuela-us-sanctions-united-nations-oil-pdvsa-a8748201.html

Shneyer, Paul A. and Virginia Barta (1981) 'The legality of the U.S. Economic Blockade of Cuba under International Law', Case Western Reserve Journal of International Law, Vol 13 Issue 3, 450-482

Toumaj, Amir (2014) 'Iran's economy of resistance: implications for future sanctions', Nov, American Enterprise Institute, 17 November, online: http://www.aei.org/publication/irans-economy-resistance-implications-future-sanctions/

Tution, Mark (2009) 'Report: US sanctions put Cubans health at risk', CNN, 2 Sept, online: http://edition.cnn.com/2009/HEALTH/09/01/amnesty.cuba.health/

UN News (2019) 'Independent UN rights expert calls for compassion, not sanctions on Venezuela', 31 January, online: https://news.un.org/en/story/2019/01/1031722

UNGA (2014) 'Human Rights and Unilateral Coercive Measures', United Nations General Assembly, A/HRC/27/L.2, 18 September, online: https://documents-dds-ny.un.org/doc/UNDOC/LTD/G14/164/28/PDF/G1416428.pdf?OpenElement

US Dept. of Treasury (2019a) 'Active Sanctions Programs', March, online: https://www.treasury.gov/resource-center/sanctions/programs/pages/programs.aspx

US Dept. of Treasury (2019b) 'Civil Penalties and enforcement information', online: https://www.treasury.gov/resource-center/sanctions/CivPen/Pages/civpen-index2.aspx

US Dept. of Treasury (2019c) 'Cuba Sanctions', Resource Center, online: https://www.treasury.gov/resource-center/sanctions/programs/pages/cuba.aspx

Vira, Varun (2010) 'Sanctions on Iran: Reactions and Impact', Critical Threats, 28 September, online: https://www.criticalthreats.org/analysis/sanctions-on-iran-reactions-and-impact

Webb, Whitney (2019) 'Former UN expert: US sanctions in Venezuela largely responsible for crisis, possible 'crime against humanity'', Mint Press, 28 January, online: https://www.mintpressnews.com/former-un-expert-us-sanctions-venezuela-largely-responsible-crisis-possible-

crime-humanity/254334/
Weiqi Zhang (2018) 'Neither friend nor big brother: China's role in North Korean foreign policy strategy', Palgrave Communications, 4, Article Number 16, online: https://www.nature.com/articles/s41599-018-0071-2
White, Nigel (2018) 'Ending the US Embargo of Cuba: International Law in Dispute', Journal of Latin American Studies, online: https://www.cambridge.org/core/journals/journal-of-latin-american-studies/article/ending-the-us-embargo-of-cuba-international-law-in-dispute/5DF4D4D5573333AD40AAC57B6F1F4FA0#

Chapter Four

MYTH AND METHOD IN STUDIES OF WAR

Syrian President Bashar al Assad, relentlessly demonised by western governments, visits an art project in tunnels created by western-backed al Qaeda groups. Douma, rural Damascus. Photo by SANA.

The chapter discusses, in two sections, the myth of neutral war reporting and some principles of method to help understand contemporary international controversies, in particular war and foreign interventions.

1. War and the Myth of Neutral Reporting

There is no such thing as a neutral discussion of a great conflict. The analyst or reporter adopts certain values, implicitly if not explicitly. Those values, which most often come from a host culture, form an interpretive lens; and they generally become more entrenched the longer the writer engages. Similarly, to speak of an 'objective view' is philosophical nonsense. All human beings bring their own subjectivity to bear when viewing the circumstances of the world. Better to speak of honest, fair and disinterested views, informed by evidence. That should, in theory, lead to better informed opinion.

There may be reasons for initial agnosticism over a foreign conflict, when key elements and players are not well known. Yet to pretend an agnostic position, after some basic study, more likely shows uncertainty or dissembling.

There are such things as small, symmetrical and civil wars, but most major and protracted conflicts involve overdetermination and aggression by big ambitious powers. That is certainly the case with the series of 21st century wars in the Middle East region, and imperial interventions provoke polarized responses.

In contemporary wars involving the big powers commentators make use of two main value sets. The first is a neo-realist justification for big power aggression. This logic says: whatever pretexts offered by the big power must be in the interest of stabilizing the international order, containing threats, and restoring economic stability by maintaining corporate privilege.

In north American culture this value set is underwritten by historic notions of 'manifest destiny' and 'exceptionalism', whether liberal or realist. Both major parties in the USA subscribe to the idea that their culture is morally superior and cannot be subject to the same rules as others. The Europeans simply referred to this as their imperial age.

The second value set typically draws on foundations of post-colonial international law, to assert the sovereignty of small states, racial and national equality, the principle of non-intervention and the human right of 'a people' to self-determination. These principles have a sound basis in current international law; 'exceptionalist' notions do not.

Nevertheless, the first set of values is well embedded in the colonial cultures; the second is championed by the former colonies, especially those with a history of anti-colonial struggle. That is why, for example, educated Latin Americans understand the dirty wars against Libya and Syria, just as they do those against Venezuela and Nicaragua. Much the same can be said for most formerly colonised peoples. They understand greedy intervention by outsiders.

What of the eight recent Middle East wars? The imperial and former colonial powers set up the Jewish colony in Palestine, at the end of the colonial era, and to this day they support its dreadful ethnic cleansing. Washington and its allies invaded Afghanistan and Iraq on false pretences, slaughtering hundreds of thousands. The same powers backed the Israeli invasions of Lebanon to suppress the Palestinian and Lebanese resistance. All the major powers moved to cripple Iran's nuclear power program, by focusing on a unilateral nuclear weapons disarmament demand which effectively said: the only regional power to possess nuclear weapons can be apartheid Israel. Even when there was a nuclear agreement, Washington resumed its economic siege, breaking all agreements and covertly backing terrorist attacks on Iran.

Salafist fanatics were contracted to destroy the Libyan and Syrian nations, and to cripple the post-2003 Iraqi state. And when an unpopular Yemeni president was ousted by a coalition of local forces, the big powers backed aggression through the vicious al Saud family in yet another terrible war of subjugation.

While the pretexts and some of the players in each of these conflicts were hidden, the basic elements could be determined by an honest and curious foreign student within a few weeks. Yet in western countries there remain terribly divided commentaries.

Many of those who back these new wars do so largely on a priori grounds. The first imperial faction says that the great power does what it must to maintain the global order. The second imperial faction (the liberals) sees a moral mission in 'saving' other peoples from their own governments or societies. A small group of western leftists even imagine that imperial wars are carried out in support of 'revolutions'. Each new pretext for war is separated from the others, so that the pattern of aggression and deceit is better hidden.

Such views prevail in a state and corporate media culture which seeks to normalize war and maintain each new set of war myths, such as imminent threats from 'weapons of mass destruction', or of unexplained and imminent great crimes. The resilience of mass media support for such arguments, across multiple wars, leads me to call them a 'colonial media'.

Those in the colonial cultures who criticize the war line, the western 'war dissidents', are often said to be biased because they speak and sympathise with the target peoples and even their governments. Whatever pluralism the colonial media might have had disappears at wartime.

There are claims that real analysis and real journalism cannot side with a people under attack, as this means 'bias' and the abandoning of a supposed ideal 'neutral' mission.

However, that brings me back to my first point. Commentators and journalists must adopt certain values and perspectives, and the honest ones spell them out. It is not 'bias' to demand respect for international law.

2. Reading International Controversies

Even well-educated people have great difficulty interpreting contemporary international controversies. They go to the corporate and state media, which mostly reflect the view of powerful states, or to human rights agencies which often amplify these same state-media messages (see the chapter in this book: 'The human rights industry in humanitarian war').

It is usually only after the dust settles that independent research begins to emerge. For example, the facts about claimed weapons of mass destruction in Iraq only emerged months after the invasion of that country in March 2003. The false accusations about Libya in 2011 were admitted by US analysts (e.g. Alan Kuperman) and by Amnesty International (France), only after NATO had bombed the country, the state had been destroyed and President Gaddafi had been publicly murdered.

One option many take is simply to stay away from such controversies. However, as the consequences may be time-critical, we are entitled to ask: what appropriate tools are available to intelligent observers to read and build their understandings?

I suggest a combination of postcolonial and forensic principles can help construct an informed and ethical approach to understanding contemporary international controversies, and in particular interventions and war.

The postcolonial principles include key elements of international law adopted in the post-colonial era, in particular: (1) the United Nations Charter (1945), on the need to defend a system of sovereign states and prevent war; (2) the Declaration on Decolonization (1960), on the rejection of colonial regimes; (3) the twin Covenants on Human Rights (1966), which both begin with the foundational right of peoples to self-determination, including sovereign control of their own resources; and (4) the subsequent body of treaty and humanitarian law, which opposes intervention in the affairs of sovereign states, and bans military and economic coercion.

In the post-1945 order, two exceptions to the ban on military intervention have been those based on 'collective security' grounds, authorized by the UN Security Council and the right of nation-states to self-defence. Chapter VII of the UN Charter restricts possible military intervention to the maintenance of 'international peace and security'.

Unfortunately, three of the five permanent members of the UN Security Council have tried to widen the exceptions to the principle of non-intervention, first by creating the doctrine of a 'Responsibility to Protect' (R2P) and second by fabricating pretexts for both 'self-defence' and R2P interventions.

The R2P doctrine does not change international law, but argues the case for intervention to prevent great crimes, such as genocide and crimes against humanity. It does this by trying to weaken the concept of sovereignty and to widen the UN Security Council's Chapter VII armed intervention powers. The principal problem in practice is that the big powers, which typically have poorly disguised ambitions to expand their influence, so as to control regions and resources. Yet advancing or defending supposed imperial prerogatives is how wars begin.

We saw the abuse of these exceptions to the rule of non-intervention in the 2003 invasion of Iraq, and in the 2011 NATO bombing and destruction of Libya. The former fabricated 'self-defence' pretexts, while the latter fabricated 'humanitarian intervention' pretexts. Those interventions had the wider effect of normalising war in the 21st century. Yet they were in fact subversions of international law, and should have attracted principled rejection.

Attempts by states to avoid anti-war norms on 'exceptional' pretexts should be regarded as illegal and illegitimate at the outset. There should be no presumption in favour of war.

When such aggression does occur, traditional forensic tools can help us understand the controversies. I have listed the key principles for such a process in Table 3. In Chapter 10 of *The Dirty War on Syria* I discussed the deceptive doctrine of a 'responsibility to protect'.

The first step must be to identify 'interested parties'. An interested party means someone engaged and with a material interest in the conflict. That includes warring states, their proxies and paid agents. It should include agencies traditionally embedded with or advising a warring party. Typically, the evidence of interested parties is excluded in law as self-serving and unreliable, as they have an interest in the outcome.

Second, sources of independent evidence can be identified and made central to an assessment. These sources are the 'gold standard' in any serious dispute. They often exist, in international conflicts, and may include dissident officials, so long as they have not themselves become party to the conflict.

Third, 'admissions against interest' can be considered,

Table 3
Relevant legal and forensic principles

Intervention is banned under international law	
Non-intervention in a sovereign state	UN Charter 1945
Right of peoples to self-determination	ICCPR and ICESCR 1966
Prohibition of colonialism, coercion and aggression	Body of international treaty and humanitarian law
There are very limited exceptions to the ban on non-intervention	
Threat to 'collective security' (e.g. invasion of a sovereign state)	UNSC may authorise intervention but only to protect the international order
Legitimate self-defence	Threat must be actual or imminent
Responsibility to Protect (R2P) - collective action to prevent great crimes	No change to international law but concept of sovereignty undermined
Forensic principles can help understand pretexts for intervention	
Identify interested parties to the conflict (includes paid and allied agencies)	Interested party = engaged and with a material interest in the conflict
Disregard the 'self-serving' claims of interested parties	Self-serving statements are unreliable, and usually inadmissible in law
Look for independent evidence	The 'gold standard' in any dispute
Make use of 'admissions against interest'	Parties sometimes make admissions

just as confessions to crimes are often accepted in law. While there are such things as false confessions, the general rule is that people will not speak against their interests, unless the admission contains some factual content. In a long conflict, such as the war on Syria, many of the key elements can now be read by admissions from US officials. The following chapter makes use of such evidence, to identify the sponsors of DAESH.

These principles draw on established rules of criminal law. They are best applied to specific controversies, such as the claims about weapons of mass destruction in Iraq. I apply them to the repeated claims of chemical weapons use in Syria (see the chapter in this book: WMD Take 2: Chemical Weapons in Syria).

Proper recognition of the principles of non-intervention in international law should form a basis for critical consideration of any 'exceptional' claim in favour of intervention and war. That is, the presumption must be firmly against intervention.

Part II

Collapse of the Dirty War on Syria

Syrian soldiers, eastern desert, Syria

Chapter Five

THE DIRTY WAR REVISITED

At the time of writing (June 2019) the Washington-led war on Syria was failing badly, only maintained by two foreign occupations which sheltered clusters of proxy militia. With this collapse, the US dream of a 'New Middle East' was fading. The destruction of an independent Syria was supposed to pave the way to regime change in Iran.

In the south, east and far north east of Syria US occupation forces (backed by air power) entered Syria in late 2014, without invitation, on the pretext of fighting terrorism. In fact, the two main terrorist groups (DAESH aka ISIS and Jabhat al Nusra aka Hayat Tahrir al Sham) had been used by Washington to weaken Damascus. This was confirmed by US intelligence files (DIA 2012). Under the pretence of fighting terrorism, the US presence prolonged it. Protected by US air power, in mid-2015, a Jabhat al Nusra coalition reinvaded Idlib in the north, while DAESH rushed in from the east to seize Palmyra. That prompted a response from Syria and her allies. Russia and Iran increased their commitments, and began to roll back the terrorist offensive. But the US maintained a border presence, blocking full liberation of the country. By late 2017, in the east and north-east, DAESH was gradually replaced by the US-sponsored 'Syrian Democratic Forces', comprising separatist Kurds and the remnants of defeated Salafist groups. In the north-west the Turkish army entered Idlib, both to protect its 'jihadist' proxies and to confront separatist Kurds.

Despite the invasions, by late 2017, an alliance comprising Syrian forces, Russia and Iran alongside the Lebanese and Iraqi resistance, had liberated all of Syria's major cities and most regions. With the help of Hezbollah, the al Qaeda groups had been driven out of the Qalamoun mountains, on Syria's border with Lebanon. Palmyra, the historic city at the heart of the Syrian desert, was liberated in mid-2016. Also by mid-2016 the gangs had been purged from the southern part of the east Ghouta region, in rural Damascus. Syria's second city Aleppo was liberated in December 2016. In October 2017 the Syrian Army reclaimed the eastern city of Deir Ezzor from DAESH. That terrorist group was declared defeated in both Syria and Iraq. It persisted in rural areas but had been expelled from all major urban areas (Mulhem 2017; Haider 2017; FT 2017). DAESH and other terror groups, according to Russian Foreign Minister Sergei Lavrov, still existed due to the 'safe haven' protection they enjoyed through the presence of US forces (Lavrov 2018). Then in early 2018 the Syrian alliance swept through the south, driving the western-backed gangs out of the rest of the East Ghouta, and from the Yarmouk, Daraa and Quneitra areas. The operation to retake Idlib was stalled in September 2018 after threats from Washington, Britain and France. Russia then began a negotiation with the government of Turkey, hoping to secure some cooperation in anti-terrorism. By April 2019 the main obstacles to complete liberation of the country were (1) the large pocket of exiled jihadists gathered in Idlib, comprising tens of thousands of fighters, protected by the Turkish Army; and (2) the SDF and DAESH remnants in eastern and southern Syria, protected by US occupation forces.

Washington was using separatist Syrian Kurds, reinforced with Turkish Kurds and the remnants of its other failed proxies, to prevent the Syrian Army reclaiming the entire country. The US had no intention of supporting an independent Kurdish state, as its officials admitted (Calamur 2017). Israel was the only regional body which supported the idea of a Kurdish state, with some Kurds in Iraq and Syria even speaking of a 'second Israel', a horrific notion for most of the Arab and Muslim World (Bengio

2017; Levinson 2017; Qurbany 2018). The very idea of 'a second Israel' conjured up the fear of more ethnic cleansing. For all these uncertainties, Syrian separatist Kurds never broke relations with Damascus (Said 2019). In the meantime the Turkish Government, which saw the Kurdish PKK as an national security threat, began to threaten Washington's Kurdish proxies. In response US President Trump announced his intention to withdraw all US troops from Syria (RFERL 2018). However he faced opposition at home and from Tel Aviv. The US occupation was still serving to disrupt more comprehensive cooperation between Syria, Iraq and Iran.

In the region, much had changed during eight years of war against Syria. As the Syrian alliance drove back the proxy armies, the Muslim Brotherhood and its patrons in Egypt and Qatar received another beating: Egypt and Iraq shifted their support towards Syria. The Saudis covertly joined with Israel against Iran. Russia – despite its friendly relations with Israel – built stronger bonds with both Syria and Iran. The Arab League, having backed the destruction of two Arab states (Libya and Syria) seemed all but dead.

This chapter revises two matters developed by The Dirty War on Syria: the character of the war on Syria, and the sponsorship of the terrorist proxy armies used throughout that war. It then addresses a third matter: the role of Russia and its relationship with the Axis.

1. The Character of the Dirty War

In *The Dirty War on Syria* I explained the disguised character of the war in some detail. The claim from Washington and embedded organisations like Human Rights Watch was that there had been a 'peaceful protest movement' for the first six months, and this later transformed into an armed citizens' revolution (Abouzeid 2011; HRW 2012). Much media propaganda (for example from Al Jazeera) repeated that story, but it was far from the truth. In fact, the largely peaceful protest movement, demanding political reforms, was infiltrated by a Muslim Brotherhood-led violent and sectarian insurrection. These two movements ran together, almost from the beginning. In early March 2011 the mosque in the border town of Daraa had been armed by Saudi Arabia (Reuters 2011; Truth Syria 2012), and police and security forces as well as civilians were shot by sectarian Islamists (Salt 2011). Independent witnesses, such as the late Father Frans Van der Lugt testified to this: 'I have seen from the beginning armed protesters in those demonstrations ... they were the first to fire on the police. Very often the violence of the security forces comes in response to the brutal violence of the armed insurgents' (Van der Lugt 2012). That violent insurrection drove the protestors off the streets in the early weeks.

The violence in Daraa copied that of an earlier Muslim Brotherhood insurrection at Hama in 1982. Subsequent mythology has called this a 'civilian massacre' of tens of thousands at the hands of President Hafez al Assad (Lefèvre 2013). However independent accounts at the time make it clear that the large-scale sectarian and anti-government violence at Hama was started by the Muslim Brotherhood. After three weeks the Syrian Army crushed this insurrection. British author Patrick Seale estimated five to ten thousand casualties at Hama. 'The guerrillas were formidable opponents. They had a fortune in foreign money ... [and] no fewer than 15,000 machine guns' (Seale 1988: 332, 335). Washington had covertly backed the uprising, through its clients which included the Saudis and Saddam Hussein. Yet US intelligence puts the casualties even lower. A US DIA report from May 1982 observed: "The total casualties for the Hama incident probably number about 2,000. This includes an estimated 300 to 400 members of the Muslim Brotherhood's elite 'Secret Apparatus'"(DIA 1982: 7). When it was over the DIA simply observed that: 'the Syrians are pragmatists who do not want a Muslim Brotherhood government' (DIA 1982: vii). They should have remembered this three decades later, in 2011.

The head of the Syrian Brotherhood, Muhammad Riyad Al-Shaqfa, issued a statement on 28 March 2011, which left no doubt that the group's aim was a sectarian-salafist 'revolution'. The enemy was 'the secular regime' and Brotherhood members 'have to make sure that the revolution will be pure Islamic, and with that no other sect would have a share of the credit after its success' (Al-Shaqfa 2011). Other foreign sectarian Islamist groups quickly joined this 'Syrian Revolution', coming at first from Lebanon and later from Turkey. A US DIA report of August 2012 said: 'The Salafist, the Muslim Brotherhood and AQI [Al Qaeda in Iraq, later ISIS] are the major forces driving the insurgency in Syria ... AQI supported the Syrian Opposition from the beginning, both ideologically and through the media' (DIA 2012). That is, officials for Washington admitted, contrary to US government public statements, that from early days the insurrection was led by sectarian and foreign extremists.

The vicious, sectarian slogans of this 'revolution' were no secret. From exile in Saudi Arabia, the Syrian Salafi Sheikh, Adnan Arour, called for a holy war against the liberal Alawi Muslims, who were said to dominate the Syrian government: 'by Allah we shall mince [the Alawites] in meat grinders and feed their flesh to the dogs' (MEMRITV 2011). His aim was also a theocratic state or caliphate. The genocidal slogan 'Christians to Beirut, Alawites to the grave' was reported in the western media from Homs as early as 5 April (Farrell 2011) and into May (Shadid and Kirkpatrick 2011; Blanford 2011). Most western media chose to ignore this, speaking of 'peaceful protestors' and then, later on, 'moderate rebels'. We now know that dozens of Syrian security forces were killed throughout April of 2011 (Narwani 2012; Narwani 2014).

We can chart much of the course of this early violence from independent sources. US Journalist Nir Rosen attacked the western consensus over the early violence, saying that the story about army defectors had been exaggerated and that claims of civilians killed were 'in fact dead opposition fighters' (Rosen 2012). Journalist Hala Jaber demonstrated very well how the civil opposition was driven off the streets by Salafist gunmen, in her account of demonstrations in Idlib in June 2011. She observed that about five thousand people turned up for a demonstration at the town of Ma'arrat al-Numan. 'Protestors' were said to have been shot by government forces the week before, as they were trying to block the road between Damascus and Aleppo. After some negotiations which disarmed and reduced the numbers of security forces in the town, 'men with heavy beards in cars and pick-ups with no registration plates,' with 'rifles and rocket-propelled grenades,' began shooting at these security forces. A military helicopter was sent in. After the clash 'four policemen and 12 of their attackers were dead or dying. Another 20 policemen were wounded'. Officers who escaped the fight were hidden by some tribal elders who had participated in the original demonstration. When the next 'demonstration for democracy' took place the following Friday, 'only 350 people turned up', mostly young men and some bearded militants (Jaber 2011). So we can see that five thousand protestors had been reduced to 350, after the Salafist attacks. Many of those who had been involved in the political reform demonstrations, when they saw the sectarian character of the 'revolution', turned back to protection of the state and the army, if not to the government. In chapters four and five of *The Dirty War on Syria* I document the beginning of the conflict, and the political reform movement.

  Syria's sectarian groups came to rely on foreign Islamists from the early months. These al Qaeda style coalitions carried out many public atrocities, publicising their murder of pro-government and minority civilians. They also blamed some of their atrocities on the Syrian Army. They had a credulous audience amongst western governments, media and 'human rights' groups. In *The Dirty War on Syria* I dedicate two chapters to their 'false flag' massacres. The Houla massacre of May 2012, for example, was carried out by the Farouq Brigade of the 'Free Syrian Army', but was falsely blamed on the Syrian Government, then used as a pretext for widespread economic sanctions. Chapter Eight of *The Dirty War on Syria* documents the accounts of fifteen independent witnesses to this crime. Some other attempts at false flags were exposed. For example there was the attempt to blame the Syrian Army for a large massacre in the Damascus suburb of Daraya, in August 2012 (Oweis 2012). Yet British journalist Robert Fisk (2012) exposed this as the slaughter of hostages in a failed prisoner exchange, by one of the 'Free Syrian Army' groups. Chapter Nine of *The Dirty War on Syria* documents the chemical weapons false flag incident at the East Ghouta, in August 2013. The general question of chemical weapon attacks is dealt with in the chapter of this book titled 'WMD Take 2: chemical weapons in Syria'.

2. The Sponsors of DAESH

In late 2014 several senior US officials admitted what had been obvious to Syrians from early days: close allies of Washington - in particular the Saudis and Qatar but also the UAE, Turkey, Israel and others - were funding and arming all the terrorist groups which had flooded into Syria in attempts to topple the government in Damascus. It is worth highlighting these admissions, as they cut through the misinformation about western support as only for 'moderate rebels' and the US claim of leading a coalition to 'fight DAESH' (GCAD 2019). After the failure of pretexts for 'humanitarian intervention', the US came to rely on this false pretext for 'protective intervention'.

DAESH, otherwise known as ISIS or ISIL, was one of the main Islamist groups set up to fight both the Iraqi and Syrian armies. As an international group it grew from al Qaeda in Iraq (AQI), later renamed the Islamic State in Iraq (ISI), until it crossed the Syrian border in late 2012 and rebranded itself as the Islamic State in Iraq and the Levant (ISIL) or the Islamic State in Iraq and Syria (ISIS). DAESH comes from the acronym in Arabic. It had a similar genesis to Jabhat al Nusra ('Victory Front'; later Jabhat Fateh al-Sham, then later still Hayat Tahrir al Sham) (CEP 2019). They were both branches of al Qaeda and committed to the backward and vicious notion of a salafist-religious state. When in late 2012 Jabhat al Nusra was proscribed by Washington as a banned terrorist group most of the other 'jihadist' anti-government armed groups in Syria protested by declaring 'we are all Jabhat al Nusra' (Zelin 2012). That confirmed the character of the armed 'Syrian revolution', as also the leading role of al Nusra in western Syria. There have been hundreds of armed groups in Syria but, with the failure of a merger between DAESH and al Nusra, the armed groups in western Syria coalesced around al Nusra while, for a time, DAESH held much of the east of the country. At one stage there were separate sponsors for separate groups. Qatar, for example, supported Ahrar al Sham; while Kuwait sponsored Liwaa al Ummah. However in Syria, ordinary people did not distinguish much between the groups, calling them either DAESH or Musalaheen (armed groups). It is in that sense that this section explains the sponsors of DAESH, along with all other terrorist groups in Syria and Iraq.

The first important admissions can be seen in a leaked US intelligence report from August 2012, which showed US satisfaction with the dominance of extremist groups in the 'Syrian Opposition', including the move towards a 'salafist principality' (an Islamic state) in eastern Syria. This would serve to 'isolate the Syrian regime' (DIA 2012). This report countered Washington's public statements about only supporting 'moderate rebels':

> The Salafist, the Muslim Brotherhood and AQI [Al Qaeda in Iraq, later ISIS] are the major forces driving the insurgency in Syria ... AQI supported the Syrian Opposition from the beginning, both ideologically and through the media ... There is the possibility of establishing a declared or undeclared Salafist principality in eastern Syria (Hasaka and Der Zor), and this is exactly what the supporting powers [The West, Gulf monarchies and Turkey] to the [Syrian] opposition want, in order to isolate the Syrian regime (DIA 2012).

Some years later General Michael Flynn, former head of the DIA, confirmed the report, saying that this was a deliberate policy of the Obama administration:

> We've allowed this extremist, you know, these extremist militants to come in ... it goes before 2012. I mean, when we were, when we were in Iraq ... it was very clear what we were, what

we were going to face. I don't know if they [the Obama administration] turned a blind eye. I think it was a decision. I think it was a wilful decision [to allow the extremists to take control] (Flynn 2016).

In late 2014, around the time that the US was sending forces to Iraq and Syria to 'fight ISIS' (GCAD 2019), several senior US officials admitted that their main regional allies were arming and financing ISIS/DAESH. However, they also tried to suggest that the US was not involved in this and was, in effect, powerless to stop its allies. That was a false excuse, for reasons I will explain below. But let's recall their stories first.

In August 2014 former US Secretary of State Hillary Clinton wrote to John Podesta that 'the governments of Qatar and Saudi Arabia ... are providing clandestine financial and logistic support to ISIL and other radical Sunni groups in the region'. She went on to maintain the fiction that the US was only backing 'moderate forces' (Clinton 2014). This linking of US allies to DAESH was repeated publicly by both the head of the US military and the US Vice President. In September 2014 General Martin Dempsey told a Congressional hearing 'I know major Arab allies who fund [ISIS]' (Rothman 2014). Senator Lindsey Graham, of the Armed Services Committee, responded with a justification, 'They fund them because the Free Syrian Army couldn't fight [Syrian President] Assad, they were trying to beat Assad' (Rothman 2014; Washington's Blog 2014). Dempsey nodded his head in agreement.

In October US Vice President Joe Biden gave a little more detail to basically the same story: our allies are supporting DAESH and we can't stop them. Biden told a public audience that Turkey, Qatar, the UAE and Saudi Arabia 'were so determined to take down Assad ... they poured hundreds of millions of dollars and tens, thousands of tons of weapons into anyone who would fight against Assad ... [including] al Nusra and al Qaeda and extremist elements of jihadis coming from other parts of the world ... [and then] this outfit called ISIL' (RT 2014; Usher 2014). As with Clinton's private email, these public statements were consistent and credible admissions, except that they tried to exempt Washington by shifting the blame to key allies.

That caveat is not credible. The DIA memo from 2012 tells us that the rise of DAESH and other extremists was looked on favourably as it could help to 'isolate' Damascus. John Kerry, the former Secretary of State and successor to Hillary Clinton, confirmed this logic in 2017. 'We saw that Daesh was growing in strength, and we thought Assad was threatened. We thought, however, we could probably manage, that Assad would then negotiate. Instead of negotiating, he got Putin to support him' (Kerry in Weiss 2017). The notion that Washington would allow its allies to arm and finance groups they claimed to be mortal enemies is absurd. The Saudis in particular are politically dependent on Washington and could not mount any major initiative without US approval, let alone one against the interests of the US. Not only that, precisely to prevent such adventures, the US systematically controls, by purchase contract and re-export license, the use of its weapons (Export.Gov 2015). Neither the Saudis nor anyone else can simply purchase US weapons and then forward them to their favourite terrorist groups without US approval. The enormous quantities of US weapons in the hands of DAESH and the others were not there due to US ignorance or oversight, shifted to DAESH by 'rogue' elements within forces that were otherwise US approved or by occasional theft from the Iraqi military. Former Israeli Defence Minister Moshe 'Bogie' Yaalon acknowledged Israeli collaboration with DAESH when he said that the terror group had 'immediately apologised' for once sending a shell into Israeli held territory (Silverstein 2017). Despite a DAESH presence in south Syria, they made no attacks on Israel. The al Qaeda groups were armed by the US through its allies because, when they attacked US targets like Syria, that served Washington's interests. Big powers making use of so-called 'Radical Islam' has a long history (Curtis 2015).

'Moderate rebels' armed by the Obama administration

had repeatedly joined al Nusra and DAESH, as well as working alongside them (Newman 2014; Anderson 2016: Ch.12). This made a farce of claims to distinguish the groups. After Syrian and Iraqi forces had driven DAESH out of the major cities, the US began a process of replacing them with another proxy group, the SDF. There were repeated reports of US helicopter airlifts of DAESH leaders along the Euphrates, taking them out of danger (UFilter 2017). Hundreds of DAESH fighters were then reported as surrendering to the SDF. At least some of these seem to have been recruited by the SDF. Others were said to have been simply set free. US media observed that 'hundreds' of DAESH fighters were then allowed to go free from the city of Raqqa, with observers speaking of a convoy comprising 50 trucks, 13 buses and 100 DAESH vehicles (CBS 2017). Former SDF spokesman Talal Silo told western media that the numbers of DAESH fighters allowed to simply leave the city of Raqqa, in a US-backed deal, was far higher than 'hundreds'. He put the number at 'about 4,000 people, all but 500 of whom were fighters' (Evans and Coskun 2017). Most of the new recruits for the SDF in the 'fight for Raqqa' were said to be 'Arabs', without further explanation (ARA 2016). Iran complained that the US had relocated some of these DAESH fighters to Afghanistan (MEMO 2018). But the US plan

The USA backed 'moderate rebels' who in turn worked with DAESH. Two degrees of separation: US Ambassador Robert Ford, FSA Colonel Abdul Jabbar al-Okaidi and ISIS leader Abu Jandal. Photo by 'FSA'.

to hold eastern Syria for as long as possible, blocking coordination between Syria and Iraq, depended on the pretext of a fight against DAESH (Khaled 2019).

Consistent support of US allies for DAESH, complained of repeatedly by Iraqis and Syrians, was confirmed by these admissions. More direct US-led coordination with DAESH is documented in the chapter of this book titled 'The US-Fighting-DAESH Deception: the crime at Jabal al Tharda'. That close relationship has to be borne in mind when considering claims that US forces somehow fought or eliminated DAESH.

3. The Role of Russia

Syria had a longstanding relationship with the Soviet Union and this passed to Russia, but practical support was weak in the first two decades that followed the collapse of the Soviet Union. Four and a half years after the war began in Syria, after seeing firm Syrian resistance against a powerful coalition of international states and jihadist-mercenaries, President Putin decided to enter the conflict directly, by use of air power, on 30 September 2015. This was a coordinated move, at the invitation of Damascus and with ground support from regional militia backed by Iran. It came after a Turkish-backed counter offensive by the gangs in the north, and covert US support for an advance by DAESH in the east (Ghanem 2015; ABC 2015). While Syria had managed to defend or retake most of the western cities, the Russian-led intervention helped turn the course of the war in Syria's favour.

What motivated Russia to provide 'aviation support to the actions of the regular Syrian army' (Sharifulin 2015)? The main stated reason was to fight terrorism and to fight it in Syria before it reached Russia (Yakovenko 2016; Fisk 2018). The background to that was Russia's own experience of an Islamist insurgency in Chechnya in the 1990s. While there had been a settlement in Chechnya, many former fighters later joined the 'jihadist' gangs in Syria, paid by the Saudis (Hauer 2018). A Lebanese analyst later noted that Iran had encouraged the Russian President to join in the fight against terrorism, with an additional incentive: to strategically weaken the US role in the region. Anees Naqqash said that Iran had suggested that 'the main weak point of the United States in the world is the Middle East region, and we are able to weaken it to a greater extent if we were to cooperate' (Naqqash 2019). A Russian analyst added that an additional objective was 'to test weapons and gain combat [military] experience' (Bershidsky 2018). A US analyst suggested Russia wanted 'to reclaim its status as a global power broker' (Frolovskiy 2019). All these are plausible and complementary. However, the Russian intervention was quite different to that of Turkey and the USA: it was based on an invitation from the recognised government of Syria and so had a firm basis in international law.

Direct Russian air power engagement in Syria not only degraded DAESH and Jabhat al Nusra, it exposed Turkish President Erdogan's backing for DAESH. In late 2015 Russia's Defence Ministry presented photographic evidence of convoys of trucks stealing Syrian oil and taking it for sale in Turkey (Brooks-Pollock 2015). So Russia introduced a strong political voice as well as a military presence. Subsequently a series of articles linked President Erdogan's son Bilal Erdogan to the oil trade with DAESH (Phillips 2016). More recently former DAESH 'prince' Abu Mansour al Maghrebi (originally from Morocco) told US academics that Erdogan's government had worked 'hand in glove with ISIS', in particular through Turkey's MIT intelligence agency, to develop a relationship in which 'both sides benefit' (Ahmed 2019).

From the Axis of Resistance side there have been criticisms and claims that Russia was either duplicitous or 'captured' by Israeli interests, because Moscow maintained its close relationship with Tel Aviv, the mortal enemy of Syria and the regional Resistance. The stronger versions of such claims are exaggerations. If Russia were really captured by Israel it would not have made such a commitment to defeating the proxy armies in Syria. Israeli leaders revelled in the chaos of Islamist groups killing Syrian and Iraqi soldiers. It is certainly true that Russia tried to limit its enemies to the internationally proscribed terrorist groups Jabhat al Nusra, DAESH 'and all other individuals, groups, undertakings and entities associated with Al-Qaida' (UNSC 2015). Russia also tried (and for most of the time succeeded) in avoiding direct conflict with US, Turkish and Israeli forces, all of whom were overtly or covertly supporting the proxy armies. They could even claim common ground, as all state parties and the UN Security Council had formally agreed to fight DAESH and al Nusra. It is logical, in a war, to limit one's enemies and so prevent the unexpected consequences of escalation.

Nevertheless, it is also true that Russia has maintained a close relationship with Israel (Krasna 2018), quite distinct to that of the resistance countries, which all consider Israel an illegitimate 'entity'. Because of its colonisation of Palestine, its invasions, its occupations of Arab lands and its regional interventions in league with the colonial powers, the Axis partners say Israel is at the root of conflict in the region (TOI 2018). Russia has a different view, and distinct strategic interests. Questioned on this, Resistance analyst Anees Naqqash said 'A commitment to the security of Israel, is different to defending Israel ... ... is [Russia] able to prevent the Resistance Axis or Syria from taking a decision to retake the Golan [Heights]? No it is not, because this also falls under international law' (Naqqash 2019). Russia's relations with Israel are a major difference, but that does not destroy the common interests that made Russia an ally of Syria, Iran, Iraq and Hezbollah. The Lebanese Resistance leader Hassan Nasrallah said as much, in early 2017:

> Russia does not classify itself as [part of the Resistance Axis] ... There is a convergence between Russia and the Resistance Axis regarding a number of fields and files, one of which is Syria. However, in other places, there is a difference of opinion. For example, in Yemen ... Russia naturally as a big state – or one of the great powers of the world – has wide-ranging relations and contacts, one of which is with Israel.

Okay – we do not fight Israel alongside Russia. When we fight Israel, we fight it ourselves. However, in Syria, there is a convergence, there is an intersection of interests ... a convergence in actual fact, regarding events in Syria. And therefore we are in agreement regarding Syria, but it is not necessary that we be in agreement in other fields (Nasrallah 2017).

Russia under President Putin has also tried to maintain its relations with the US, but it faced another power game from Washington: the effort to divide Russia from western Europe (Brzezinski 1997). Russia has also pursued strategic and business interests with Syria's enemies, Turkey (under President Erdogan) and Saudi Arabia. Some of this has helped Syria, for example in moving the centre of international diplomacy to Astana, by including both Iran and Turkey. For all these reasons I suggest that Russia cannot be considered a member of the Axis of Resistance but, at least for its commitment in Syria, must be considered a strong ally of the Resistance.

Russia has made a dedicated effort to protect Syria and there have been substantial sacrifices. We cannot ignore the fact that many Russians in Syria have paid the ultimate price. There have been several hundred Russian casualties in Syria. That includes aircraft pilots, soldiers and civilians. Notable examples include the young special forces officer, Senior Lieutenant Alexander Prokhorenko, who called in an airstrike on himself, as he was discovered by a DAESH gang near Palmyra (Dearden 2016). Then there was pilot Major Roman Filipov, who was killed 'during combat with terrorists' in Idlib. There is film of him detonating a grenade as he was about to be captured by the al Nusra gang (RT 2018). Syrian people have shown deep appreciation for these sacrifices.

In August 2018 the Russian military said that over the previous three years it had deployed 63,000 troops in Syria, had attacked 121,000 terrorist targets and had killed 86,000 'militants'.

As a sign of the relentless propaganda war the British-backed 'Syrian Observatory for Human Rights' (a Syrian exile funded by British intelligence) claimed at least 7,928 civilians and 10,069 combatants had been killed by Russian air strikes (BBC 2018). There is no end to the propaganda war, especially on casualty figures.

The Syrian Arab Army (SAA) has carried the greatest share of casualties in defending and reclaiming their land from foreign aggression. The SAA represents the 'Syrian Arab' nation, pluralist and 'secular', which includes members from all communities and religions. Contrary to the claims of mass defections and disintegration, the army held together as a nationalist force, despite tremendous casualties. Notwithstanding the invaluable assistance of allies, most of the gains in liberating Syria's cities and towns were fought for, won and paid in blood by the hundreds of thousands of young Syrians, who defended a nation which provides them with identity, education and a range of shared services.

The Syrian Government apparently has, but does not publish, a martyr's list. Yet every town and suburb has its public display of soldiers who fell defending their country. Most estimates of soldiers and national defence force casualties are well over 100,000; that is, around a quarter of the estimated 400,000 killed. Casualties amongst the armed groups and their families (always masquerading as 'civilians') are probably double this, in excess of 200,000. The top photo on the cover of this book shows a billboard commemorating the SAA and National Defence Force (NDF) martyrs from the southern Damascus suburb of Dwella.

Unlike western expeditionary forces in the Middle East, the SAA did not invade other countries, they did not demand 'regime change' in other parts of the world and they did not set out to 'kill their own people', as the imperial propaganda has it. They defended their communities and their nation, with that historical Syrian pluralism which placed nation above religion or sect. From this writer's observations in seven visits to Syria, the Syrian Arab Army remains the most popular entity in the country. Almost every family has a relative martyred or wounded in fighting the vicious proxy armies. I wrote about the army, the government and the opposition in Chapters 3 and 5 of *The Dirty War on Syria*.

Syria as a pluralist nation, both in its modern form and with a long tradition, brings its own distinct character to the Axis of Resistance, which includes religious parties and an Islamic Republic. President Assad has reaffirmed his commitment to secularism and Pan Arabism, which he says neither excludes religion nor is a narrow 'ethnic' concept of Arabism. Indeed, he maintains that that a key goal of the war was to destroy this regional Pan-Arabism. The enemies of Syria and pan-Arabism, he says, 'focused on the ethnic issue and took away from the pan-Arabism, the most important civilized aspects in it which are related to the cultural aspect, language, geography, history and other things' (Assad 2017).

Criticisms of Syria's strong state, built in the face of decades of war with Israel and violent insurrection from salafists, now look rather hollow. A weak or tyrannical state would have been destroyed by those eight years of war. The Syrian Arab Army, drawing on contemporary Syrian Arab identity, played a crucial role in maintaining national unity during the crisis. Despite great wartime damage, Syria has demonstrated the will and capacity to defend itself and rebuild, consistent with its long traditions of self-reliance. Syria's allies have also played an important role in defeating Washington's latest aggression. All that underlines the need for a permanent and strong regional alliance. Small states cannot resist alone.

Bibliography

ABC (2015) 'UNESCO condemns Islamic State militant's killing of Palmyra's antiquities chief Khaled Assad', ABC News, 20 August, online: https://www.abc.net.au/news/2015-08-20/unesco-condemns-islamic-state-killing-palmyra-antiquities-assaad/6710664

Abouzeid, Rania (2011) 'Syria's Revolt, how graffiti stirred an uprising', *Time*, 22 March

Ahmed, Nafeez (2019) 'Erdogan worked "hand in glove" with ISIS in Syria, claims former emir', INSURGE Intelligence, 2 April, online: https://medium.com/insurge-intelligence/erdogan-worked-hand-in-glove-with-isis-in-syria-claims-former-emir-e83c0e6b9c3d

Al-Shaqfa, Muhammad Riyad (2011) 'Muslim Brotherhood Statement about the so-called 'Syrian Revolution'', General supervisor for the Syrian Muslim Brotherhood, statement of 28 March, online at: http://truthsyria.wordpress.com/2012/02/12/muslim-brotherhood-statement-about-the-so-called-syrian-revolution/

Anderson, Tim (2016) The Dirty War on Syria, Global Research, Montreal

Anderson, Tim (2017) 'Implausible Denials: The Crime at Jabal al Tharda. US-led Air Raid on Behalf of ISIS-Daesh Against Syrian Forces', Global Research, 17 December, online: https://www.globalresearch.ca/implausible-denials-the-crime-at-jabal-al-tharda-us-led-air-raid-on-behalf-of-isis-daesh-against-syrian-forces/5623056

ARA (2016) 'Over 1,000 new fighters join Syrian Democratic Forces in fight for Raqqa', ARA News, 10 December, online: http://aranews.net/files/2016/12/over-1000-new-fighters-join-syrian-democratic-forces-in-fight-for-raqqa/

Assad, Bashar al (2017) 'President al-Assad: Main goal of war on Syria is undermining pan-Arabism and affiliation', SANA, 14 November, online: https://sana.sy/en/?p=118174

BBC (2018) 'Russia says 63,000 troops have seen combat in Syria', 22 August, online: https://www.bbc.com/news/world-middle-east-45284121

Bengio (2017) 'Kurdistan, the New Israel?', Tablet, 23 September, online: https://www.tabletmag.com/jewish-news-and-politics/245328/kurdistan-the-new-israel

Bershidsky, Leonid (2018) 'Putin's Goals in Syria Went Beyond Saving Assad', *Moscow Times,* 5 January, online: https://www.themoscowtimes.com/2018/01/05/putins-goals-in-syria-went-beyond-saving-assad-a60121

Blanford, Nicholas (2011) 'Assad regime may be gaining upper hand in Syria', *Christian Science Monitor*, 13 May, online: http://www.csmonitor.com/World/Middle-East/2011/0513/Assad-regime-may-be-gaining-upper-hand-in-Syria

Brooks-Pollock, Tom (2015) 'Russia unveils 'proof' Turkey's Erdogan is smuggling Isis oil across border from Syria', *The Independent,* 4 December, online: https://www.independent.co.uk/news/world/europe/russia-releases-proof-turkey-is-smuggling-isis-oil-over-its-border-a6757651.html

Brzezinski, Zbigniew (1997) *The Grand Chessboard: American Primacy and Its Geostrategic Imperatives*, Basic Books, New York

Calamur, Krishnadev (2017) 'Why Doesn't the U.S. Support Kurdish

Independence?', *The Atlantic*, 20 October, online: https://www.theatlantic.com/international/archive/2017/10/us-kurdish-independence/543540/

CBS (2017) 'US quietly let hundreds of ISIS fighters flee Raqqa', 14 November, online: https://www.cbsnews.com/news/report-us-allowed-isis-fighters-escape-raqqa-sdf-deal/

CEP (2019) 'Nusra Front (Jabhat Fateh al-Sham)', Counter Extremism Project, online: https://www.counterextremism.com/threat/nusra-front-jabhat-fateh-al-sham

Clinton, Hillary (2014) 'Re: Here's what I mentioned', Wikileaks, email from Hillary Clinton to John Podesta, 17 August, online: https://wikileaks.org/podesta-emails/emailid/7243

Curtis, Mark (2015) *Secret Affairs: Britain's Collusion with Radical Islam*, Serpent's Tail, London

Dearden, Lizzie (2016) 'Body of Russian special forces officer who 'ordered air strike on himself' to kill Isis militants returned home', *The Independent*, 30 April, online: https://www.independent.co.uk/news/world/europe/russian-special-forces-officer-ordered-air-strike-on-himself-to-kill-isis-militants-surrounded-body-a7008106.html

DIA (1982) 'Syria: Muslim Brotherhood Pressure Intensifies', Defence Intelligence Agency (USA), May, online: https://syria360.files.wordpress.com/2013/11/dia-syria-muslimbrotherhoodpressureintensifies-2.pdf

DIA (2012) 'Department of Defence Information Report, Not Finally Evaluated Intelligence, Country: Iraq', Defence Intelligence Agency, August, 14-L-0552/DIA/297-293, Levant report, online at:http://levantreport.com/2015/05/19/2012-defense-intelligence-agency-document-west-will-facilitate-rise-of-islamic-state-in-order-to-isolate-the-syrian-regime/

Evans, Dominic and Orhan Coskun (2017) 'Defector says thousands of Islamic State fighters left Raqqa in secret deal', Reuters, 8 December, online: https://www.reuters.com/article/us-mideast-crisis-syria-defector/defector-says-thousands-of-islamic-state-fighters-left-raqqa-in-secret-deal-idUSKBN1E12AP

Export.Gov (2015) 'Dual Use Export Licenses', US Export Agency, online: http://www.export.gov/regulation/eg_main_018229.asp

Farrell, Shane (2011) 'Lebanese Christians react to regional instability', Now Media, 5 April, online: https://now.mmedia.me/lb/en/reportsfeatures/lebanese_christians_react_to_regional_instability

Fisk, Robert (2012) 'Inside Daraya - how a failed prisoner swap turned into a massacre', 29 August: http://www.independent.co.uk/voices/commentators/fisk/robert-fisk-inside-daraya--how-a-failed-prisoner-swap-turned-into-a-massacre-8084727.html

Fisk Robert (2018) 'To Putin, Assad's enemies in Syria are the same as Russia's in Chechnya', *The Independent*, 5 March, online: https://www.independent.co.uk/voices/putin-russia-ghouta-assad-syria-chechnya-shaun-walker-enemies-the-same-a8240311.html

Flynn, Michael (2016) 'Transcript: Michael Flynn on ISIL', Al Jazeera, 13 January online: https://www.aljazeera.com/programmes/headtohead/2016/01/transcript-michael-flynn-160104174144334.html

Frolovskiy, Dmitriy (2019) 'What Putin Really Wants in Syria', *Foreign Policy*, 1 February, online: https://foreignpolicy.com/2019/02/01/what-putin-really-wants-in-syria-russia-assad-strategy-kremlin/

FT (2017) 'Iraq announces defeat of ISIS', *Financial Times*, 10 December, online: https://www.ft.com/content/d6636416-dcf3-11e7-a8a4-0a1e63a52f9c

GCAD (2019) 'Global Coalition Against DAESH', online: https://theglobalcoalition.org/en/

Ghanem, Mohammad Alaa (2015) 'Syria: An Opportunity in Idlib', The Atlantic Council, 3 April, online: https://www.atlanticcouncil.org/blogs/menasource/syria-an-opportunity-in-idlib

Haider, Syed (2017) 'The defeat of DAESH in Syria and Iraq', *Daily Times*, 27 November, online: https://dailytimes.com.pk/147727/defeat-daesh-syria-iraq/

Hauer, Neil (2018) 'Chechen and North Caucasian Militants in Syria', Atlantic Council, 18 January, online: https://www.atlanticcouncil.org/blogs/syriasource/chechen-and-north-caucasian-militants-in-syria

HRW (2012) 'Open Letter to the Leaders of the Syrian Opposition, Human Rights Watch, Washington, 20 March, online: http://www.hrw.org/news/2012/03/20/open-letter-leaders-syrian-opposition

Khaled, Ahmad Al (2019) 'US Has a Plan for Eastern Syria, and It Relies on ISIS', Global Research, 24 March, online: https://www.globalresearch.ca/us-eastern-syria-relies-isis/5672489

Krasna, Joshua (2018) 'Moscow on the Mediterranean: Russia and Israel's Relationship', Russian Foreign Policy papers, Foreign Policy Research Institute, Philadelphia, June, online: https://www.fpri.org/wp-content/uploads/2018/06/krasna2018.pdf

Lavrov, Sergei (2018) 'Russia says Nusra terrorists 'recovering strength' in US-controlled zone in S Syria', Press TV, 19 February, online: https://www.presstv.com/DetailFr/2018/02/19/552938/Russia-Syria-US-Jabhat-Fateh-alSham-alTanf-Rukban-Daesh

Lefèvre, Raphaël (2013) *Ashes of Hama: The Muslim Brotherhood in Syria*, Oxford University Press, Oxford

Levinson, Adam Valen (2017) 'The "second Israel" dream: Kurdistan and 21st century secessions', Salon, 12 November, online: https://www.salon.

com/2017/11/12/the-second-israel-dream-kurdistan-and-21st-century-secessions/
MEMO (2018) 'Iran: US moved Daesh militants to Afghanistan', Middle East Monitor, 7 December, online: https://www.middleeastmonitor.com/20181207-iran-us-moved-daesh-militants-to-afghanistan/
MEMRITV (2011) 'Syrian Sunni Cleric Threatens: "We Shall Mince [The Alawites] in Meat Grinders"', YouTube, 13 July, online: https://www.youtube.com/watch?v=Bwz8i3osHww
Mulhem, Suliman (2017) 'A Closer Look at How Russia and the Syrian Army Defeated Daesh', 14 December, online: https://sputniknews.com/analysis/201712141060004673-russia-syrian-army-daesh-defeat/
Naqqash, Anees (2019) 'Hezbollah-linked Analyst on reality of Russia's alliance with Iran/Hezbollah', Middle East Observer, 11 March, online: http://middleeastobserver.net/video-senior-analyst-close-to-hezbollah-on-reality-of-russian-alliance-with-iran-resistance-axis-english-subs/
Narwani, Sharmine (2012) 'Questioning the Syrian "Casualty List"', 28 Feb, online: http://english.al-akhbar.com/content/questioning-syrian-%E2%80%9Ccasualty-list%E2%80%9D
Narwani, Sharmine (2014) Syria: The hidden massacre, RT, 7 May, online: http://rt.com/op-edge/157412-syria-hidden-massacre-2011/
Nasrallah, Hassan (2017) 'Nasrallah: Russia and 'Resistance axis' agree on Syria, but not Israel & Yemen', Middle East Observer, 23 February, online: https://middleeastobserver.net/translation-nasrallah-russia-and-resistance-axis-agree-on-syria-but-not-israel-yemen/
Newman, Alex (2014) '"Moderate" Rebels Armed by Obama Join al-Qaeda, ISIS', New American, 21 November, online: http://www.thenewamerican.com/world-news/asia/item/19583-moderate-rebels-armed-by-obama-join-al-qaeda-isis
Oweis, Khaled Yacoub (2012) 'Syria activists report 'massacre' by army near Damascus', 25 August: http://www.reuters.com/article/2012/08/25/us-syria-crisis-killings-idUSBRE87O08J20120825
Phillips, David L. (2016) 'Research Paper: Turkey-ISIS Oil Trade', *The Huffington Post*, 14 December, online: https://www.huffpost.com/entry/research-paper-turkey-isi_b_8808024
Qurbany, Arif (2018) 'How can Kurdistan become a second Israel?', RUDAW, 7 November, online: http://www.rudaw.net/english/opinion/11072018
Reuters (2011) 'Syria says seizes weapons smuggled from Iraq', 11 March, online: http://www.reuters.com/article/2011/03/11/us-syria-iraq-idUSTRE72A3MI20110311?hc_location=ufi
RFERL (2018) 'Trump's Syria Withdrawal Announcement Criticized By Allies, Praised By Putin', Radio Free Europe Radio Liberty, 20 December, online: https://www.rferl.org/a/trump-syria-troop-pullout-islamic-

state-russia-turkey-iran/29666375.html
Rothman, Noah (2014) 'Dempsey: I know of Arab allies who fund ISIS', YouTube, 16 September, online: https://www.youtube.com/watch?v=nA39iVSo7XE
RT (2012) '89% vote in favor of new Syrian Constitution', 27 February online: https://www.rt.com/news/syria-referendum-constitution-results-307/
RT (2014) 'Anyone but US! Biden blames allies for ISIS rise', 3 October, online: https://www.youtube.com/watch?v=1Il8nLZNPSY
RT (2018) '"This is for the boys!' Video allegedly shows Su-25 pilot's last stand with grenade explosion', 4 February, online: https://www.rt.com/news/417852-russian-pilot-last-stand-grenade/
Said, Rodi (2019) 'Syrian Kurds seek Damascus deal regardless of U.S. moves', 5 January, Reuters, online: https://www.reuters.com/article/us-mideast-crisis-syria-kurds/syrian-kurds-seek-damascus-deal-regardless-of-us-moves-idUSKCN1OY1ET
Salt, Jeremy (2011) Truth and Falsehood in Syria, The Palestine Chronicle, 5 October, online: http://palestinechronicle.com/view_article_details.php?id=17159
Seale, Patrick (1988) *Asad: the struggle for the Middle East,* University of California Press, Berkeley
Shadid, Anthony and David D. Kirkpatrick (2011) 'Promise of Arab Uprisings Is Threatened by Divisions', *New York Times,* 21 May, online: http://www.nytimes.com/2011/05/22/world/middleeast/22arab.html?pagewanted=all
Sharifulin, Valeriy (2015) 'Only aviation support will be provided to regular Syrian army — Russian lawmaker', TASS, 30 September, online: http://tass.ru/en/politics/824875
Silverstein, Richard (2017) 'Former Israeli Defense Minister Confirms Israeli Collaboration with ISIS in Syria', *Tikun Olam,* 23 April, online: https://www.richardsilverstein.com/2017/04/23/breaking-former-israeli-defense-minister-confirms-israeli-collaboration-isis-syria/
TOI (2018) "Iran's Rouhani calls Israel a 'cancerous tumor' established by West", *Times of Israel,* 24 November, online: https://www.timesofisrael.com/irans-rouhani-calls-israel-a-cancerous-tumor-established-by-west/
Truth Syria (2012) 'Syria – Daraa revolution was armed to the teeth from the very beginning', BBC interview with Anwar Al-Eshki, YouTube interview, video originally uploaded 10 April, latest version 7 November, online: https://www.youtube.com/watch?v=FoGmrWWJ77w
UFilter (2017) 'US helicopters transfer DAESH members from eastern Syria', Uden Filter, 5 November, online: http://ufilter.blogspot.com.au/2017/08/us-helicopters-transfer-daesh-members.html
UNSC (2015) 'Resolution 2249 (2015) Adopted by the Security Council at its

7565th meeting, on 20 November 2015', United Nations Security Council, S/RES/2249 (2015), online: https://www.un.org/en/ga/search/view_doc.asp?symbol=S/RES/2249(2015)

Usher, Barbara Plett (2014) 'Joe Biden apologised over IS remarks, but was he right?' BBC News, 7 October, online: http://www.bbc.com/news/world-us-canada-29528482

van der Lugt, Frans (2012) 'Bij defaitisme is niemand gebaat', from Homs, 13 January, online: https://mediawerkgroepsyrie.wordpress.com/2012/01/13/bij-defaitisme-is-niemand-gebaat/

Washington's Blog (2014) 'Top U.S. Military Official: Our Arab "Allies" Support ISIS', 16 September, online: http://www.washingtonsblog.com/2014/09/top-u-s-military-official-arab-allies-support-isis.html

Weiss, Phillip (2017) 'US watched ISIS rise in Syria and hoped to 'manage' it — Kerry on leaked tape', Mondoweiss, 11 January, online: https://mondoweiss.net/2017/01/watched-manage-leaked/

Yakovenko, Alexander (2016) 'Russia went to Syria to fight terrorists. We are succeeding', *The Guardian,* 16 October, online: https://www.theguardian.com/commentisfree/2016/oct/15/syria-russian-ambassador-aleppo-isis

Zelin, Aaron Y. (2012) 'Rally 'Round the Jihadist', *Foreign Policy*, 11 December, online: https://foreignpolicy.com/2012/12/11/rally-round-the-jihadist/

The crushing of Aleppo's al Qaeda groups led to street celebrations. Photo RT.

Chapter Six

THE LIBERATION OF ALEPPO

The liberation of Syria's second city from al Qaeda gangs in December 2016 was a major turning point in the conflict. After the liberation of Homs, Qusayr and Palmyra, definitive reverses began to destroy the morale of both the 'jihadists' and their sponsors. Not even religious fanatics are keen to join a losing cause.

Throughout 2016, as Damascus regained some sense of security, a shocking war raged on in Aleppo. As usual, the western media lied incessantly, focussing exclusively on that part of the city held by the al Qaeda groups which held a maximum of 300,000 people (about 20% of the then population of the city). Small groups of armed men surrendered to take advantage of a possible amnesty, as dozens of residents passed out through Syrian- and Russian army-controlled humanitarian corridors. Those checkpoints were run by commando units, including those of General Suheil al Hassan's Tiger Forces, as the check points still faced jihadist suicide car-bombs, as they had from DAESH in Palmyra.

Typically, there were almost no western media stories about how the 1.5 million in the government-held parts of Aleppo were faring. Over April-May many dozens of people were murdered across the city as civilian areas and major hospitals were bombed by the NATO-backed 'rebels'. They were even filmed firing their 'hell cannons' while saying 'throw it on the civilians' (Syrian Reporters 2016; HOS 2019b).

It is worth recounting some of the barrage of propaganda that accompanied western-backed efforts to prevent or at least stall the liberation of this ancient city, especially the 'hospital wars' propaganda, before turning to the final liberation of the city.

1. The Hospital Wars

Over April-May dozens were killed across Aleppo. From the early days of their occupation these gangs called 'rebels' by most western media but 'DAESH' or 'musalaheen' (armed groups) by most Syrians -- complained that the people of Aleppo hated them. 'Abu Sadek', a member of the 'Liwa Suqooral-Sha'ba' gang in Bustan al-Basha, told a US reporter: 'The Aleppans here, all of them, are loyal to the criminal Bashar, they inform on us, they tell the regime where we are, where we go, what we do, even now ... If God wasn't with us, we would have been wiped out a long time ago' (Abouzeid 2012). Similarly, a British reporter observed another gang leader, 'Abu Ali Sulaibi,' telling scared civilians: 'You are all informers ... I know you cross back to government side and report on us'. Another gang member told the western media: 'I know they hate us. They blame us for the destruction. Maybe they are right, but had the people of Aleppo supported the revolution from the beginning this wouldn't have happened' (Abdul-Ahad 2012). Lack of popular support is fatal to a revolution, less so it seems for fanatics.

Meanwhile, western media ran fantasy stories about the besieged city. If you believed the western corporate media you might think that the Syrian Government, for some unknown reason, has been bombing its own hospitals (ABC Radio National 2016), and had killed Aleppo's only paediatric surgeon. Nothing could be further from the truth.

The Syrian Arab Army (SAA) mounted a large operation – backed by the Russians and reinforced by regional and local militias – to reclaim those sections of the city held by Islamist fighters since 2012. Almost half Aleppo's population had been displaced but there were still about 1.7 million residents. Syrian-Russian operations were set up to evacuate civilians from east

Aleppo through humanitarian corridors some months before the final operation (Geopolitics 2016).

The withdrawal of the Saudi-backed 'High Negotiations Committee' from the Geneva peace talks on 21 April was followed the very next day by a pre-emptive counter-offensive. Many hundreds of rockets were fired into government-held areas by a coalition led by the internationally banned terrorist organisation, Jabhat al Nusra. These attacks came mostly from 'hell cannons', which shoot large gas canisters filled with explosives and at times chemicals. They caused havoc, killing and wounding many people in the streets, residential areas, schools and hospitals. The Syrian Army responded by shelling the al Nusra hideouts.

Aleppo Doctor Dr Nabil Antaki estimated that 1.5 million were still living in the government-controlled western parts of the city, with up to another 300,000 in the gang-controlled eastern areas. He complained bitterly that the western media 'only talk about loss of life in east of Aleppo which is entirely controlled by al Nusra. The three quarters of Aleppo under Syrian Government control, where numerous paediatricians are practising are of no consequence'(Cattori 2016). He was referring to the string of bomb attacks on major state hospitals including Ibn Rushd, al Dabbit and al Razi. Many dozens of people were killed and injured. Those attacks were filmed by Syrian and Russian people on the ground, but very little of this reached the western media. Dr Antaki wasn't the only Aleppo doctor who was upset. The Aleppo Medical Association, on its Facebook page, denounced the western propaganda campaign, posting photos of their outrage. Twenty doctors in front of the heavily damaged al Dabbit Hospital declared their support for the Syrian Army. Their signs – in English, Italian and German as well as Arabic – read: 'Syrian Arab Army represents me', 'Long live Syria, long live Aleppo', 'Terrorists are killing our children', 'Armed opposition is destroying our civilisation', 'No to armed opposition' (AMA 2016).

Yet the story of supposed Russian or Syrian air attacks on the 'al Quds hospital' gained prominence in the western media. Stories were fuelled with information from the French group

Aleppo Medical Association (AMA) doctors stand with Syrian soldiers, demanding an end to western misinformation about the Aleppo attacks. Photo AMA.

Médecins Sans Frontières (MSF, Doctors without Borders) and the UK- and US Government-funded group, the 'White Helmets', which regularly celebrated their 'revolution' with Jabhat al Nusra (Webb 2017; Beeley 2018; HOS 2019a).

The 'al Quds hospital' building is in the southern al-Sukkari district, a stronghold of Jabhat al Nusra for some years. Many Aleppans had never heard of it. Dr Antaki says: 'This hospital did not exist before the war. It must have been installed in a building after the war began' (Antaki and Cattori 2016). MSF reports seem to confirm this. This facility was neither state run nor a registered facility. Nevertheless, MSF representatives Pablo Marco and Muskilda Zancada claimed: 'Al Quds hospital has been functional for more than 4 years so it was basically impossible that this information was not known ... the facts are pointing to this being a deliberate attack' (Stirling 2016). Their 'facts' came from armed groups in Aleppo.

Indeed, MSF-backed medical facilities in Syria have almost exclusively been in al Nusra held areas, such as Douma, north east of Damascus. MSF provided money but not doctors.

There is some debate as to whether clinics or hospitals run to service banned terrorist organisations have protection under international humanitarian law. Certainly, US law does not allow it. A few years back the US jailed US doctor Rafig Sabir for 25 years after it emerged that he had been 'on call' to treat al Qaeda fighters in Saudi Arabia (USCA 2011). Registered hospitals certainly do have such protection, and it is a crime to attack them. However, this protection disappears when the facility becomes militarised. The Red Cross makes it clear that 'civilian objects are protected against attack, unless and for such time as they are military objectives' (ICRC 2019).

All three air forces that claimed to be bombing terrorist groups in Syria – Russia, Syria and the USA – denied involvement in the 'al Quds hospital' incident. The USA had engaged in bombing some areas around Aleppo (RT 2016) but is not known to have carried out attacks on Jabhat al Nusra, which was well embedded with the proxy armies Washington likes to call 'moderate rebels'.

'Al Quds hospital' in 2016: neither a pile of rubble, nor a designated hospital. Photo Jabhat al Nusra.

There were other serious discrepancies in the 'al Quds hospital' story. Pablo Marco for MSF told CNN and PBS that 'there were two barrel bombs that fell close to the hospital ... then the third barrel bomb fell in the entrance'. Barrel bombs are supposedly dropped by helicopters. Yet the MSF press release spoke of an 'airstrike ... [which] brought down the building ... leaving a pile of rubble'. Reports of the death toll ranged from 14 to 50 (in Stirling 2016). Of course, the MSF spokespeople were passing on stories relayed to them by the armed groups which controlled the clinic.

Contrary to western stories about 'Aleppo's last paediatrician' (Drury 2016), there were dozens of paediatricians in Aleppo's main public hospitals (Antaki and Cattori 2016; Makhoul-Yatim 2016). The al Quds facility was a field hospital for the armed groups (Turbeville 2016); and it was not a pile of rubble. As Rick Sterling (2016) pointed out, photos showed that the facility was still standing, after the alleged air attack. It appeared a heavily sand-bagged building. Further, Russian satellite imagery showed the damaged building was in much the same state back on 15 October 2015. If this is correct, the MSF-backed 'al Quds hospital' suffered no air attack on 27 April.

Russian satellite imagery shows 'al Quds hospital' in the al Sukkari district had the same damage six months before the alleged airstrike. Photo RT.

'Al Quds hospital' in October 2017

This writer visited that building in October 2017, after liberation of the city and while the building was under reconstruction. There was substantial internal and peripheral damage, but the building was structurally sound (see photo above). Only the front room at the top lacked a roof. There was no collapse of walls or floors, or of the elevator shaft, as one might expect from an air attack. Restoration was taking place on the facade and windows. I was told it had been a small private hospital, under construction when it was taken over in 2012.

The scale of coverage of the 'al Quds hospital' story obscured the ugly fact that several much larger public hospitals in Aleppo were being bombed by the gangs. The former smokescreen covered up the latter poorly reported massacres. It is not that there was no western coverage of the actual hospital attacks, the coverage was just removed to the very margins of western stories.

Take the devastating bombing of al Razi hospital, which Al Alam (2016) reported as killing 4 and wounding 38, in days of 'rebel' shelling which left 57 dead and 150 injured. The Wall

Street Journal mentioned western Aleppo casualties and al Razi in an article which led by blaming Russia for the alleged 'airstrike' on 'al Quds hospital'. The WSJ spent the next 28 paragraphs on that incident. Buried at paragraph 30 was this reference, from an anti-Syrian source: 'shells had [also] hit the Al-Razi Hospital, a facility in a government-held neighbourhood where many wounded were being treated' (Dagher 2016).

A report of the bombing of al Dabbit hospital did make it into the UK Independent. This hospital was said to be in 'regime-controlled Aleppo'. The report opened: 'At least 19 civilians have been killed at a hospital and other parts of government-controlled Aleppo in shelling attributed to Islamist rebels' (Dearden 2016). The Syrian news agency SANA reported on 3 May that the death toll from the bombing of al Dabbit hospital had risen to 16 dead and 68 injured (SANA 2016; Turbeville 2016). Hardly mentioned in the western media was the bombing of the large Ibn Rushd hospital, but the Russian TV channel ANNA filmed the actual bombing and Latin American media ran that video (ANNA 2016). YouTube later closed down ANNA Television's video account.

The attacks on Aleppo were extensive, well beyond hospitals. Vicar of Aleppo Mons. Georges Abou Khazen said 'we have been under continuous bombardment over the past few days in Aleppo with civilian deaths, injuries and destruction'. He pointed his finger at the groups backed by the West, along with Turkey and Saudi Arabia, saying that 'These bombings ... are from the front of the so-called "moderates" and ... in reality [they] are no different from other jihadists [Islamic State (IS) and the Nusra Front]' (Abou Khazen 2016).

The gangs fired hundreds of rockets into the main part of Aleppo, gassed the Kurdish areas of the city and publicly beheaded a 12-year-old Palestinian boy, Abdullah Issa, accused of being a spy for one of the Palestinian militias which fought alongside the SAA (BBC 2016). But the gangs were losing and the region's public mood was hardening. Syrian civil opposition leader Moustafa Kelechi (not allied to the armed groups) said that the battle of Aleppo was 'a war to crush the Takfiri groups' bones' (FARS News 2016).

2. The Liberation of Aleppo

By late 2016, at the cost of many young lives, Syrian forces took back the eastern part of the city of Aleppo, occupied by NATO- and Saudi-backed terrorists for more than four years. Syrian soldiers were backed by the Russians, but there were no air attacks in the final weeks. Syrian ground forces, with help from Hezbollah and Palestinian-Syrian militia, bore most of the sacrifice of the fighting in those final days. In the chapter of this book titled 'The Human Rights Industry in Humanitarian War' I discuss a misleading UN report prepared on the liberation of the city.

After a storm of western government and media misinformation (claims of massacres, mass executions and 'civilians targeted') over the evacuation of around 100,000 civilians and many thousands of terrorists, the UN Security Council authorised some 'independent observers' to monitor the process. The Syrian President gave amnesties to some who surrendered, while others chose the option of traveling to a type of temporary internal exile in Idlib, with their families, in a fleet of what The Atlantic called 'menacing green buses', while mourning 'the fall' of Aleppo (Attar 2017). Outgoing UN Secretary General Ban Ki-Moon, a close ally of Washington, claimed in his final press conference that 'Aleppo is now a synonym for hell' (VOA 2016). Those claims were based on stories from NATO's desperate jihadists.

Syrian, Iranian, Russian and independent reporters on the ground – including Maytham al Ashkar, Shadi Halwi, Asser Khatab, the late Khaled Alkhateb, Ali Musawi, Lizzie Phelan, Murad Gazdiev, Vanessa Beeley, Eva Bartlett, Jan Oberg, Carla Ortiz and the late Mohsen Khazaei – told us a different story, which bore little resemblance to the western apocalyptic stories. As Syrian forces smashed the al Qaeda lines, the trapped civilians streamed out. They published interviews and videos of long lines of people leaving east Aleppo and finding relief, food and shelter with the Syrian Arab Army. Tired and relieved, they celebrated and told their stories to anyone who cared to listen (Cenci 2016; Phelan 2016; Beeley 2016; Telesur 2016; Doucet 2016; Oberg 2017; Van Wagenen 2017). Russia and Iran handed out many tons of food, clothing, blanket and shelter aid. By contrast, western countries generally gave nothing. The al Qaeda groups had rejected all aid from the Syrian alliance.

Civilians had been prohibited from leaving the al Qaeda enclave and a number were shot dead when they tried to do so. The armed gangs had food reserves but kept it for their fighters. Arms factories, including toxic chemicals, were found and were being made safe. Some of the armed men were taken into custody, but most were shipped out to Idlib. When the hell cannons fell silent, and no more home-made gas cylinder mortars landed in the heart of the city, there was elation and dancing in the streets, shown widely on social media (Syrian Girl 2016). A US State Department spokesman claimed he had not seen this.

Much of the western media, reflecting the view of their governments, solemnly reported on 'the fall of Aleppo' (Attar 2017). According to this line, the Syrian victory over the al Qaeda groups was a great tragedy. That bias tries to hide what should have been an obvious point, even admitted by US officials: that every single armed group in Syria (whether 'moderate' or 'extremist') had been armed and financed by the US and its allies, in an attempt to overthrow the Syrian Government and weaken the Syrian state (e.g. Biden in RT 2014).

The final evacuations of Aleppo – which included an exchange of civilians besieged for 20 months in the Idlib towns of Foua and Kefraya for remaining NATO-jihadists in eastern Aleppo – were organised between Russia and Turkey (Bassam and Davison 2017). But as some of the last exchanges took place, in April 2017, the gangs committed a terrible massacre at Rashidin. Buses full of Shi'a Muslim civilians from Foua and Kefraya were attacked by a suicide bomber as they waited to cross into the city of Aleppo. The Syrian government had secured their exit from

Idlib in exchange for the release of gang members captured in Zabadani. The gangs and their supporters once again tried to blame the Syrian Army for their own crime. This was after the Syrian government had worked to supply, protect and ultimately rescue the residents of those towns. More than 120 civilians, including children, were killed in a terrible pattern of killing and 'false flag' claims, established by the gangs from the beginning of the conflict (Davison 2017; Press TV 2017). The residents of Foua and Kefraya had been constantly menaced and attacked, simply for their Shi'a religion. The year before the 'Army of Conquest' (an Idlib coalition led by Jabhat al Nusra) had threated to 'wipe them out'. 'A massacre is inevitable ... [the gangs] are always sending them threats on walkie-talkies', said Mohammad Hassan Taqi, head of the towns' crisis committee (Bulos 2016). Seven months later his dreadful prediction came true.

When this writer visited Aleppo in early October 2017, life was returning to the city. From west to east it was quite peaceful, but with vigilant SAA reinforcements on the western and north-western sides of the city. The internally displaced persons (IDP) camp at Jebrin, which had previously housed people escaping from the eastern parts of the city, had been mostly emptied, but partially refilled by displaced people coming from Raqqa and other parts to the east. Visits to several of the damaged and functioning hospitals showed a common pattern. Aleppo MP Fares Shehabi told us that the gangs typically looted Aleppo's hospitals of their medical supplies and then used them (due to their solid construction) for command centres, also in some cases for torture centres.

The large French hospital was in ruins. A local guard and a worker at the nearby Cancer hospital confirmed to me multiple media reports that it had been looted by the armed groups and then hit by a Jabhat al Nusra suicide car bomb in November 2012. Similarly, the Eye Hospital in al Marja (East Aleppo) had been looted and then used as command centre for Nusra-FSA. It was still standing but badly damaged (Anderson 2017). Al Zarzour hospital (see photo following page) had been burnt out from the inside. A local woman told me it had been used for organ

Al Zarzour hospital, Aleppo

trafficking. Later, Maxim Grigoriev, of the Russian Foundation for the Study of Democracy, presented a report to the UN showing that the UK-US-funded White Helmets were deeply involved in the organ trafficking business. (Sputnik 2018).

* The Cancer Hospital (of the Syrian Cancer Society of Aleppo) and the nearby Labour hospital (for government employees) were both looted by FSA-Nusra gangs in 2012.
* The Labour hospital was later used to house refugees but was empty when we arrived (Anderson 2017).
* The large Ibn Rushd hospital had been bombed by FSA-Nusra gangs in April 2016, but appeared mostly intact, as was the Aleppo University Heart Hospital.
* The Al Dabbit maternity hospital was hit by an FSA-Nusra rocket in 2016 (Turbeville 2016) but seems have been quickly repaired. It was operating normally, when we arrived (Anderson 2017).
* The large al Kindi hospital (a specialist cancer facility) was completely destroyed by al Nusra truck bombs in December 2013. The gangs placed video online of the bombing, as those filming celebrated its destruction (Jabhat al Nusra 2013).

Nevertheless, both the displaced people and the refugees in Turkey returned more rapidly to Aleppo than to any other part of Syria. Even the BBC, in a small story, recognised the joy with which some IDPs were returning to their homes as the city was being liberated (Doucet 2016). Christmas was celebrated in the city for the first time in many years. The UN's International Organization for Migration (IOM) reported that 600,000 returned to Aleppo in the first seven months of 2017 (IOM 2017; Kennedy 2017). The following year US media reported 'tens of thousands' of refugees returning to Aleppo from Germany (CBS News 2018).

After the liberation of Aleppo the dynamic of international peace talks shifted, away from a US brokered process and towards talks between the engaged regional powers: Iran, Russia and Turkey. The so-called 'Astana process' began in January 2017, just after the liberation of Aleppo and with the backing of UN Security Council resolution 2336 (UNSC 2016). From Washington the Obama administration played little role in the endgame over Aleppo. Its regime change proxy war was failing.

Bibliography
ABC Radio National (2016), 'Syrian city of Aleppo running out of food as regime forces surround city', 20 July, online: http://www.abc.net.au/radionational/programs/breakfast/syria's-aleppo-running-out-of-food/7643402

Abdul-Ahad, Ghaith (2012) "The people of Aleppo needed someone to drag them into the revolution', *The Guardian*, 29 December, online: https://www.theguardian.com/world/2012/dec/28/aleppo-revolution-abu-ali-sulaibi

Abou Khazen, Georges (2016) 'Vicar of Aleppo: "moderate" front no better than jihadists, bombing civilians and not seeking peace', Asia News IT, 15 February, online: http://www.asianews.it/news-en/Vicar-of-Aleppo:-moderate-front-no-better-than-jihadists,-bombing-civilians-and-not-seeking-peace-36685.html

Abouzeid, Rania (2012) 'Aleppo's Deadly Stalemate: A Visit to Syria's Divided Metropolis', *Time*, 14 November, online: http://world.time.com/2012/11/14/aleppos-deadly-stalemate-a-visit-to-syrias-divided-metropolis/

Al Alam (2016) 'VIDEO: 57 Civilians killed, 150 Injured in Continued Terrorist Attacks on Aleppo', online: http://en.alalam.ir/news/1812988

AMA (2016) 'A solidarity stand for Aleppo Doctors', Aleppo Medical Association, 6 May, online: https://www.facebook.com/pg/Aleppodoctors.org/photos/?tab=album&album_id=1174868069211596

Anderson, Tim (2016) *The Dirty War on Syria*, Global Research, Montreal

Anderson, Tim (2017) 'Aleppo Hospitals', Facebook photo set, 8 October, online: https://www.facebook.com/timand2037/media_set?set=a.10212875196127629&type=3

ANNA (2016) Video of bombing of Ibn Rushd hospital, [ANNA's YouTube account was blocked; the video was online here: https://www.youtube.com/watch?v=afEd5HBb-ik]

Antaki, Nabil and Silvia Cattori (2016) 'Aleppo Doctor Attacks Western Media for Bias, Censorship and Lies', Global Research, 1 May, online: http://www.globalresearch.ca/aleppo-doctor-attacks-western-media-for-bias-censorship-and-lies/5522736

Attar, Lina Sergie (2017) 'Grieving for Aleppo, One Year After Its Fall', *The Atlantic*, 31 December, online: https://www.theatlantic.com/international/archive/2017/12/syria-aleppo-assad/549437/

Bassam, Laila and John Davison (2017) 'Syrian rebels, Shi'ite villagers evacuated from towns under swap deal', Reuters, 14 April, online: https://www.reuters.com/article/us-mideast-crisis-syria-evacuation/syrian-rebels-shiite-villagers-evacuated-from-towns-under-swap-deal-idUSKBN17G0BY

BBC (2016) 'Syria conflict: Boy beheaded by rebels "was fighter"', 21 July, online: http://www.bbc.com/news/world-middle-east-36843990

Beeley, Vanessa (2016) 'The Liberation of East Aleppo – Vanessa Beeley on UK Column', ZComm, 16 December, online: https://zcomm.org/zblogs/aleppo-the-liberation-of-east-aleppo-vanessa-beeley-on-uk-column/

Beeley, Vanessa (2018) 'Vanessa Beeley Meets the White Helmets and Armed Group Leader in Dara'a Al Balad', 21st Century Wire, 17 October, online: https://21stcenturywire.com/2018/10/17/syria-exclusive-vanessa-beeley-meets-the-white-helmets-and-armed-group-leader-in-daraa-al-balad/

Bulos, Nabih (2016) '"A massacre is inevitable": Punishing siege drags on for two Shiite villages in Syria', *Los Angeles Times*, 23 September, online: https://www.latimes.com/world/middleeast/la-fg-syria-fuah-siege-20160922-snap-story.html

Cattori, Silvia (2016) 'Aleppo Doctor Attacks Western Media for Bias, Censorship and Lies', Information Clearing House, 1 May, online: http://www.informationclearinghouse.info/article44597.htm

CBS News (2018) 'Safe or not, Syrian refugees slowly start coming home', 2 February, online: https://www.cbsnews.com/news/syrian-refugees-returning-aleppo-isis-beaten-lingering-dangers/

Cenci, Federico (2016) 'INTERVIEW: 'Aleppo Is Celebrating, Free From Terrorists. The Western Media Misinformed', Zenit, 26 December, online: https://zenit.org/articles/interview-aleppo-is-celebrating-free-from-terrorists-the-western-media-misinformed/

Dagher, Sam (2016) 'Hospital Hit as Fighting Engulfs Syria's Largest City', *Wall Street Journal*, 28 April, online: http://www.wsj.com/articles/syria-hospital-hit-in-airstrike-blamed-on-russia-1461841686

Davison, John (2017) 'Bombing of Syrian bus convoy kills dozens outside Aleppo', Reuters, 15 April, online: https://in.reuters.com/article/mideast-crisis-syria/bombing-of-syrian-bus-convoy-kills-dozens-outside-aleppo-idINKBN17H04U

Dearden, Lizzie (2016) 'Syrian civil war: Hospital in regime-controlled Aleppo partly destroyed by rebel shelling as more civilians killed', *The

Independent, 3 May, online: https://www.independent.co.uk/news/world/middle-east/syrian-civil-war-hospital-in-regime-controlled-aleppo-partly-destroyed-by-rebel-shelling-as-more-a7011546.html

Doucet, Lysee (2016) 'Syria: Celebrations as families return to homes in Aleppo', BBC, 6 December, online: https://www.bbc.com/news/av/world-middle-east-38218086/syria-celebrations-as-families-return-to-homes-in-aleppo

Drury, Flora (2016) 'The final moments of Aleppo's last paediatrician caught on chilling CCTV footage showing moment Russian bombs struck hospital', *Daily Mail*, 3 May, online: https://www.dailymail.co.uk/news/article-3569698/The-final-moments-Aleppo-s-paediatrician-caught-chilling-CCTV-footage-showing-moment-Russian-bombs-struck-hospital.html

FARS News (2016) 'Dissident Leader Sees Army Victories in Aleppo "Syria's Winning Card in Geneva"', 23 July, online: http://en.farsnews.com/newstext.aspx?nn=13950502000650

Geopolitics (2016) 'Trapped Aleppo residents begun flowing through 1st humanitarian corridor', 31 July, online: https://geopolitics.co/2016/07/31/trapped-aleppo-residents-begun-flowing-through-1st-humanitarian-corridor/

HOS (2019a) 'Best White Helmets = al Qaeda compilation', Hands Off Syria YouTube channel, 13 January, online: https://www.youtube.com/watch?v=vg_3gyhPQbk&bpctr=1554247205

HOS (2019b) 'Terror gang in Aleppo fires hell cannon, February 2016', Hands off Syria, YouTube, 26 March, online: https://www.youtube.com/watch?v=a7R7VrMLTz8&feature=youtu.be

ICRC (2019) 'Rule 10. Civilian Objects' Loss of Protection from Attack', International Committee of the Red Cross, Customary IHL, online: https://www.icrc.org/customary-ihl/eng/docs/v1_rul_rule10

IOM (2017) 'Over 600,000 Displaced Syrians Returned Home in First 7 Months of 2017', 11 August, online: https://www.iom.int/news/over-600000-displaced-syrians-returned-home-first-7-months-2017

Jabhat al Nusra (2013) 'Syria - 2013/12/20 - FSA terrorists blow up Al-Kindi Hospital in Aleppo', 'Syria General' at Vimeo, online: https://vimeo.com/246317584

Kennedy, Merrit (2017) 'U.N.: More Than 600,000 Syrians Have Returned Home In 2017', NPR, 11 August, online: https://www.npr.org/sections/thetwo-way/2017/08/11/542828513/u-n-more-than-600-000-syrians-have-returned-home-in-2017

Makhoul-Yatim, Amara (2016) 'Nabil Antaki, the Syrian doctor who refused to leave Aleppo', France 24, 21 May, online: http://www.france24.com/en/20160520-syria-aleppo-nabil-antaki-doctor-maristes-civilians-civil-war

Oberg, Jan (2017) 'Testimony on the Liberation of Aleppo: How the Media Distorts and Manipulates Reality', Global Research, 14 January, online: https://www.globalresearch.ca/testimony-on-the-liberation-of-aleppo-how-the-media-distorts-and-manipulates-reality/5568305

Phelan, Lizzie (2016) 'Street celebrations in Aleppo on news of Syrian Army retaking east of city', RT, 12 December, online: https://www.rt.com/news/370084-aleppo-liberation-reports-celebrations/

Press TV (2017) 'Syria urges UN to hold responsible those behind deadly bus attack', 16 April, online: https://www.presstv.com/Detail/2017/04/16/518316/Syria-UN-UNSC-Kefraya-Foua-Idlib-Aleppo

RT (2014) 'Anyone but US! Biden blames allies for ISIS rise', 3 October, online: https://www.youtube.com/watch?v=1l18nLZNPSY

RT (2016) 'US A-10s bombed city of Aleppo' on Wednesday, shifted blame onto Moscow – Russian military, Russian Television, 11 February, online: https://www.rt.com/news/332109-russian-jets-isis-warlords/

SANA (2016) '16 civilians killed, 68 wounded in terrorist attacks on Aleppo neighborhoods and a hospital', Syrian Arab News Agency, 3 May, online: http://sana.sy/en/?p=76237

Syrian Reporters (2016) in Vanessa Beeley 'Syria: The Real US NATO Creators of Hell in Aleppo', The Wall Will Fall, 30 April, online: https://thewallwillfall.org/2016/04/30/syria-the-real-us-nato-creators-of-hell-in-aleppo/

Sputnik (2018) 'White Helmets Engaged in Looting, Human Organ Trafficking in Syria – Watchdog', 21 December, online: https://sputniknews.com/middleeast/201812211070877298-un-syria-white-helmets-human-trafficking-plundering/

Stirling, Rick (2016) 'About Bias and Propaganda on Syria: Open Letter to MSF/Doctors without Borders', Dissident Voice, 4 May, online: https://dissidentvoice.org/2016/05/about-bias-and-propaganda-on-syria/

Syrian Girl (2016) 'The Truth About Aleppo. Victory Tribute', at Hands Off Syria (2017) YouTube, 18 June, online: https://www.youtube.com/watch?v=ufqCCPA1jAs

Telesur (2016) 'Bolivian Filmmaker Debunks Mainstream Lies on Syria', 31 December, online: https://www.telesurenglish.net/news/Bolivian-Filmmaker-Debunks-Mainstream-Lies-on-Syria-20161231-0002.html

Turbeville, Brandon (2016) 'A Tale Of Two Hospitals: Fabricated Bombing Incident vs. Open Terrorist Targeting Of Facilities In Aleppo?', Global Research, 5 May, online: https://www.mondialisation.ca/a-tale-of-two-hospitals-fabricated-bombing-incident-vs-open-terrorist-targeting-of-facilities-in-aleppo/5523687

UNSC (2016) 'Resolution 2336 (2016) Adopted by the Security Council at its 7855th meeting, on 31 December 2016', United Nations Security Council, 31 December, online: http://unscr.com/en/resolutions/doc/2336

USCA (2011) 'UNITED STATES of America, Appellee, v. Abdulrahman FARHANE, also known as "Abderr Farhan," and Rafiq Sabir, Defendants-Appellants', United States Court of Appeals, Second Circuit. FindLaw, 4 February, online: http://caselaw.findlaw.com/us-2nd-circuit/1554703.html

Van Wagenen, William (2017) 'Yes, Aleppo was Liberated', The Libertarian Institute, 6 July, online: https://libertarianinstitute.org/articles/yes-aleppo-liberated/

VOA (2016) 'UN's Ban Calls Aleppo "Synonym for Hell" in Final News Conference', Voice of America, 16 December, online: https://www.voanews.com/a/united-nations-secretary-general-calls-aleppo-synonym-hell/3639492.html

Webb, Whitney (2017) 'James Le Mesurier: The Former British Mercenary Who Founded The White Helmets', MintPress, 31 July, online: https://www.mintpressnews.com/james-le-mesurier-british-ex-military-mercenary-founded-white-helmets/230320/

Chapter Seven

THE US-FIGHTING-ISIS DECEPTION:
The Crime at Jabal al Tharda

The author with commanding officer Colonel Nihad Kanaan at Mount Tharda in 2017. Photo Sinan Saeed.

That close US allies were arming and financing DAESH/ ISIS was admitted by several senior US officials in 2014, as I explained in Chapter Five: *The Dirty War Revisited*. Since then, Iraqi, Syrian and Iranian sources complained bitterly and repeatedly that US forces were also directly aiding DAESH. This was denied or simply not reported in the western media. However, a 2016 air attack on Syrian troops behind the city of Deir Ezzor proved this close and covert collaboration. This crime gave the lie to claims that Washington was 'fighting ISIS'.

On 17 September 2016 a carefully planned US-led air raid on Jabal al Tharda (Mount Tharda), overlooking Deir Ezzor airport, slaughtered more than 100 Syrian soldiers and delivered control of the mountain to DAESH. After that surprise attack, the terrorist group held the mountain for almost a year, but did not manage to take the airport or the entire city. US-led forces admitted the attack but claimed it was all a 'mistake'. However uncontested facts, eye witness accounts and critical circumstances show that claim was a lie. This chapter sets out the evidence of this crime, in the context of Washington's historical use of mercenaries for covert actions, linked to the doctrine of 'plausible deniability'.

Syrian eyewitness accounts from Deir Ezzor deepen and confirm this simple fact: the US-led air raid on Syrian forces at Jabal al Tharda on 17 September 2016 was no mistake but rather a well-planned and effective intervention on behalf of DAESH. After days of careful surveillance a devastating missile attack followed by machine gunning of the remaining Syrian soldiers helped DAESH take control of the strategic mountain that same day.

Mercenary forces - like DAESH and the other jihadist groups in Iraq and Syria - have been a staple of US intervention since the early decades of the Cold War, deployed in more than 25 conflicts, such as those of the Congo, Angola and Nicaragua. Whatever their claimed aims and ideologies, they allowed for the 'multiplication' of US power and were associated with the doctrine of 'plausible deniability', where the formal denial of the mastermind role in covert operations minimised damage to domestic public opinion and international relations (Voss 2016: 37-40). That doctrine was discussed during the 1976 Church Committee hearings into CIA covert operations (especially assassinations and coups) and resurfaced during the Iran-Contra scandal of the 1980s (Hart 2005; Dorn 2010). The key idea behind the doctrine is to be able 'to use violence without directly incriminating the [contracting] regime' (Ron 2002). The use of terrorist proxy armies in Iraq and Syria, both overtly and covertly supported by US forces, is thoroughly consistent with this history.

By September 2016 a US-led coalition had been active in both Iraq and Syria for more than two years, supposedly to help Iraq fight DAESH, but without permission to enter Syria. The foreign powers tried to side-step that legal problem by claiming the invitation from Iraq allowed them to conduct cross border raids against DAESH (Payne 2017). By this time the Russian air force had been assisting Syria for almost a year against multiple terrorist groups, all of them, as senior US officials would admit (Biden in RT 2014 and Usher 2014; Dempsey in Rothman 2014), armed and financed by US allies.

Contrary to its stated aims, there is little evidence the US-led coalition did anything to fight DAESH in Syria. Washington's group sat back and watched DAESH twice take over Palmyra (in 2015 and 2016), then did nothing to help the Syrian Army take back Palmyra and Deir Ezzor. Most US activity focused on bombing Syrian infrastructure and helping a Kurdish-led separatist force (the SDF) replace DAESH in the city of Raqqa. On the other hand, the 17 September air raid positively helped DAESH attempts to wrest the remaining parts of Deir Ezzor from the Syrian Army.

US, Australian, British and Danish forces quickly admitted their role in that attack, but claimed the slaughter of over 100 Syrian soldiers was a 'mistake'. Now mistakes in war do happen. However they are usually associated with a single, unprepared incident. This attack was well-planned, sustained and achieved a key objective in the attempt to drive 'the Syrian regime' from Deir Ezzor. Assisting extremists to create an 'Islamic State' in eastern Syria, US intelligence wrote back in August 2012, was 'exactly' what Washington wanted to do so as 'to weaken the regime in Damascus' (DIA 2012).

One year later, as Syrian forces re-took the whole of Deir Ezzor city from DAESH, I spoke with Colonel Nihad Kanaan the commanding officer at Jabal al Tharda on that day, one of 35 survivors of the US-led attack. He confirmed the US admissions that surveillance aircraft had overflown the mountain days before. He also said that the Syrian Army had held the mountain for many months and that their position was clearly marked with Syrian flags. One year later he still showed shock at recalling how the attack aircraft returned to finish off his wounded comrades with line-of-sight machine-gunning (Kanaan 2017).

That Washington could block most western media from serious study of this treacherous attack, simply by saying 'sorry, mistake', is testament to the near absence of critical media voices at a time of war. The surprise attack was treacherous, not only to the Syrians whom the US had promised not to attack, but also to the western populations who mostly believed what their governments were saying: that they were in Iraq and Syria 'to fight ISIS'.

It was not that the denials over the crime at Jabal al Tharda were particularly 'plausible', just that they had been made. Formal denial was enough, it seems, to stop the western corporate and state media in its tracks. The practice of 'plausible deniability' was never so much intended to fool those familiar with the facts, as it was to set up a shield of formal denial which might be used to deflect or discredit 'potentially hostile' investigations (Voss 2016: 40; Bogan and Lynch 1989: 205). In past and present propaganda wars, less importance is given to independent evidence than to insistent repetition, denunciation and distraction.

This account is a prosecuted case, not reportage where one side says this and the other side says that. Its conclusion is announced at the outset and supporting evidence is provided. Readers are entitled to see all evidence, including the cover story of the criminals. While this crime and its authors can be convincingly established by the following uncontested facts, a review of what took place from the Syrian perspective is included to deepen readers' understanding of the conflict.

Uncontested facts

There are eight elements of this massacre where the facts are virtually uncontested:

* First, the attack was on the forces of a strategic opponent, whom the US wished to overthrow, weaken or 'isolate';

* Second, there was no semblance of provocation;
* Third, this was a well-planned operation, with days of advance surveillance;
* Fourth, the attack was sustained and effective, meeting conventional military objectives;
* Fifth, there was both immediate and longer term benefit to DAESH;
* Sixth, the US gave false locality information to the Russians before the attack, and their 'hotline' to Russia was defective during the attack;
* Seventh, the US made false claims about being unable to identify Syrian troops;
* Eighth, the US 'investigation' was hopelessly partisan, self-serving and forensically useless; there was no attempt to even contact the Syrian side.

Let's look at each element in a little more depth

1. The attack was on a strategic opponent

This was no 'friendly fire accident'. The Syrian forces were seen as adversaries. The political leadership of the US-led operation had called for the dismissal or overthrow of the Syrian Government and had provided material support to armed opponents of the Government since mid-2011. The terrorist group DAESH was engaged in a campaign to create an Islamic State in the region and that objective was shared by Washington. US intelligence, in August 2012, had expressed satisfaction at extremist plans for a 'salafist principality' (i.e. an Islamic State) in eastern Syria, 'in order to isolate the Syrian regime' (DIA 2012). The US had not admitted providing finance and arms to ISIS / DAESH, but several senior US officials acknowledged in 2014 that their 'Arab allies' had done so (Anderson 2016: Ch.12). After the attack US and Australian officials referred to their victims as forces aligned with the 'Syrian regime' (Johnston 2016; Payne 2017), reinforcing the fact that the assailants did not recognise Syrian soldiers as part of a legitimate national army.

2. There was no suggestion of provocation

There was no suggestion of any provocation, as had happened in previous 'mistakes'; for example where a pilot had mistaken gunfire or fireworks for a hostile attack. This attack was premeditated.

3. It was a well-planned operation, with substantial surveillance

All sides agree this was a carefully planned operation, with surveillance taking place days in advance. Colonel Nihad Kanaan, the Syrian Arab Army commanding officer on 'Post Tharda 2' (a military post on the second of three peaks of Tharda mountain range) that day, told this writer that US-coalition surveillance aircraft were seen 'repeatedly circling' the area on 12 September, 5 days before the attack (Kanaan 2017). US reports confirm this. On the day of the attack the New York Times cited US Central Command saying that 'coalition forces believed they were striking a DAESH fighting position that they had been tracking for a significant amount of time before the strike' (Barnard and Mazzetti 2016). A US military report, some weeks after the attack, said a 'remotely piloted aircraft' (RPA) was sent to 'investigate' the area the day before and two RPAs revisited the same area on the 17th, identifying two target areas with tanks and personnel (Coe 2016: 1).

Australian Defence Minister Marise Payne wrote that 'target identification was based on intelligence from a number of sources', and that the US-led group had 'informed Russian officials prior to approving air strikes on the DAESH position' (Payne 2017). Australian Chief of Joint Operations Vice-Admiral David Johnston pointed out that his country's contribution to the attack had included 'an Australian E7 Wedgetail airborne early warning and control and 2 FA-18 hornet strike fighters' (Johnston 2016). The Wedgetail E-7 is based on a Boeing 737 and came into operation in 2015. It is an intelligence and control aircraft said to have 'tonnes of electronic wizardry' (Military Shop 2014) and to have 'the most advanced air battlespace management capabilities in the world' (RAAF 2017). All this speaks of a well-planned and technologically capable operation.

Further, surveillance of the area over two years meant the US group was well aware of the strategic troop placements. Kuwait based journalist Elijah Magnier, who had followed the battles around Deir Ezzor, said that defence of the airport depended on four interconnected Syrian army positions on the Tharda mountain range. Largely because of these elevated fire power positions the 'daily attacks' by DAESH on the airport had failed (Porter 2016: 6). Fabrice Balanche, a leading French expert on Syria, adds that the Syrian Army had held positions along the Tharda range 'from March 2016 until the US air strikes', when DAESH took control (in Porter 2016: 6).

4. The attack was sustained and effective, meeting conventional military objectives

The attack was carried out for an extended period and destroyed the Syrian Arab Army post, killing more than 100 soldiers and destroying tanks and all heavy equipment (O'Neill 2016; Kanaan 2017). The Syrian commander says the attack 'continued for 1.5 hours, from 5.30 to 7pm', as night fell (Kanaan 2017). There is some disagreement over exact times. Syrian Army Command said the attack began at about 5pm while US CentCom said the attack began earlier but 'was halted immediately when coalition officials were informed by Russian officials that it was possible the personnel and vehicles targeted were part of the Syrian military' (Barnard and Mazzetti 2016). However the US military confirms that this sunset attack was extended, lasting for just over an hour (Coe 2016: 1).

The Syrian command said at first that 62 soldiers had been killed and 100 injured (RT 2016). Within a short time the numbers killed had been raised to 'at least 80' (Killalea 2016). In addition, three T-72 tanks, 3 infantry vehicles and anti-aircraft guns and 4 mortars were destroyed (MOA 2016). A surviving solider said he saw planes 'finishing with machine guns our soldiers who tried to take refuge ... I saw with my own eyes the death of about 100 soldiers' (SFP 2016). Colonel Kanaan puts the final number of dead at 123, with 35 survivors (Kanaan 2017). The US side did not bother reporting numbers killed, with General Richard Coe at first mentioning '15 dead regime loyalists' (Watkinson 2016) then later simply saying 'Syrian regime/aligned forces were struck' (Coe 2016: 2). There is no report of ISIS forces on the mountain being struck by the coalition aircraft that day; nor any day over the next year.

5. The attack created immediate and longer term benefit to ISIS

The Syrian side made it clear that the massacre had allowed an almost simultaneous ISIS attack on and takeover of the hill. After planes had pounded the Syrian Army position on the mountain, ISIS quickly moved in and took full control of the mountain range (FNA 2016a). Within hours they had posted a video of themselves standing on the bodies of the Syrian soldiers killed by the air strikes (Charkatli 2016). While the US side failed to comment on the immediate consequence of their attack, they did not contradict the Syrian and Russian reports. Colonel Nihad Kanaan confirms that, as the US strikes were being carried out, ISIS attacked the Syrian Army post at Tharda 2. Survivors had to flee, as they did not have time to repel the DAESH attack (Kanaan 2017). Syrian Army defences prevented DAESH from taking the airport, but Syrian forces did not retake the mountain until early September 2017, when the Syrian Army broke the siege and began to liberate the entire city (Brown 2017).

6. False information to and delayed communications with Russia

The US military report admits that 'incorrect information [was] passed to the Russians' about the locale of the attack. They said:

> the strikes would occur 9 kilometres south of DAZ 'airfield'. However this information was incorrect, as the strikes were planned approximately 3 to 6 kilometres south of the airfield and 9 kilometres

The US-Fighting-ISIS Deception

south of Dayr az Zawr city. This may have affected the Russian response to the notification and caused considerable confusion in the DT process (Coe 2016: 3).

Brigadier General Richard Coe agreed with reporters that this misleading information prevented a Russian intervention: 'had we told them accurately, they would have warned us', he admitted (Porter 2016: 4). Providing false information to Russia was quite consistent with a plan to protect the attack from any unwanted interference.

After that, there was yet another 'mistake'. The US military admitted there was a half hour delay in responding to a Russian alarm (that the US was striking Syrian forces) on their specially constructed 'hotline'. The US military tried to shift blame for this delay to the Russian caller:

> when the Russians initially called at 1425Z, they elected to wait to speak to their usual point of contact (POC) rather than pass the information immediately to the Battle Director. This led to a delay of 27 minutes, during which 15 of the 37 strikes were conducted (Coe 2016: 3).

The less benign view of this event was that the 'hotline' was left unattended during the attack. Haddad (2017) reported that: 'During the attack, a hotline between Russia and US forces was reportedly left unattended for 27 minutes' (Haddad 2017). Certainly Russia had to ring twice to pass on the urgent message (McLeary 2016) and, by that time, the attack was virtually complete.

7. The US made false claims about non-identification of Syrian forces

The US military apologia relies heavily on claims that, despite their several days of surveillance, they identified 'irregular forces' on the mountain. US General Coe claims that 'in many ways, the group looked and acted like the (Islamic State) forces we have been targeting for the last two years' (Dickstein 2016). Echoing this story, Australian Vice-Admiral David Johnston, Chief of Joint Operations said 'in many ways these forces looked and acted like DAESH fighters the coalition has been targeting for the last 2 years. They were not wearing recognisable military uniforms or displaying identifying flags or markings' (Johnston 2016). Colonel Kanaan said they had flags flying. The US military confirms this, admitting that they received a report about sighting a 'possible [Syrian] flag ... 30 minutes prior to the strike', but did nothing about it (Coe 2016: 2). Could 'doing nothing' have been just another 'mistake', in such a well-planned operation? It tends to corroborate the case for a deliberate strike, with some attempt at cover up, for 'plausible deniability'.

8. The US 'investigation' was hopelessly partisan

A brief report issued in November exonerated US forces of any wrongdoing. It did admit some critical facts, as noted above. But this was the US military investigating itself. US General Richard Coe said 'We made an unintentional, regrettable error, based on several factors in the targeting process' (Watkinson 2016). The 'errors' relied upon were a series of random or 'human' mistakes and misidentification of the Syrian troops, supposedly because they were dressed in an irregular way. No attempt was made to contact the Syrian side (Coe 2016; Dickstein 2016). By reference to principles of criminal law some admissions made in this report are important and would be admissible evidence in a criminal trial. But the conclusions of the US report are entirely 'self-serving' and 'recent inventions' after the event. For that reason they are forensically worthless.

Summing up, the US-led air attack was a pre-meditated, brutal and effective massacre of the armed forces of a declared opponent. It gave an immediate and longer term advantage to one of the terrorist groups the US and its allies (as Biden and Dempsey admitted) were covertly supporting. Even before we consider the Syrian perspective, these uncontested facts destroy the feeble claim that this well planned and treacherous crime was a 'mistake'. The US military admits that it gave false information to its Russian counterparts, then admits that its 'hotline' did not function properly during the attack. Despite all their sophisticated technology and days of surveillance, they pretended they could not distinguish between entrenched Syrian troops and terrorist DAESH gangs. They admitted they had a report of a Syrian flag, but claim they just neglected it. Having carried out a devastating attack on Syrian forces that day, allegedly by mistake, they did not return even once over the following year to attack the ISIS encampment on the mountain. This is as flimsy a cover story as any criminal has ever presented in court. If the commanders of this appalling massacre ever faced criminal charges, no independent tribunal could fail to convict.

The cover story

The 'defence' case centres around three matters. First, Washington said that the 2014 request for assistance against DAESH from the Government of Iraq gave authority to the US coalition to venture into Syria. Second, they insist that there was no intent to kill Syrian soldiers. Third, they argue that their slaughter of soldiers was due to poor intelligence and mistaken identification. Other aggravating factors were random 'errors'. Then, by way of general excuse, and alluding to the supposed bases of human error, there was reliance on the 'complexity' of the situation. US CentCom, in its apologia, said 'Syria is a complex situation' (RT 2016); a phrase echoed by Australian Prime Minister Turnbull who said 'it is a very complex environment' (Killalea 2016). None of this is compelling but, as was mentioned at the outset, the history of 'plausible deniability' rests not so much on its actual plausibility as on formal denials; that is thought sufficient to distract, intimidate and raise doubts.

The US apologia was repeated by its collaborators. Australian involvement in Syria had already been criticised at home (Billingsley 2015). After the attack on Jabal al Tharda, this writer wrote to ask Australian Prime Minister Malcolm Turnbull about the massacre and the legal basis for the Australian air force presence in Syria. Defence Minister Marise Payne responded on 4 May 2017, addressing the legal question in the following way. Australia's presence in Syria, the Minister claimed, came from a request made by the Government of Iraq for international assistance against DAESH/ISIS: 'The legal basis for ADF operations against DAESH in Syria is the collective defence of Iraq ... The Government of Syria has, by its failure to constrain attacks upon Iraqi territory originating from DAESH bases within Syria, demonstrated that it is unable to prevent DAESH attacks' (Payne 2017).

Indeed, two Iraqi ministers of foreign affairs had made requests to the UN Security Council in June 2014 (Zebari 2014) and again in September 2014 (al Ja'fari 2014). Those requests referred to 'thousands of foreign terrorists of various nationalities' coming across the border from eastern Syria (Zebari 2014). Both requests also stressed the need to respect national sovereignty. So the US-led forces might have relied on this argument, had they helped Syria reclaim its eastern cities and regions from DAESH. However, as noted above, they did not.

On the general legal authority question there is one relevant matter. The Australian side was not so confident about its own law before the strike. Two weeks before the attack it was said that the chief of the Australian Defence Forces, Mark Binskin, had 'fears that Australian Defence Force members could be prosecuted in Australian courts for military actions that are legal internationally [sic]' (Wroe 2016). They were considering this matter two years after they had committed forces to Iraq and Syria and two weeks before the attack.

The general apologia for the massacre relied on a supposed lack of intent. 'We had no intent to target Syrian forces,' said US Air Force Brigadier General Richard Coe. He blamed, in part, the soldiers' form of clothing. 'The group looked and acted like the (Islamic State) forces we have been targeting for the last two years' (Dickstein 2016). In addition, Coe claimed, the soldiers displayed 'friendly' interactions with other groups in an Islamic

State 'area of influence.' He blamed the massacre on 'human factors,' including miscommunications and an optimistic view of the intelligence (Dickstein 2016).

Taking the 'mistake' cover story at face value (i.e. assuming that the attack was aimed at ISIS, and defending Syrian forces), some western commentators quickly suggested the massacre of Syrian soldiers represented an alarming turn to US coalition air support for the 'Syrian regime'. Time magazine said 'the location of the strike in Deir al-Zour suggested the raid could have been a rare, even unprecedented attempt to assist regime forces battling ISIS'. Similarly, Faysal Itani, senior fellow at the Atlantic Council tweeted: 'U.S. airstrikes on ISIS in such close proximity to regime positions are unusual. Arguably constitute close air support for regime' (Malsin 2016). Following the same logic, but in open disbelief, Russia's UN Ambassador Vitaly Churkin asked:

> Why would, all of a sudden, the United States chose to help the Syrian Armed forces, defending Deir Ezzor? After all they did nothing when ISIL was advancing on Palmyra ... All of a sudden the United States decides to come to the assistance of Syrian armed forces defending Deir Ezzor? (Hamza 2016).

Of course, they did not decide to do that, nor did they 'assist' Syrian forces. Nor did Russia believe the attack was a mistake. Damascus was also under no such illusions. President Bashar al Assad, invoking the wider antagonistic role of the US, said the surprise attack 'was a premeditated attack by the American forces ... the raid continued more than one hour, and they came many times' (Haddad 2017).

The US report of November 2016 became the core of explanations from US collaborators in the attack. Australian Vice-Admiral David Johnston gave more detail on Australian involvement in the Jabal al Tharda attack before he presented the official US version of events (Johnston 2016). The coalition air contingent, which included Australian aircraft, had 'conducted multiple air strikes against what was believed to be DAESH fighters near Deir Ezzor', he said. The Australian contingent had included 'an Australian E7 Wedgetail airborne early warning and control and 2 FA-18 hornet strike fighters', along with aircraft from the US, UK and Denmark. These planes carried out the attack 'under the coordination and control of the US combined air operations centre' (Johnston 2016). The Australians were thus deeply involved in intelligence and coordination.

Johnston repeated the self-exonerating conclusions of the US report: 'The air strikes were conducted in full compliance with the rules of engagement and the laws of armed conflict'. The investigation found that the decisions that identified the targets as DAESH fighters were 'supported by the information available at the time ... [there was] no evidence of deliberate disregard of targeting procedures or rules of engagement' (Johnston 2016). He repeated the line that the situation on the ground in Syria was 'complex and dynamic. In many ways these forces looked and acted like DAESH fighters ... They were not wearing recognisable military uniforms or displaying identifying flags or markings' (Johnston 2016).

A typical shallow Australian media review of the incident would admit that 'something went badly wrong'; but then asserted, based more on loyalty than anything else: 'no credible person suggest the RAAF pilots committed war crimes; everyone knows things go wrong in war' (Toohey 2016). Yet some independent, more detailed western commentaries expressed stark disbelief at the cover story. David MacIlwain complained about the failure of media scrutiny of Australia's role in Iraq and Syria, asking why US coalition forces had not returned immediately to the mountain to correct their 'mistake' (Macilwain 2016). Lawyer James O'Neill said, far from a mistake, 'what happened at Deir Ezzor is entirely consistent with the long-standing American aim of regime change in Syria' (O'Neill 2016).

This 'error' which killed over 100 soldiers who were defending Deir Ezzor from ISIS, was the only serious attack on what US coalition forces 'believed to be DAESH fighters' near Deir Ezzor city. US-led forces would do nothing to help liberate Deir Ezzor. The 'innocent massacre' story just does not accord with known facts.

The Syrian Perspective

For those not bound by wartime propaganda attempts to demonise or prohibit the 'enemy' media (a demand which results in reliance on US, British and French media), a Syrian perspective on the crime at Jabal al Tharda helps deepen our understanding. Sources in this section are Syrian, Lebanese, Iraqi, Iranian and Russian. We can address the Syrian perspective from a wider view, taking into account the particulars of the attack and of events after that attack.

In the wider view the Syrian side has seen the US as the mastermind of all terrorist groups in Syria, making use of regional allies, in particular Saudi Arabia, Qatar, Israel and Turkey. The Syrian armed forces make little distinction between DAESH and the western Syria jihadist groups, which collaborate from time to time and whose members pass from one to the other, depending mainly on pay rates (Lucente and Al Shimale 2015). When Aleppo was liberated DAESH flags were seen alongside those of the al Nusra-led coalition (RT 2016a). Both international terrorist groups fought together for many years with the other jihadist groups which western governments had tried to brand as 'moderate rebels' (e.g. Paraszczuk 2013; Safadi 2015). The Syrian Government has regularly expressed 'strong condemnation' of US attacks on civilians and infrastructure, calling the group a 'rogue coalition' which had added 'new bloody massacres' to its record of 'war crimes and crimes against humanity' (RT 2017).

US forces mounted several direct attacks on Syrian forces, over 2015-2017. An online investigative group has compiled information of four such attacks between mid-2015 and mid-2017: on Saeqa airbase in Deir Ezzor (December 2015); on Jabal al Tharda (September 2016); on Shayrat Airbase (April 2017) and an attack on an SU-22 aircraft near Tabqa (June 2017) (MMM

2017). In June 2017 the US group also attacked Syrian forces near the southern al Tanf border crossing (Islam Times 2017). All attacks had different pretexts.

US bombing in Deir Ezzor at the time of the Jabal al Tharda attack (in the name of anti-ISIS operations) was notable for its destruction of infrastructure, in particular the destruction of seven bridges across the Euphrates in September and October 2016 (Syria Direct 2016; SANA 2016). Syrian Army sources told Iranian media that the US aimed to extend its influence in the region and stop the Syrian Army's advance, as well as to cut supply routes between the provinces and separate Deir Ezzor's countryside from the city (FNA 2016a). Syrian General Aktham told me that the US bombing of bridges was to isolate Deir Ezzor, when the city was under siege from ISIS (Aktham 2017).

Direct US support for DAESH had been reported many times in Iraq over 2014-2015. This was mainly to do with arms drops and helicopter evacuation assistance, as Iraqi forces struggled to contain a strong ISIS offensive. Iraqi MP Nahlah al Hababi said in December 2014 that the US coalition was 'not serious' about air strikes on ISIS; she added that 'terrorists are still receiving aid from unidentified fighter jets in Iraq and Syria' (FNA 2015a). In February 2015 there were multiple and more specific reports. The Salahuddin Security Commission said that 'unknown planes threw arms ... to the ISIL' in Tikrit city (FNA 2015c). Majid al Gharawi, an Iraqi MP on the country's Security and Defence Commission said that the US was 'not serious' in its anti-ISIS fight, and that it wanted to prolong the war to get its own military bases in Mosul and Anbar (FNA 2015b). Jome Divan, member of the Sadr bloc in the Iraqi parliament, said the US coalition was 'only an excuse for protecting the ISIL and helping the terrorist group with equipment and weapons' (FNA 2015b). Khalef Tarmouz, head of the al Anbar Provincial Council, told Iranian media that his Council had discovered weapons that were made in the USA, Europe and Israel, in areas liberated from ISIS in the al Baghdadi region (FNA 2015b). Hakem al Zameli, head of the National Security and Defence Committee, reported that

Iraqi forces had shot down two British planes carrying weapons for ISIS, and that US planes had dropped weapons and food for ISIS in Salahuddin, al Anbar and Diyala provinces (FNA 2015b). In other words, within a few months of the US military re-entering Iraq in late 2014, on a 'fight ISIS' pretext, there were several reports of exactly the reverse from senior Iraqi figures. Although these reports were in English, none of them reached the western media. Apparently those channels had no interest in listening to those actually affected by DAESH, or perhaps they just saw it as unthinkable that their own governments were lying to cover up their support for terrorism.

On the Jabal al Tharda massacre, the Syrian Government immediately said that the strike was no mistake but 'a very serious and flagrant aggression' which had aided DAESH (Barnard and Mazzetti 2016). President Assad said the troops were deliberately targeted, pointing out that there had been an hour of bombing (Watkinson 2016). 'It was a premeditated attack by the American forces, because ISIS was shrinking', said the Syrian President (Haddad 2016). Russian President Vladimir Putin suggested the attack must have been deliberate:

> Our American colleagues told us that this airstrike was made in error. This 'error' cost the lives of 80 people and, also just 'coincidence', perhaps, ISIS took the offensive immediately afterwards ... [But] how could they make an error if they were several days in preparation? (Putin in RT 2016).

Russian spokesperson Maria Zakharova said the attack showed the world that 'The White House is defending ISIS' (FNA 2016a). More detail was hinted at. President of the Syrian Parliament, Hadiya Khalaf Abbas, said that Syrian intelligence had intercepted an audio recording between the US and ISIS before the airstrike on Deir Ezzor (Christoforou 2016). Syrian UN Ambassador Bashar al Jaafari denounced the attack as a movement from proxy aggression to "personal aggression", lamenting the

US renunciation of the Russian-US agreement of 9 September to combat al Nusra and ISIS (Mazen 2016).

The detail of eye-witness evidence gives a fuller picture. In October 2017, as the Syrian Army was liberating Deir Ezzor city, Syrian film-maker Sinan Saed and I interviewed Colonel Nihad Kanaan at Jabal al Tharda, where the attack took place. He told us they had seen US coalition surveillance aircraft on 12 September. On the day of the attack:

> Five Coalition aircraft began attacking the site. The fifth aircraft had a synchronized [line of sight] machine gun ... I had 2 T-72 tanks, 2 BMP tanks, a 57mm gun on its base, and a 60mm mortar on a base. The aircraft first began attacking the arsenal. They did this by circling the site at very close distance. Once they were done targeting the arsenal, they began targeting the soldiers with perfect precision (Kanaan 2017).

He says the raid continued for 1.5 hours, using missiles, bombs and machine guns. As the attack took place, ISIS launched 'a very heavy attack' from the north-west shoulder of the mountain, using 'all types of weapons — 14.5 mm, mortars, BKC machine guns and every other weapon they had. This was happening at the same time. They [ISIS] were attacking the post while the aircraft were bombing from above' (Kanaan 2017).

DAESH was using the US-coalition air strikes as cover as they advanced on the army posts, showing 'connection and coordination between the US Coalition and ISIS'. The post fell and the airport was then cut off from the Maqaber road. 'Then 2 aircraft bombed the actual airport from the Tharda 2 post' (Kanaan 2017).

Colonel Kanaan's group was flying Syrian flags, as the US military would later admit.

When the Coalition aircraft attacked the post, the

post had 3 Syrian flags up - one at the entrance, one in the middle and one at the forefront, and the soldiers were wearing the official military uniforms of the Syrian Arab Army ... It is not true what the media reported, that the attack was a mistake. It was very clear that their target was the Syrian army and the Syrian soldiers. The Syrian flags were there, and the Syrian army uniforms were showing, and the site was so obviously belonging to the Syrian army. At the same time, ISIS were attacking us under their cover; the Coalition aircraft didn't even shoot one bullet at them (Kanaan 2017).

There were other eye witnesses. A wounded solider saw dozens of his comrades being finished off with aircraft machine gunning (SFP 2016). Two days before speaking with Colonel Kanaan I had met Doctor Abd al Najem al Abeid, surgeon and head of Deir Ezzor health. As he rushed to the surgery from a group meeting I asked him a question about which I was embarrassed: 'Have you seen any sign of the US coalition helping remove DAESH [ISIS] from Deir Ezzor?' I asked it this way because I wanted the answer to an open question for a western audience. But as I asked I also apologised, because I knew that the question, to an educated Syrian, would be rather insulting. He immediately said that the US forces had only helped ISIS and that he had seen the attack on Jabal al Tharda. He had watched in shock for more than half an hour, as the aircraft attacked the strategic mountain base he knew was guarding the city (Abeid 2017). After that he rushed off to surgery to dig DAESH drone shrapnel from the abdomen of a young boy.

After the massacre, reports of US forces providing logistic and intel support to ISIS, aiding regroupings and evacuations, came from all along the Euphrates in late 2017, as Syrian forces took back Deir Ezzor. In September Press TV reported that the US had evacuated 22 DAESH commanders from Deir Ezzor. This writer was in the city for 4 days in late October, as it was being liberated. On 26 August a US air force helicopter was reported as taking two DAESH commanders 'of European origin' with family members. On 28 August another 20 DAESH field commanders were also taken by US helicopters from areas close to the city (Press TV 2017a). Then in November Muhammad Awad Hussein told Russian media he had seen US helicopters evacuate more DAESH fighters, after an airstrike outside al Mayadin, a city south of Deir Ezzor (Press TV 2017b). The anti-Syrian Government and British-based Syrian Observatory for Human Rights confirmed that US helicopters were transferring DAESH fighters out of eastern Syria. Four DAESH members, including three Egyptians, and a civilian were taken from a house in Beqres, a suburb of Deir Ezzor which had been used as an arms depot (UFilter 2017).

Lebanese and Iranian media corroborated these reports. US forces were backing up ISIS with intelligence during the Syrian Army troops' operation to liberate the town of Albu Kamal in Southeastern Deir Ezzor, according to the Secretary-General of Iraq's al-Nujaba Resistance Movement Sheikh Akram al-Ka'abi. The al-Mayadeen news network quoted Sheikh al-Ka'abi saying that the US forces tried hard to push the Syrian army's operation in Albu Kamal towards failure, and that US forces were targeting pro-government resistance forces before the Albu Kamal battle, in ultimately unsuccessful attempts to block their advances (FNA 2017).

In late 2017 the Russian Defence Ministry announced it had evidence that 'the US-led coalition provides support for the terrorist group Islamic State'. The US military had twice rejected Russian proposals to bomb identified DAESH convoys retreating from al Bukamal, saying that they enjoyed the protection of international law. That shielding of the terrorist group and its heavy weapons allowed them to regroup and carry out new attacks (TNA 2017). At the same time the US backed deals by the Kurdish-led SDF militia to allow ISIS fighters and their families to leave Raqqa for other parts of the region (Paterson 2017).

A senior Syrian General in Deir Ezzor confirmed to me helicopter evacuations from three points on the east bank of the Euphrates: south Deir Ezzor, east al Mayadeen and al Muhassan.

The US-Fighting-ISIS Deception

He also spoke of US satellite intelligence being passed to ISIS. From this catalogue of US coordination and collaboration I asked him: 'you must feel that you are fighting a US command?' '100%' he responded (General SR 2017).

Palmyra after liberation from DAESH, April 2016. In the centre is a DAESH execution rack.

AXIS OF RESISTANCE

Assessment

As the Syrian Army liberated eastern Syria over 2016-2017, the US military tried to slow its advance by a series of covert and overt actions. The massacre of more than 100 soldiers at Jabal al Tharda was one of five direct US attacks on Syrian forces since 2015. Mistakes do happen in war, but this was no isolated mistake. The US-led attack on this strategic anti-ISIS base, protecting Deir Ezzor city, was a pre-meditated slaughter of Syrian forces which allowed DAESH to advance its plan to take the city. As it happened, Syrian Army defences meant that they did not do that. A series of uncontested facts make it clear this was a well-planned and deliberate strike, in support of DAESH. The US military gave false information to its Russian counterparts about the attack, left their 'hotline' unattended and hid evidence that showed they knew Syrian forces held the mountain. Having destroyed Syrian forces on that base, they did not return to attack DAESH on the mountain. Their cover story was weak and, while it served to block investigation by the western media, does not hold up to any serious scrutiny. No independent tribunal would fail to convict US coalition commanders of this bloody massacre.

US and Australian denials over their responsibility for the 17 September 2016 massacre at Jabal al Tharda are not credible, on any close examination. However they did serve their immediate purpose. Most of the western corporate and state media was stopped in its tracks. Yet the crime was 'entirely consistent with the long standing American aim of regime change in Syria ... [and] the Australian Government provided a willing chorus to the regime change demands of the Americans' (O'Neill 2016). North American, British and Australian arms sales to the chief ISIS sponsors, the Saudis, could proceed without interruption or scrutiny (Begley 2017; Brull 2017). The Cold War doctrine of 'plausible deniability', as on many previous occasions, helped deflect 'potentially hostile' investigations. Nevertheless, I urge closer examination of this crime, using conventional principles of criminal law, considering the uncontested evidence and ignoring the intimidation of war propaganda. Particularly adventurous western observers might even read the Syrian perspective, drawing on Syrian, Lebanese, Iraqi, Iranian and Russian sources. That would help deepen their understandings of the conflict.

Bibliography

Al Abeid, Abd al Najem (2017) Interview with this writer, Deir Ezzor Hospital, 21 October. Dr al Abeid was, at this time, head of Deir Ezzor Health and a surgeon at the city's main hospital.

Al Ja'fari, Ibrahim al-Usharqir (2014) 'Annex to the letter dated 20 September 2014 from the permanent representative of Iraq to the United Nations addressed to the President of the Security Council', United Nations Security Council, S/201/691, 20 September, online: https://www.justsecurity.org/wp-content/uploads/2015/12/Iraq-Letter-Requesting-US-Help-09202014.pdf

Aktham, General (2017) Interview with this writer, 21 October, Deir Ezzor

Barnard, Anne and Mark Mazzetti (2016) 'U.S. admits airstrike in Syria, meant to hit ISIS, killed Syrian troops', *New York Times*, 17 September, online: https://www.nytimes.com/2016/09/18/world/middleeast/us-airstrike-syrian-troops-isis-russia.html

Begley, Patrick (2017) 'Senate pressures Defence for answers on Saudi Arabian military deals', *Sydney Morning Herald*, 30 March, online: http://www.smh.com.au/federal-politics/political-news/senate-pressures-defence-for-answers-on-saudi-arabian-military-deals-20170329-gv996s.html

Billingsley, Anthony (2015) 'Australian bombs won't bring peace to Syria, so why do it?', The Conversation, 31 August, online: http://theconversation.com/australian-bombs-wont-bring-peace-to-syria-so-why-do-it-46674

Bogen, David and Michael Lynch (1989) 'Taking Account of the Hostile Native: Plausible Deniability and the Production of Conventional History in the Iran-Contra Hearings', *Social Problems*, Vol. 36, No. 3 June, pp. 197-224

Brown, Matt (2017) 'Syria breaks Islamic State siege on eastern city, opens a new phase in the war', ABC News, 6 September, online: http://www.abc.net.au/news/2017-09-06/syria-breaks-is-siege-deir-ezzor-opens-a-new-phase-in-the-war/8876668

Brull Michael (2017) 'Christopher Pyne Spruiks Aussie Arms To Saudi Arabia As UN Warns Of Impending Yemen Famine', New Matilda, 13 November, online: https://newmatilda.com/2017/11/13/christopher-pyne-spruiks-aussie-arms-to-saudi-arabia-as-un-warns-of-impending-yemen-famine/

Charkatli, Izat (2016) 'Video: ISIS militants cheer atop Syrian soldiers killed by US air strikes', Al Masdar, 18 September, online: https://www.almasdarnews.com/article/video-isis-militants-cheer-atop-syrian-soldiers-killed-us-air-strikes/

Christoforou, Alex (2016) 'Syrian MP: 'Syrian intelligence intercepted audio recording between US and ISIS before airstrike on Deir ez-Zor', The Duran, 26 September, online: http://theduran.com/syrian-mp-syrian-intelligence-intercepted-audio-recording-between-us-isis-airstrike-deir-ez-zor/

Coe, Richard (2016) 'Memorandum for USAFCENT/CC', Centcom, 2 November, online: http://www.centcom.mil/Portals/6/media/REDACTED_FINAL_XSUM_Memorandum__29_Nov_16___CLEAR.pdf

DIA (2012) 'Intelligence report 'R 050839Z Aug 2012', Levant Report, August, online: https://levantreport.com/2015/05/19/2012-defense-intelligence-agency-document-west-will-facilitate-rise-of-islamic-state-in-order-to-isolate-the-syrian-regime/

Dickstein, Corey (2016) 'Investigation: US, coalition airstrikes likely killed Syrian government forces', *Stars and Stripes*, 29 November, online: https://www.stripes.com/news/investigation-us-coalition-airstrikes-likely-killed-syrian-government-forces-1.441745

Dorn, Walter (2010) 'Plausible Deniability Plausible Deniability or How Leaders May Try to or How Leaders May Try to Conceal Their Roles Conceal Their Roles', ICC Prosecutor presentation, 18 May, Walter Dorn, online:http://walterdorn.net/pdf/PlausibleDeniability_PPT_ICC-OTP_Presentation_Dorn_ReducedSize_18May2010_10June2011.pdf

Fadel, Leith (2016) 'US Coalition knew they were bombing the Syrian Army in Deir Ezzor', Al Masdar News, 27 September, online: https://www.almasdarnews.com/article/us-coalition-knew-bombing-syrian-army-deir-ezzor/

FNA (2015a) 'Iraqi Hezbollah: Unidentified Planes Supplying ISIL with Arms from Saudi Arabia', Fars News Agency, 10 January, online: http://en.farsnews.com/newstext.aspx?nn=13931020001065

FNA (2015b) 'Iraq's Popular Forces Release Photo of Downed US Chopper Carrying Arms for ISIL', Fares News Agency, 28 February, online: http://en.farsnews.com/newstext.aspx?nn=13931209001345

FNA (2015c) 'Iraqi Army Downs 2 UK Planes Carrying Weapons for ISIL', Fars News Agency, 23 February, online: http://en.farsnews.com/newstext.aspx?nn=13931204001534

FNA (2016a) 'Syrian people to file lawsuit against US over Deir Ezzor massacre', FARS News Agency, 5 October, online: https://www.sott.net/article/330331-JASTA-blowback-Syrian-people-to-file-lawsuit-against-US-over-Deir-Ezzur-massacre

FNA (2016b) 'Source Discloses Coordination between US, ISIL in Attacking

Syrian Army in Deir Ezzur', Fars News Agency, 18 September, online: http://en.farsnews.com/newstext.aspx?nn=13950628000914

FNA (2017) 'Iraqi leader accuses US of providing intel to terrorists', Fars News Agency, 26 November, online: http://en.farsnews.com/newstext.aspx?nn=13960905001064

General SR (2017) Interview with this writer, Deir Ezzor, 22 October. I have kept this Syrian General's name private.

Haddad, Tareq (2017) 'At least 30 dead in Deir ez-Zour after Isis launches biggest attack in Syria for months', International Business Times, 14 January, online: http://www.ibtimes.co.uk/least-30-dead-deir-ez-zour-after-isis-launches-biggest-attack-syria-months-1601091

Hamza (2016) 'Russia's ambassador Vitaly Churkin exposes US actions in Syria', YouTube, 18 September, online: https://www.youtube.com/watch?v=i4LVLajdhek

Hart, Gary (2005) 'Intelligence Abuse Déjà Vu', Huff Post, 21 December, online: https://www.huffingtonpost.com/gary-hart/intelligence-abuse-deja-v_b_12686.html

Islam Times (2017) 'US Attacks on Syrian Forces in Al-Tanf a Blatant International Law Breach', 11 June, online: http://islamtimes.org/en/doc/article/644956/

Johnston, David (2016) 'Vice Admiral David Johnston speaks about the investigation findings', ABC TV, 30 November, online: http://www.abc.net.au/news/2016-11-30/vice-admiral-david-johnston-speaks-about-syria-investigation/8077656

Kanaan, Nihad (2017) Interview with this writer at Mount Tharda (Deir Ezzor, Syria), 23 October. Colonel Nihad Kanaan was the Syrian Arab Army commanding officer at Post Tharda 2 on 17 September 2016.

Killalea, Debra (2016) 'Syria air strikes mistake: At least 80 dead, Russia, US cast blame', News Corp, 19 September, online: http://www.news.com.au/world/middle-east/syria-air-strikes-mistake-at-least-80-dead-russia-us-cast-blame/news-story/9470b270a7b4fc3e260878475f8274b3

Lucente, Adam and Zouhir Al Shimale (2015) 'Free Syrian Army decimated by desertions', Al Jazeera, 11 November, online: http://www.aljazeera.com/news/2015/11/free-syrian-army-decimated-desertions-151111064831800.html

Macilwain, David (2016) 'Australia clears itself of blame in Deir ez-Zor bombing, watches on as Palmyra falls to ISIS', Russian Insider, 12 December, online: http://russia-insider.com/en/aleppo-palmyra/ri18136

Malsin, Jared (2016) 'How a Mistaken U.S.-Led Air Attack Could End the Syria Cease-Fire', *Time*, 18 September, online: http://time.com/4498493/how-a-mistaken-u-s-led-air-attack-could-end-the-syria-cease-fire/

Mazen (2016) 'Al-Jaafari: US-led coalition aggression on Syria means moving from a proxy aggression into "personal aggression", SANA, 21 September, online: http://sana.sy/en/?p=88633

McLeary, Paul (2016) 'Russia Had to Call U.S. Twice to Stop Syria Airstrike', *Foreign Policy*, 20 September, online: https://foreignpolicy.com/2016/09/20/russia-had-to-call-u-s-twice-to-stop-syria-airstrike/

Military Shop (2014) 'WHEN THE "SHIT GOT REAL" FOR AUSTRALIA'S WEDGETAIL', 1 October, online: https://www.militaryshop.com.au/blog/read/n/WHEN-THE-SHIT-GOT-REAL-FOR-AUSTRALIAS-WEDGETAIL.html

MMM (2017) '"Mistakes" behind 4 US attacks on Syrian Forces', Monitor on Massacre Marketing, 19 June, online: http://libyancivilwar.blogspot.com.au/2017/06/mistakes-behind-4-us-attacks-on-syrian.html

MOA (2016) 'U.S. ALLIES "VOLUNTEER" TO SHARE (millimetric) BLAME FOR DEIR EZZOR ATTACK', WorldInWar, 20 September, online: http://www.worldinwar.eu/u-s-allies-volunteer-to-share-millimetric-blame-for-deir-ezzor-attack/

O'Neill, James (2016) 'Was Syrian air strike a "mistake"'? and why does Australia loyally plead guilty? Independent Australia, 22 September, online: https://independentaustralia.net/politics/politics-display/was-syrian-air-strike-a-mistake-and-why-does-australia-loyally-plead-guilty,9501

Paraszczuk, Joanna (2013) 'Syria Analysis: Which Insurgents Captured Menagh Airbase — & Who Led Them?', EA Worldview, 7 August, online: http://eaworldview.com/2013/08/syria-feature-which-insurgents-captured-the-menagh-airbase/

Paterson, Stewart (2017) 'The Great ISIS exodus: investigation reveals 250 fighters and 3,500 of their family members were driven out of Raqqa in coalition deal and are now "spreading across Syria and beyond"', *Daily Mail*, 14 November, online: http://www.dailymail.co.uk/news/article-5078691/Hundreds-ISIS-fighters-smuggled-Raqqa.html

Payne, Marise (2017) Letter to this writer, 4 May, Marise Payne was at that time the Australian Minister for Defence

Porter (2016) 'US strikes on Syrian troops: Report data contradicts 'mistake' claims', Middle East Eye, 6 December, online: http://www.middleeasteye.net/news/us-strike-syrian-troops-report-data-contradicts-mistake-claims-1291258286

Press TV (2017a) 'US Evacuates 22 DAESH commanders from Dayr al-Zawr: report', 7 September, online: http://www.presstv.com/Detail/2017/09/07/534383/US-Syria-Daesh-Dayr-Zawr

Press TV (2017b) 'US airlifted DAESH cmdrs. In Syria to safety: witnesses', 8 November, online: http://www.presstv.com/Detail/2017/11/08/541403/

Syria-Mayadin-Daesh-commanders-US-airlift

Putin in RT (2016) 'Putin: West responsible for Middle East instability and terrorism in Europe' Russian Television, 12 October, online: https://www.rt.com/news/362554-putin-west-syria-war/

RAAF (2017) 'E-7A Wedgetail', Royal Australian Air Force, online: https://www.airforce.gov.au/Technology/Aircraft/B737-Wedgetail/?RAAF-yFLAkgbpvuhRf7dG5J3kHi1Q4caywtso

Ron, James (2002) 'Territoriality and Plausible Deniability: Serbian Paramilitaries in the Bosnian War', in Bruce B. Campbell and Arthur D. Brenner (2000) Death Squads in Global Perspective: murder with deniability, Palgrave MacMillan, London

Rothman, Noah (2014) 'Dempsey: I know of Arab allies who fund ISIS', YouTube, 16 September, online: https://www.youtube.com/watch?v=nA39iVSo7XE

RT (2014) 'Anyone but US! Biden blames allies for ISIS rise', 3 October, online: https://www.youtube.com/watch?v=1l18nLZNPSY

RT (2016) 'US-led coalition aircraft strike Syrian army positions, kill 62 soldiers – military', Russia Today, 17 September, online: https://www.rt.com/news/359678-us-strikes-syrian-army/

RT (2016a) 'RT crew's footage reveals ISIS & Al-Nusra flags planted on Aleppo's frontline', Russian Television, 10 October, online: https://www.rt.com/news/362205-aleppo-isis-snipers-exclusive/

RT (2017) 'Damascus denounces US-led coalition for adding "new bloody massacres" to their "war crimes" record', Russian Television, 13 November, online: https://www.rt.com/news/409657-damascus-us-led-coalition-massacres/

Safadi, Mowaffaq (2015) 'Don't rely on Syria's "moderate" fighting force. It doesn't exist', The Guardian, 17 December, online: https://www.theguardian.com/commentisfree/2015/dec/16/dont-rely-syria-moderate-fighting-force-anti-isis

SANA (2016) 'US-led coalition continues targeting Syrian infrastructure by destroying al-Syasia bridge in Deir Ezzor', Syrian Arab News Agency, 7 October, online: http://sana.sy/en/?p=89914

SFP (2016) 'A Syrian survivor soldier from Deir Ezzour attack: "The U.S.-coalition warplanes were finishing the wounded [Syrian soldiers] by machine gun"', Syrian Free Press, 22 September, online: https://syrianfreepress.wordpress.com/2016/09/22/deirezzour-saa-survivor/

Syria Direct (2016) 'US-led coalition destroys two bridges in IS-held Deir e-Zor, leaving civilians in the lurch', 29 September, online: http://syriadirect.org/news/us-led-coalition-destroys-two-bridges-in-is-held-deir-e-zor-leaving-civilians-in-the-lurch/

TNA (2017) 'US directly supports IS terrorists in Syria – Russian Defence

Ministry', Tasnim News Agency, 14 November, online: https://www.tasnimnews.com/en/news/2017/11/14/1574055/us-directly-supports-daesh-terrorists-in-syria-russian-defense-ministry

Toohey, Paul (2016) 'A war crime in Syria with Aussie jets? Unlikely', News Corp, 24 September, online: http://www.news.com.au/national/a-war-crime-in-syria-with-aussie-jets-unlikely/news-story/cb53e264badc0cc9d99fe747f67ee49f

UFilter (2017) 'US helicopters transfer DAESH members from eastern Syria', Uden Filter, 5 November, online: http://ufilter.blogspot.com.au/2017/08/us-helicopters-transfer-daesh-members.html

Usher, Barbara Plett (2014) 'Joe Biden apologised over IS remarks, but was he right?' BBC News, 7 October, online: http://www.bbc.com/news/world-us-canada-29528482

Voss, Klaas (2016) 'Plausibly deniable: mercenaries in US covert interventions during the Cold War, 1964-1987, *Cold War History*, Vol 16, No 1, 37-60

Watkinson, William (2016) 'The US-led coalition said it attacked troops loyal to Bashar al-Assad in error on 17 September', International Business Times, 29 November, online: http://www.ibtimes.co.uk/us-military-admits-it-targeted-killed-loyalist-syrian-forces-by-mistake-deir-ez-zor-1594076

Wroe, David (2016) ' Australian forces to expand Islamic State strikes after fears military members could be prosecuted', *Sydney Morning Herald*, 1 September, online: http://www.smh.com.au/federal-politics/political-news/australian-forces-to-expand-islamic-state-strikes-after-fears-military-members-could-be-prosecuted-20160831-gr605c.html

Zebari, Hoshyar (2014) 'Annex to the letter dated 25 June 2014 from the Permanent Representative of Iraq to the United Nations addressed to the Secretary General', United Nations Security Council, S/2014/440, online: http://www.securitycouncilreport.org/atf/cf/%7B65BFCF9B-6D27-4E9C-8CD3-CF6E4FF96FF9%7D/s_2014_440.pdf

Chapter Eight

WMD TAKE TWO

Chemical Weapons in Syria

Exclusive - Assad linked to Syrian chemical attacks for first time

"According to a document seen by Reuters ... the United Nations ... did not name any commanders or officials ... Now a list has been produced ... according to a source famliar with the inquiry ... the lislt, which has been seen by Reuters but has not been made public, was based on a combination of evidence ... according to the source, who declined to be identified due to the sensitivity of the issue. Reuters was unable to independently review the evidence or to verify it."

Fake news: how they do it. Independent evidence never backed the claims by 'jihadists' and their western sponsors that the Syrian Army used chemical weapons; but that did not deter an insistent colonial media.

How do we know that every single allegation of Syrian Government use of chemical weapons use (i.e. 2013 to 2019) was a fabrication? By ignoring, so far as possible, the propaganda storm of the warring parties and focusing on independent evidence and admissions.

Millions of words have been written about chemical weapons in Syria, and many are still confused. How can the average person understand this controversy? Rather than debate at length each incident, I suggest some basic forensic principles can help us 'cut to the chase'. In particular, we should ignore the endless partisan stories and pay more attention to the genuinely independent evidence.

I investigated and wrote about the early stages of this issue back in 2013, then published a chapter on it in my 2016 book, *The Dirty War on Syria*. On the basis of the evidence I concluded that the August 2013 incident in East Ghouta was fabricated by the anti-government 'jihadist' groups, in an attempt to attract greater NATO support, as had happened in Libya.

In a diplomatic move, Russia persuaded Syria to give up its actual chemical weapon stock (held as a deterrent against Israel) and indeed that stockpile was certifiably destroyed in 2014. But this did not put an end to the allegations. Similar accusations came from the sectarian Islamist groups, particularly in 2017 and 2018, as the Syrian Army drove them out of the country's cities.

We are entitled to consider the circumstances of these claims. We must be sceptical particularly because many were fooled by the very same governments over claims of 'weapons of mass destruction' (WMD) in Iraq. The 'chemical weapons' allegations are similar, in that they refer to banned WMDs and seem to provide a pretext for military intervention. Other extraordinary allegations (unexplained civilian massacres) were argued to justify the NATO bombing of Libya. In each case exceptional claims have been used to justify (or cover up) what would otherwise be seen as a transparent aggression.

Regarding the allegations against Syria, we should observe that none of the chemical weapons claims were linked to any conventional military objectives. Such weapons are simply unsuited to urban warfare. This was quite different from the circumstances of the Iran-Iraq war of the 1980s. There the US helped Saddam Hussein use chemical weapons against Iran's mass troop movements ('human waves'), and against the Kurds of Halabja (Harris and Aid 2013; Tan 2008).

I suggest that some standard legal-forensic principles can help us disentangle the claims and counter-claims. These involve (a) identifying interested parties, and discounting their promotional 'evidence' as self-serving; (b) identifying genuinely independent evidence, whether from witnesses or technical experts; and (c) making use of 'admissions against interest'. These are standard concepts in criminal law.

In practice it means putting to one side ALL the claims and arguments of interested parties. That is, ignore everything said by the Syrians, Russians, Iranians and their media; and put aside everything said by the armed groups and their supporters, including that from the governments and media of the USA, Britain, France, Saudi Arabia, the UAE, Qatar, Turkey and Israel. We also have to ignore paid agents of the warring parties, such as the Aleppo Media Centre (paid by NATO governments), the Syrian Observatory for Human Rights (paid by Britain), 'Bellingcat' (paid by the US Government) and others. This includes Human Rights Watch and Amnesty International, which are both closely linked to the US State Department and have both repeatedly helped sell false pretexts for war. For example, Amnesty International backed the false 'incubator babies' story that helped drive the 1990-91 Gulf war against Iraq; in 2011 they backed (but later retracted) false allegations against Libyan President Muammar Gaddafi; and in 2012 they praised the NATO occupation of Afghanistan (Anderson 2018).

What do we have left? Genuinely independent evidence! Let's look at that evidence in the four most publicised chemical weapons claims: Khan al Asal (2013), East Ghouta (2013), Khan Sheikoun (2017) and Douma (2018).

Khan al Asal

The first alleged use of sarin gas in Syria was in April 2013 at Khan al Asal, on the western outskirts of Aleppo city. The Syrian government reported to the UN that anti-government armed groups had used sarin gas, killing 25 and wounding dozens more, both soldiers and civilians. In May 2013 investigator Carla del Ponte, former chief prosecutor of international criminal law tribunals against Rwanda and Yugoslavia, confirmed that the UN had evidence of the 'rebel' use of sarin gas. Also in May 2013 Turkish police reported finding a 2kg canister of sarin, after raiding the homes of Jabhat al Nusra (al Qaeda) members in Turkey (Anderson 2016: 199-201). At that stage there appeared independent evidence that anti-government armed groups had introduced nerve gas to the conflict.

In response, the UN sent weapons inspectors to Damascus in August 2013. However, just as these inspectors arrived in Damascus, a sarin incident was staged in the East Ghouta area. Video and photos were published of sick or dead children, and the armed groups and their sponsors blamed the incident on the Syrian Army. Syria denied it. The armed groups claimed up to 1,400 were killed; yet only eight bodies were reported buried (ISTEAMS 2013). Syrians questioned the origins of the pictured children, as the area in question had long been a war zone and ghost town, with no schools. It was suspected that these may have been kidnapped children (ISEAMS 2013). This incident overshadowed and delayed the Khan al Asal investigation, and led to an international crisis which was partly resolved by the Russian proposal to destroy Syria's chemical stockpiles.

East Ghouta

UN Investigation of this second major allegation, the August 2013 East Ghouta incident, was given priority over the earlier Khal al Asal investigation. Nevertheless, in December 2013 the UN team presented a report on those and several other reported incidents from that year. Because of divisions at the Security Council, the investigators were asked to report on the actual incidents, without seeking to cast blame. They found that chemical weapons had been used on five occasions (Khan al Asal, East Ghouta, Jobar, Saraqueb and Ashrafieh Sahnaya), and on three of those occasions they were used against 'civilians and soldiers' (UNMIAUCWSAA 2013). Only the armed groups were attacking Syrian soldiers. That independent finding discredited a key argument from the Obama White House, that only the Syrian government had the capacity to launch a sarin attack.

Two additional independent reports undermined the August 2013 accusations. A January 2014 report by MIT scientists Richard Lloyd and Professor Theodore Postol found that the improvised rockets used had a range of only 2 kilometres and so 'could not possibly' have been fired at the East Ghouta site from any of the closest Syrian Army positions, as had been suggested by the White House report. Richard Lloyd had been a UN Weapons Inspector, while Professor Ted Postol had been a forensic advisor to the US military. They were acknowledged experts whose independence was unquestionable. A third independent report came from famous investigative journalist Seymour Hersh. His report ('Whose Sarin', December 2013) found that many in the US intelligence community did not believe the White House report, which omitted all reference to the evidence of sarin possessed by Jabhat al Nusra (al Qaeda). 'When the attack occurred al Nusra should have been a suspect, but the [Obama] administration cherry-picked intelligence to justify a strike against Assad,' he wrote (Hersh 2013).

So, when stripped of the clamour from the warring parties and their supporters, the independent evidence regarding the East Ghouta incident of August 2013 lines up against the al Qaeda groups, which controlled much of the East Ghouta area and wanted a pretext for greater military assistance from NATO.

Khan Sheikoun

We can apply the same principles to the third highly publicised incident, the alleged sarin attack on Khan Sheikoun (Idlib). This served as the pretext for President Trump's 7 April

2017 missile attack on Shayrat airbase in Syria. By this time Syria, with help from Russia and Iran, was driving back the armed 'jihadists'. These groups and their supporters, in particular the US government and various paid 'information activists' claimed it was an attack by the Syrian airforce; the Syrians denied it. Once again it was a claimed Syrian Army attack that had no military significance.

What did the independence evidence say? Once again Professor Ted Postol issued a report, the main focus of which was White House reports from the Trump administration. After analysing the allegations, video and wind evidence he issued a rebuttal, which said: 'the nerve agent attack described in the White House report did not occur as claimed. There may well have been mass casualties from some kind of poisoning event, but that event was not the one described by the WHR' (Postol 2017a). As with the East Ghouta incident, Syrians suspected that kidnap victims held by the al Qaeda groups were being used in these 'false flag' attacks. Later Postol issued a second and a third report. Taking into account further information argued by the jihadists in Idlib, and other US allies, he concluded: 'the WHR was fabricated without input from the professional intelligence community' (Postol 2017b).

In the Khan Sheikhoun case US agencies used each other to lend the appearance of 'corroboration'. So the US- and UK-funded groups, the White Helmets, provided 'evidence' of the Sarin attack to both the UN's OPCW and to the US group Human Rights Watch (2017). There is substantial photographic and video evidence that the White Helmets are close affiliates of the armed Islamist groups in Syria, in particular of Jabhat al Nusra (Beeley 2018; Hands Off Syria 2019). However for the purpose of this analysis it is sufficient to observe that their major funders are the governments of the UK and the USA, active parties in the war against the Syrian Government. That alone disqualifies the White Helmets as a source of independent evidence. Nor is Human Rights Watch (HRW) an independent NGO. It is closely linked to the US foreign policy elite and the US State Department, and its leader Kenneth Roth has issued a series of demonstrably false claims about Syria, during the long war (see the chapter in this book 'The Human Rights Industry in Humanitarian war').

The OPCW would later report that there had been use of a 'sarin like substance' in Khan Sheikhoun (OPCW 2017). However they relied on evidence provided by the White Helmets, as no-one from the OPCW visited the site. This problem was discussed by another clearly independent expert, former UN weapons inspector Scott Ritter. Prior to the 2003 invasion of Iraq Ritter, a US citizen, had warned that Iraq did not possess significant weapons of mass destruction. He was ignored then, but was later proven correct. In mid-2017 Ritter wrote that the Human Rights Watch claim that 'the material cause of the Khan Sheikhoun event is a Soviet made KhAB-250 chemical bomb' must be false as:

> if a KhAB-250, or any other air delivered chemical bomb had been used at Khan Sheikhoun, there would be significant physical evidence of that fact, including the totality of the bomb casing, the burster tube, the tail fin assembly and parachute (Ritter 2017).

The OPCW was therefore:

> in no position to make the claim … [that] a sarin like substance was used at Khan Sheikhoun, a result that would seemingly compensate for both the lack of a bomb and the amateurish theatrics of the rescuers (Ritter 2017).

The main reason for this was that there was a broken 'chain of custody' in taking samples from the site, out of Syria to the OPCW (Ritter 2017). That act was carried out by the obviously non-independent White Helmets.

We see once again that, when the shrill propaganda is removed, and we pay attention to genuinely independent evidence, another attempt at a 'weapons of mass destruction' scandal is exposed. The partisan sources mislead us.

The Douma hospital

The fourth and final widely-publicised, alleged chemical weapons incident was said to have been carried out just as the Syrian Army was about to liberate the city of Douma from al Qaeda and its allied 'jihadists'. This was the alleged 7 April 2018 attack on Douma hospital. Notice that the Syrian Army, by this time, with Russian and Iranian help, had been steadily driving the armed groups out of the urban centres. Once again, any Syrian military rationale for the use of chemical weapons was absent. Yet that is what the Douma-based 'Army of Islam', their ally. the banned Jabhat al Nusra terrorist group, and their western sponsors claimed.

Once again the armed groups and their White Helmet partners issued video which showed people rushing around the hospital reception area, washing others, including children, with water. The White House and associated media and US- and UK-funded agencies (including the BBC, CNN, Bellingcat and the US-based 'Syrian American Medical Society') repeated the jihadists' stories. The 'Army of Islam' media group, the Ghouta Media Centre, put out the story that 'hundreds' were killed and injured by a 'barrel bomb containing sarin' (Embury-Denis 2018). A White House statement duly affirmed:

> The United States assesses with confidence that the Syrian regime used chemical weapons in the eastern Damascus suburb of Duma on April 7, 2018, killing dozens of men, women, and children … information points to the regime using chlorine in its bombardment of Duma, while some additional information points to the regime also using the nerve agent sarin (White House 2018).

Most western media ran with this. The story was revised to a 'chlorine bomb', after a photo of an unexploded tank was shown in a building.

After the Syrian Army took control of Douma, 11-year old Hassan Diab, one of the children in that video would denounce the story, saying he was dragged into his unexpected film role and experienced no toxic chemicals. Yet, because he contradicted the jihadists claims, western media suggested he was an 'unwitting pawn' (Barker 2018). However, alongside this child, no less than twelve hospital staff told media in Damascus and in The Hague that there had been no chemical attack (RT 2018b). Several of them flew to The Hague to repeat this evidence. These doctors and nurses said, in various ways, that there had been an extended filmed commotion at reception; but there had been no air attack on the hospital, there were no fatalities and there had been no evidence of chemical weapons (RT 2018b). The British Guardian called this an 'obscene masquerade', organised by Russia. Other western agencies claimed that these witnesses had been pressured by the Syrian Government (Wintour 2018). Before this particular controversy is dismissed we might observe that hospital staff in Douma could not have survived had they been known government sympathisers. It is well known that both religious minorities and government supporters were murdered by the Army of Islam and Jabhat al Nusra. In that sense those medical staff were likely fairly independent

In any case, not long after the area was liberated the UN's OPCW went in and made their report. First they found no trace of any nerve agent: 'no organophorphorous nerve agents or their degradation products were detected' (OPCW 2018). So much for the claims from the 'Ghouta Media Centre' and the White House. But what about the chlorine backup story? The UN team did find 'various chlorinated organic chemicals ... from two sites'. However 'the FFM cannot confidently determine whether or not a specific chemical was used as a weapon' (OPCW 2018). This report was misused by some media to pretend that the UN group had found that chlorine was used as a weapon. Yet others pointed out that 'chlorinated organic chemicals' are found in most households, including as cleaning agents in hospitals. Although under great pressure in New York, the UN team rejected the Douma WMD story.

Nevertheless, relying on the general spin over the OPCW report, the BBC (2018) headlined: 'Douma attack was chlorine gas – watchdog'. This story was a misrepresentation of the OPCW report. It was soon deleted from BBC websites; but not before it had been picked up by other sites (e.g. MyVueNews 2018). In 2019 an OPCW engineers report came to light. It investigated the claim that two chlorine cylinders found in Douma had been dropped from an aircraft. After observing the cylinder and holes in the roof the engineers concluded 'there is a higher probability that both [chlorine] cylinders were manually placed at those two locations rather than being delivered from aircraft' (OPCW 2019: 8).

To wrap up five disgraceful years of chemical weapons propaganda, forensic principles entitle us to look at independent statements, or 'admissions against interest', by the warring parties. That includes statements from military leaders in the USA and the UK. US Defence Secretary James Mattis, for example, both before and after the Douma incident, said that he had 'no evidence' Syria had used sarin, but was relying on media, including social media stories. On 3 February 2018 Mattis was reported as saying: 'We have other reports from the battlefield from people who claim it's been used. We do not have evidence of it. We're looking for evidence of it' (Burns 2018). In April, just days after the Douma claims, he told the US Congress: 'We are not engaged on the ground there so I cannot tell you that we have evidence, even though we certainly had a lot of media and social media indicators that either chlorine or sarin were used' (RT 2018a). Is it credible that the US Government, after five years of claims and counter-claims, had no better intelligence than social media reports?

Two former British military leaders were more direct. They expressed incredulity at the Douma claims, even though those claims had been backed by their own government. That fact makes them both independent. Former SAS commander British General Jonathan Shaw asked:

> Why would Assad use chemical weapons at this time? He's won the war. That's not just my opinion, it is shared by senior commanders in the US military. There is no rationale behind Assad's involvement whatsoever. He's convinced the rebels to leave occupied areas in buses. He's gained their territory. So why would he be bothering gassing them? (Basu 2018).

A similar opinion was expressed and developed further by Lord Alan West, former senior British government security advisor and former head of the British Navy:

> Just before he [President Assad] goes in and takes it [the Douma area] all over, apparently he decides to have a chemical attack. It just doesn't ring true, it seems extraordinary because, clearly he would know that there is likely to be a response from the allies ... what benefit is there for his military? Most of the rebel fighters, this disparate group of Islamists, have withdrawn, there are a few women and children left around. What benefit is there is doing what he did [sic]? I find that extraordinary. Whereas we know that in the past some of the Islamic groups have used chemicals, and of course there would be huge benefit for them in labelling an attack as coming from Assad, because they would guess quite rightly that there would be a response from the US, as there was last time, and possibly from the UK and France ... The reports that came from there were from the White Helmets who, let's face it, are not neutrals, you know, they are very

much on the side of the disparate groups who are fighting Assad (NewsVoice 2018).

These are genuinely independent assessments from two military experts. 'Similar fact' principles of criminal law further entitle us to apply their rationales over Douma to the earlier claims made by the same armed groups in the same area. That is, there is a pattern of behaviour from these armed groups, involving repeated fabricated claims, in the hope of stalling Syrian Army advances and gaining greater foreign military support. This 'similar fact' pattern increases confidence in the evidence that says they have been fabricating claims against the Syrian Army from 2013.

When we remove the clamour of the warring parties, their media and their paid propagandists, the independent evidence points in one direction: every single claim of chemical weapon use by the Syrian Army was a fabrication. As Alan West said, the al Qaeda aligned groups wanted to attract greater western military support. Western governments and media either promoted or went along with this extended 'WMD' hoax. The scandal served to hide naked US-led aggression against Syria. Western audiences were played, for the second time in a decade, over a 'Weapons of Mass Destruction' scam. Most took the bait.

Bibliography
Anderson, Tim (2016) *The Dirty War on Syria*, Global Research, Montreal
Anderson, Tim (2018) 'Syria: the human rights industry in "humanitarian war"', Centre for Counter Hegemonic Studies, Research paper 1/18, online: https://counter-hegemonic-studies.net/humanitarian-war-rp-1-18/
Barker, Anne (2018) 'Syrian war: The boy at the centre of conflicting tales about alleged Douma chemical attack', ABC News, 29 April, online: https://www.abc.net.au/news/2018-04-28/hassan-becomes-face-of-information-war-surrounding-syria-douma/9705538
Basu, Joy (2018) '"He's WON the WAR"– British general claims Assad DIDN'T use chemical weapons', *The Daily Star*, 15 April, online: https://www.dailystar.co.uk/news/latest-news/696049/syria-war-assad-theresa-may-world-war-three-douma-missile-attack
Beeley, Vanessa (2018) 'Whitewashing the White Helmets – Peter Ford, Former

UK Ambassador to Syria Responds to UK Government Statement', 21st Century Wire, 23 July, online: https://21stcenturywire.com/2018/07/23/whitewashing-the-white-helmets-peter-ford-former-uk-ambassador-to-syria-responds-to-uk-government-statement/

Burns, Robert (2018) 'US has no evidence of Syrian use of sarin gas, Mattis says', Associated Press, 3 February, online: https://apnews.com/bd533182b7f244a4b771c73a0b601ec5

Embury-Denis, Tom (2018) 'Trump warns of "big price to pay" as he blames Assad, Putin and Iran for alleged Syria chemical weapons attack', *The Independent,* 9 April, online: https://www.independent.co.uk/news/world/americas/us-politics/donald-trump-syria-civil-war-chemical-weapons-attack-putin-assad-iran-russia-civilians-killed-douma-a8294806.html

Hands off Syria (2019) 'Best White Helmets = al Qaeda compilation', 13 January, YouTube: https://www.youtube.com/watch?v=vg_3gyhPQbk&bpctr=1548055546

Harris, Shane and Matthew Aid (2013) 'CIA Files Prove America Helped Saddam as He Gassed Iran', *Foreign Policy,* 26 August, online: https://foreignpolicy.com/2013/08/26/exclusive-cia-files-prove-america-helped-saddam-as-he-gassed-iran/

Hersh, Seymour (2013) 'Whose Sarin?' *London Review of Books,* Vol 35 No 24, 19 December, online: https://www.lrb.co.uk/v35/n24/seymour-m-hersh/whose-sarin

Human Rights Watch (2017) 'Mounting Evidence Syrian Forces Were Behind Khan Sheikhoun Attack', 6 September, online: https://www.hrw.org/news/2017/09/06/mounting-evidence-syrian-forces-were-behind-khan-sheikhoun-attack

ISTEAMS (2013) 'Independent Investigation of Syria Chemical Attack Videos and Child Abductions', 15 September, online: http://www.globalresearch.ca/STUDY_THE_VIDEOS_THAT_SPEAKS_ABOUT_CHEMICALS_BETA_VERSION.pdf

Lloyd, Richard and Theodore A. Postol (2013) 'Possible implications of faulty US Technical Intelligence in the Damascus Nerve Agent Attack of August 21, 2013', MIT Science, Technology and Global Security Working Group, 14 January, online: https://www.documentcloud.org/documents/1006045-possible-implications-of-bad-intelligence.html

MyVueNews (2018) 'Syria war: Douma attack was chlorine gas – watchdog' 6 July, online: http://www.myvuenews.com/syria-war-douma-attack-was-chlorine-gas-watchdog/

NewsVoice (2018) 'Admiral Lord West Casts Doubt on Syria Attack Intelligence - BBC News', 18 April, YouTube: https://www.youtube.com/watch?v=_6sJKKspTEc

OPCW (2017) 'REPORT OF THE OPCW FACT-FINDING MISSION IN SYRIA REGARDING AN ALLEGED INCIDENT IN KHAN SHAYKHUN, SYRIAN ARAB REPUBLIC, APRIL 2017', S/1510/2017, 29 June, online: https://www.opcw.org/sites/default/files/documents/Fact_Finding_Mission/s-1510-2017_e_.pdf

OPCW (2018) 'OPCW issues fact finding mission reports on chemical weapons use allegations in Douma, Syria in 2018 and in al-Hamadaniya and Karm al-Tarrab in 2016', 6 July, online: https://www.opcw.org/media-centre/news/2018/07/opcw-issues-fact-finding-mission-reports-chemical-weapons-use-allegations

OPCW (2019) 'Engineering assessment of two chlorine cylinders observed at the Douma incident', posted at Centre for Counter Hegemonic Studies, 27 February, online: https://counter-hegemonic-studies.net/opcw-douma-eng-1/

Postol, Theodore (2017a) 'Khan Sheikhoun, Syria: The nerve agent attack that did not occur', Global Research, 19 April, online: https://www.globalresearch.ca/khan-sheikhoun-syria-the-nerve-agent-attack-that-did-not-occur/5585818

Postol, Theodore (2017b) 'A critique of "false and misleading" White House claims about Syria's use of lethal gas', TruthDig, online: https://www.truthdig.com/videos/a-critique-of-false-and-misleading-white-house-claims-about-syrias-use-of-lethal-gas/

Ritter, Scott (2017) 'Ex-weapons inspector: Trump's sarin claims built on "lie"', *The American Conservative*, 29 June, online: https://www.theamericanconservative.com/articles/ex-weapons-inspector-trumps-sarin-claims-built-on-lie/

RT (2018a) 'Mattis: No evidence on Syria chemical attack, but I believe there was one', 12 April, Youtube: https://www.youtube.com/watch?v=vWlXTBaN1Sc

RT (2018b) 'No attack, no victims, no chem weapons: Douma witnesses speak at OPCW briefing', 26 April, YouTube: https://www.youtube.com/watch?v=kSZrMfdgw64

Tan, Vivian (2008) 'Feili Kurds in Iran seek way out of identity impasse', UNHCR, 28 May, online: https://www.unhcr.org/news/latest/2008/5/483d60872/feili-kurds-iran-seek-way-identity-impasse.html

UNMIAUCWSAA (2013) 'Final report', United Nations Mission to Investigate Allegations of the Use of Chemical Weapons in the Syrian Arab Republic, 12 December, online: https://unoda-web.s3.amazonaws.com/wp-content/uploads/2013/12/report.pdf

Webb, Whitney (2018) 'White Helmets Currently Staging "False Flag" Chemical Attack in Idlib', MintPress News, 11 September, online: https://www.mintpressnews.com/white-helmets-chemical-attack-idlib/249121/

White House (2018) 'United States Government Assessment of the Assad Regime's Chemical Weapons Use', 13 April, online: https://www.whitehouse.gov/briefings-statements/united-states-government-assessment-assad-regimes-chemical-weapons-use/

Wintour, Patrick (2018) '"Obscene masquerade": Russia criticised over Douma chemical attack denial', *The Guardian*, 27 April, online: https://www.theguardian.com/world/2018/apr/26/obscene-masquerade-russia-criticised-over-douma-chemical-attack-denial

Chapter Nine

THE HUMAN RIGHTS INDUSTRY IN 'HUMANITARIAN WAR'

Al Qaeda boss thanks US-UK-funded White Helmets, who are the "hidden soldiers of our revolution". This was part of his speech commemorating the 6th anniversary of the Jihadist insurgency in Syria. Small armies of 'humanitarians' and 'media activists' were recruited in support of the dirty war on Syria. Photo: Jabhat al Nusra. https://www.youtube.com/watch?v=cpuxbyNIO8

Humanitarian war – war said to be waged on the basis of disinterested and altruistic motives, and these days based specifically on the doctrine of a 'responsibility to protect' - has helped drive an expansion of heavily funded human rights agencies, effectively operating more as corporate public relations bodies than NGOs. Large agencies such as the US-based group Human Rights Watch (HRW) and Amnesty International have little of the accountability, participatory nature or independence of traditional community-based NGOs. They are or have become large corporations embedded with powerful states, in particular the USA. Some other more specific agencies, purpose-built for the Syrian war, have also received many millions of dollars from those same powerful states and linked corporations, to support humanitarian war.

Bricmont points out that the UN's key purpose, to prevent wars of aggression, has been subverted by doctrines of 'humanitarian intervention' (Bricmont 2006). Heningsen refers to a 'human rights industrial complex', drawing on the good intentions of 'hard-working and extremely well educated individuals' (Heningsen 2016). This style of 'human rights' promotion is big business. Amnesty International, now deeply embedded with the US State Department, spends around 280 million Euros per year (Amnesty 2017a); Human Rights Watch, closely aligned to the Democrat side of US politics, boasts over US$220 million in assets (HRW 2017: 5); while the White Helmets is a paramilitary, first aid and public relations group set up by a former British soldier, which was paid more than US$100 million for its Syrian war activities by both the British and US governments (Beeley 2017d).

A problem for serious discussion, during a conflict, is what we might call 'vexatious propaganda', which attempts to impose barriers on debate. Just as a vexatious litigant tries to monopolise argument in the courts, so vexatious propaganda, by constant repetition of its themes, tries to monopolise the themes of conflict discussion. In the case of the Syrian conflict, such attempts to control debate have come from media aligned to states committed to the overthrow of the Syrian government. This propaganda has been extreme, as it must be to evade the normal constraints of international law. So for example, even though it was well established by independent evidence that the terrorist group Jabhat al Nusra first brought sarin gas into Syria, in early 2013 (Barnard 2013; BBC 2013), Washington-aligned media later insisted, mimicking the White House line, that 'only the Syrian government' had the capacity to launch sarin gas attacks (Plummer 2013, RT 2013). And even though independent evidence on the August 2013 chemical weapons incident in East Ghouta positively disproved Syrian Army involvement (Anderson 2016: Chapter Nine), nothing stops vexatious propaganda from insisting that Syria defend itself against endless fabrications. Discussants can contest the allegations, but they cannot change the reiteration, which embeds the allegations irrespective of refutation. Nevertheless, this chapter insists on undertaking an interrogative analysis of the propaganda industry that destroys reasonable debate over the conflict.

This human rights industry has helped market the recent Middle East wars, particularly the extended proxy war on Syria. Underlying such wars is a modernist doctrine which empowers neo-colonial voices, agents of domination dressed up as independent mediators. The great contradiction of this western project, undertaken in the name of human rights, is its disregard for the first article of the International Bill of Human Rights: the right of peoples and nations to self-determination (UN HRC 1984). In face of this apparent constraint, the contemporary notion of a 'responsibility to protect' was created (UN 2005; Bass 2009), and has unleashed new pretexts for military intervention.

Two important practical implications of international 'human rights' advocacy over Syria have been, first, that the popular memes of the war (e.g. 'the government is killing its own people') are given greater weight than forensic fact. Second, there is the insistent denial by the state sponsors of terrorism in Syria that the Syrian state ('regime') has any right to use its national army to defend the Syrian people or to liberate its cities from their proxy armies. This is an extraordinary contention, yet it goes unquestioned. I won't waste more time on it.

This chapter will characterise the human rights industry as a key legitimacy driver of the normalised 'humanitarian wars' of the 21st century, illustrating the phenomenon through the activity of some prominent human rights agencies during the war on Syria. Independent evidence shows that pro-intervention propaganda over a series of critical incidents has been consistently one-sided, breaching elementary principles of fair assessment and amplifying partisan stories throughout the war. Whatever abuses might have been committed by the Syrian Army and its allies, any chance of a balanced perspective on these has been swamped by the 'humanitarian war' narrative. A target nation with no strong international voice or allies has little chance of being heard.

On the other side, human rights agencies embedded with the big powers have rarely questioned the gross breaches of international law carried out by their sponsoring states. Instead, partisan and contrived reports continue to fuel humanitarian war, while inviting repeated 'false flag' atrocities to create the 'exceptions' thought necessary to breach international law and sovereign rights (see Anderson 2016: Chapters 8 and 9). The first part of this chapter will discuss the human rights pretexts for 'humanitarian war' and its normalised conflicts of interest; the second will document sufficient examples of extreme bias and active fabrication to prove the partisan character of some key agencies. The global agencies discussed are Amnesty International and Human Rights Watch, while the purpose-built agencies are The Syria Campaign and Tthe White Helmets.

Human rights pretexts for humanitarian war

Humanitarian war is not new; its roots can be traced to the European liberal imperialism of the 19th century, as also to the appeal of high-sounding pretexts for 'realist' imperialism. Liberalism's theoretical emphasis on individualism, a non-interventionist state and peaceful exchange tends to mask its colonial history. For example the English liberal, John Stuart Mill, famous for his writings on individual freedom, called British colonialism 'the best affair of business in which the capital of an old and wealthy country can engage'; adding 'the same rules of international morality do not apply ... between civilised nations and barbarians' (Sullivan 1983: 601). This version of liberalism imagined that 'barbarians have no rights as a nation, except a right to such treatment ... [to] fit them for becoming one' (Mill

1874: 252-253). Mill believed in virtuous British intervention, for example to 'mediate in the quarrels ... [and] intercede for mild treatment of the vanquished' (Mill 1859: 2).

That 'civilising mission' legacy was adopted by the North American traditions of 'exceptionalism', distinct from European imperial traditions and in favour of evangelised missions of 'freedom'. Despite its colonial era purchases (e.g. Louisiana) and conquests (e.g. Mexico, Cuba), the United States of America consistently rejected the status of an imperial or colonial power. The self-image of an exceptional state, a 'shining light on the hill', remained central (Gamble 2012). This tells us that North American power places greater emphasis on modernist idealism than the Europeans, who often still defend their imperial legacies. The US, on the other hand, pretends that it has no imperial legacy. In that sense it appears, at least nominally, more consistent with the post-colonial body of international law developed through the United Nations, after 1945.

Contemporary war propaganda therefore draws on this idealism, albeit for traditional ends: to elevate the mission of the aggressor, and to disqualify resistance, in particular from existing state governments defending their own sovereign territories and peoples. It includes co-opting the contemporary, popular norms of 'human rights' and subsuming them in imperial-modernist language, such that all such human rights problems are 'ours' to protect. The delicate matter of the self-determination of peoples and nations is thus collapsed into insistent narratives of 'failed' or 'fragile' states, from which peoples must be rescued from their very own 'dictators', elected or not.

Yet imperialism is imperialism. In what came to be known as the 'American Century', and with a hoped for 'New American Century' (Pitt 2003), there has been alternation between a 'realist' version, where goals and methods are more direct, and a liberal version, where there is consolidation of hegemonic ideology. Traditional pretexts of the civilising mission and actual aims of excluding competitors remain, but with succeeding phases of assertion and legitimation. In the contemporary context, with a looming energy crisis and Washington 'losing' Iran to that country's Islamic Revolution, there was a declaration from 'liberal' Washington that the Persian Gulf region was central to 'the vital interests of the United States of America' (Carter 1980). This claim for US extraterritorial privilege, practised in the Americas for over a century, was formalised and extended to the Middle East region. After the collapse of the Soviet Union and the apparent rise of a unilateral global system, the concept of a New American Century began to include complete control of the resource rich–Middle East region. This was no longer about simple control of particular oilfields or gas pipelines, but rather domination of an entire region. Terrorism claims and demands for unilateral disarmament provided pretexts for the 'realist' invasions of Afghanistan and Iraq. A 'New Middle East' would be created through 'creative destruction'—implicitly, creating sectarian violence (Karon 2006; Nazemroaya 2006). A senior US general spoke of Pentagon plans to take over 'seven countries in five years', beginning with Iraq and Syria and ending with Iran (Clark 2007).

However, liberal imperial doctrine had been re-shaped in the 1990s in the Balkans, where claims of extreme crimes had provided the pretexts for NATO moving in to dismantle the Socialist Federal Republic of Yugoslavia, playing on ethnic divisions (Oberg 2014). Human rights agencies embedded with US foreign policy bodies began to play a more important role. Supposed western inaction over the 1994 mass killings in Rwanda helped boost western demands for intervention while in fact the US had supported the 'regime change' that followed the Rwandan massacres (Philpot 2013).

Humanitarian intervention arguments reshaped traditional debate lines over US foreign policy. In 2000 former Human Rights Watch director Holly Burkhalter argued, in a 'white paper' on behalf of the US State Department, that Washington should engage more in military intervention on 'humanitarian' grounds, supposedly to prevent great crimes. Her position was more assertive than that of the US military, which argued a more cautious line, linked to US interests (CFR 2000). The resurgent idea of 'humanitarian intervention' thus began to erode the older distinction between militarist 'hawks' and diplomatic 'doves'.

Popular western revulsion at the Bush administration's 2003 invasion of Iraq on a notorious false disarmament pretext (Hoeffel 2014) allowed US liberals to seize the initiative. Greater legitimacy had to be built into the New Middle East project. The notion of 'smart power', to counter the uglier 'realist' approach, was spelt out by Suzanne Nossel, an official with Human Rights Watch who later worked with Hillary Clinton in the US State Department and in 2012, became head of Amnesty International (USA). In a 2004 article she argued for a reassertion of US 'liberal internationalism'. Washington should offer 'assertive leadership', in the tradition of 'exceptionalism', to drive a range of goals, but 'unlike conservatives, who rely on military power as the main tool of statecraft, liberal internationalists see trade, diplomacy, foreign aid, and the spread of American values as equally important' (Nossel 2004). This multifaceted approach was consistent with the Pentagon doctrine of 'Full Spectrum Dominance' (Garamone 2000), linking military to economic, political and communications hegemony.

The US State Department drove the new doctrine of a 'responsibility to protect' (R2P) through a UN committee. The 'International Commission on Intervention and State Sovereignty' in 2001 posed the idea of 'sovereignty as responsibility', with a focus on violence within weak and new states. The 'World Summit' of 2005 then declared that states had the responsibility to prevent great crimes but, if they failed, the international community should be 'prepared to take collective action ... through the Security Council' (UN 2005: 138-139). Much of this text was adopted in UN Security Council resolution 1674 the following year (UNSC 2006).

However in its substance the R2P is an imperial doctrine which seeks to normalise war and enhance the prerogatives of the big powers to intervene. Edward Luck argues that there is no necessary contradiction between this doctrine and state sovereignty. However he admits a tension is posed, in that R2P ideas 'might be used by powerful states ... to justify coercive interventions undertaken for other reasons' (Luck 2009: 17). Indeed, the R2P does not change international law, but it does attract greater attention to the Chapter VII intervention powers of the Security Council. The doctrine does promote 'a new norm of customary international law', (Loiselle 2013: 317-341), even suggesting an obligation to intervene.

The first experiment subsequent to the crafting of this norm was seen in NATO's 2011 destruction of Libya, a small country with the highest living standards in Africa. The pretext here was alleged civilian massacres, in the wake of a jihadist insurrection in eastern Libya. The British Guardian, a key supporter of 'humanitarian intervention', claimed that 'hundreds of civilians' had been killed in 'protests' (Cronogue 2012). Amnesty International, for its part, supported the claims of 'killings, disappearances, and torture' (Amnesty 2011: 8). Amnesty International backed the intervention in Libya, while pretending an 'even handed' criticism of the tiny country and powerful NATO forces. Kovalik observes that Amnesty called for 'immediate action' by the UN against Gaddafi, then made some mild admonishments to NATO during the bombing campaign (Kovalik 2012). The storm of accusations and intervention claims rapidly led to UN Security Council resolution 1973, which called for the protection of civilians through a 'no fly zone'. Exploiting this 'civilian protection' mandate, NATO bombers intervened, the Libyan government was overthrown and Gaddafi was publicly murdered. Secretary of State Hillary Clinton publicly gloated over the President's death (Daly 2011). However NATO had grossly overstepped the UNSC mandate.

The false pretexts for this war were soon exposed. Genevieve Garrigos of Amnesty International (France) admitted there was 'no evidence' to back her group's earlier claims that Gaddafi had used 'black mercenaries' to commit massacres (Cockburn 2011; Forte 2012; Edwards 2013). US academic Alan Kuperman demonstrated that Gaddafi's crackdown on the Islamist insurrection in eastern Libya was 'much less lethal' than had been suggested. Indeed, contrary to the popular western narrative, Gaddafi had not threatened a civilian massacre and had 'refrained from indiscriminate violence'. By later estimates, of the almost one thousand casualties in the first seven weeks, only about three percent were women and children (Kuperman 2015). It was when Libyan government forces were about to regain the east that NATO intervened. Ten thousand more people were killed after the NATO intervention, and the Libyan state was destroyed. 'No evidence or reason' came out to support the claim that Gaddafi planned mass killings (Kuperman 2015). The UNSC had been deceived, and the trust placed in NATO was betrayed.

This immediate abuse of the R2P in practice caused dismay. Dunne and Gelber say that the Libyan experience undermined the idea of an R2P 'norm', with the NATO shift from a 'no fly zone' to regime change 'betraying' the UN trust and showing the partisan nature of intervention (Dunne and Gelber 2014: 327-328). Brown agrees, saying that the Libyan intervention demonstrates that the suggested 'apolitical nature' of a responsibility to protect 'is a weakness not a strength ... the assumption that politics can be removed from the picture is to promote an illusion and thus to invite disillusionment' (Brown 2013: 424-425). The doctrine lost its intellectual gloss. Nevertheless, with a Democrat administration in Washington and an incipient proxy war in Syria, 'humanitarian war' arguments were not dead. Feeling betrayed by the experience on Libya, Russia and China would block 'no fly zone' proposals for Syria, at the Security Council. Yet even if a UN Security Council resolution were not possible, the 'moral' arguments for humanitarian intervention in Syria were well in train.

Normalised conflicts of interest

The US-led 'smart power' interventions in Libya and Syria illustrate very well how, in a neoliberal era, traditionally understood conflicts of interest are ignored. Washington moved rapidly into the Syrian conflict, at first providing 'non-lethal' support to anti-government groups, then providing arms directly to some of those groups; and all that while selling billions of dollars of arms to the Saudis, who had armed Syria's Islamist insurrection from the beginning (see Anderson 2016b). Despite being a belligerent party, the US Government pretended to act as an arbiter of the war. The US and its allies (especially Britain and France) also funded a range of 'media activists', information sources and 'human rights' advocates. The independence of these agencies was compromised by their belligerent patrons.

That conflict of interest was also seen in the United Nations commission set up in mid-2012 to assess the human rights situation in Syria. In early 2012 the UN appointed US diplomat Karen Koning AbuZayd to co-chair, with Brazilian Paulo Pinheiro, a Geneva-based UN Commission on Syria, replacing the former in-country Special Mission (UNSMIS), led by Norwegian General Robert Mood. The appointment of AbuZayd was a partisan move by the UN administration as, by that time, the US was backing the armed opposition in Syria. The replacement of UNSMIS by an AbuZayd-led Commission was important because a massacre of villagers al Houla, outside Homs city, was to be the first major test of the 'responsibility to protect' doctrine against Syria. The AbuZayd-Pinherio commission tried to blame unidentified government aligned thugs, but without substantial evidence, motive or names (HRC 2012: 20). The report was strongly criticised at the UNSC, with Russia, China and India refusing to accept it as a basis for action against Syria. Fifteen independent eye-witnesses had publicly identified Farouq Brigade (FSA) leaders and local collaborators as having committed the crime (Anderson 2016a: Ch. 8). That same armed group had declared a boycott on, and threatened reprisals against, those who participated in, Syria's 2012 national assembly elections.

Five years later the AbuZayd-led commission tried to portray as a 'crime' the liberation of the city of Aleppo from al Qaeda aligned groups. The commission falsely claimed that there had been 'daily air strikes' on the eastern part of Aleppo city, leading up to its liberation (HRC 2017: 19). Yet it was reported widely in foreign media that air strikes on the east part of the city were suspended on 18 October (BBC 2016; Xinhua 2016). NPR's Merrit Kennedy (2016) reported 'several weeks of relative calm' during the 'humanitarian' pause, aimed at evacuating civilians. The 'resumption' of airstrikes almost one month later was aimed at the armed groups in rural Aleppo, not on the shrinking parts of the city held by the al Qaeda aligned sectarian jihadists (Pestano 2016; Graham-Harrison 2016). Nevertheless, al Qaeda aligned 'media activists' claimed the city was being bombed (CNN 2016). The UN commission, as Gareth Porter pointed out, 'did not identify sources for its narrative ... [but rather] accepted the version of the events provided by the 'White Helmets'', a jihadist auxiliary funded by the US and UK governments (Porter 2017). This was a feature of the wider cycle of war reporting.

Washington's openly stated ambition, since mid-2011, to overthrow the Syrian Government led by Bashar al Assad ('Assad must go') taints all the agencies and advocates that take money from the big power. This is simple logic, but in this case the obvious must be stated. Agencies which support US Government policy and practice are more likely to get finance; those against will not. No agency engaged with the polemics of the Syrian conflict can claim to be independent if it is on the payroll of governments committed to the overthrow of the Syrian Government. Nor can those committed to the 'revolution' claim independence as sources of information.

Western-financed sources

For example, a large part of the western media coverage of the conflict relied on a single source, Rami Abdul Rahman, a Syrian exile based in England, who calls himself the Syrian Observatory for Human Rights (SOHR). Many of the stories about Syrian body counts, 'regime' atrocities and huge collateral damage come from this man (Skelton 2012; Christensen 2016). Yet for the first few years of the conflict Abdul Rahman flew the flag of the Muslim Brotherhood led 'Free Syrian Army' on his

THE HUMAN RIGHTS INDUSTRY IN 'HUMANITARIAN WAR'

website (SOHR 2015; see graphic below). He claimed to collect information from a network of associates in and around Syria. It is logical to assume these are also mostly anti-Government people. Western advocates often claim that Syrian, Russian and Iranian sources are to be disqualified for their bias; but they rarely say the same of sources linked to and embedded with the anti-Syrian Government armed groups. That is an untenable position. Abdul Rahman admitted early on that he gets 'small subsidies from the European Union and one European country that he declines to identify' (MacFarquar 2013). As he lives in England that latter source is most likely an agency of the UK government.

Syrian Observatory for Human Rights (SOHR, Ramil Abdul Rahman). Funding: "small subsidies from the European Union and one European country that he declines to identify" (NYT). No research training. Based in Britain.

Syrian Network for Human Rights (SNHR, Fadel Abdul Ghani). Funding: "unconditional grants and donations from individuals and institutions. No research training. Based in Britain

Bellingcat (Elliot Higgins). Funding: Soros OSF and NED (US Congress). No research training. Based in Britain.

Human Rights Data Analysis Group (HRDAG). Funding: Soros OSF and NED (US Congress). Based in United States.

Key 'sources' used by Amnesty International and the US co-chaired UN Human Rights Commission on Syria. Key sources of 'information' on Syria are funded by and linked to the same governments that provide weapons to the armed groups.

Like the SOHR, the Syrian Network for Human Rights (SNHR) is another virtual one-man band based in England. It claims to be 'independent, non-partisan, non-governmental' and is run by Syrian exile Fadel Abdul Ghani (SNHR 2016). The tiny group trumpets 'accountability' yet its sources of funding are nowhere declared. The only thing made public seems to be that: 'SNHR funds its work and activities through unconditional grants and donations from individuals and institutions' (MOA 2017). More recently, even that sentence was removed from the group's website. Abdul Ghani is closely linked to jihadist groups and so is a clear partisan player. He told a journalist in 2013 that US air strikes on Syria were necessary, even if they killed civilians. Using the first person to speak of the armed opposition he added: 'If we don't try to take out Assad's missiles and tanks, [Assad] will continue using them against civilians' (Scaturro 2013). A method note on the SNHR site admits that the group cannot collect reliable data from Syria. They say 'the likelihood of documenting military victims from the opposition is rather slim' as the SNHR cannot get to battlefronts and because of 'the secrecy of the armed opposition'. Similarly, Syrian Army and allied militia victims cannot be calculated due to 'the absence of a clear methodology' (SNHR 2017). Like Abdul Rahman, Abdul Ghani has no training in research. They both compile 'data' in a fairly ad hoc manner from their own partisan networks.

Nevertheless, UN commissioned groups and Amnesty International make use of 'data' from the SOHR, the SNHR and another similarly compromised US-based group called the Human Rights Data Analysis Group (Price, Gohdes and Ball 2014). This HRDAG gets funding from US foundations, including George Soros' Open Society Foundation, and directly from the US Government through the Congress-funded National Endowment for Democracy (NED) (HRDAG 2017). That group, in turn, said 'four sources were used for this analysis ... Syrian Center for Statistics and Research (CSR-SY), Damascus Center for Human Rights Studies (DCHRS), Syrian Network for Human Rights (SNHR) and the Violations Documentation Center (VDC) (Price,

Gohdes and Ball 2016: 1). Those are all anti-Syrian government sources, networked together. Similarly, an untrained researcher and blogger Elliot Higgins, with his small group called Bellingcat, reinforces the US 'war narrative' against Syria. Higgins admits that his group receives money from (amongst others) the Open Society Foundation (run by billionaire George Soros) and from the US government-funded NED (Higgins 2017). The graphic on page 161 shows this network of partisan and western government funded sources. Collaboration in a one-sided war narrative was sought and bought from these and other agencies. Let us turn now to the role of the larger, better known human rights agencies.

Selling humanitarian war: Human Rights Watch and Amnesty International

These large agencies are corporations dedicated to projects concerning political legitimacy. They are, or have become, deeply embedded with powerful states, in part with a view to 'civilise' but more importantly to legitimise globalist agendas. They attract hundreds of millions of dollars from western states and multinational companies and have no real community or democratic accountability. At times of war their most important role becomes prominent: to legitimise the globalist intervention and disqualify the resistance.

The role of Human Rights Watch (HRW) and Amnesty International (Amnesty) during the 'smart power' interventions against Libya and Syria may have caught some by surprise; but there was a longer history to their support for US foreign policy. Because the Syrian conflict has been so protracted, and so reliant on sustained ideological pretext, it has served to highlight the partisan role of these agencies. This section explains how both Human Rights Watch and Amnesty International have become embedded in Washington's 'humanitarian wars'. It presents sufficient evidence of their partisan character.

Human Rights Watch

Human Rights Watch is a New York based corporation

funded mainly by other US corporations and foundations. Unlike the National Endowment for Democracy, it is not directly government-funded; however, it works closely with Washington. In 2010 billionaire George Soros donated $100 million to the agency (Strom 2010), no doubt giving Soros significant leverage in the group. Indeed, after HRW founding member Aryeh Neier left the group to become President of Soros's Open Society Foundation, Ken Roth rose to Executive Director. He remained in that position for the next 24 years (1993-2017). The HRW budget in 2016 was $76 million and its assets were $234 million (HRW 2016a: 15). It maintains close links to the Democrat side of US politics and to the foreign policy elite group, the Council on Foreign Relations (CFR). On the board and a former chairperson is James Hoge, editor of Foreign Policy magazine from 1992-2009. Many other HRW board members are from the US corporate elite. Some donors want the group to focus on a particular area. In 2016 about 90% of the company's assets were 'restricted' by donors (HRW 2016b); that means restricted in time or dedicated to particular projects.

HRW can therefore be said to represent a corporatised, US based lobby on rights issues, catering to the wealthy and closely aligned to US foreign policy (Anderson 2010). Despite its refusal of government funds, conflicts of interest are apparent. For example, HRW director Ken Roth regularly attacks US foreign policy enemies, but was criticised for saying little about President Obama's killer drone program (Bhatt 2014b). The main objects of HRW in Latin America, for many years, were Cuba and Venezuela; HRW mostly ignored Colombia, key US ally and the biggest killer of journalists, trade unionists and lawyers (Anderson 2010). At times the political motivation has been explicit. The 2008 HRW report on Venezuela under President Chavez mainly focused on issues of political discrimination in employment and the judiciary (HRW 2008). It was criticised by more than 100 academics (including this writer) for not meeting 'even the most minimal standards of scholarship, impartiality, accuracy or credibility' (Acuña et al 2008). HRW responded: the report was written, according to HRW Director for the Americas, José Miguel Vivanco, 'because we wanted to demonstrate to the world that Venezuela is not a model for anyone' (Roth 2008).

A similar letter, a few years later, met a similar response. 130 academics led by two Nobel Peace laureates asked HRW to close the 'revolving door' it had with the US Government (Pérez Esquivel et al 2014). They again criticised HRW for ignoring gross abuses by the US Government, while singling out US foreign policy opponents, such as Venezuela. The critics demonstrated repeated interchange of US officials (presidential advisers, US ambassadors, military, and CIA and State Department staff) with HRW, demanding that the group close its 'revolving door' by banning or imposing 'cooling off periods' for 'those who have crafted or executed U.S. foreign policy' (Pérez Esquivel et al 2014). Roth (2014) rejected any idea of a conflict of interest, saying HRW had a great diversity of staff. Nor did he see any problem with HRW having Javier Solana, a former head of NATO, on its board (Bhatt 2014a). Only with the transition from Obama to Trump (that is, from a liberal to a realist regime), did the more Democrat-aligned HRW shift ground. Indeed the US, for the first time in 27 years, was listed as a 'major human rights abuser' when Trump had been in office for just a few days (Moran 2017).

Here are three areas of HRW activity during the war on Syria which demonstrate that the group's integration with Washington has been put into practice. First there is the patently false account HRW gave for the start of armed conflict in Syria. In a March 2012 report, which included some token criticism of the armed jihadists, HRW asserted that 'the protest movement in Syria was overwhelmingly peaceful until September 2011' (HRW 2012). A mass of independent evidence shows this assertion to be quite false.

The late Jesuit priest, Father Frans Van der Lugt, who lived for more than 40 years in Syria before he was murdered by Jabhat al Nusra (al Qaeda) in Homs in 2014:

> I have seen from the beginning armed protesters in those demonstrations ... they were the first to

fire on the police. Very often the violence of the security forces comes in response to the brutal violence of the armed insurgents (van der Lugt 2012).

Similarly, the Ankara-based Australian academic Jeremy Salt wrote, in October 2011:

The claim that armed opposition to the government has begun only recently is a complete lie. The killings of soldiers, police and civilians, often in the most brutal circumstances, have been going on virtually since the beginning (Salt 2011).

Another priest, Belgian Father Daniel Maes - who was resident at the 6th century Mar Yakub monastery in Qara, 90km north of Damascus - said there was 'no civil uprising' in Syria, the violence was foreign paid and contrived (Azizi and Maes 2017). Independent voices in a conflict are important.

The 'peaceful protestor taking up arms' myth was dismantled by independent researchers and journalists. Rather, the armed jihadists had infiltrated political reform demonstrations. The Saudi-armed insurrection in Daraa (Anderson 2016b) spread into Homs in early April 2011. General Abdo Khodr al-Tallawi (with his two sons and a nephew), Syrian commander Iyad Kamel Harfoush and off-duty Colonel Mohammad Abdo Khadour were killed by jihadists (Narwani 2014). On 11 April North American commentator Joshua Landis (2011) reported the death of his wife's cousin, a soldier in Baniyas. Compiling information on soldier deaths, independent journalist Sharmine Narwani reported that in April 2011 eighty-eight Syrian soldiers were killed 'by unknown shooters in different areas across Syria' (Narwani 2014). In June 2011 journalist Hala Jaber reported on the 'armed jihadists' who had infiltrated demonstrations in Idlib, shooting unarmed police (Jaber 2011). These violent jihadist agents drove the peaceful protests off the streets. HRW (2012) recognises nothing of this.

Second, there was the issue of Qatar's morgue photos, released in January 2014. These photos, presented by an anonymous defector code-named 'Caesar', purported to show thousands of 'opposition' prisoners in Syria who had been tortured to death by 'the regime'. Many of the photos seemed to come from a morgue attached to a major hospital in Damascus. 'Caesar' was given asylum by the tiny oil-rich monarchy of Qatar, a major sponsor of the jihadist groups (Shapiro 2013; Dickinson 2014). The story was thus sponsored by a belligerent party and uncorroborated. Qatar hired some British lawyers to provide a 'bootstraps' seal of approval. Thus it was reported that 'senior war crimes prosecutors say photographs and documents provide "clear evidence" of systematic killing of 11,000 detainees (Black 2014). Forensic science experts were said to have examined and authenticated samples of 55,000 digital images, comprising about 11,000 victims. 'Overall there was evidence that a significant number of the deceased were emaciated and a significant minority had been bound and/or beaten with rod-like objects', the Qatari financed report said (Black 2014). Dozens of photos were widely publicised, but the full file was not made public.

Almost two years later HRW got the full file, and ran much the same story, except for one important extra detail. Almost half the photos, HRW admitted, were those of 'dead army soldiers or members of the security forces', or the victims of 'explosions, assassinations ... fires and car bombs' (HRW 2015: 2-3). This had never been mentioned before and, for the rest of the HRW report, was not mentioned again. Without making public the full file, HRW said that 'the largest category of photographs, 28,707 images, are photographs of people Human Rights Watch understands to have died in government custody'. Those photos had a consistent numbering pattern to them and there were 'multiple photographs of each body', sometimes as many as twenty. These photos were estimated to 'correspond to at least 6,786 separate dead individuals' (HRW 2015). However HRW, while admitting that at least 27,000 photos of dead bodies did not depict prisoners of 'the regime', proceeded to ignore them. HRW simply said 'this

US bomb damage in Kobane (below) presented as Syrian 'barrel bomb' damage (left)

Israeli bombing of Gaza (above right) presented as Syrian 'barrel bomb' damage in Aleppo (left)

Ken Roth's 'barrel bomb' campaign: photo switching

report focuses on analyzing the first category of photographs in greater detail' (HRW 2015: 3). The casual reader of the HRW report might not even have noticed the admission that almost half these secret photos had nothing to do with 'industrial scale' killing of 'opposition' people (Black 2014). It was a particularly brazen deceit by HRW to maintain the original story, when they knew better. Rick Sterling (2016) pointed out that partisan publicity over these photos came on the eve of peace negotiations.

A third area of evidence, showing the partisan character of HRW information on Syria, is the recycled and rebadged photos of HRW Director Ken Roth. Columnist Yalla La Barra writes that, over 2014 and 2015, Roth became obsessed with Syria's President Assad and the theme of 'barrel bombs'. According to La Barra's count, Roth made 65 posts on Twitter about Assad and 'barrel bombs' during 2014, and 135 in 2015. This did not include other anti-Syrian comments, including Assad's alleged 'use of chemical weapons against his own people' (La Barra 2015). The suggested motive for the alleged crime of 'barrel bombing' is unclear. The constant reference is to a supposedly improvised bomb, typically dropped on a building from a helicopter. In most senses that is little different from any other sort of bomb during war. However the meaning suggested by Roth and others is that it is either an 'indiscriminate' bomb, or a bomb only dropped (for some unexplained reason) on civilians.

In any case, Roth's tweets were insistent, biased and reckless. The head of HRW said little about Saudi Arabia, Qatar, USA, UK and France arming all kinds of extremist jihadist groups in Syria. His focus, like that of Washington, was the Syrian Government. He made a series of reckless errors, as shown in the adjacent photos. In early 2015 he posted a photo of bombed out Kobane (a.k.a. Ayn al Arab, the Kurd-Arab city which had resisted ISIS attacks, then suffered US bombing) suggesting it was damage from Syrian 'barrel bombs' (MOA 2015a). Soon after that Roth posted Israeli bombing damage on the Gaza strip, suggesting it was damage from 'Assad's barrel bombs' in Aleppo (Johnson 2015; MOA 2015b). That photo switching is shown in

Kenneth Roth
@KenRoth

Here, for comparison, is an example of Aleppo's destruction after Assad's barrel bombs. trib.al/TEkotQN

SYRIA-CONFLICT

After his 'Gaza as Aleppo' post, Roth posts as 'Assad's barrel bomb' damage in the Hamidyeh neighbourhood of Aleppo as local popular committee fighters ... try to defend the traditionally Christian district ... [from] Islamic State group jihadists' (below)

the adjacent photo. Soon after that Roth posted as 'Assad's barrel bomb' damage in Aleppo a photo which was originally titled by the US Getty agency 'destruction in the Hamidiyeh neighbourhood of Aleppo as local popular committee fighters ... try to defend the traditionally Christian district ... [from] Islamic State group jihadists' (MOA 2015c). That 'reinterpretation' is shown in the adjacent photo. Three 'mistakes', all in the one direction, are enough to illustrate the partisan activity of the HRW director.

If that were not enough, Roth tried to link President Assad to the 1945 nuclear attack on Hiroshima. On 9 August 2015 he posted a photo of post-bomb Hiroshima, with the comment 'For the planners of the Hiroshima bomb (like Assad today) the point was to kill civilians' (Roth 2015). The attempt to link Syria to a notorious US crime was extreme cynicism. Roth's behaviour illustrates well the partisan and unreliable reporting by his group of the Syrian conflict. HRW remains deeply embedded with Washington, especially with the State Department and the liberal side of US politics. The evidence cited here demonstrates the agency's partisan character. It cannot be regarded as an independent source.

Amnesty international

Amnesty International began in 1961 as a non-government letter writing agency, campaigning for 'prisoners of conscience'. It foreswore 'political' involvement, but this seems to have changed, at least by the time of the First Gulf War (1990-91). Since then the group has collaborated in pretexts for several US-led wars.

Amnesty claims independence from governments, and many branches do not accept government money. However the group has received many millions of dollars from the British Government, the European Commission, and from the governments of the Netherlands, the USA, Israel (NGO Monitor 2012) and Sweden (Ferrada de Noli 2015). Clearly some states exercise influence. For example, the Israeli government 'funded the establishment and activity of the Amnesty International branch in Israel in the 1960s and 70s', after which Israel's Foreign

Ministry relayed instructions and further funds to this Amnesty branch (Blau 2017). Amnesty International globally raises and spends around 280 million Euros per year (Amnesty 2017a), getting its funds from a range of supporters including several western governments, the highly politicised 'Open Society' groups run by George Soros and the pro-Israel 'American Jewish World Service' (Source Watch 2014).

Jean Bricmont, author of the 2006 book Humanitarian Imperialism, observes that, before the 2003 US invasion of Iraq, both Amnesty International and HRW pretended a 'neutral' position, urging 'all belligerents' to abide by the rules of war (Bricmont 2006). They chose to say nothing about an aggression which was characterised as 'illegal' by the then Secretary General of the United Nations, Kofi Annan (MacAskill and Borger 2004). An Amnesty official confirmed this stance of taking 'no position on the use of armed force or on military interventions in armed conflict, other than to demand that all parties respect international human rights and humanitarian law' (Bery 2012). Amnesty similarly ignored the external interference in Syria, including the arming of terrorist groups (Sterling 2015). It then proceeded to present a highly partisan commentary on the conduct of war, ignoring what the Nuremberg Tribunal had called 'the supreme crime,' a war of aggression.

By the 21st century the Amnesty leadership was well embedded in US state and foreign policy and cross-linked to HRW. One of the US Democrat 'smart power' doctrine advocates Suzanne Nossel, for example, moved from Chief Operating Officer at Human Rights Watch to Deputy Assistant Secretary for International Organisations at the US Department of State, before becoming Executive Director of Amnesty International (USA) (HRI 2012). By 2017 Amnesty USA employed seven current and former US Government officials (Open Secrets 2017).

Amnesty effectively had no-one 'on the ground' during the Syrian conflict, with one exception. In late 2016, during the battle for Aleppo, media coordinator for Amnesty in Australia Samuel Hendricks told this writer 'we do not currently have staff on the ground in Syria ... it is simply not feasible ... [however] our senior crisis response adviser Donatella Rovera, has crossed the border into Syria 10 times ... [and] we've been 'documenting atrocities since the conflict began' (Hendricks 2016). However Rovera only went [illegally] into the jihadist held northern areas of Syria. She had prepared the group's partisan and misleading reports about Libya; the discredited claims that Amnesty France would later retract (Cockburn 2011; Kuperman 2015). Yet she was contracted to prepare a set of similar stories on Syria. On the basis of her visits and testimony from jihadist-controlled areas, Amnesty reported alleged 'ongoing crimes against humanity' by the Syrian Army (Amnesty 2012a).

Other than Rovera's reports and some interviews outside Syria, Amnesty relied on those same sources embedded in the 'regime change' project, including Rami Abdul Rahman's 'Syrian Observatory for Human Rights'. Although the SOHR does not reveal its method, Amnesty researcher Neil Sammonds claimed Abdul Rahman's 'information on the killings of civilians is very good, definitely one of the best, including the details on the conditions in which people were supposedly killed' (MacFarquar 2013). Sammonds does not demonstrate any basis for concluding that information from this openly partisan source was 'very good'.

Salil Shetty, Secretary General of Amnesty International, claimed that Amnesty investigates 'in a very systematic, primary, way where we collect evidence with our own staff on the ground ... [with] corroboration and cross-checking from all parties ... it's very important to get different points of view and constantly cross check and verify the facts' (Shetty 2014). Yet, contrary to these claims, the group relied on third party evidence from sources closely linked to armed groups in Syria, in particular the SOHR and the SNHR. Scottish academic Tim Hayward criticises Amnesty claims that its research has been 'systematic', from 'primary sources', verified by corroboration and cross checked with all parties concerned. He concluded that Amnesty research on Syria does not qualify on any of those counts (Hayward 2017).

Let's look at several areas of Amnesty activity which

demonstrate the group's partisan integration with Washington. First the group has a track record of backing false pretexts for US-led wars. Amnesty pretended to corroborate an important pretext for US intervention in the 'First Gulf War' (1990-91), to drive the Iraqi army from Kuwait. This was the notorious televised lie by Kuwaiti 'Nurse Nayirah' that Iraqi soldiers had taken over a Kuwait hospital and, wanting to seize valuable medical equipment, threw babies out of incubators and left them to die on the cold floor. This story was supported by the London secretariat of Amnesty, claiming they had corroboration for 'Nayirah'. Former Amnesty (USA) board member Francis Boyle (2002) says the group 'rammed' it through without proper scrutiny. In fact, 'Nayirah' was the daughter of Kuwait's ambassador to the USA. After the military intervention, including a huge massacre of retreating Iraqi soldiers within Iraq, the 'Nurse Nayirah' story was exposed as an exercise in fabrication using PR firm Hill and Knowlton to coach 'Nayirah' in her lines (Stauber and Rampton 2002; Regan 2002).

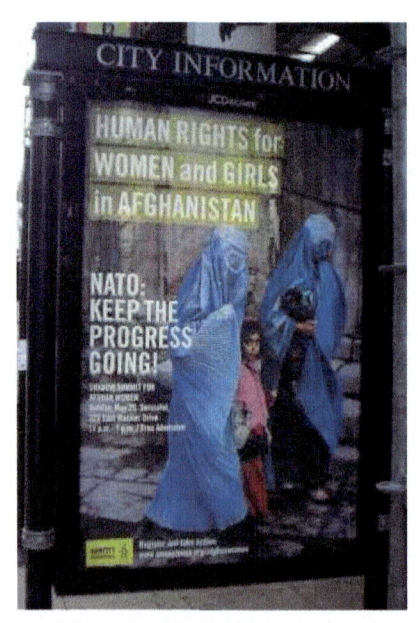

Amnesty International praises NATO's ten year military occupation of Afghanistan, in 2012.

In 2012 then new Director of Amnesty (USA), Suzanne Nossel, launched a campaign supposedly in support of the rights of women and girls in Afghanistan. Amnesty's billboards at the time of the 2012 NATO summit in Chicago declared 'NATO: keep the progress going!' The not too subtle corollary was to praise NATO's ten year military occupation of the country, on a pretext dreamed up by then US President George W. Bush. Outraged obser-

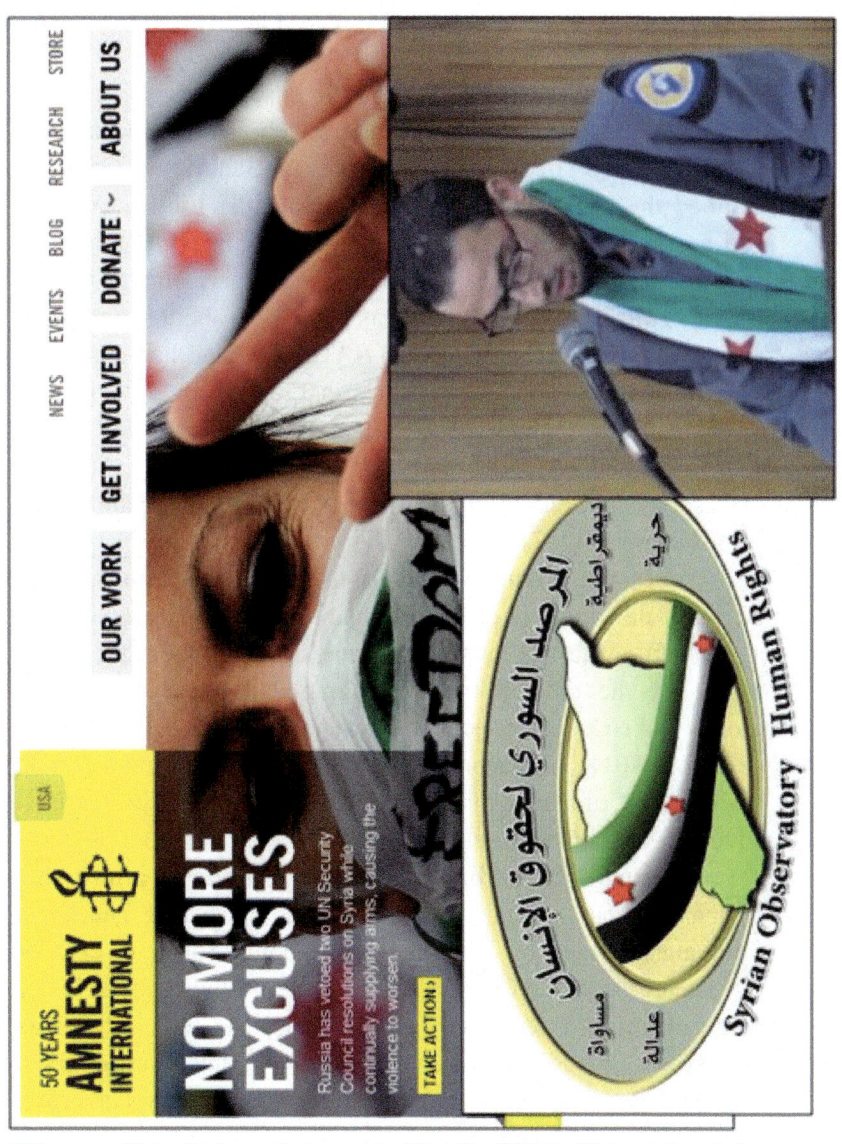

What conflict of interest? Amnesty, like the 'White Helmets' and the 'Syrian Observatory' (SOHR), flies the red starred 'revolution' flag.

vers branded this as Amnesty 'shilling for US wars' (Wright and Rowley 2012). The group later admitted it had sent a 'confusing' message (Colucci 2012).

Amnesty also corroborated the false stories about Libya, campaigning strongly against the government of Muammar Gaddafi. Head of Amnesty (France), Genevieve Garrigos, claimed the Libyan president was threatening Libyan civilians and had used 'black mercenaries' to kill civilians. At this time, Al Jazeera (owned by the monarchy of Qatar, which also funded Libya's armed Salafist groups) was telling lies about shootings at a Benghazi demonstration. After NATO bombing had destroyed the Libyan state, Garrigos admitted that there was 'no evidence' to support the claims over 'black mercenaries' (Teil 2011; Timand2037 2012; Kuperman 2015). In a similar way, Amnesty ran a series of unreliable and partisan stories to inflame the war on Syria (Sterling 2017).

Second, aligning itself to its openly partisan sources, Amnesty flew the flag of armed jihadists on its websites, next to a 'peaceful protestor' flashing a peace sign (see photo preceding page). By the time of this 2012 graphic 'Free Syrian Army' groups had engaged in sectarian killings, using genocidal slogans (Blanford 2011; Anderson 2016a: 123) 'Fight bad guys' would became one of Amnesty's slogans, a not too subtle, populist advocacy of 'humanitarian war'.

Using jihadist-linked sources, Amnesty joined the US-based groups Avaaz, Human Rights Watch and The Syria Campaign, funded by US billionaire George Soros, to call for UN Security Council Chapter Seven (armed) action against Syria, while claiming it remained 'even-handed'. As with Libya, the pretext was defending civilians: 'the main victims of a campaign of relentless and indiscriminate attacks by the Syrian army' (Amnesty 2012b).

Third, Amnesty adopted the claims of current and former sectarian jihadists that there were mass hangings at a small prison in Saydnaya. 'Up to 13,000 secretly hanged in Syrian jail, says Amnesty' was the headline (Chulov 2017). While the death penalty exists in Syria and no doubt many of those convicted of murder during the conflict have been executed, this exaggerated claim must have been designed to attract scandalous publicity, again in support of expanded western intervention. Amnesty had joined its interviews with a few dozen anonymous people in Turkey to 'data' provided by the jihadist-aligned, UK-based Syrian Network for Human Rights. Amnesty alleges there were 'extermination policies' resulting in 'the deaths of hundreds – probably thousands – of detainees' (Amnesty 2017: 7). From the vague 'hundreds – probably thousands' the report scales up to 'between 5,000 and 13,000', before finally planting a headline of 'up to 13,000' (Amnesty 2017; Turbeville 2017). This was a transparent exercise in number manipulation and extremist language.

Russian Foreign Ministry spokeswoman Maria Zakharova said the report 'does not correspond to reality ... [appearing to be] the result of mathematical calculations on the basis of testimony of unnamed people' (Press TV 2017). Independent observer Peter Ford, the former UK ambassador to Syria, asked why this report came just as the peace talks in Astana seemed to be making some progress? Amnesty had used anonymous witnesses in Turkey and, according to Ford, those 'nameless sources are wrong on basic information'. The former ambassador had visited Saydnaya several times and says the prison there was far smaller than Amnesty suggested. The building he saw at Saydnaya 'could not possibly accommodate more than ten percent of those numbers' [10,000 to 20,000] (Sputnik 2017).

Analysts asked how it was possible that there were no detailed previous reports of these 'mass executions', and on what information were the numbers based? Key source the UK-based SNHR presents no clear method of data collection and does not make detailed information publicly available. Only 95 were given names (MOA 2017). Amnesty presented some rather wild guesses, based on anonymous interviews and a notorious partisan, exile source. These were not the acts of a professional or impartial body.

Custom built agencies: 'The Syria Campaign' and the 'White Helmets'

Several custom-built agencies were set up and most often funded by western governments, specifically to service the 'war narrative' needs of the Syrian conflict. This section will not make a comprehensive documentation of all those agencies. Rather, it will demonstrate the embedded nature of two (The Syria Campaign and the White Helmets), providing evidence of how they have systematically misled the public.

The Syria Campaign is a Wall Street (New York) agency set up to run an online 'war narrative' campaign, with eye-catching video and graphics. Their speciality is in marketing. Key messages are that the Syrian government is by far the worst human rights abuser, and that the great majority of Syria's refugees are running from the Syrian Army and President Assad. Their data, once again, comes from partisan agencies, in particular the SNHR and the SOHR (TSC 2017). Packaged messages along these lines have been picked up by much of the western media (e.g. Naylor 2015).

The Syria Campaign (TSC) was set up by people linked to Avaaz, through a mother company called 'Purpose'. The New York group adds some 'Syrian' credibility through links to a few jihadist 'activists', such as photographer Khaled Khatib (Morningstar 2015). With funds from the Soros groups, they were anti-Syria and pro-regime change from the start. In June 2014 TSC tried to block Facebook from hosting Bashar al Assad's presidential election campaign page (Rushe and Jalabi 2014). Avaaz, The Syria Campaign and The White Helmets shared campaigns for a Libyan-styled 'no fly zone', making often outlandish claims. Without any credible evidence Avaaz claimed 'women in Syria are being forced to stand in front of tanks and act as human shields before they're stripped and raped by soldiers' (Avaaz 2013). This was while sectarian and pseudo-Islamists were openly boasting about their kidnapping and raping Syrian women and girls, crimes backed by fatwas from their pseudo-religious leaders (Chumley 2013).

TSC has been active in the recycling of war photos. In

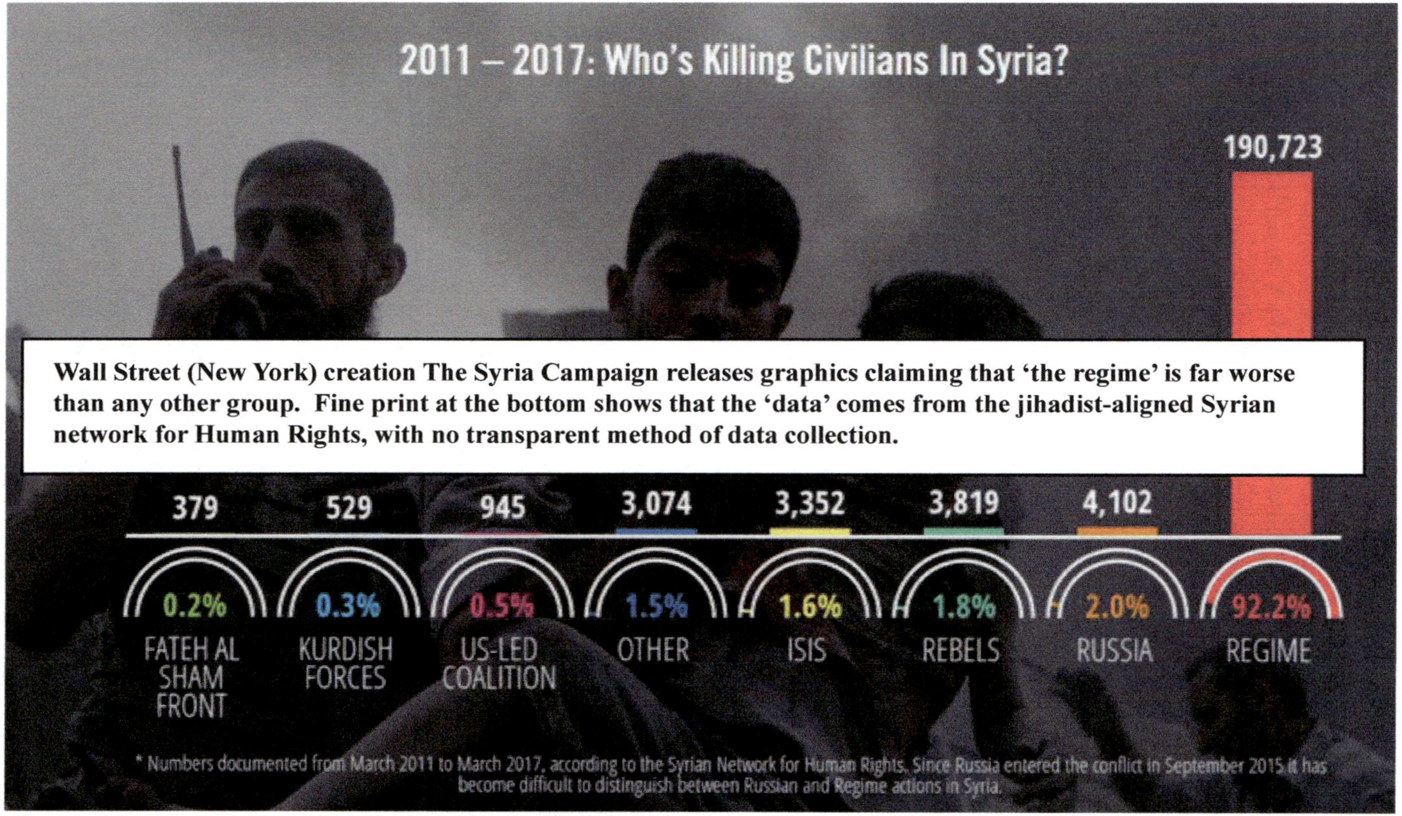

2011 – 2017: Who's Killing Civilians In Syria?

Wall Street (New York) creation The Syria Campaign releases graphics claiming that 'the regime' is far worse than any other group. Fine print at the bottom shows that the 'data' comes from the jihadist-aligned Syrian network for Human Rights, with no transparent method of data collection.

379	529	945	3,074	3,352	3,819	4,102	190,723
0.2%	0.3%	0.5%	1.5%	1.6%	1.8%	2.0%	92.2%
FATEH AL SHAM FRONT	KURDISH FORCES	US-LED COALITION	OTHER	ISIS	REBELS	RUSSIA	REGIME

* Numbers documented from March 2011 to March 2017, according to the Syrian Network for Human Rights. Since Russia entered the conflict in September 2015 it has become difficult to distinguish between Russian and Regime actions in Syria.

'The Syria Campaign': nice graphics but worthless data

August 2015 Avaaz and TSC ran photos of dead children's bodies in building rubble, claiming they were victims of Syrian Government attacks on Islamic Front-held East Ghouta (countryside Damascus) in 2015. That same photo had been used a year earlier to illustrate a story of ISIS having massacred 700 tribespeople in Deir Ezzor (Chronicle 2014). Tracked back further, the same photo was claimed in March 2014 by Getty News and photographer Khaled Khatib, said to portray child victims of earlier 'barrel bombing' in Aleppo (Getty Images 2014). Khatib is described as an 'activist' who operates in areas occupied by Free Syrian Army armed groups, and an 'Aleppo member of "Syrian Civil Defence"', aka the White Helmets (al Khatib 2015; Laughland 2015).

In an attempt to prove that the millions of Syrian war refugees were mostly running from the Syrian Government, TSC (2015a) commissioned a poll in Germany. In the poll, 889 Syrian refugees were said to have been interviewed in Berlin, Hanover, Bremen, Leipzig and Eisenhüttenstadt. Candidates 'were approached on entering or leaving registration centers'. However the survey does not specify how sampling choices were made; nor does it provide a sampling error (TSC 2015b). Where there is no clear statement of sampling method and no calculated sampling error there is no basis for asserting that any survey represents a broader population. The results are then almost useless, except as anecdotes.

The poll cover note, headline and graphics highlight a claim that '70% of refugees are fleeing Assad' (TSC 2015a). This is a false characterisation of the actual survey which, in its questions, does not even mention 'Assad' (TSC 2015b). Second, those whom the refugees fear do not add up to 100. Nevertheless, the three relevant questions seem to be number 9 ('Who was responsible for the fighting?), number 14 ('Who did you fear getting arrested or kidnapped by?'), and number 18 ('What was the main reason for you to leave Syria?'). In questions 9 and 14 there were multiple options, so results tally to much more than 100. (TSC 2015b; see also Anderson 2016c). In responses to Question 9, 70% identified 'Syrian Army and allied groups' as 'responsible for the fighting'. However 82% also identified other armed groups (ISIS, al Nusra, FSA, YPG, other rebels). Removing the Kurdish YPG, which had until then generally fought terrorism in coordination with the Syrian Army, the total is 74% anti-government armed groups. With Question 14, 77% said they feared 'getting arrested or kidnapped by' the 'Syrian Army and its allied groups'. However, the combined total of feared anti-government groups is 82% and, if we add the YPG, 90%. The answers to both questions suggest these respondents feared anti-government armed groups more than they feared the Syrian Army. This is the reverse of the impression conveyed by '70% ... fleeing Assad'. Yet most journalists ran with the TSC press release headline. For example, *Deutsche Welle* reported: 'Survey leaves no doubt: Syrians are fleeing Assad' (Fuchs 2015).

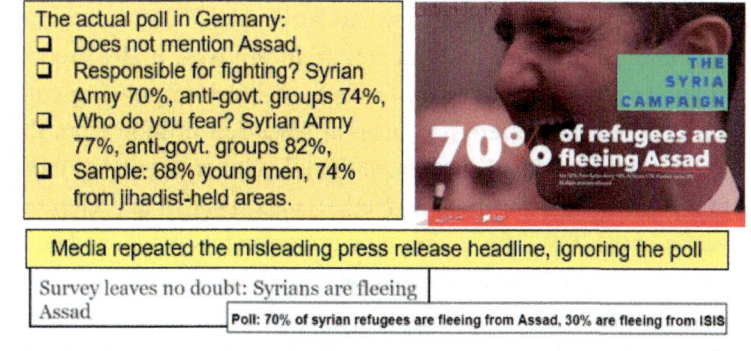

The actual poll in Germany: ❏ Does not mention Assad, ❏ Responsible for fighting? Syrian Army 70%, anti-govt. groups 74%, ❏ Who do you fear? Syrian Army 77%, anti-govt. groups 82%, ❏ Sample: 68% young men, 74% from jihadist-held areas.	70% of refugees are fleeing Assad THE SYRIA CAMPAIGN
Media repeated the misleading press release headline, ignoring the poll	
Survey leaves no doubt: Syrians are fleeing Assad	Poll: 70% of syrian refugees are fleeing from Assad, 30% are fleeing from ISIS

The Syrian Campaign proves the opposite of its press release, even with a heavily biased sample; more refugees in Germany say they were fleeing armed groups than the Syrian Army.

Further, the TSC poll was on its face highly unrepresentative. Those Syrians interviewed in Germany were mostly young men, and most of them from jihadist held areas. Women and children barely exist in this poll. The poll states that 74% were from areas held by anti-government armed groups, and 68% were young men. There were hardly any from the government held areas of Tartus, Latakia and Sweida; and Damascus was seriously under-represented (TSC 2015b; Anderson 2016c) (see photo above). In summary, the TSC poll did not show that most refugees

181

were 'fleeing Assad'. To the contrary, and despite the seriously biased cohort, the poll suggested that those sampled were more fearful of anti-government armed groups.

The White Helmets (TWH) is a group famous for its self-promoting video and photos of members rushing from the scene of a bombing with children in their arms. They claim to have rescued '70,000 people' from Syrian government bomb attacks (RT 2016). Yet their videos hide the fact that there is a real Syrian civil defence (linked to the fire brigade, with red helmets) which serves almost the whole country (Beeley 2017a). The western created 'cuckoo' 'Syrian Civil Defence' is a jihadist auxiliary, founded by former British soldier-mercenary James le Mesurier, and exclusively associated with the al Qaeda held areas of western Syria (Webb 2017). At first the group hid its sources of finance but over 2015-2016 it was revealed that most came from USAID and the British Government (Beeley 2015c; Beeley 2016a). Despite claiming independence and humanitarian motives, a 2017 report counted about $120 million in funds from western governments. From 2014 to 2017 there had been at least $23 million from the US Government, $80 million from the UK Government and more than $16 million from the EU, Netherlands, Danish and German governments (2CW 2017); the same governments which had been arming the jihadist groups ('moderate rebels').

Several White Helmet associates in Syria—Mosab Obeidat, Khaled Diab, and Farouq al Habib—have strong links to the armed groups and their funders. Obeidat worked for Qatar's Red Crescent for some years, then 'with the US Department of State in Jordan' (MayDay Rescue 2015). Diab also worked for the Qatar's Red Crescent, where he was accused of providing about $2.2 million to terrorist groups in Syria (Cartalucci 2013). Habib was a member of the 'Homs Revolutionary Council' (Beeley 2015c). TWH shared with HRW the theme that 'Assad's barrel bombs ... are the greatest threat to Syrians' (Roth 2015a).

TWH are also deeply involved in the recycled war photos game. Immediately after Russian air support for the Syrian Army began, on 30 September 2015, the White Helmets published a photo on its Twitter account, depicting a bleeding girl and claiming she was injured during a Russian airstrike. This false claim was immediately exposed by Russian media, as the photo had been first published five days before the air strikes (Sputnik 2015). Throughout 2016 video and photographs appeared showing men in White Helmets uniforms not only mingled in alongside and helping the jihadist groups - including in the torture and murder of Syrian soldiers and civilians - but switching their medic uniforms for armed group logos and weapons. That is, the armed fighters were themselves White Helmets personnel. There are now compilations of many dozens of such photos (e.g. COS 2017; SWB 2017). One White Helmets self-promotion video, supposedly showing rescue attempts on a baby, was denounced by Swedish Doctors for Human Rights as showing 'medical malpractice and misuse of children for propaganda aims' (Ferrada de Noli 2017).

This photo switching has misled UN agencies. On 19 August 2015 TWH posted a picture of a damaged building in Aleppo, saying 'arrived at the scene of the blast ... about one dozen barrel bombs have torn a whole block apart'. The words and picture were adopted and re-posted by the UN's Humanitarian Affairs Office (UNOCHA 2015; see photo following page). However, that picture had been published 28 months earlier, attributed to the jihadist-linked Aleppo Media Centre (CSM 2013). The AMC, in turn is funded by the Washington based Syrian exile group the SEO, and the French Government (Beeley 2016b). The reliability of the 2013 photo-story is also in doubt. However, we do know that (1) the 2015 photo-story, with its text, has been dishonestly recycled by the White Helmets, and that (2) this fabrication was (probably unwittingly) adopted and propagated by a UN agency.

If there were any doubt about their partisan and jihadist credentials, the head of al Qaeda in western Syria, Abu Jaber al Sheikh, praised TWH as 'hidden soldiers of the revolution' (Vino 2017). After the eastern part of Aleppo city was liberated and almost 100,000 civilians came flooding out, a number of Syrian, Iranian, Russian and independent journalists were there to ask

The Monitor's View

Looking for Obama's agenda in Syria

As killings in Syria worsen, more people look to Obama for action preparation for action doesn't start with the White House.

By the Monitor's Editorial Board | APRIL 14, 2013

April 14, 2013

UNOCHA
@UNOCHA

Arrived at the scene of the blast... about one dozen barrel bombs have torn a whole tower block apart. #ShareHumanity

August 8, 2015

2:26 PM - 19 Aug 2015

UN Office for the Coordination of Humanitarian Affairs (OCHA) copies 'White Helmets' recycled photo, posted 28 months earlier by the jihadist-linked (US SEO and French Government-funded) 'Aleppo Media Centre'.

White Helmets recycled photo reposted by UN agency

them about their experiences. Former residents of occupied east Aleppo called them 'Nusra front [al Qaeda] civil defence', saying they worked together with the armed groups and rarely provided any assistance to ordinary people (Beeley 2017c). Over May-June 2017 the White Helmets were filmed attending executions in Aleppo and Daraa and, in the latter case, parading severed heads and dismembered bodies before dumping them in a garbage heap (Live Leak 2015; O'Connor 2017; Beeley 2017b).

The White Helmets also played a role in taking samples from the site of a chemical weapons incident in Idlib (Khan Sheikhoun) to the OPCW, a UN agency in Turkey. Syria and Russia say the aim was to blame the Syrian Airforce for the attack. This story was backed by the White House and its embedded agencies, such as Bellingcat; but it was rejected by independent US experts Ted Postol and Scott Ritter. Postol, a Pentagon forensic consultant, said whatever chemical was used had not come from the air, but had been detonated on the ground (Postol 2017). Former US arms inspector Scott Ritter said intervention by the partisan White Helmets had destroyed the integrity of the chain of command of tissue samples, so the OPCW was in no position to judge from where it came (Ritter 2017). Professor Paul McKeigue, examining the UN's OPCW/JIM report, rejected the suggested sarin 'finger-printing' exercise (which sought to link the Syrian sarin stocks, disposed in 2014, with the samples provided by the jihadists in Idlib). He also concluded that US-provided flight path data for Syrian aircraft was 'incompatible' with the air strike story (McKeigue 2017). The White Helmets misled the OPCW, just as they had misled the UNOCHA. Once again, these were partisan, paid groups in action.

Concluding Remarks

'Humanitarian war' has a long colonial and neo-colonial history, but requires strong ideological campaigns and renewed doctrine. To this end, 'human rights' groups have been both co-opted and created for legitimising purposes. Human Rights Watch and Amnesty International are the most prominent examples of a human rights industry embedded with US foreign policy. In the proxy war on Syria, other purpose-built public relations groups have been created, like The Syria Campaign and the White Helmets, funded by the big powers and associated western foundations. Together these groups form a highly politicised industry, which seeks to bury or 'normalise' its conflicts of interest. The joint project has been an attempt to legitimise western military intervention on humanitarian pretexts, avoiding the non-intervention and anti-war principles of the United Nations. The project seeks to disqualify or demoralise resistance to imperial strategy, aiming at division or destruction of independent states in the process of building a US-led 'New Middle East'. The evidence of fabrications and partisan campaigns carried out by this network is massive. Yet war propaganda has never relied on reason and evidence.

Bibliography

2CW (2017) 'Secret £1bn UK War Chest Used to Fund the White Helmets and Other "Initiatives"', 21st Century Wire, 13 March, online: http://21stcenturywire.com/2017/03/13/secret-1bn-uk-war-chest-used-to-fund-the-white-helmets-and-other-initiatives/

Acuña, Rodolfo et al (2008) 'More Than 100 Latin America Experts Question Human Rights Watch's Venezuela Report', Venezuela Analysis, 17 December, online: https://venezuelanalysis.com/analysis/4051

Amnesty (2011) 'LIBYA: THE BATTLE FOR LIBYA: KILLINGS, DISAPPEARANCES AND TORTURE', 13 September, online: https://www.amnesty.org/en/documents/MDE19/025/2011/en/

Amnesty (2012a) 'Syria: Fresh evidence of armed forces' ongoing crimes against humanity', 13 June, online: https://www.amnesty.org/en/latest/news/2012/06/syria-fresh-evidence-armed-forces-ongoing-crimes-against-humanity/

Amnesty (2012b) 'SYRIA: INDISCRIMINATE ATTACKS TERRORIZE AND DISPLACE CIVILIANS', 19 September, online: https://www.amnesty.org/en/documents/mde24/078/2012/en/%20/

Amnesty (2017) 'Human Slaughterhouse: Mass Hangings And Extermination At Saydnaya Prison, Syria', 7 February, online: https://www.amnesty.org/en/documents/mde24/5415/2017/en/

Amnesty (2017a) 'Global Financial Report 2016', Amnesty International, online:

https://www.amnesty.org/en/2016-global-financial-report/

Anderson, Tim (2010) 'How Credible Is Human Rights Watch on Cuba?', *Monthly Review* Online, 16 February, online: https://mronline.org/2010/02/16/how-credible-is-human-rights-watch-on-cuba/

Anderson, Tim (2016a) *The Dirty War on Syria*, Global Research, Montreal

Anderson, Tim (2016b) 'Daraa 2011: Syria's Islamist Insurrection in Disguise', Global Research, 16 March, online: http://www.globalresearch.ca/daraa-2011-syrias-islamist-insurrection-in-disguise/5460547

Anderson, Tim (2016c) 'How "The Syria Campaign" Faked Its "70% Fleeing Assad" Refugee Poll' Global Research, 17 September, online: http://www.globalresearch.ca/how-the-syrian-campaign-faked-its-70-fleeing-assad-refugee-poll/5546220

Avaaz (2013) 'For the women of Syria', 20 June, online: https://secure.avaaz.org/en/syria_the_last_straw_r/

Azizi, Bahar and Fr. Daniel Maes (2017) 'Sott.net Interview with Father Daniel in Syria: "There Never Was a Popular Uprising in Syria"', SOTT, 24 June, online: https://www.sott.net/article/354637-Sott-net-Interview-with-Father-Daniel-in-Syria-There-Never-Was-a-Popular-Uprising-in-Syria

Barnard, Anne (2013) 'Syria and Activists Trade Charges on Chemical Weapons', *New York Times*, 19 March, online: http://www.nytimes.com/2013/03/20/world/middleeast/syria-developments.html?pagewanted=all

Bass, Gary J. (2008) *Freedom's Battle: the origins of humanitarian intervention*, Vintage Books, New York

BBC (2013) UN's Del Ponte says evidence Syria rebels "used sarin", 6 May, online: http://www.bbc.com/news/world-middle-east-22424188

BBC (2016) 'Syria war: Russia halts Aleppo bombing for humanitarian pause', 18 October, online: http://www.bbc.com/news/world-middle-east-37689063

Beeley, Vanessa (2015c) 'Syria's white helmets: war by way of deception – Part 1', 21st century Swire, 23 October, online: http://21stcenturywire.com/2015/10/23/syrias-white-helmets-war-by-way-of-deception-part-1/

Beeley, Vanessa (2016a) 'Who are Syria's White Helmets? (terrorist linked)'? 21st century Wire, 21 June, online: http://21stcenturywire.com/2016/06/21/who-are-the-syria-white-helmets/

Beeley, Vanessa (2016b) '"Aleppo Media Centre" Funded By French Foreign Office, EU and US', 20 September, online: http://21stcenturywire.com/2016/09/20/exclusive-aleppo-media-centre-funded-by-french-foreign-office-eu-and-us/

Beeley, Vanessa (2017a) 'The REAL Syria Civil Defence, Saving Real Syrians,

Not Oscar Winning White Helmets, Saving Al Qaeda', Global Research, 2 April, online: http://www.globalresearch.ca/the-real-syria-civil-defence-saving-real-syrians-not-oscar-winning-white-helmets-saving-al-qaeda/5583020

Beeley, Vanessa (2017b) 'WHITE HELMETS: Severed Heads of Syrian Arab Army Soldiers Paraded as Trophies – Endorsed by Channel 4', 21st century Wire, 21 June, online: http://21stcenturywire.com/2017/06/21/white-helmets-severed-heads-of-syrian-arab-army-soldiers-paraded-as-trophies-endorsed-by-channel-4/

Beeley, Vanessa (2017c) 'SYRIA WHITE HELMETS HAND IN HAND WITH AL QAEDA', YouTube, 22 January, online: https://www.youtube.com/watch?v=OBkn78q_t_Q

Beeley, Vanessa (2017d) 'WHITE HELMETS: Taxpayers Funds Used to Finance Terrorism in Syria?', 21st Century Wire, 25 October, online: http://21stcenturywire.com/2017/10/25/white-helmets-taxpayers-funds-used-finance-terrorism-syria/

Bery, Sunjeev (2012) 'A Critic Gets it Wrong on Amnesty International and Libya', Amnesty International USA, 2 November, online: http://blog.amnestyusa.org/middle-east/a-critic-gets-it-wrong-on-amnesty-international-and-libya/

Bhatt, Keane (2014a) 'The Revolving Door at Human Rights Watch', Counterpunch, 11 July, online: http://www.counterpunch.org/2014/07/11/the-revolving-door-at-human-rights-watch/

Bhatt, Keane (2014b) 'A Shared Culture of Conflict of Interest', FAIR, 1 September, online: http://fair.org/extra/a-shared-culture-of-conflict-of-interest/

Blau, Uri (2017) 'Documents Reveal How Israel Made Amnesty's Local Branch a Front for the Foreign Ministry in the 70s', Haaretz, 18 March, online: http://www.haaretz.com/israel-news/.premium-1.777770

Black, Ian (2014) 'Syrian regime document trove shows evidence of "industrial scale" killing of detainees"', *The Guardian,* online: https://www.theguardian.com/world/2014/jan/20/evidence-industrial-scale-killing-syria-war-crimes

Blanford, Nicholas (2011) 'Assad regime may be gaining upper hand in Syria', *Christian Science Monitor,* 13 May, online: http://www.csmonitor.com/World/Middle-East/2011/0513/Assad-regime-may-be-gaining-upper-hand-in-Syria

Boyle, Francis (2002) Interview with Dennis Bernstein, *Covert Action Quarterly,* Number 73 Summer 2002, pp. 9-12, 27.

Bricmont, Jean (2006) *Humanitarian Imperialism: using human rights to sell war,* NYU Press, New York

Brown, Chris (2013) 'The Anti-Political theory of Responsibility to Protect',

Global Responsibility to Protect, Vol 5, Issue 4, 423-442

Bush Centre (2017) 'Afghan Women's Project', George W. Bush Presidential Centre, online: http://www.bushcenter.org/explore-our-work/fostering-policy/afghan-womens-project.html

Cartalucci, Tony (2013) 'UN's Syria "Aid" Appeal is Bid to Relieve Trapped Terrorists', Land Destroyer, 17 December, online: http://landdestroyer.blogspot.com.au/2013/12/syria-uns-aid-appeal-is-bid-to-relieve.html

Carter, Jimmy (1980) 'The State of the Union Address Delivered Before a Joint Session of the Congress', The American Presidency Project, 23 January, online: http://www.presidency.ucsb.edu/ws/?pid=33079

CFR (2000) Humanitarian Intervention: crafting a workable doctrine, A Council Policy Initiative, Council on Foreign Relations, Washington

Christensen, Beau (2016) 'Propaganda spin cycle: "Syrian Observatory for Human Rights" is funded by US and UK governments', SOTT, 23 September, online: https://www.sott.net/article/329117-Propaganda-spin-cycle-Syrian-Observatory-for-Human-Rights-is-funded-by-US-and-UK-governments

Chulov, Martin (2017) 'Up to 13,000 secretly hanged in Syrian jail, says Amnesty', *The Guardian,* 7 February, online: https://www.theguardian.com/world/2017/feb/07/up-to-13000-secretly-hanged-in-syrian-jail-says-amnesty

Chumley, Cheryl K. (2013) 'Islamic cleric decrees it OK for Syrian rebels to rape women', *Washington Times,* 3 April, online: http://www.washingtontimes.com/news/2013/apr/3/islamic-cleric-decrees-it-ok-syrian-rebels-rape-wo/

Chronicle (2014) 'Islamic State Group "Executes 700" in Syria', 18 August, online: http://www.chronicle.co.zw/islamic-state-group-executes-700-in-syria/

Clark, Wesley (2007) *A Time to Lead: for duty, honor and country,* St. Martin's Press, London

CNN (2016) 'Syria: Aleppo pounded by "heaviest bombardment" since war began', 21 November, online: http://edition.cnn.com/2016/11/20/middleeast/syria-aleppo-airstrikes/index.html

Cockburn, Patrick (2011) 'Amnesty questions claim that Gaddafi ordered rape as weapon of war', *The Independent,* 23 June, online: http://www.independent.co.uk/news/world/africa/amnesty-questions-claim-that-gaddafi-ordered-rape-as-weapon-of-war-2302037.html

Colucci, Vienna (2012) 'We Get It', Amnesty International, 19 May, online: http://blog.amnestyusa.org/asia/we-get-it/

COS (2017) 'Massive White Helmets Photo Cache Proves Hollywood Gave Oscar to Terrorist Group', Clarity of Signal, 27 February, online: https://clarityofsignal.com/2017/02/27/massive-white-helmets-photo-cache-proves-hollywood-gave-oscar-to-terrorist-group/

Cronogue, Graham (2012) 'Responsibility to Protect: Syria, the Law, Politics and Future of Humanitarian Intervention Post-Libya', *Journal of International Humanitarian Legal Studies*, Volume 3 issue 1, 124-159

CSM (2013) 'Looking for Obama's agenda in Syria', *Christian Science Monitor*, 14 April, online: https://www.csmonitor.com/Commentary/the-monitors-view/2013/0414/Looking-for-Obama-s-agenda-in-Syria

Daly, Corbett (2011) 'Clinton on Qaddafi: "We came, we saw, he died"', CBS, 20 October, online: http://www.cbsnews.com/news/clinton-on-qaddafi-we-came-we-saw-he-died/

Dickinson, Elizabeth (2014) 'The Case Against Qatar', *Foreign Policy*, 30 September, online: http://foreignpolicy.com/2014/09/30/the-case-against-qatar/

Dunne, Tim and Katherine Gelber (2014) 'Arguing Matters: The responsibility to protect and the Case of Libya', *Global Responsibility to Protect*, 6, 326-349

Edwards, Dave (2013) '"Limited But Persuasive" Evidence - Syria, Sarin, Libya, Lies', Media Lens, 13 June, online: http://www.medialens.org/index.php/alerts/alert-archive/alerts-2013/735-limited-but-persuasive-evidence-syria-sarin-libya-lies.html

Ferrada de Noli, Marcello (2015) 'Swedish Doctors for Human Rights on biased allegations of "war crimes" put forward by Amnesty International against Russia', The Indicter, December, online: http://theindicter.com/swedish-doctors-for-human-rights-on-the-allegations-of-war-crimes-put-forward-by-amnesty-international-against-russia/

Ferrada de Noli, Marcello (2017) 'White Helmets Video: Swedish Doctors for Human Rights Denounce Medical Malpractice and Misuse of Children for Propaganda Aims', The Indicter, 6 March, online: http://theindicter.com/white-helmets-video-swedish-doctors-for-human-rights-denounce-medical-malpractice-and-misuse-of-children-for-propaganda-aims/

Forte, Maximilian (2012) *Slouching Towards Sirte: NATO's War on Libya and Africa*, Baraka Books, Quebec

Fuchs, Richard (2015) 'Survey leaves no doubt: Syrians are fleeing Assad', *Deutsche Welle*, 11 October, online: http://www.dw.com/en/survey-leaves-no-doubt-syrians-are-fleeing-assad/a-18775789

Gamble, Richard M. (2012) *In Search of the City on a Hill: The Making and Unmaking of an American Myth*, Bloomsbury Academic, London

Garamone, Jim (2000) 'Joint Vision 2020 Emphasizes Full-spectrum Dominance', US Department of Defence, 2 June, online: http://archive.defense.gov/news/newsarticle.aspx?id=45289

Getty Images (2014) Syria Conflict, Photograph 479335513, Khaled Khatib/

AFP/Getty Images, 18 March, online: http://www.gettyimages.com. au/detail/news-photo/the-bodies-of-two-syrian-children-lie-in-the-rubble-of-a-news-photo/479335513?license

Graham-Harrison, Emma (2016) 'Aleppo airstrikes restart as Russia announces major Syria offensive', *The Guardian,* 16 November, online: https://www.theguardian.com/world/2016/nov/15/aleppo-airstrikes-resume-as-russia-announces-major-syria-offensive

Hayward, Tim (2017) 'How We Were Misled About Syria: Amnesty International', blog, 23 January, online: https://timhayward.wordpress.com/2017/01/23/amnesty-internationals-war-crimes-in-syria/

Hendricks, Samuel (2016) 'Your Aleppo appeal?' personal email communications with this writer, 21-22 December

Heningsen, Patrick (2016) 'Introduction: Smart Power & The Human Rights Industrial Complex', 21st century 19 April, online: http://21stcenturywire.com/2016/04/19/an-introduction-smart-power-the-human-rights-industrial-complex/

Higgins, Elliot (2017) 'Bellingcat has received money from the following: OSF, Meedan, NED [etc]', Twitter, 6 February, online: https://twitter.com/EliotHiggins/status/828554441485869056

Hoeffel, Joseph (2014) *The Iraq Lie: How the White House Sold the War,* Progressive Press, San Diego

HRC (2012) 'Oral Update of the Independent International Commission of Inquiry on the Syrian Arab Republic', Human Rights Commission, 26 June, online: http://www.ohchr.org/Documents/HRBodies/HRCouncil/CoISyria/OralUpdateJune2012.pdf

HRC (2017) 'Report of the Independent International Commission of Inquiry on the Syrian Arab Republic' [Aleppo report], A/HRC/34/64, 2 February, online: https://documents-dds-ny.un.org/doc/UNDOC/GEN/G17/026/63/PDF/G1702663.pdf?OpenElement

HRDAG (2017) Human Rights Data Analysis Group: funding' online: https://hrdag.org/

HRI (2012) 'Suzanne Nossel Executive Director of Amnesty International USA', Human Rights Investigations, 30 September, online: https://humanrightsinvestigations.org/2012/09/30/suzanne-nossel-executive-director-of-amnesty-international-usa/

HRW (2008) 'A Decade Under Chávez: Political Intolerance and Lost Opportunities for Advancing Human Rights in Venezuela', September, online: https://www.hrw.org/sites/default/files/reports/venezuela0908web.pdf

HRW (2012) 'Open Letter to the Leaders of the Syrian Opposition, Human Rights Watch, Washington, 20 March, online: http://www.hrw.org/news/2012/03/20/open-letter-leaders-syrian-opposition

HRW (2015) 'If the Dead Could Speak: Mass Deaths and Torture in Syria's Detention Facilities'. Human Rights Watch, 16 December, online: https://www.hrw.org/report/2015/12/16/if-dead-could-speak/mass-deaths-and-torture-syrias-detention-facilities

HRW (2016a) 'Human Rights Watch annual report 2016', online: https://www.hrw.org/sites/default/files/news_attachments/english_annual_report-2016.pdf

HRW (2016b) 'Human Rights Watch, Inc., Financial Statements Year Ended June 30, 2016', online: https://www.hrw.org/sites/default/files/supporting_resources/financial-statements-2016.pdf

HRW (2017) Financial Statements, year ended 30 June 2016, Human Rights Watch Inc, online: https://www.hrw.org/sites/default/files/supporting_resources/financial-statements-2016.pdf

Jaber, Hala (2011) 'Syria caught in crossfire of extremists', Sunday Times, 26 June, online: http://www.thesundaytimes.co.uk/sto/news/world_news/Middle_East/article657138.ece

Johnson, Adam (2015) 'HRW tries to pass off IDF crimes as Assad "barrel bombs"', Twitter, 8 May, online: https://twitter.com/adamjohnsonNYC/status/596909627318640640

Karon, Tony (2006) 'Condi in Diplomatic Disneyland', Time, 26 July, online: http://content.time.com/time/world/article/0,8599,1219325,00.html

Kennedy, Merrit (2016) 'After Rocky Pause, Airstrikes Resume On Syria's Aleppo', NPR, 15 November, online: http://www.npr.org/sections/thetwo-way/2016/11/15/502129917/after-rocky-pause-airstrikes-resume-on-syrias-aleppo

Khatib al, Khaled (2015) 'Fleeing the frontline, Marea's poorest seek refuge in orchards', Syria Direct, 15 September, online: http://syriadirect.org/news/fleeing-the-frontline-marea%E2%80%99s-poorest-seek-refuge-in-orchards/

Kovalik, Daniel (2012) 'Amnesty International and the Human Rights Industry', Counterpunch, 8 November, online: https://www.counterpunch.org/2012/11/08/amnesty-international-and-the-human-rights-industry/

Kuperman, Alan J. (2015) 'Obama's Libya Debacle', *Foreign Affairs*, 16 April, online: https://www.foreignaffairs.com/articles/libya/2015-02-16/obamas-libya-debacle

La Barra, Yalla (2015) 'Human Rights Watch's Kenneth Roth's Obsession with Bashar Al-Assad and Barrel Bombs', Yalla la Barra, 28 August, online: https://yallalabarra.wordpress.com/2015/08/28/human-rights-watchs-kenneth-roths-obsession-with-bashar-al-assad-and-barrel-bombs/

Landis, Joshua (2011) 'The Revolution Strikes Home: Yasir Qash'ur, my wife's cousin, killed in Banyas', Syria Comment, 11 April, online: http://www.joshualandis.com/blog/the-revolution-strikes-home-yasir-

qashur-my-wifes-cousin-killed-in-banyas/
Laughland, Oliver (2015) 'US should use radar to warn civilians of Syrian barrel bombs, group demands', *The Guardian*, 28 February, online: http://www.theguardian.com/world/2015/feb/27/us-military-warn-civilians-incoming-syria-air-strikes
Live Leak (2015) 'Syria - So-called "White Helmets" facilitate.an.al Nusra.execution', 6 May, online: http://www.liveleak.com/view?i=fd8_1430900709
Loiselle, Marie-Eve (2013) 'The Normative Status of the Responsibility to Protect After Libya', *Global Responsibility to Protect,* Vol 5, Issue 3, 317-341
Luck, Edward C. (2009) 'Sovereignty, Choice, and the Responsibility to Protect', *Global Responsibility to Protect* 1, pp. 10–21
MacAskill, Ewan and Julian Borger (2004) 'Iraq war was illegal and breached UN charter, says Annan', *The Guardian,* 16 September, online: https://www.theguardian.com/world/2004/sep/16/iraq.iraq
MacFarquar, Neil (2013) 'A Very Busy Man Behind the Syrian Civil War's Casualty Count', *New York Times*, 9 April, online: http://www.nytimes.com/2013/04/10/world/middleeast/the-man-behind-the-casualty-figures-in-syria.html
MayDay Rescue (2015) 'Mosab Obeidat', 26 August, online: http://www.maydayrescue.org/content/mosab-obeidat
McKeigue, Paul (2017) 'Khan Sheikhoun Chemical Attack: Guest Blog Featuring Paul McKeigue's Reassessment', Tim Hayward, 22 December, online: https://timhayward.wordpress.com/2017/12/22/khan-sheikhoun-chemical-attack-guest-blog-featuring-paul-mckeigues-reassessment/
Mill, John Stuart (1859) 'A Few Words on Non-intervention', Fraser's Magazine, reprinted in Foreign Policy Perspectives, Libertarian Alliance, No. 8, London, online: http://www.libertarian.co.uk/lapubs/forep/forep008.pdf
Mill, John Stuart (1874) Dissertations and Discussions: Political, Philosophical, and Historical, Vol 3, John W. Parker and Son, New York, online: http://www.thelatinlibrary.com/imperialism/readings/mill.html
MOA (2015a) 'Human Rights Watch Accuses Syria Of "Barrel Bomb" Damage Created By U.S. Attacks', 27 Feb, online: http://www.moonofalabama.org/2015/02/human-rights-watch-accuses-syria-of-barrel-bomb-damage-created-by-us-attacks.html
MOA (2015b) 'Human Rights Watch Again Accuses Syria Of "Barrel Bomb" Damage Done By Others', 9 May, online http://www.moonofalabama.org/2015/05/human-rights-watch-again-accuses-syria-of-barrel-bomb-damage-done-by-others.html
MOA (2015c) 'HRW's Kenneth Roth Continues Unfounded Accusations With

Another False Picture', 15 May, online: http://www.moonofalabama. org/2015/05/hrws-kenneth-roth-continues-unfounded-accusations-with-another-false-picture.html

MOA (2017) 'Hearsay Extrapolated - Amnesty Claims Mass Executions In Syria, Provides Zero Proof', Moon of Alabama, 7 February, online: http://www.moonofalabama.org/2017/02/amnesty-report-hearsay.html

Morningstar, Cory (2015) 'SYRIA: Avaaz, Purpose & the Art of Selling Hate for Empire', Aletho News, 27 January, online: https://alethonews.wordpress.com/2015/05/10/syria-avaaz-purpose-the-art-of-selling-hate-for-empire/

Moran, Rick (2017) 'Human Rights Watch Labels U.S. a "Human Rights Abuser" Because of Trump', PJ Media, 14 January, online: https://pjmedia.com/trending/2017/01/14/human-rights-watch-labels-us-human-rights-abuser-because-of-trump/

Narwani, Sharmine (2014) Syria: The hidden massacre, RT, 7 May, online: http://rt.com/op-edge/157412-syria-hidden-massacre-2011/

Naylor, Hugh (2015) 'Islamic State has killed many Syrians, but Assad's forces have killed more', *Washington Post*, 5 September, online: https://www.washingtonpost.com/world/islamic-state-has-killed-many-syrians-but-assads-forces-have-killed-even-more/2015/09/05/b8150d0c-4d85-11e5-80c2-106ea7fb80d4_story.html?utm_term=.6b4bde8c4b47

Nazemroaya, Mahdi Darius (2006) Plans for Redrawing the Middle East: The Project for a 'New Middle East', Global Research, 18 November, online: http://www.globalresearch.ca/plans-for-redrawing-the-middle-east-the-project-for-a-new-middle-east/3882

NGO Monitor (2012) 'Breaking Its own Rules: Amnesty's Researcher Bias and Govt Funding', 4 June, online: http://www.ngo-monitor.org/reports/breaking_its_own_rules_amnesty_s_gov_t_funding_and_researcher_bias/

NGO Monitor (2016) 'Amnesty International', 27 November, online: http://www.ngo-monitor.org/ngos/amnesty_international/

Nossel, Suzanne (2004) 'Smart Power: reclaiming liberal internationalism', *Foreign Affairs,* March-April, online: https://www.foreignaffairs.com/articles/united-states/2004-03-01/smart-power

Oberg, Jan (2014) 'NATO and the Destruction of Yugoslavia', Global Research, 31 October, online: http://www.globalresearch.ca/nato-and-the-destruction-of-yugoslavia-where-it-all-went-wrong-and-lessons-were-never-learnt/5411123

O'Connor, Tom (2017) 'Syria's White Helmets, subject of Oscar winning film, caught dumping dead soldiers, fire volunteer', Newsweek, 22 June, online: http://www.newsweek.com/oscar-win-white-helmets-syria-volunteer-dump-bodies-rebels-628407

Open Secrets (2017) 'Employer search: Amnesty International USA', 12 May, online: https://www.opensecrets.org/revolving/search_result.php?priv=Amnesty+International+USA

Pérez Esquivel, Adolfo et al (2014) 'The Corruption of Human Rights Watch', Consortium News, 13 May, online: https://consortiumnews.com/2014/05/13/the-corruption-of-human-rights-watch/

Pestano, Andrew V. (2016) 'Aleppo airstrikes resume after 3-week pause', UPI, 15 November, online: http://www.upi.com/Top_News/World-News/2016/11/15/Aleppo-airstrikes-resume-after-3-week-pause/8561479211543/

Philpot, Robin (2013) Rwanda and the New Scramble for Africa: From Tragedy to Useful Imperial Fiction, Baraka Books, Montreal

Pitt, William Rivers (2003) 'The Project for the New American Century', Information Clearing House, 25 February, online: http://www.informationclearinghouse.info/article1665.htm

Plummer, Brad (2013) 'Everything you need to know about Syria's chemical weapons', *Washington Post,* 5 September, online: https://www.washingtonpost.com/news/wonk/wp/2013/09/05/everything-you-need-to-know-about-syrias-chemical-weapons/?utm_term=.a7df48808641

Porter, Gareth (2017) 'A Flawed UN investigation on Syria', Consortium News, 11 march, online: https://consortiumnews.com/2017/03/11/a-flawed-un-investigation-on-syria/

Postol, Ted (2017) 'The Nerve Agent Attack that Did Not Occur', 18 April, Washington's Blog, online: http://www.washingtonsblog.com/2017/04/67102.html

Press TV (2017) 'Russian Foreign Ministry rejects Amnesty "fake" report of mass hangings in Syria', 9 February, online: http://www.presstv.ir/Detail/2017/02/09/509848/Russia-Syria-Maria-Zakharova-Amnesty-International-

Price, Megan; Anita Gohdes and Patrick Ball (2014) 'Updated Statistical Analysis' of Documentation of Killings in the Syrian Arab Republic Commissioned by the Office of the UN High Commissioner for Human Rights, August, online: http://www.ohchr.org/Documents/Countries/SY/HRDAGUpdatedReportAug2014.pdf

Price, Megan; Anita Gohdes and Patrick Ball (2016) 'Technical Memo for Amnesty International Report on Deaths in Detention', Human Rights Data Analysis Group, 17 August, online: https://hrdag.org/wp-content/uploads/2016/08/HRDAG-AI-memo-2.pdf

Regan, Tom (2002) 'When contemplating war, beware of babies in incubators', *Christian Science Monitor,* 6 September, online: https://www.

csmonitor.com/2002/0906/p25s02-cogn.html

Ritter, Scott (2017) 'Ex-Weapons Inspector: Trump's Sarin Claims Built on "Lie"', *The American Conservative*, 29 June, online: http://www.theamericanconservative.com/articles/ex-weapons-inspector-trumps-sarin-claims-built-on-lie/

Roth, Kenneth (2008) 'HRW Response to Criticisms of our Venezuela Work', Human Rights Watch, 29 December, online: https://www.hrw.org/news/2008/12/29/hrw-response-criticisms-our-venezuela-work

Roth, Kenneth (2014) 'Letter to Nobel Laureates', 3 June, online: https://www.coolloud.org.tw/node/79465

Roth, Ken (2015) 'For the planners', Twitter, 9 August, online: https://twitter.com/kenroth/status/630544175851769857

Roth, Kenneth (2015a) 'Barrel Bombs, Not ISIS, Are the Greatest Threat to Syrians', *New York Times*, 5 August, online: http://www.nytimes.com/2015/08/06/opinion/barrel-bombs-not-isis-are-the-greatest-threat-to-syrians.html?_r=1

RT (2013) 'German intelligence concludes sarin gas used on Assad's orders – reports', 2 September, online: https://www.rt.com/news/germany-syria-sarin-intelligence-326/

RT (2016) '"We don't hide it": White Helmets openly admit being funded by Western govts', 19 October, online: https://www.rt.com/news/363363-white-helmets-funded-west/

Rushe, Dominic and Raya Jalabi (2014) 'Facebook pressured to refuse access to Assad campaign in Syria election', *The Guardian*, 2 June, online: http://www.theguardian.com/world/2014/jun/02/facebook-bashar-al-assad-campaign-syria-election

Salt, Jeremy (2011) Truth and Falsehood in Syria, The Palestine Chronicle, 5 October, online: http://palestinechronicle.com/view_article_details.php?id=17159

Scaturro, Michael (2013) 'Why Human Rights Groups Don't Agree on What to Do About Syria', *The Atlantic*, 5 September, online: https://www.theatlantic.com/international/archive/2013/09/why-human-rights-groups-dont-agree-on-what-to-do-about-syria/279360/

Shapiro, Jeremy (2013) 'The Qatar problem', *Foreign Policy*, 28 August, online: http://foreignpolicy.com/2013/08/28/the-qatar-problem/

Shetty, Salil (2014) 'Amnesty International chief - western govts hypocritical, inconsistent on Syria', Worlds Apart, 21 September, online: https://www.youtube.com/watch?v=Unl-csIUmp8

Skelton, Charlie (2012) 'The Syrian opposition: who's doing the talking?', *The Guardian*, 13 July, online: https://www.theguardian.com/commentisfree/2012/jul/12/syrian-opposition-doing-the-talking

SNHR (2016) 'Syrian Network for Human Rights', online: http://sn4hr.org/

SNHR (2017) 'Syrian Network for Human Rights: work methodology', online: http://sn4hr.org/public_html/wp-content/pdf/english/SNHR_Methodology_en.pdf

SOHR (2015) Syrian Observatory for Human Rights, online: http://www.syriahr.com/en/

Source Watch (2014) 'Amnesty International: Discussion', online: http://www.sourcewatch.org/index.php/Talk:Amnesty_International

Sputnik (2015) 'Soros-funded "White Helmets" NGO caught faking 'civilian casualties of Russian airstrikes' in Syria', 30 September, online: http://www.sott.net/article/302997-Soros-funded-White-Helmets-caught-faking-Syria-casualties-report

Sputnik (2017) 'Amnesty Report on Syrian Prison Deaths Questioned by Ex UK Ambassador to Syria', 15 February, online: https://sputniknews.com/world/201702151050686212-amnesty-international-syria-report-not-credible/

Stauber, John and Sheldon Rampton (2002) 'How PR Sold the War in the Persian Gulf', Chapter 10 in Toxic Sludge is Good for You, Common Courage Press, Monroe, Maine, excerpt on the First Gulf War is online here: http://www.prwatch.org/books/tsigfy10.html

Sterling, Rick (2015) 'Eight Problems with Amnesty's Report on Aleppo Syria', Dissident Voice, 14 May, online: http://dissidentvoice.org/2015/05/eight-problems-with-amnestys-report-on-aleppo-syria/

Sterling, Rick (2016) 'The Caesar Photo Fraud that Undermined Syrian Negotiations', Counterpunch, 4 March, online: https://www.counterpunch.org/2016/03/04/the-caesar-photo-fraud-that-undermined-syrian-negotiations/

Sterling, Rick (2017) 'Amnesty International Stokes Syrian War', Consortium News, 11 February, online: https://consortiumnews.com/2017/02/11/amnesty-international-stokes-syrian-war/

Strom, Stephanie (2010) 'Soros to Donate $100 Million to Rights Group', *New York Times*, 6 September, online: http://www.nytimes.com/2010/09/07/business/07gift.html

Sullivan, Eileen P (1983) 'Liberalism and Imperialism: J. S. Mill's Defense of the British Empire', *Journal of the History of Ideas*, Vol. 44, No. 4 (Oct. - Dec.), 599-617

SWB (2017) 'White Helmets Exposed as Extremists: 65 Facebook profiles of Their Members', Syrian War Blog, 14 November, online: http://syrianwar1.blogspot.com.au/2017/11/white-helmets-exposed-as-extremists-65.html

Teil, Julian (2011) 'Lies behind the "Humanitarian War" in Libya: There is no evidence! (Part 1), NATO Crimes In Libya', YouTube, Interview with Soliman Bouchuiguir, October 15, online: https://www.youtube.com/

watch?v=j4evwAMIh4Y
Timand2037 (2012) '"Humanitarian Intervention" in Libya - the duplicitous game', YouTube, 15 March, online: https://www.youtube.com/watch?v=hNbUnTelwJU
TSC (2015a) 'Care about refugees? Listen to them', 9 October, online: https://diary.thesyriacampaign.org/what-refugees-think/
TSC (2015b) 'Listen To Refugees – First Survey of Syrian Refugees in Europe', survey results spreadsheet, The Syria Campaign, online: https://docs.google.com/spreadsheets/d/1WYn4N7STdP2eW3EYdX86Gsb6lxE4VrcNvZ4aEczsFwI/edit#gid=833561282
TSC (2017) '2011–2017: Who's Killing Civilians In Syria?', The Syria Campaign, accessed 1 August 2017, online: http://whoiskillingciviliansinsyria.org/
Turbeville, Brandon (2017) 'Amnesty International "Human Slaughterhouse" Report Lacks Evidence, Credibility, Reeks Of State Department Propaganda', Activist Post, 8 February, online: http://www.activistpost.com/2017/02/amnesty-international-human-slaughterhouse-report-lacks-evidence-credibility-reeks-of-state-department-propaganda.html
UN HRC (1984) CCPR General Comment No. 12: Article 1 (Right to Self-determination), The Right to Self-determination of Peoples, online: http://www.refworld.org/docid/453883f822.html
UN (2005) 2005 World Summit Outcome, 60/1, 24 October, online: http://www.un.org/womenwatch/ods/A-RES-60-1-E.pdf
UN (2005) 2005 World Summit Outcome, 60/1, 24 October, online: http://www.un.org/womenwatch/ods/A-RES-60-1-E.pdf
UNOCHA (2015) 'Arrived at the scene of the blast', Twitter, 19 August, online: https://twitter.com/UNOCHA/status/634114213112221696
UNSC (2006) Resolution 1674, online: http://www.securitycouncilreport.org/atf/cf/%7B65BFCF9B-6D27-4E9C-8CD3-CF6E4FF96FF9%7D/Civilians%20SRES1674.pdf
van der Lugt, Frans (2012) 'Bij defaitisme is niemand gebaat', from Homs, 13 January, online: https://mediawerkgroepsyrie.wordpress.com/2012/01/13/bij-defaitisme-is-niemand-gebaat/
Vino, Jorge (2017) 'Leader of Al-Qaeda in Syria calls the White Helmets "the hidden soldiers of the revolution"', 20 March, YouTube, online: https://www.youtube.com/watch?v=cpuxgbyNlO8
Webb, Whitney (2017) 'James le Mesurier: the former British mercenary who founded The White Helmets', Mint Press, 31 July, online: https://www.mintpressnews.com/james-le-mesurier-british-ex-military-mercenary-founded-white-helmets/230320/
Wright, Ann and Coleen Rowley (2012) 'Amnesty's Shilling for US Wars',

Consortium News, 18 June, online: https://consortiumnews.com/2012/06/18/amnestys-shilling-for-us-wars/

Xinhua (2016) 'News Analysis: Suspended Russian airstrikes encourage rebels to unleash major offensive in Aleppo', 29 October, online: http://news.xinhuanet.com/english/2016-10/29/c_135788805.htm

Chapter Ten

THE PSEUDO-LEFT AND THE 'SYRIAN REVOLUTION'

Some western liberals and Trotskyists pay homage to Yassin al-Haj Saleh, an intellectual leftist of the 'Syrian Revolution'. In fact Saleh represented only a tiny part of Syria's left. He was 'persecuted' because he aligned himself with the 1980 and 2011 bloody uprisings by the sectarian Muslim Brotherhood, and their international Salafist (al Qaeda) supporters. In the end he had to flee for his life from those same sectarian terrorists.

With popular forces in Syria and Iraq destroying the globalised proxy armies, some ideologues in colonial cultures keep alive the romantic idea of a 'Syrian Revolution', that somehow tragically failed. This is also a myth propagated by the Muslim Brotherhood and their western sponsors, to cover the otherwise naked aggression against Syria.

It is a myth that matters much less since the war has turned in Syria's favour, as such propaganda has much less capacity to incite deeper, uninvited foreign intervention in Syria. Yet it seems important for the self-image of small groups of western pseudo-leftists, who committed themselves to the cause of 'red-washing' Washington's latest war of aggression, backed by the most reactionary forces in the region.

By pseudo-leftist I mean fanatical ideologues who cling to their fantasies, showing little interest in what the masses of ordinary

Why we call them 'the imperial left'

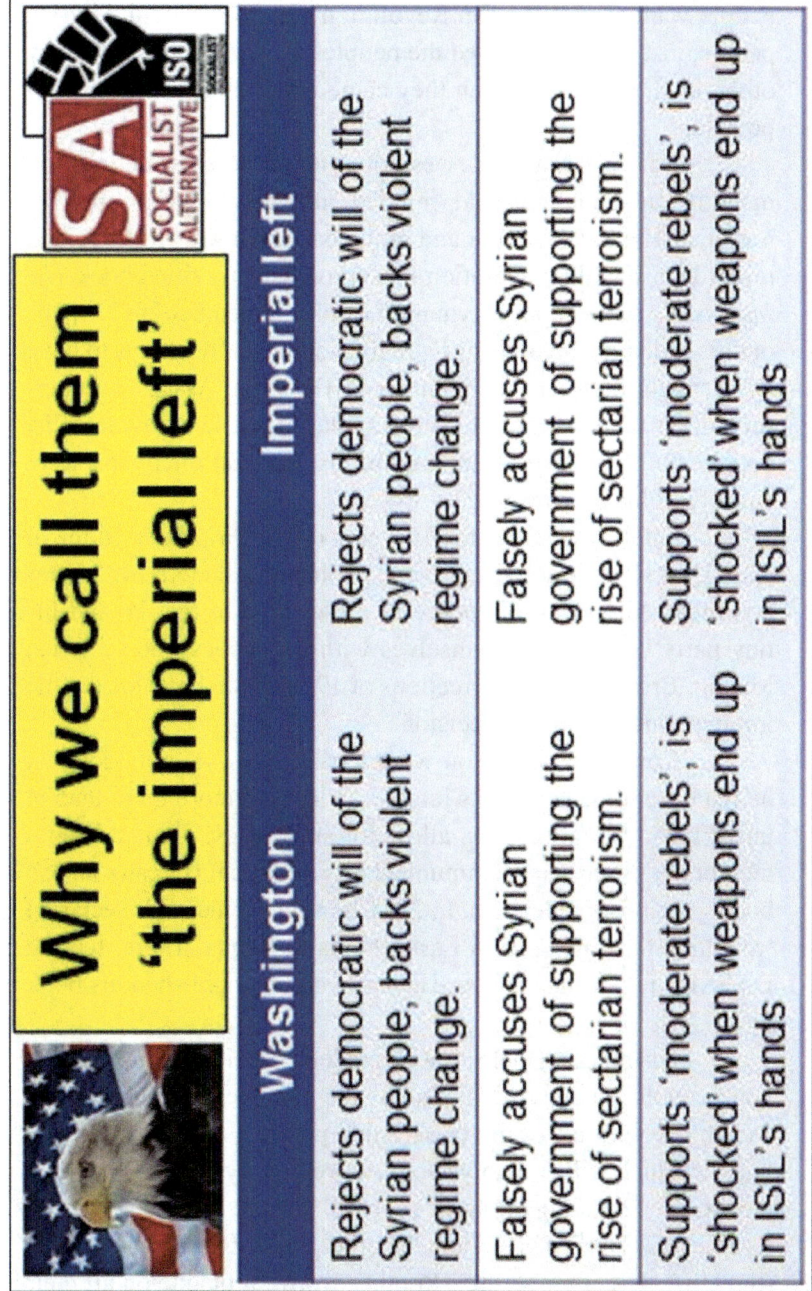

Washington	Imperial left
Rejects democratic will of the Syrian people, backs violent regime change.	Rejects democratic will of the Syrian people, backs violent regime change.
Falsely accuses Syrian government of supporting the rise of sectarian terrorism.	Falsely accuses Syrian government of supporting the rise of sectarian terrorism.
Supports 'moderate rebels', is 'shocked' when weapons end up in ISIL's hands	Supports 'moderate rebels', is 'shocked' when weapons end up in ISIL's hands

Historically, the main achievement of the western left was to oppose imperial war; however hybrid wars and 'colour revolutions' fooled most of them.

people want. Those 'Syrian Revolution' fans betrayed the Syrian people, just as they betrayed the people of Libya, Cuba and many other small countries, when they came under attack from the big powers.

But imagine the western pseudo-leftist's delight on meeting an apparently like-minded individual Syrian such as Yassin al-Haj Saleh, author and proud backer of what he imagined might be a socialist revolution in Syria. His aptly titled book *The Impossible Revolution* (Haymarket Books September 2017) spells out his failed dream and angry disillusionment. He claims to have been caught between 'the hammer of Bashar al Assad's counter-revolution and the anvil of his reactionary Islamic fundamentalist opponents'. On closer examination, his personal dilemmas seem entirely of his own making.

Saleh was jailed for 16 years (1980-96) under Hafez al Assad, for what he and his fans and publisher call 'activism'. Does this mean 'dissident' or 'peaceful protestor'? In fact he and his tiny party had aligned themselves with the bloody and sectarian Muslim Brotherhood insurrections of 1979-1982. Let's look at the implications of that bad decision.

Conditions in prison were terrible he says, but adds that he read 'hundreds of books [and] ... I learned more there than at university'. Not all prisons allow for such study. He had been a member of the Syrian Communist Party (Political Bureau), and so boasts socialist credentials. In 2011 he again joined this sectarian 'revolution', moving from East Ghouta to Raqqa. There, fearing DAESH, he left the country. He survived and published his book in 2017.

Haymarket Books, a well credentialed left US publishing house, calls Yassin Al-Haj Saleh 'the intellectual voice of the Syrian revolution'. In the book Saleh presents a bleak portrait – but one which will probably appeal to western cynicism – of "three monsters ... treading on Syria's corpse': (1) the Assad regime and its allies, (2) DAESH/ISIS and the other jihadists, and (3) the West (the USA, UK, France, etc). In other words, a plague on all their houses. Such cynicism, if popular, is weak analysis.

Pseudo-Leftists and the 'Syrian Revolution'

We know from independent Turkish pollsters TESEV that, by the end of 2011, only 5% of Syrians supported 'violent protest', the lowest figure in the region (c.f. 33% in Tunisia and 31% in Palestine) (TESEV 2012: 15). The big influx of foreign jihadists in 2012 would have hardened popular views even further against 'jihadist' violence. And we know that the Syrian Arab Army, after some relatively small defections in the first year, did not fracture on religious grounds, as the Salafists had hoped.

The key problems with promotion of a figure like Saleh, to keep afloat the romantic idea of a failed 'revolution', are these: (a) the self-serving story hides who this new hero is and what forces in Syria he might represent; (b) the idealistic narrative (for a 'democratic and egalitarian Syria', etc) hides the actual historical forces of the Syrian insurrections; and (c) in particular, it whitewashes Saleh's own foolish collaboration with sectarian Islamists.

Most of Saleh's arguments appear in an extended interview with Ashley Smith in the US journal, International Socialist Review. Smith is a member of the US International Socialist Organization, a Trotskyist group drawing on the ideas of the late Tony Cliff. Prominent amongst those ideas is Cliff's theory of 'state capitalism', which suggests that there has never been a true 'socialist' revolution and that all capitalist and 'state capitalist' nation-states must be smashed and rebuilt. That doctrine is consistent with attacks on each and every state, progressive or otherwise, as also with alliances with imperialism and reactionary forces. To what extent that sort of Trotskyism is consistent with Saleh's view is another matter.

However we know these things about Saleh. First, his Communist Party (Political Bureau) faction was a tiny 'Maoist' splinter from Syria's main Communist Party, back in the late 1970s. The main reason for this split was that Saleh's faction wanted to 'form an alliance' with the Muslim Brotherhood, as they engaged in a series of sectarian attacks on the Syrian state (Gambill 2001). Most Syrian communists sided with the Ba'ath socialist party state. However Saleh and his former leader, Riyad al Turk, persisted in their subordinate 'alliance' with the al Qaeda linked Muslim Brotherhood, well into the 2000s (Pace 2005).

What precisely was Syria's Muslim Brotherhood doing, back in 1979? Let's read it from the late British writer Patrick Seale: 'The artillery school massacre of June 1979 marked the start if full-scale urban warfare against Alawis [and] against Ba'ath party officials ... when cornered they often blew themselves up with grenades ... In Aleppo between 1979 and 1981 terrorists killed over 300 people, mainly Baathists and Alawis but including a dozen Islamic clergy who had denounced the murders' (Seale 1988: 324-325). Hardly progressive credentials. All other opposition parties, including most communists, rejected the Muslim Brotherhood's sectarian terror; but not Saleh's sect. Collaboration with the Muslim Brotherhood terrorists is why Saleh received a long jail term in 1980, not because he was simply an 'activist'.

Muslim Brotherhood terror has been romanticised over the years. At the end of the 1979-1982 attacks a final Brotherhood insurrection at Hama city was put down by Hafez al Assad. Revisionist historians these days, including many western writers, claim there was a large 'civilian massacre' at Hama in May 1982. For example, author Rafaël Lefèvre (2013: 77) credulously reports: 'While initial reports suggested 10,000 civilians were killed, other reports put the number as high as 40,000'. This is poor revisionist history.

Seale (1988: 333-334) observes that Hama 1982 was a serious conflict, not a 'civilian massacre'. The Hama insurrection 'was a last ditch battle' for the Brotherhood and it 'raged for three grim weeks ... many civilians were slaughtered in the prolonged mopping up ... in nearly a month of fighting about a third of the historic inner city was demolished'. On overall casualties he notes that 'government forces too suffered heavy losses to snipers ... and grenades', while total losses of life were controversial even at the time, 'with government sympathisers estimating a mere 3,000 and critics as many as 20,000'.

The 'civilian massacre' mythology tries to hide the Brotherhood's hand in initiating the violence, as recurred in Daraa and

Homs in 2011. US intelligence back in 1982 had no such illusions. Of course, the US had quietly backed those who financed and armed the Brotherhood's attacks on Syria (the Saudis, the King of Jordan, Saddam Hussein and others). But Washington's intelligence was dry and pragmatic, in its final assessment of May 1982:

> the Islamic Revolution in Syria, the Nom de Guerre for the Muslim Brotherhood ... [spoke of] the rebels' seizure of the city and the execution of some 50 "spies and informers" ... about 3,000 government forces had been killed, according to the communique ... [However] the total casualties for the Hama incident probably number about 2,000. This includes an estimated 300-400 members of the Muslim Brotherhood's elite Special Apparatus ... the Syrian Government defeated the fundamentalist[s] ... most Syrians, regardless of their difference with the present government, do not want the Muslim Brotherhood in power ... [but] the Syrian dissidents' modus operandi will continue to be terrorism, particularly bombings and assassination (DIA 1982: 6-8).

Even if Saleh was relatively young in 1980, many of the political prisoners with whom he shared prison time would have belonged to the Muslim Brotherhood. He was certainly not unaware of their approach to 'revolution' when he joined their next major insurrection in 2011. Indeed he says 'When the [2011] revolution broke out I went into hiding ... [and] while I was writing I was directly involved in the struggle' (Smith 2017). His greatest claim to fame was to be one of the founders of the 'Local Coordinating Councils' (LCCs), indeed he says he was 'the main author of the first political statement LCCs issued in June 2011' (Smith 2017). This tells us that the apparently secular language of the LCCs masked the faces of Muslim Brotherhood and al Qaeda fanatics.

In any case, we know that the LCCs were little more than

a fig leaf on the thoroughly sectarian insurrection, dominated by Syrian Muslim Brotherhood groups until 2012. Then they were displaced from leadership by their international jihadist partners, in the form of Jabhat al Nusra (al Qaeda in Syria, set up as a support group for the Syrian Salafis) and DAESH / ISIS, an outreach of al Qaeda in Iraq (AQI). As I wrote in my book *The Dirty War on Syria* (Anderson 2016: 83-84), the LCCs were seen as having a mainly media or PR role in 2011 (Asi Abu Najm 2011) and, by 2013, they were embedded with the Islamist groups, mainly reporting on jihadist casualties (LCC 2013).

Yassin al-Haj Saleh says he fled from East Ghouta to Raqqa, before leaving the country. However his early presence in Douma (East Ghouta) demonstrates how reliant he had become on his Salafist partners. For many years Douma had been dominated by Jaysh al Islam, in alliance with Jabhat al Nusra. Although the civilian population there has been decimated, from many thousands fleeing the conflict, it remained one of the few areas in Syria with a substantial social base for sectarian extremists. The same might be said about Raqqa. Both areas had a strong, reactionary culture, with women in burkas and many families preferring to send their children to a Salafist-led mosque than to a school.

The US certainly knew from early days that this 'revolution' (1) was being led by extremists and (2) wanted to create a sectarian Islamic state in eastern Syria. US intelligence in August 2012 observed that 'Internally, events are taking a clear sectarian direction. The Salafist, the Muslim Brotherhood and AQI are the major forces driving the insurgency in Syria' (DIA 2012 in Hoff 2015).

Washington knew it and most Syrians knew it. The head of the Syrian Brotherhood, Muhammad Riyad Al-Shaqfa, issued a statement on 28 March 2011, which made clear that the Brotherhood's target was the secular state. The enemy was 'the secular regime', he said, and Brotherhood members 'have to make sure that the revolution will be pure Islamic, and with that no other sect would have a share of the credit after its success' (Al-Shaqfa 2011).

The sectarian internationalists of Jabhat al Nusra (al Qaeda in Syria) appeared in Homs in early 2011, specifically to help the Farouq Brigade (then the largest 'FSA' group) with its infamous genocidal slogan 'Alawis to the grave, Christians to Beirut' and consistent genocidal practice: the sectarian murder of supposedly apostate Muslims and the ethnic cleaning of Christians. Those slogans and practice were reported in the English language media as early as 5 April 2011 (Farrell 2011) and in the New York Times in May (Shadid and Kirkpatrick 2011). Tens of thousands of Syrian Christians from Homs were indeed driven to Beirut (CNA 2012). Claims that the 'Assad regime' was behind the sectarianism were simply dishonest. Whatever their views of the Ba'athist system, most Syrians, and particularly the minorities, swung behind the Syrian army very quickly.

As international jihadists (mainly from the Arab world, North Africa, the Caucasus and Europe) joined the Syrian Salafis in large numbers in mid-2012, even the western media began reporting that these were fanatics, not revolutionaries. In Aleppo the 'Free Army' leaders were complaining that the Syrian President had at least '70 percent' support in Aleppo (Bayoumy 2013); that the local people were 'loyal to the criminal Bashar' (Abouzeid 2012); and that the people were 'all informers ... they hate us. They blame us for the destruction' (Ghaith 2012). But, they went on to say, they had God on their side. James Foley, himself subject to a theatrical style execution by DAESH in 2014, reported two years earlier that the FSA 'rebels' had little public support. Indeed one leader promised Aleppo 'would burn', because the people there did not support the 'revolution' (Foley 2012). Unpopularity is fatal to a revolution but only inconvenient to a fanatic.

It is impossible that Saleh – an ideological fanatic, but an educated fanatic – did not know all this. Even if he himself was not a sectarian Islamist, he knew that the extreme sectarians with whom he collaborated in 1979 and again in 2011 were leading his 'revolution'.

Saleh maintains his own self-serving myths about the conflict: that the 'Assad regime' was the source of sectarian violence, that Sunni Muslims and Kurds were oppressed, and that the US and its minions really supported the Assad Government. Saleh claims that the Obama administration (despite its repetitive and imperious 'Assad must go' demands) really wanted 'regime preservation not regime change' (Saleh in Smith 2017).

It is hard to see how any reasonable person can take this seriously. We even have admissions from senior US officials, including former Vice President Biden and former head of the US military Martin Dempsey, that the 'Arab Allies' of the US financed every jihadist group from the 'Free Army' to DAESH / ISIS, precisely to get rid of Assad. More recently, former Qatari Foreign Minister Hamad Bin Jassim admitted that Qatar coordinated with the Saudis, Turkey and the US to support all the anti-Government 'jihadist' forces (Syriana Analysis 2017).

Saleh's former mentor, Riyad al Turk (who 'liked' the Saudi-backed Lebanese Prime Minister Rafiq Hariri), was calling for US military assistance in 2005 to help 'the opposition' get rid of the Assad Government (Pace 2005). Of course he did not represent the Syrian Opposition. In the Damascus Declaration (2005), amongst harsh criticisms of the Baathist system, most Syrian opposition groups specifically renounced violent attacks on the state and recourse to foreign intervention. The Muslim Brotherhood and its hangers on, in contrast, always wanted a violent insurrection, with foreign assistance.

Saleh's claim to fame as a secular communist against 'the regime' is undermined by how unrepresentative his small group was of Syria's communists. He, like al Turk, criticises most other communists who 'supported the regime' (Smith 2017). So how much support did his faction have? Al Turk maintained 'we don't announce how many members we have' (Pace 2005), but Gambill (2001) suggests it was 'very little'.

Syria's main Communist Party split in the mid-1980s (over Gorbachev's policies) into two groups. Both stood candidates in the Peoples' Congress (Majlis al Shaab) elections of 2007, 2012 and 2016, gaining 8, 11 and 4 MPs out of 250, respectively. That indicates that Syria's main communist parties had electoral support of between 80,000 and 140,000 Syrian voters (IDEA 2017; Syrian Parliament 2017). They certainly had more support than Saleh, who eventually fled both Jaysh al Islam and then DAESH. We have no way of knowing exactly how much support there ever was for the Communist Party (Political Bureau), or its successor the 'Syrian Peoples Democratic Party'. But ask yourself, how many genuinely secular Marxists would collaborate with sectarian, al Qaeda styled Islamists?

The inescapable conclusion is that Saleh's romanticised ideas failed and he was lucky to escape with his life. He certainly would have been in danger from both the Syrian Army and DAESH. But he and his tiny faction did not represent any significant part of the Syrian left. They were distinguished mainly by their collaboration with the Brotherhood groups and their al Qaeda allies, before they disappeared entirely from the scene.

After his successive failures Saleh blames everyone (Bashar al Assad, alQaeda/ISIS, western governments) but himself. Yet it seems he has become a useful figure for western pseudo-leftists who never could identify an actual Syrian armed group to support. They can now point to Saleh and say 'Look, there really was a left revolution in Syria! There he is!'

Pseudo-leftists in western countries – who for years held on to the Washington-promoted fiction of a 'Syrian Revolution' – were desperate for a token Syrian 'hero' on which to hang their fantasies. That could be an ex-Islamist or an ex-communist; they don't look too closely to see where these people come from. This desperation highlights their failure to confront actual history, and to care about the things that matter to ordinary people. That indeed is the problem with all fanatics.

Bibliography

Abouzeid, Rania (2012) 'Aleppo's Deadly Stalemate: A Visit to Syria's Divided Metropolis', *Time,* 14 November, online: http://world.time.com/2012/11/14/aleppos-deadly-stalemate-a-visit-to-syrias-divided-metropolis/

Al-Shaqfa, Muhammad Riyad (2011) 'Muslim Brotherhood Statement about the so-called 'Syrian Revolution", General supervisor for the Syrian Muslim Brotherhood, statement of 28 March, online at: http://truthsyria.wordpress.com/2012/02/12/muslim-brotherhood-statement-about-the-so-called-syrian-revolution/

Amazon (2017) Promotion and reviews of Saleh's book 'The Impossible Revolution', online: https://www.amazon.com/Impossible-Revolution-Yassin-al-Haj-Saleh/dp/160846850X

Anderson, Tim (2016) *The Dirty War on Syria,* Global Research, Montreal

Asi Abu Najm (2011) 'Syria's Coordination Committees: a Brief History', Al Akhbar, 1 October, online: http://english.al-akhbar.com/node/764

Bayoumy, Yara (2013) 'Insight: Aleppo misery eats at Syrian rebel support', Reuters, 9 January, online: http://www.reuters.com/article/2013/01/09/us-syria-crisis-rebels-idUSBRE9070VV20130109

CNA (2012) 'Syrian violence drives 50,000 Christians from homes', Catholic News Agency, online: http://www.catholicnewsagency.com/news/syrian-violence-drives-50000-christians-from-homes/

Damascus Declaration (2005) 'The Damascus Declaration for Democratic National Change', English version in Joshua Landis blog 'Syria Comment', 1 November, online: http://faculty-staff.ou.edu/L/Joshua.M.Landis-1/syriablog/2005/11/damascus-declaration-in-english.htm

DIA (1982) 'Syria: Muslim Brotherhood pressure intensifies', Syria360, May, online: https://syria360.files.wordpress.com/2013/11/dia-syria-muslimbrotherhoodpressureintensifies-2.pdf

Farrell, Shane (2011) 'Lebanese Christians react to regional instability', Now Media, 5 April, online: https://now.mmedia.me/lb/en/reportsfeatures/lebanese_christians_react_to_regional_instability

Foley, James (2012) 'Syria: Rebels losing support among civilians in Aleppo', PRI, 16 October, online: https://www.pri.org/stories/2012-10-16/syria-rebels-losing-support-among-civilians-aleppo

Gambill, Gary C. (2001) 'Dossier: Riyad al Turk', *Middle East Intelligence Bulletin*, Middle East Forum, Vol 3 No 9, September, online: https://www.meforum.org/meib/articles/0109_sd1.htm

Ghaith, Abdul-Ahad (2012) 'The people of Aleppo needed someone to drag them into the revolution', *The Guardian*, 28 December, online: http://www.theguardian.com/world/2012/dec/28/aleppo-revolution-abu-ali-sulaibi

Hoff, Brad (2015) '2012 Defense Intelligence Agency document: West will facilitate rise of Islamic State "in order to isolate the Syrian regime"', Levant Report, 19 May, online: https://levantreport.com/2015/05/19/2012-defense-intelligence-agency-document-west-will-facilitate-rise-of-islamic-state-in-order-to-isolate-the-syrian-regime/

IDEA (2017) 'Syrian Arab republic, Total vote, Parliamentary elections, 1994-2016, online: https://www.idea.int/data-tools/question-countries-view/437/274/ctr

LCC (2013) 'Dignity Strike ... We make our revolution by our own hands', Local Coordination Committees of Syria, December, online: http://www.lccsyria.org/3528

Lefèvre, Rafaël (2013) Ashes of Hama: the Muslim Brotherhood in Syria, Hurst and Company, London

Pace, Joe (2005) 'Riyad al Turk, interviewed by Joe Pace on Mehlis, the Opposition, Ghadry', Joshua Landis Page, October 22, online: http://joshualandis.oucreate.com/syriablog/2005/10/riad-al-turk-interviewed-by-joe-pace.htm

Seale, Patrick (1988) *Asad: the struggle for the Middle East,* University of California Press, Berkeley

Shadid, Anthony and David D. Kirkpatrick (2011) 'Promise of Arab Uprisings Is Threatened by Divisions', *New York Times,* 21 May, online: http://www.nytimes.com/2011/05/22/world/middleeast/22arab.html?pagewanted=all

Smith, Ashley (2017) 'Revolution, counterrevolution, and imperialism in Syria, Interview with Yassin al-Haj Saleh', *International Socialist Review,* Issue #107 online: https://isreview.org/issue/107/revolution-counterrevolution-and-imperialism-syria

Syrian parliament (2017) Syrian Peoples' Assembly, online: https://web.archive.org/web/20121008210031/http://parliament.sy/forms/cms/viewStatistics.php ; and Inter-Parliamentary Union (2016) 'SYRIAN ARAB REPUBLIC: Majlis Al-Chaab (People's Assembly)', online: http://archive.ipu.org/parline-e/reports/2307_E.htm; and as compiled in Wikipedia 'Syrian parliamentary elections' 2007 / 2012 / 2016, online: https://en.wikipedia.org/wiki/Syrian_parliamentary_election,_2007

Syriana Analysis (2017) 'Hamad Bin Jassim: We Supported Al-Qaeda in Syria', online: https://www.youtube.com/watch?v=9f33l30kQxg

TESEV (2012) 'The perception of Turkey in the Middle East 2011', Türkiye Ekonomik ve Sosyal Etüdler Vakfı, Istanbul, February, online: http://tesev.org.tr/en/yayin/the-perception-of-turkey-in-the-middle-east-2011/

Chapter Eleven

REFUGEES AS WEAPONS OF WAR

Syrian family from Deir Ezzor, refugees on the Greek island of Lesvos, July 2016. They told me they fled from DAESH.

Civilian populations are always displaced by war; but in the war on Syria their situation was 'weaponised' into an instrument of war propaganda and power politics. The Turkish government of Recep Tayyip Erdoğan, having entered the war on Syria with its own regional ambitions, successfully leveraged the Europeans for military cooperation and finance in 2015 by releasing a wave of displaced peoples from Syria and other countries. The US-funded group 'The Syrian Campaign' then sponsored an opinion poll in Germany which pretended to show that the refugees were 'Fleeing Assad' (TSC 2015).

In fact, their poll showed no such thing. Refugees were being used as instruments of war.

In mid-2015 the European states, most of which had backed the war on Syria, became consumed with their own concerns and debates about borders, refugees and migrants. In 2016 they promised Erdoğan $6 billion (Hurriyet Daily News 2018), an effective ransom to hold back this human tide. Having backed the al Qaeda armies against Damascus, Erdoğan claimed the Syrian refugees were fleeing the 'cruelty, oppression and violence' of the Assad government (*Daily Sabah* 2018), as he pressured Europe with sustained political demands.

Over 2018-19 Erdoğan maintained this refugee threat in an attempt to stall off the looming Syrian-Iranian-Russian operation against his 'jihadist' proxies in Idlib. He was holding that province as a bargaining chip, using what had become a Turkish protectorate within Syria as a 'security zone'. However Turkish analysts Haldun Solmazturk and Celalettin Yavuz said his further blackmail of the Europeans was unlikely to succeed. Both Syria and Russia had announced that they would soon put an end to the al Qaeda- (a.k.a. 'Hayat Tahrir al Sham') controlled zone (Xinhua 2019). With more displaced peoples returning to Syria, this game was reaching its limits.

But would the Europeans reflect on their role in fomenting the war on Syria? In April 2016 Syria's Grand Mufti, Sheikh Ahmed Badreddin Hassoun, told this writer: 'Tell [the Europeans] to stop the war on Syria. The refugees will stop within one day. Within one month they will return' (Hassoun 2016). His words were reinforced by Professor Francis Boyle: 'All these refugees are fleeing because the United States government has been destroying their states' (in Nevradakis 2016). These messages contradict some popular western myths, that the Syrian conflict was a 'civil war', that the Syrian Government was mainly responsible for the refugees, that displaced people were 'fleeing the regime' and that the western powers were playing some angelic, humanitarian role. But Sheikh Hassoun and Professor Boyle were right. As soon as Aleppo city was liberated in December 2016, hundreds of thousands began to return home (IOM 2017; Kennedy 2017).

It is widely acknowledged that the Syrian refugees arriving in Europe would prefer to go home. It has even been reported that many refugees in Germany have trouble when they try to do so (ABC 2016). Some in Canada and many in Lebanon say they want to return (Tharoor 2016; Holt 2016). So how might we best appreciate the links between war and refugees?

Those concerned for refugees cannot ignore the wars that drive them, especially when they share responsibility for those wars. Most of the Europeans powers backed the wars in Afghanistan, Iraq, Libya and Syria, causing massive displacement of peoples, a fraction of which ended up as refugees in Europe.

1. War Mythology and Displacement Crises

It is essential to understand the character of the Middle East wars to properly appreciate and address the refugee phenomenon in Europe. This is especially the case with wars where, even after many years, almost every tragedy and accusation is contested, and official war narratives remain poles apart.

For example, if Europeans accept the myth that there is simply a 'civil war' in Syria they would regard the flood of refugees from that country as an external imposition; perhaps a threat but in any case, an external development which must be met, probably with some mix of regulation and 'charity'. If, on the other hand, that war were recognised as an attempt by the NATO countries to overthrow yet another Middle Eastern government, there might be greater reflection on European responsibility for both the war and the refugees. Observers would be more conscious of the aggravation of this mass displacement by the European states, which had backed the many thousands of internationalised 'jihadists', often wrongly called 'rebels' or 'opposition'. Whether deliberate or due to ignorance, politicians and the media misrepresent the character of the Middle East wars and their relationship to displacement through several inter-related and self-serving myths: that a 'civil war' in Syria has little to do with Europe, that Middle Eastern peoples pose a threat to European peoples and that the priority must be to block the refugees, rather than end the wars.

It is logical to imagine that people would flee from terrorist groups who sloganize and carry out their threats to publicly chop off heads and declare war on minorities and other 'unbelievers'. Indeed, very soon after the genocidal slogans of 2011 in Homs ('Alawites to the grave, Christians to Beirut') and the violence of the first 'Free Syrian Army' groups, 50,000 Christians were said to have been driven to Lebanon (CNA 2012).

Nevertheless, in propaganda wars, the images of such tragedies get turned on their heads. As addressed earlier, the US-funded organisation called The Syria Campaign (TSC) helped drive a claim that most of the Syrian refugees were 'Fleeing Assad'. One of several interlocked groups (Avaaz, Purpose, the White Helmets) which campaigned for a Libyan-style 'no fly zone' in Syria, this one worked for NATO intervention (see Sterling 2015). The group commissioned a poll in Germany, which was carried out by German academic Heiko Giebler. In it, 889 Syrian refugees were said to have been interviewed in Berlin, Hanover, Bremen, Leipzig and Eisenhüttenstadt. Candidates 'were approached on entering or leaving registration centers'. However the survey does not specify how the sampling choices were made, nor is there any mention of a sampling error (TSC 2015). Yet without a clear sampling method and a stated sampling error, we cannot know to what extent the survey might represent a broader population. The results are then almost useless, except as anecdotes.

Again, the actual survey (TSC 2015) begins with a false characterization: that '70% of refugees are fleeing Assad'. It had no question at all about 'Assad' The Syria Campaign's headline and graphics have drawn, very loosely, on some combination of three questions. In response to question 18 ('what was the main reason for you to leave Syria?'), 69% said that 'the main reason' for leaving Syria was an 'imminent threat' to life, but without an identified source of that threat. In Question 9 ('who was responsible for the fighting?'), 70% identified 'Syrian Army and allied groups' as 'responsible for the fighting'. However this was

215

a multiple option question in which we also see that 82% have identified other armed groups (ISIS, al Nusra, FSA, YPG, other rebels). If we remove the Kurdish YPG, which has not fought the Syrian Army, the total is 74% anti-government armed groups. Question 14 ('who did you fear getting arrested or kidnapped by?') shares the 'multiple option' structure of Question 9. Here 77% said they feared 'getting arrested or kidnapped by' the 'Syrian Army and its allied groups'. However, the combined total of those fearing the anti-government groups is 82% and, if we add the YPG, 90%. In other words, the answers to both questions suggest these respondents feared the anti-government armed groups more than they feared the Syrian Army. Most likely many feared getting caught in the crossfire.

So, even before we examine the representative validity of the poll, there is no basis in any of those three questions – or anywhere else in the poll – for saying that '70% of refugees are fleeing Assad'. To the contrary, the poll shows that more are fleeing anti-government armed groups. This contradicts The Syria Campaign's quite dishonest headline. Nevertheless, a Deutsche Welle report faithfully noted: 'Survey leaves no doubt: Syrians are fleeing Assad' (Fuchs 2015). Apparently this reporter did not read the survey.

Further internal analysis, combined with UNHCR (2016) data on the wider Syrian refugee population, shows The Syria Campaign's survey to have been quite unrepresentative, and therefore providing no basis for claims about the wider Syrian refugee population. As Table 2 shows, the respondents in Germany had massive over-representation from young men. Put together we see a 1.76 over-representation of males and a 2.25 over-representation of people between 15 and 55 (UNHCR: 18-59; TSC: 15-55). Women and children barely exist in this poll. The poll also shows that 51% came alone to Europe, 61% had no children and that 68% (0.78 x 0.88) were young men between 15 and 35 years old.

Table 4: Syria refugee population profile, 2015

	UNHCR, Syrian refugee registration (4.8 million)	TSC survey, Germany, October (889)
Male	50%	88% (1.76 overrep)
15-35 years old	n.a.	78%
18-59 / 15-55 years old	44%	99% (2.25 over-rep)
Sources: UNHCR 2016; TSC 2015		

Other data within the poll indicates that 74% were from areas held by anti-government armed groups, as they reported government shelling. There is no credible evidence that suggests the Syrian Army shells areas which do not contain armed anti-government groups. That is reinforced by Question 1 on area of origin, which shows hardly any respondents (just 19 people) from Tartus, Latakia and Sweida, areas which in 2015 had a combined population (swollen, from internal refugees) of at least 5 million. Respondents from Damascus (170 or 19%) are also seriously under-represented. Damascus in 2015 held over six million, or almost one-third of Syria's population at that time. There were many displaced people in all these areas, controlled by the Government. On the other side, we can see an over-representation of respondents from Hasakah (164 or 19%). There are certainly a lot of refugees from the Hasakah district, in large part due to the presence of ISIS and Turkish-Kurd clashes; but with a population of half a million, less than 10% that of Damascus, that northern area had almost equal numbers of respondents. In other words, the TSC survey has a very large over-representation of young men, many from 'jihadist' held areas. Quite a number of them may be former fighters.

Putting this all together we can conclude that the poll commissioned by The Syria Campaign (2015) did not show anything like '70% fleeing Assad'. To the contrary, results of the poll (TSC 2015) suggested that more amongst that cohort were fearful of anti-government armed groups. On top of that, that poll was unrepresentative of the Syrian refugee population, as it contained a very large group of young men from 'jihadist' held areas, many of whom had indeed come under Syrian Army fire. Reasons for corruption of the data most likely include a combination of biased selection of respondents in Germany (selection was made by the associates of a partisan group) and a possible over-representation of young men and former fighters amongst the actual cohort of refugees arriving in those German cities. The absence of a sampling process and a stated sampling error simply underlines the unprofessional nature of the survey.

Other western polls of Syrians and refugees during the conflict have looked for acceptance or approval of outside military intervention. They have used 'push poll' techniques (loaded questions) and their sampling methods are often obscure. For example the British ORB poll of 2014 suggested that 'Three in Five Syrians Support International Military Involvement' (ORB 2014: Table 1). ORB's undisclosed sampling method, erratic claims and inconsistency with other polls casts doubt on its results. Their 2014 poll showed 4% support for ISIS/DAESH (4% agreed that ISIS/DAESH 'best represented the interests and aspirations of the Syrian people') yet, that number rose dramatically in 2015, when 21% were said to view the terrorist group 'positively' (ORB 2015: Table 3). That sort of support for a foreign-led group, best known for its massacres of opponents and 'unbelievers', is simply not credible, and does not sit with the other genuinely independent polls, such as the Turkish poll which showed (before the arrival of DAESH) 5% support for attacks on the government (TESEV 2012). Nor does it fit with most of the Syrian Opposition's rejection of such violence (Damascus Declaration 2005).

If it is imagined that most Syrian refugees were 'fleeing Assad' then the illegal foreign-backed attacks on Syria might not seem so bad. Yet the weight of evidence is strongly against those claims. First, the great bulk of displaced Syrians remain within Syria, where they overwhelmingly flee to government-controlled areas, for example, to Damascus, Sweida, Western Aleppo and the coast. The population of jihadist-held Eastern Aleppo, over 2015-2016, was estimated at somewhere between 40,000 (Chulov 2015) and 300,000 (Rycroft 2016), compared to 1.5 million in western Aleppo (Cattori 2016). The UNHCR at 31 December (2016) put Syrian refugees at 4.8 million and internally displaced Syrians at 6.6 million (IDMC 2016). The vast majority of these displaced people have sought shelter with Syrian Government agencies.

2. Displaced peoples: A threat to Europe or victims of European policy?

It is necessary to acquire some perspective on the relationship between displaced people and refugees arriving in Europe as a whole, in order to assess the links between the war in Syria and the mass movements of people. A Eurocentric focus on refugee arrivals is insufficient.

Let us look at the origins of the displaced peoples. In 2015, the top three countries of origin of people seeking asylum in EU countries were Syria, Afghanistan and Iraq (Eurostat 2016), all countries subject to NATO-backed invasions and interventions. The UK, Norway and Germany participated in the invasion of Afghanistan; another 18 European countries (Poland, Spain, UK, Albania, Bulgaria, Czech Republic, Denmark, Estonia, Georgia, Hungary, Italy, Latvia, Lithuania, Macedonia, the Netherlands, Portugal, Romania and Slovakia) assisted the USA in its invasion and occupation of Iraq; and at least another three (the UK, France and Germany) have backed anti-government armed groups in Syria.

In 2015, one in three asylum seekers in Europe came from Syria (Eurostat 2016). However, these were quite a small fraction of the number of displaced peoples arriving in Europe. Table 3 shows us that asylum seekers in Europe from Afghanistan, Iraq and Syria for 2015 were between 3.3% and 5% of the total numbers of displaced peoples (IDPs + refugees). That is, the impact on Europe of the movements of displaced peoples from the wars in which Europeans themselves have engaged is relatively small.

Table 5: Displaced peoples in and from Afghanistan, Iraq and Syria as at December 2015

	Afghanistan	Iraq	Syria
Population	31.3 million	36.4 million	18.5 million
Internally displaced	1.17 million	4.40 million	6.6 million
Refugees	2.69 million	277,000	4.18 million
Seeking asylum in Europe, 2015 *	178,230	121,535	362,775
Asylum seekers (Eu) as % of IDPs + refugees, 2015	5.03 %	3.32 %	3.36 %

Source: UNHCR 2016, UNHCR 2016a, UNHCR 2016b, IDMC 2016, *Eurostat 2016

It is apparent from the IDP figures that the countries under attack carry most of the burden of displaced peoples. Neighbouring countries then carry the next greatest burden of refugees. Syria has had its fair share. After the US-led invasion of Iraq, Syria took around 2 million Iraqi refugees. A UNHCR survey in late 2010 showed that many Iraqi refugees in Syria were reluctant to return home (Wilkes and Dobbs 2010), while the Syrian Arab Red Crescent estimates that, prior to March 2011 there were still 1.2 million in Syria, the majority unregistered with the UNHCR (al-Saadi 2014).

The UNHCR reported 28,919 Iraqi refugees in Syria in

mid-2014 after two years of war, but the Syrian Arab Red Crescent said the number was around 450,000. Most were getting aid from local agencies (al-Saadi 2014). Even after many years of war in Syria, thousands of Iraqi refugees were still occasionally fleeing into the 'relative safety' of Syria, for example in Hasakah, which also held other Syrian IDPs (Hasan and Alazroni 2016).

In the case of Afghanistan, most refugees went to Pakistan but most of those (about 4.7 million since 2002) have since returned (UNHCR 2016c). With the Syrian conflict, the great majority of the four million refugees have been camped in Jordan, Lebanon and Turkey, often in very poor conditions. Another 6.6 million IDPs were cared for within Syria. In late 2015 thousands of refugees were returning to war-torn Daraa, in south Syria, because of a lack of supplies in Jordan's al Zaatari camp. Indeed 'departures [from that camp] by far outnumbered arrivals' (AP 2015). This illustrates the fact that the impact of displacement within the region has been around 20 times greater than that of refugee arrivals in Europe.

The Syrian arrivals in Europe in 2015 (about one third of one million asylum seekers) seem to have been driven by some combination of war events in Syria plus internal government practice in Turkey. Around 80% of the arrivals in 2015 came from Turkey, and almost none directly from Syria (Bajekal 2015). Table 3 shows the monthly numbers of Syrian sea arrivals in Europe between April 2015 and 2016. The high numbers do correlate to certain war events. First was the invasion by a Turkey-Saudi-Qatari sponsored 'Army of Conquest' (Jaysh al Fatah), an alliance of Jabhat al Nusra and various 'FSA' groups, launched from Turkey into northern Syria in March-April 2015. This militia soon took over much of Idlib and large parts of Hama, driving many people south to Homs and Damascus, west to the Syrian coast or north into Turkey. In May 2015, despite a supposedly 'anti-DAESH' US air power presence, DAESH took over Palmyra. Further, over July-September the Government of Turkey carried out attacks on the Turkish Kurds, along the Syrian border. This war activity must have contributed to displacement and refugee flows within Turkey. However, the timing of the transformation of these mass movements must be questioned. One important indicator of the likely manipulation of these peoples is the fact that President Erdogan was able to reverse the flows after the conclusion of the 2015-16 refugee agreement with EU leaders. The deal was that the EU would pay Turkey six billion Euros plus some political concessions to contain refugees from various countries, the largest group being from Syria (Alkousaa et al 2016). Turkey already held a 'reservoir' of 2.2 million refugees (Bajekal 2015).

Table 6: Syrian sea arrivals in Europe, 2015-2016

	Syrians arriving by sea in Europe (000s)
April 2015	13.5
May	17.9
June	31.3
July	54.9
August	107.8
September	147.1
October	211.6
November	151.2
December	108.7
January 2016	67.4
February	57.1
March	26.9
April	3.6
Source: UNHCR 2016d	

The 2015 'spike' of Syrian refugees thus correlates to important war events, which must have driven many people from their homes. Conversely, the decline in European arrivals correlates with Russian air power entering Syria and with the Syrian alliance beginning to turn back the armed groups. From this point onwards more displaced people returned home. Importantly, it also links to the Turkey-EU agreements, finalised in March 2016 (Hurriyet Daily News 2018). That dramatic wind-down or exodus of people from Turkey in early 2016 is best explained by controls imposed by the Turkish state. It is easy to see how the Turkish government played the issue to its advantage. A later data set shows the 2015 'spike' of Syrian arrivals more starkly. From almost 600,000 refugees in 2015, the 'illegal entries' had fallen to 19,000 by 2017 (Statista 2019). The UN also recorded a counter movement of another 600,000 returning to Aleppo in the first seven months of 2017 (IOM 2017).

Table 7: Syrian 'illegal entries' to Europe, 2010-2017

	Syrians entering Europe (000s)
2010	0.86
2011	1.6
2012	7.9
2013	25.5
2014	78.9
2015	594.1
2016	88.55
2017	19.45
Source: Statista 2019	

The invited intervention of Russian air power in Syria began on 30 September 2015 and was more or less consistent over following months. This period is associated with a steady decline in sea arrivals. There is thus a negative correlation between European sea arrivals and the liberation of the previously 'jihadist' held areas. We can conclude that the war offensives in northern Syria and southern Turkey may have contributed to the spike in Turkey-Europe asylum seekers, but also that internal Turkish policy considerations must have facilitated the big outflow and its fairly rapid reversal.

The deal with Turkey may have initially 'worked' because Mr Erdogan had the power to turn off the 'tap' he had most likely helped turn on. However the European attempt to avoid its responsibilities under the refugee convention is causing a number of problems: Turkey was hardly a 'safe haven' for repatriation, the commitments to numbers of refugees accepted was not met; and there was European dissatisfaction with a selection process which led them to receive 'serious medical cases, or refugees with very little education' (Alkousaa et al 2016).

3. Stop the refugees or end the wars?

Greater involvement of Russian air power and greater Iranian assistance with ground forces led to a turning of the military tide in favour of Syria over 2015-16. After that there began to be reports of Syrians returning to their homes. Those returns provide evidence that ending the war on Syria is foundational to resolving the refugee problem.

As with the internally displaced, it is logical that refugees flee war and jihadists, following years of well-publicised atrocities against civilians. Public mutilations and beheadings must be intended to terrify. Anecdotal evidence that refugees want to go home is widespread. Video interviews with individual refugees show many non-politicised statements, such as: 'I miss everything', 'I want to go back and see my friends and family in Syria', 'I wish to come back to the lovely country when the war will end', and 'Just stop the war ... we don't want to go to Europe' (e.g. Holt

2016). Even the above-mentioned and flawed survey of refugees in Germany records a large majority wanting to go home. Top of their conditions for return was, unsurprisingly, that 'the war has to stop' (TSC 2016). The most logical understanding is that 'going home' means to the Syria of recent decades, before the conflict.

Wider evidence of refugee or IDP returns has emerged since Syria's alliance reclaimed hundreds of villages and towns from the jihadists. Some of the impetus was due to poor conditions in the refugee camps. In October 2015 several dozen per day were returning from Jordan to Daraa, preferring to face war at home than starvation in Jordan's al Zaatari camp. At the same time, 94,000 returned to Syria from Turkey, half of these to Kobani after ISIS was defeated there; while another 140,000 left Lebanon, some for Turkey and some for Syria (AP 2015). In January 2016 hundreds of displaced families returned home to parts of Damascus, after some ceasefires took effect (AP 2016). After six months of Russian air power support for the Syrian forces, dozens of 'reconciliations' (ceasefires or surrenders) had been signed and, with the relative calm, there were steady returns of IDPs. In March dozens of families returned to rural Hama, after jihadist groups had been ejected under Syrian Government 'reconciliations' (Syrian Observer 2016). More than 1,000 IDPs were said to be returning home every day (Valiente 2016).

In April 2016 Syria's Deputy Prime Minister told the IOM that 1.7 million IDPs had returned to their homes, the government was constructing more than 500 temporary shelters and another 2,000 houses in Damascus and Homs (SANA 2016a). In May Syrian Reconciliation Minister Ali Haidar reported that 35,000 families were expected to return home, after improvements in the security situation (SANA 2016b). This writer saw convoys of people returning to Hama from rural Aleppo in October 2017. The various reports show an ongoing trend towards return of IDPs and refugees, once they are reassured that the conflict has abated. That should reinforce calls to prioritise ending the conflict, as the key means of stemming the movement of displaced persons and refugees.

The conduct of the war on Syria caused confusion over

the displaced peoples, aggravating the refugee crisis in several ways:

- The terrorism fomented by sponsors of the jihadist groups has 'blown back' to Europe and Turkey, helping provoke further European intervention and generating fear of terrorists joining the waves of refugees.
- Disinformation campaigns over the responsibility for this conflict have helped inflame European prejudiced reactions to asylum seekers.
- Militarised responses to the refugee phenomenon (the multi-national naval presence between Turkey and Greece) enhanced European fears of an emigrant 'threat', reinforcing NATO hostility to the Syrian state.

We have seen an aggravation of the war-drives-refugees phenomenon, with consistent disinformation over the proxy war on Syria and its links to the European refugee crisis of 2015. Terrorism fomented by NATO and the Gulf monarchies against Syria has blown back, helping provoke further European intervention and greater displacement. Disinformation about the series of Middle East wars drove confusion and fear about the refugees.

Looking at displacement more broadly, we can see that the burden has fallen far more heavily on the war targeted countries and their neighbours. Only about 3 to 5 percent of displaced peoples from Afghanistan, Iraq and Syria became sea-arrivals in Europe, in the peak year of 2015. Some of the spike in 2015 arrivals might be linked to war events in Syria and Turkey in the first half of 2015. However as 80% of sea-arrivals in Europe came from Turkey, the Turkish government's management of refugees within Turkey was a significant factor. The Turkey-EU deal over refugee management led to a strong, controlled decline in sea arrivals. The Turkish Government most likely knew how to turn on and turn off the 'tap'. There was no positive correlation between increased arrivals in Europe and the entry of Russian air power into the war in Syria; in fact there was a negative correlation. There is evidence of significant returns of IDPs within Syria, as Syrian forces advanced against the western-backed jihadist groups, with ceasefires, 'reconciliation' agreements and the liberation of hundreds of towns and villages.

Western liberals often imagine that assimilating refugees from other countries is a great charity, but that is not the case when western governments are fuelling the wars which drive those refugees. Archbishop Jean-Clément Jeanbart, the Melkite Archbishop of Aleppo, said he was 'not happy' to see Syrians driven out of their own country. He would rather see western countries 'making more efforts to allow the Syrian population to stay in Syria' (in Vaillancourt 2016).

The USA and several of the European powers were in large part responsible for the creation and aggravation of the Middle East displacement crisis, which produced a European refugee crisis. Many millions were affected, yet no real solution is conceivable without addressing the roots of the problem. The Middle East wars must be fully understood, along with their aggravating factors. European and NATO acceptance of their responsibility in driving both the wars and the displaced peoples remains central to any lasting solution.

Bibliography

ABS (2016) 'Syrian Refugees Who Want to Return Home Are Stuck in Germany', 1 June, online: http://abcnews.go.com/International/wireStory/syrian-refugees-return-home-stuck-germany-39522124

Al Saadi Yazan (2014) 'Iraqi refugees in Syria: Between a rock and a hard place', Al Akhbar, April 11, online: http://english.al-akhbar.com/node/19388

Alkousaa, Riham; Giorgos Christides; Ann-Katrin Müller; Peter Müller; Maximillian Popp; Christoph Schult; and Wolf Wiedmann-Schmidt (2016) 'The Many Failures of the EU-Turkey Refugee Deal', *Spiegel Online*, 26 May, online: http://www.spiegel.de/international/europe/the-refugee-deal-between-the-eu-and-turkey-is-failing-a-1094339.html

AP (2015) 'Syrian refugees return home due to intolerable conditions in host nations', *Indian Express*, 5 October, online: http://indianexpress.

com/article/world/world-news/syrian-refugees-return-home-due-to-intolerable-conditions-in-host-nations/

AP (2016) 'Video: 100s of displaced Syrians families return home in Damascus', *Globe and Mail,* 20 Jan, online: http://www.theglobeandmail.com/news/world/hundreds-of-syrian-families-return-to-homes-near-damascus-as-part-of-truce/article28283547/

Bajekal, Naina (2015) 'Why the E.U. Is Offering Turkey Billions to Deal With Refugees', *Time,* 19 October, online: http://time.com/4076484/turkey-eu-billions-dollars-refugee-slow/

Cattori, Silvia (2016) 'Aleppo Doctor Attacks Western Media for Bias, Censorship and Lies', Information Clearing House, 1 May, online: http://www.informationclearinghouse.info/article44597.htm

Chulov, Martin (2015) 'The worst place in the world? Aleppo in ruins after four years of Syria war', *The Guardian,* 12 March, online: https://www.theguardian.com/world/2015/mar/12/worst-place-in-world-aleppo-ruins-four-years-syria-war

CNA (2012) 'Syrian violence drives 50,000 Christians from homes', Christian News Agency, 27 March, online: http://www.catholicnewsagency.com/news/syrian-violence-drives-50000-christians-from-homes/

Daily Sabah (2018) 'Erdoğan lashes out at EU for not helping refugees', 21 June, online: https://www.dailysabah.com/turkey/2018/06/21/erdogan-lashes-out-at-eu-for-not-helping-refugees

Damascus Declaration (2005) 'The Damascus Declaration for Democratic National Change', English version in Joshua Landis blog 'Syria Comment', 1 November, online: http://faculty-staff.ou.edu/L/Joshua.M.Landis-1/syriablog/2005/11/damascus-declaration-in-english.htm

Eurostat (2016) Record number of over 1.2 million first time asylum seekers registered in 2015, online: http://ec.europa.eu/eurostat/en/web/products-press-releases/-/3-04032016-AP

Fuchs, Richard (2015) 'Survey leaves no doubt: Syrians are fleeing Assad', *Deutsche Welle,* 11 October, online: http://www.dw.com/en/survey-leaves-no-doubt-syrians-are-fleeing-assad/a-18775789

Hasan, Mustafa and Qusai Alazroni (2016) 'Iraqis flee Mosul clashes for relative safety of Syria', 27 May, online: http://www.unhcr.org/news/latest/2016/5/57482e0e4/iraqis-flee-mosul-clashes-relative-safety-syria.html

Hassoun, Ahmad Badreddin Hassoun (2016) Personal conversation with Syrian Grand Mufti Hassoun and this writer, 12 April, Damascus

Holt, Kate (2016) "I want to go home': Syrian refugees in Lebanon', *The Guardian,* 12 March, online: http://www.theguardian.com/global-development/gallery/2016/mar/12/syrian-refugees-in-lebanon-want-to-go-home-zahle

Hurriyet Daily News (2018) 'EU agrees to give Turkey second tranche of 3 billion Euro for Syrian refugees', 29 June, online: http://www.hurriyetdailynews.com/eu-agrees-to-give-turkey-second-tranche-of-3-billion-euros-for-syrian-refugees-133939

IDMC (2016) 'Syria IDP Figures Analysis', Internal Displacement Monitoring Centre, update as at 19 September, online: http://www.internal-displacement.org/middle-east-and-north-africa/syria/

IOM (2017) 'Over 600,000 Displaced Syrians Returned Home in First 7 Months of 2017', 11 August, online: https://www.iom.int/news/over-600000-displaced-syrians-returned-home-first-7-months-2017

Kennedy, Merrit (2017) 'U.N.: More Than 600,000 Syrians Have Returned Home In 2017', NPR, 11 August, online: https://www.npr.org/sections/thetwo-way/2017/08/11/542828513/u-n-more-than-600-000-syrians-have-returned-home-in-2017

Nevradakis, Michael (2016) 'Human Rights Lawyer Francis Boyle on US War Crimes, the Refugee Crisis in Europe and More', Truthout, 4 April, online: http://www.truth-out.org/news/item/35486-human-rights-lawyer-francis-boyle-on-us-war-crimes-the-refugee-crisis-in-europe-and-more?tmpl=component&print=1

ORB (2014) 'Three in Five Syrians Support International Military Involvement', ORB International, July, online: http://www.opinion.co.uk/article.php?s=three-in-five-syrians-support-international-military-involvement

ORB (2015) 'ORB/IIACSS poll in Syria and Iraq gives rare insight into public opinion', ORB International, July, online: http://www.opinion.co.uk/article.php?s=orbiiacss-poll-in-iraq-and-syria-gives-rare-insight-into-public-opinion

Rycroft, Matthew (2016) 'Eastern Aleppo City is now encircled by the regime...300,000 people are now effectively besieged', UK Government, 25 July, online: https://www.gov.uk/government/speeches/eastern-aleppo-city-is-now-encircled-by-the-regime300000-people-are-now-effectively-besieged

SANA (2016a) 'Ghalawanji: 1.7 million displaced citizens returned to their areas, 11 April, online: http://sana.sy/en/?p=74121

SANA (2016b) 'Reconciliation Minister: 35,000 families expected to return home in Southern Damascus', 12 May, online: http://sana.sy/en/?p=77091

Statista (2019) 'Illegal entries between border-crossing points (BCPs) from Syria detected in the European Union (EU) from 2010 to 2018 (in 1,000 people)', February, online: https://www.statista.com/statistics/454917/illegal-border-crossing-between-bcps-to-the-eu-by-nationality-syria/

Sterling, Rick (2015) 'Seven Steps of Highly Effective Manipulators', Dissident

Voice, 9 April, online: http://dissidentvoice.org/2015/04/seven-steps-of-highly-effective-manipulators/

Syrian Observer (2016) 'More villagers return home as Hama reconciliations push forward', 24 March, online: http://syrianobserver.com/EN/News/30758/More_Villagers_Return_Home_Hama_Reconciliations_Push_Forward

TESEV (2012) 'The perception of Turkey in the Middle East 2011', Türkiye Ekonomik ve Sosyal Etüdler Vakfi, Istanbul, February, online: http://www.tesev.org.tr/the-perception-of-turkey-in-the-middle-east-2011/Content/236.html

Tharoor, Ishaan (2016) 'Some Syrian refugees in Canada already want to return to the Middle East', *Washington Post,* 26 January, online: https://www.washingtonpost.com/news/worldviews/wp/2016/01/26/some-syrian-refugees-in-canada-already-want-to-return-to-the-middle-east/

TSC (2015) 'Listen to Refugees - First Survey of Syrian Refugees in Europe', survey results spreadsheet, The Syria Campaign, online: https://docs.google.com/spreadsheets/d/1WYn4N7STdP2eW3EYdX86Gsb6lxE4VrcNvZ4aEczsFwI/edit#gid=833561282

UNHCR (2016) 'Global Focus, Syrian Arab Republic', United Nations High Commission for Refugees, update as at 19 September, online: http://reporting.unhcr.org/node/2530#_ga=1.245483460.1547106981.1474264789

UNHCR (2016a) 'Global Focus, Iraq', United Nations High Commission for Refugees, update as at 19 September, online: http://reporting.unhcr.org/node/4505#_ga=1.250864198.1547106981.1474264789

UNHCR (2016b) 'Global Focus, Afghanistan', United Nations High Commission for Refugees, updated as at 19 September, online: http://www.unhcr.org/pages/49e486eb6.html

UNHCR (2016c) 'Afghanistan Fact Sheet 2015', United Nations High Commission for Refugees, August, online: http://www.unhcr.org/protection/operations/50002021b/afghanistan-fact-sheet.html

UNHCR (2016d) 'Refugees/Migrants Emergency Response – Mediterranean', United Nations High Commission for Refugees, update as at 19 September, online: http://data.unhcr.org/mediterranean/country.php?id=83

Vaillancourt, Philippe (2016) 'Archbishop tells Canada: accepting refugees won't help Syria', *Catholic Herald,* 2 May, online: http://www.catholicherald.co.uk/news/2016/05/02/archbishop-tells-canada-accepting-refugees-wont-help-syria/

Valiente, Alexandra (2016) 'Syrian front: Over 1000 IDPs return home daily', 30 March, Uprooted Palestinians, online: http://uprootedpalestinians.blogspot.com.au/2016/03/syrian-front-over-1000-idps-return-home.

html

Wilkes, Sybella and Leo Dobbs (2010) 'Iraqi refugees in Syria reluctant to return to home permanently: survey', UNHCR, 8 October, online: http://www.unhcr.org/news/latest/2010/10/4caf376c6/iraqi-refugees-syria-reluctant-return-home-permanently-survey.html

Xinhua (2019) 'Turkey's Erdogan hopes for EU support in Syria by raising refugee threat: analysts', 23 February, online: http://www.xinhuanet.com/english/2019-02/23/c_137844765.htm

Part III:

The West Asian Alliance

Chapter Twelve

THE FUTURE OF PALESTINE

Jerusalem: Zionist troops decide who is and who is not allowed to visit the al Aqsa mosque.

The claim that Israel has a 'right to exist' is a contrived myth. In fact, apartheid states are crimes against humanity and must be dismantled. The pertinent question, addressed by this chapter is: what are the prospects for a democratic Palestine? By democratic Palestine I mean a state where all citizens have equal rights; given the destruction of any real basis for an Arab state in Palestine, it most likely means a single state.

I begin by reviewing the foundations of the Israeli state, including its racial ideology, the character of the Palestinian resistance, the 'moral equivalence' and false reformist arguments of 'left Zionism'; and then the prospects for a democratic Palestine. The analysis identifies the key challenges of Zionist military occupation, powerful western allies, a fanatical Zionist mission and disunity amongst Palestinian factions and their allies. On the other hand the strengths are ongoing Palestinian resistance, the growing legitimacy of Palestine, the commitment of regional allies and the vulnerability of Israel's allies to exposure of Zionist crimes. In sum the future of Palestine is clouded with divisions, pain and sacrifice; but it remains far from hopeless.

The situation in Palestine is often portrayed in clichés: 'religious conflict', 'helpless victims' and 'terrorism'. None of these really help us understand the situation. But it is not too complicated. The roots of the conflict lie in a traditional project of colonisation, supported by Britain and the USA. It is aggravated by public brutality and ongoing dispossession. The last seven decades of dreadful conflict and violence do show currents and counter-currents, principally those of ethnic cleansing and resistance. A proper reading of these currents might help us see what prospects there might be for a democratic and peaceful Palestine.

Despite decades of brutalising assaults, Palestinian resistance to the racial Israeli state has not diminished, let alone disappeared. Indeed, in the middle of an apparently desperate situation, there are some rays of hope. The resistance in Gaza and in south Lebanon has set boundaries on the north and south expansion of the sectarian state. Meanwhile, Palestinians in the occupied territories remain on their land and steadfastly resist (sumud), while the new colonists cheer on each new seizure of Palestinian land. Three generations of resistance now shape social relations.

On the one hand there is conflict and violence, linked to polarised colonial and anti-colonial struggles. On the other, there is a strange air of normality in the major Arab cities in the West

Bank – Ramallah, Hebron and Nablus – islands in a landscape of fences, walls, classified racial zones, feeder roads and army bases. Dozens of walls throughout the West Bank protect the Zionist colonies. Unlike in Jerusalem, which is a heavily policed 'mixed' zone, life in those Arab cities goes on with little day to day Israeli presence. Yet the storm troops come at night.

1. The European colony in Palestine

There is no need to waste too much time debating whether the Jewish state of Israel is a racial, apartheid regime. It has been well established that it is built on 'racial' privilege and has developed its thoroughgoing apartheid system by means of steady ethnic cleansing. The Adalah (2017) group, for example, has documented more than 65 laws that make Israel a racist state. The most recent authoritative report from the United Nations - by US lawyers Richard Falk and Virginia Tilley (2017) - makes it clear that Israel is indeed an 'apartheid state' and, therefore, a crime against humanity. The apartheid system must be dismantled. The claim that Israel has a 'right to exist' as a 'Jewish,' i.e. racial, state is a fraudulent claim without international legal basis.. As Falk and Tilley (2017) point out: 'the situation in Israel-Palestine constitutes an unmet obligation of the organized international community to resolve a conflict partially generated by its own actions'.

While Palestine has an ancient history, with the city of Jericho, founded perhaps 10,000 years ago, and with the holy city of Jerusalem captured by a variety of empires over the centuries, the current state of Israel has a peculiar contemporary history. After the British and French captured the Levant and other Arab lands from the Ottoman Empire, in the early 20th century, they began a series of partitions with a view to forestalling the emergence of any unified Arab state. The allocation of lands to the Zionist movement of European Jews and the subsequent creation of 'Israel' was a colonial venture that took place at the end of the colonial era.

All 13 of Israel's Prime Ministers since 1948 have come from European families. Not one came from a family which had lived in Palestine for more than one generation. Yet they all claimed a 'right of return' to a mythical ancestral land.

Zionism was and is a mostly secular, colonial project, but it drew on religious myth and came about after centuries of anti-Jewish discrimination within Europe. The religious myths were derived from Biblical texts (Genesis 15:18 referred to promised lands) and from the cult of Second Temple Revivalism, one strand within contemporary Judaism, which holds that the Jewish people will not have their social and spiritual vindication until their Second Temple, destroyed in the Roman era, is reconstructed in Jerusalem (Isaacs 2005).

European Zionists managed to extract the Balfour Declaration of 1917 promising them land in the Levant that the British Government had seized from the Ottomans. Politically, however, and as a keen British journalist of the 1920s pointed out, when it reaffirmed the Balfour Declaration in the 1920s, the British objective was 'to establish in a strategic corner in the Near East a body of people in close coalition with the British' (Jefferies 2014). This same British administration, headed by David Lloyd George, would similarly frustrate Irish independence claims with a partition in the island's north, maintained by Protestant 'loyalists'. The partition of India in the late 1940s and the creation of Pakistan was also aimed at maintaining a British ally in the region, as part of the 'great game' against the influence of the Soviet Union (Singh Sarila 2005). The French, for their part, created an artificial Christian majority in Lebanon, imagining that the little country would maintain loyal to Europe and France.

A lot has been written about Zionism (e.g. Hertzberg 1959; Hart 2005), the British in Palestine (e.g. Tuchman 1956; Segev 1999), the Balfour declaration (e.g. Jefferies 2014; Anderson 2017), the Nazi Holocaust (e.g. Gilbert 2014; Arad, Gutman and Margaliot 2014) and the independence struggles of the Arab peoples (e.g. Hourani 1991; Provence 2005; Khalidi et al 2010). This chapter will only briefly refer to that history, enough for a context to the contemporary creation of the Jewish state and the repression of a possible Arab state.

The missionary force behind the creation of a Jewish state in Palestine had two rationales. The first was a Zionist mission to colonise (or to 're-occupy') what were claimed as ancestral lands, based on scriptural history. The second was to seek refuge from centuries of discrimination against European Jews, which had its appalling culmination in the Nazi Holocaust of 1933-1945. That long standing discrimination had been generated throughout the Holy Roman Empire, where Jews were blamed for various things, including the killing of Jesus of Nazareth (Adams and Heß 2018). European Jews were often barred from holding land and public office, and were expelled from various European countries (Nirenberg 2013; Trachtenberg 2014). The Nazi Holocaust, an attempted genocide of European Jews, has been well documented, despite the conditions of war and the destruction of records and human remains (Gutman, and Berenbaum 1998). There is no doubt that great crime occurred; nor is there any doubt that European Jews in the 1940s were seeking safe refuge from persecution in Europe. Yet none of that justified the dispossession and ethnic cleansing of the Arab people of Palestine.

Contrary to popular myth, the United Nations did not 'create' the state of Israel. In the late 1940s the British passed their League of Nations 'mandate' on Palestine to the newly formed United Nations. The UN formed a committee which reported on the 'Future Government of Palestine'. The majority report from this committee formed the basis of UNGA resolution 181, which recommended the creation of an Arab state, a Jewish state and a 'Special Regime' of international status for Jerusalem (UNGA 1947). Even though the population of Palestine in 1946 was 65% Arab and 33% Jewish, with 'no clear territorial separation of Jews and Arabs by large contiguous areas', the committee recommended that the area for the Jewish state be 55.5% of the total area of Palestine. Injustice to the Arab population, therefore, began with an unbalanced UN report and resolution that provided a veneer of legitimacy on what was to come. It was also controversial at the time. Resolution 181 passed on 29 November 1947 with 33 votes in favour, 13 against and 10 abstentions (Hammond 2010; UNGA

1947). Nonetheless, both the British and the UN had opened the door for the Zionist groups' seizure of the territory of historic Palestine.

On 14 May 1948, David Ben-Gurion, head of the Jewish Agency, proclaimed the establishment of a State of Israel. The declaration was immediately recognised by the government of the US, then the USSR and gradually many others. Almost a year later Israel was admitted as a member of the United Nations. However, 25 states (Arab, Muslim and African states) have never recognised Israel, while seven countries (Iran, Chad, Cuba, Morocco, Tunisia, Oman and Qatar) subsequently revoked their earlier recognition (JVL 2018). Both preceding and accompanying the declaration, a terrible wave of Zionist violence (Arab Palestinians call it al Nakba, the Catastrophe) swept the Palestinian people from hundreds of villages and from the land which they now call '1948 Palestine' (Sa'di, and Abu-Lughod 2007; Pappe 2006: Ch 4).

Israeli historian Ilan Pappe has thoroughly documented the ethnic cleansing operation and, in particular, its planning. It was directed by a 'fourth and final' plan in March 1948 to 'ethnically cleanse the country as a whole'. Ben Gurion, leader of this operation, believed 80-90% of the British mandatory territory was needed and in 1947 he said that 'only a state with at least 80% Jews' would be 'a viable and stable [Jewish] state' (Pappe 2006: xii-xiii, 26, 48). To this end Plan C had called for the killing of Palestinian political leaders, senior officials, inciters and financial supporters and the damaging of transport, water wells, mills, villages, clubs and cafes (Pappe 2006: 28). The fourth and final plan (Plan Dalett, 10 March 1948) added:

> These operations can be carried out in the following manner: either by destroying villages (by setting fire to them, by blowing them up, and by planting mines in their debris), and especially of those population centres ... In case of resistance, the armed force must be wiped out

and the population expelled outside the borders of the state. (Pappe 2006: 39; also Vidal 1997).

The outcome, highlighted by the Deir Yassin massacre of 9 April, where 107 villagers were killed, was a series of expulsions in which 531 villages and eleven urban neighbourhoods were destroyed and 800,000 Palestinians became refugees (Pappe 2006: xiii; Vidal 1997). The foundation of Israel, therefore, was built on a partial genocide and ethnic cleansing of the non-Jewish population of Palestine. Much later the former President of the World Jewish Congress, Nahum Goldmann, reported his colleague David Ben Gurion as saying:

> Why should the Arabs make peace? If I were an Arab leader I would never make terms with Israel. That is natural: we have taken their country ... They only see one thing: we have come here and stolen their country. Why should they accept that? They may perhaps forget in one or two generations' time, but for the moment there is no chance (in Goldmann 1978: 99).

The new Israeli state was not accepted by its Arab neighbours, who were taking in large numbers of refugees. And Israel had internal problems from the beginning. There was a failed attempt to create a constitution, then resort to a set of 'basic laws' which established some principles, while leaving others unresolved. The two key rationales for the racial state were spelt out: refuge and the 'return from exile': that is, refuge from the Nazi genocide and broader European persecution, and return to a supposedly ancestral land. In its Declaration of Independence Israel is called a 'state of Jewish immigration'. The Zionist 'Law of Return', drafted by Ben-Gurion 'in the shadow of the Holocaust', argued that 'whomever the Nazis called a Jew and sent to the death camps was to be offered refuge' (Clayman 1995; Knesset 2014). However, most of the early Zionist leadership came from Eastern

European families; they and their families, like Ben Gurion, had been immigrants to Palestine before the Second World War. Ben-Gurion did not otherwise try to define who was a Jew. Clearly many of the subsequent European, Russian and American Jews who made use of that privileged migration regime had not been 'sent to the death camps'.

Greater religious and essentialist racial overtones were added, with the idea that this law was for 'the in-gathering of exiles' (Knesset 2014), based on the myth that the ancestors of all Jewish people had been driven from the Levant, back in 70AD. Historical and genealogical evidence was then put forward in attempts to prove such a common ancestry.

Zionist racial 'science' adapted to the needs of the political project. Conventional Zionist historians these days maintain that all Jews have a common genetic makeup which comes from the Levant (e.g. Ostrer 2001). This theory tries to link the European (Ashkenazi) and Mediterranean (Sephardic) Jews to those of the Levant. It claims that that those who were driven out of Palestine by the Romans, after the destruction of the Second Temple, went into exile along the Rhine river and other parts of Europe. World Jewry at the turn of the 21st century was estimated at 13 million, with 5.7m in the USA and 4.7 in Israel, but all were said to be biologically linked to ancestors in the Levant (Ostrer 2001). The implication is that European Jews might be said to be 'returning' to their ancestral home (e.g. Entine 2013; Rubin 2013).

Yet this 'consensus' has been seriously undermined. Professor Shlomo Sand, in his book The Invention of the Jewish People (Sand 2010), studied an earlier idea that Palestinian Arab villagers were descended from Jewish farmers. This was suggested by early Zionists David Ben Gurion and Chaim Weizmann, when they made common cause with Palestinian Arabs, before the creation of Israel. Yet Sand could find little evidence either of that or of the collective 'exile'. He went on to argue that European Jews most likely were the descendants of those subject to mass conversions in north east Turkey, Europe and North Africa (Cohen 2009; Sand 2010). This explanation has support from historians who observed that millions of Jews lived in all the far reaches of the Roman Empire, the great majority outside Judea. Judaism was also a faith exported 'to Yemen, Ethiopia, India and China'. Myths evolved about some of those as 'lost tribes' (Ostrer and Skorecki 2012:). The 'Rhineland Theory' tried to maintain the European Jewish link to Palestine but was contradicted by the 'Khazar Theory' of mass conversions in the Caucasus. Other arguments for the even wider origins of Europeans Jews drew on genetic, linguistic and documented evidence. Judaism, it seems, was more given to proselytising in the past than at present. Evidence for past 'mass conversions' undermines the 'common ancestry' theory and supports the view that Jewishness (like Christianity) spread more as a religion than through racial migration (Entine 2013, Rubin 2013). Yet Jewishness also became a supra-religious identity.

Eran Elhaik used Geographical Population Structure (GPS) technology to study the geographical origins of Yiddish, the language of Ashkenazic Jews. His findings draw on some common genetic disorders in Iranian and Ashkenazic people which, through genetic evidence, show that Ashkenazic DNA comes from mixtures of Jews in Iran, Greece and North East Turkey (Elhaik 2016). More dramatically, others have concluded that, at the time of the destruction of the second temple in 70AD, more than 90% of Jews were living outside Judea, mainly in southern Europe (Ghose 2013). Their DNA analyses show, through maternal haplo-group evidence, that all the major sources of Ashkenazi mitochondrial DNA

> have ancestry in prehistoric Europe, rather than the Near East or Caucasus ... thus the great majority of Ashkenazi maternal lineages were not brought from the Levant, as commonly supposed, nor recruited in the Caucasus, as sometimes suggested, but assimilated within Europe (Costa et al 2013).

This evidence for a greater diversity of Jewish origins

outside the Levant is quite strong. Yet perhaps even more significant have been the Zionist efforts to construct a loyal racial 'science', which might bolster the Zionist project and its 'right to return' regime. This effort privileges Jews and, without even any pretence at science, excludes Palestinian Arabs. The latter are often simply dismissed as uncivilised people without culture or law. It is a terrible irony that Jewish people, who suffered so much from racial theorising and genocidal practice in Europe, should create racial myths to justify their own colonial project.

Racial 'science' came to obsess many Zionists, as it did the persecutors of the Jews in Nazi Germany. The purported special people with special rights and a historical mission was always a manufactured device. Today, orthodox Zionists and neo-Nazis are those most upset at critiques of racial 'science'. For example, former Ku Klux Klan leader David Duke rejects the idea that Jewishness might be religious and not racial. He supports the Zionist consensus, maintaining the essentialist idea of Jews as a separate race (Bridges 2016). Such 'science' is readily turned to racist purpose, to reject those outside the special class. That is why we see striking similarities between the essentialist racism of, for example, the Nazi ideologist Julius Streicher and the Zionist historian Benzion Netanyahu. They set up similar classes of superior and inferior peoples, demonising their 'racial' enemies. In both cases this ideology laid a common foundation for ethnic cleansing and genocidal practice (see Table Eight).

The inability of the Jewish state to clearly define who is a Jew has led to significant internal tensions. For the purpose of citizenship this task has been passed to the supervision of orthodox rabbis. The Jewish-Israeli population, said to be around 50% European, 30% Sephardic and 23% from the Levant (Ostrer 2001: 891), is dominated by Europeans. There is significant European prejudice against both Separdim and the Arab Jews for their cultural and religious differences (Shasha 2010; Masalha 2017). On top of that, there is a large group of around one million Russian and Ukrainian migrants, who came after the great depressions in Russia of the 1990s. They were welcomed by the Israeli elite, as

Table 8
Racial ideologies: The basis for ethnic cleansing

Julius Streicher (1885-1946). Nazi ideologist, executed for spreading hatred of the Jewish people.	Benzion Netanyahu (1910-2012). Zionist historian and father of Benjamin Netanyahu.
As a child 'a first suspicion came into my life that **the essence of the Jew** was a peculiar one ... Who were the money lenders? They were those who were driven out of the temple by Christ himself ... [they] never worked but live on fraud ... The God of the Jews is ... the God of hatred.' (Streicher 1938, 1945)	'He has no respect for any law ... in the desert he can do as he pleases. The tendency towards conflict is **the essence of the Arab**. He is an enemy by essence ... It doesn't matter what kind of resistance ... what price he will pay. His existence is one of perpetual war.' (Derfner 2012)

helping with the Jew-Arab numbers game, but it seems that many were economic migrants. On arrival as many as half were not seen as Jewish, so they were forced to submit to a conversion process, as a condition of citizenship (Reeves 2013). The pressure of non-Jewish immigrants, on top of the growing Arab population inside Palestine, was said to be adding to the pressure on Israel 'to choose between being a 'Jewish' state and a democracy' (Brownfeld 2000).

Zionists often attempt to conscript Jewish people to their cause, and accuse others of racism if they oppose Israel. This requires a peculiar logic. For example Julie Nathan, Research Officer for the Executive Council of Australian Jewry, claims that Zionism 'is not separate from Judaism ... Zionism is an intrinsic component of Judaism' (Nathan 2017a). In that view of the world, any calls for an end to the 'colonial apartheid state' means the 'ethnic cleansing' of Jewish people (Nathan 2017b). In this way, rejection of the Jewish apartheid state's supposed 'right to exist' is falsely painted as a genocidal threat to the Jewish people.

Ethnic cleansing in Palestine has changed over time, but its ambitions remain. The often cited Yinon Plan of 1982 was not so much a plan as a reiteration of older Zionist ambitions, to create a 'Greater Israel' (Eretz Yisrael), a Jewish State stretching from 'from the Brook of Egypt [the Nile River] to the Euphrates' (Herzl 1960: 711). Oded Yinon, a senior Israeli advisor, wrote of what he saw as a civilizational crisis of the 'West', during the cold war. Israel, for its part, could only 'survive as a state' if it seized the 'immense opportunities' to extend its territory against a fragmented 'Moslem Arab world', which he claimed was 'built like a temporary house of cards put together by foreigners' (Yinon 1982). He did not recognise that Israel had been far more decisively built by foreigners.

The Allon Plan, which set out parameters for absorption of the occupied West Bank, was put to an Israeli cabinet in the wake of the Zionist victory in the 1967 war. Labor Minister Yigal Allon opposed the idea of delegating the Palestinian problem to Jordan, seeing that country's monarchy as an unreliable partner. Instead he suggested that Israel begin to carve the West Bank into an Israeli-controlled strip along the Jordan river, with permanent Jewish colonies ('settlements') and army bases strategically placed across all the Palestinian territories. He said 'the last thing we must do is to return one inch of the West Bank' (Auerbach 1991; Shlaim 2001). On that basis negotiation could be opened for a separate and subordinate Palestinian entity (Pedatzur 2007). This plan was not accepted by the Israeli cabinet but its initial aim of colonising 40% of the West Bank became de facto Labor policy for many years (Reinhart 2006: 51).

Immediately after the 1967 conflict, Israel began to build illegal settlements and demolish Palestinian housing in the annexed areas of East Jerusalem. Yet the UN has not shifted from its position since 1967 that the Palestinian residents of East Jerusalem are under belligerent occupation and therefore protected by the 4th Geneva Convention (AIC 2011: 5-6). UN Security Council Resolution 242 (1967) demanded the 'withdrawal of Israel armed forces from territory occupied in the recent conflict' and emphasised 'the inadmissibility of the acquisition of territory by war' (UNISPAL 1967). Disregarding this resolution, successive Israeli governments began to colonise the Occupied Palestinian Territories. A range of devices – purchase under duress, seizure for state purposes, penal confiscations – were used to seize land. The large number of feeder roads, military bases and buffer zones also expanded the territory taken by the colonizers. Best informed estimates today of the Palestinian land occupied in flagrant violation of international law (categorised under Israeli law as 'Category C', for exclusive Israeli use) is now over 60% of the West Bank. This includes more than 200 colonies, both 'authorised' and 'non-authorised', containing around 600,000 'Israeli citizens', of which over 200,000 live in those parts of the West Bank around Jerusalem, which have been more recently annexed by the separation wall (DG EXPO 2013; TOI 2016; BTSELEM 2017).

After Israel's forced withdrawal from South Lebanon in 2000, Tel Aviv decided to concentrate on steadily encircling and dominating the West Bank and Gaza. It realised that, in the post-colonial world, there were some limits on replicating the mass ethnic cleansings of 1948 and 1967. Yet the steady colonisation and popular uprisings acted to discredit both the Oslo accords and the notion of a 'two state solution' (Bishara 2001: 11-12).

In this context Israel began to construct its notorious 700km 'Separation Barrier', supposedly to protect Israelis from Palestinian 'terrorism', but also to annex more territory. The Israeli government ignored an advisory opinion from the International Court of Justice, saying that the barrier would be a violation of international law (UN News Centre 2004). This wall is these days a multilayered system of fences, with an average 60m exclusion zone, and concrete walls in the urban areas. It extends deep into the West Bank, enclosing all of Palestinian East Jerusalem and linking up with the large colony of Adumim. The wall put about 100,000 Palestinians in enclaves, while cutting off many more from their land, homes and workplaces. The Jewish colonists have privileged access to most of the gates and roads that pass through the wall, deepening the apartheid character of Israel (Hever 2007: 15-17, 20-21, 52-56). It makes even more complex the level of policing of Palestinians according to residence and Israeli determined rights of movement. There are at least 5 categories of Palestinian rights of movement, reflected in their Israeli-issued ID cards (Hever 2007: 12-13).

The 'Zone A' areas (only Arabs allowed) are reminiscent of the 'Bantustans' of Apartheid South Africa. Put up as a substitute for racial equality, these 'homelands' created municipalities with local government roles, similar to those of the current Palestinian Authority. While suggesting 'independent' status, they actually segregated and stripped black South Africans of their citizenship. Their leaders were rejected as 'puppets of the apartheid regime' (Phillips, Lissoni and Chipkin 2014). The current occupied territories—isolated, non-viable islands, dependent on and controlled by the colonial state—are remarkably similar. Yet Zionists do not see it this way. Israeli and Jewish populations are encouraged to believe that, in the colonial manner, military conquest entitles Israel to Arab lands. Yet that colonial notion has been repudiated by contemporary international law. See photo page. 248.

2. Palestinian Resistance

In the face of relentless Zionist pressure to empty Palestine of its non-Jewish population, it is only Palestinian resistance that has slowed the ethnic cleansing. Resistance is passive, active and underestimated. First there is the simple fact of Palestinians remaining on their land. This is often referred to as sumud, steadfastness or resilient resistance. It has been said that too little attention is paid to this autonomous resistance, including 'adaptation' by women and families, in the face of extreme

Ramallah has become 'Zone A'. Under the Israeli apartheid regime, Ramallah has become 'Zone A', for Arabs only. "The entrance for Israeli citizens is forbidden, dangerous to your lives and is against the Israeli law".

violence, by simply 'asserting Palestinian culture and identity' (Ryan 2015).

Then there is active (including armed) resistance. There is no doubt this is legitimate, in context of the violent colonisation. It is well recognised by international law. Vicious, at times genocidal incitements are made by Zionist leaders, further indicating their support for repeated attacks on Palestinian communities. These attacks are, in large part, to make Palestinian territories 'uninhabitable' and so drive them from the 'promised lands' (Wadi 2018). In that context both remaining and fighting back represent resistance. The Apartheid State occupies more Arab land than before, yet the uprisings in Palestine show that the new 'settlements', their military bases and feeder roads are not safe (Bishara 2001: 24). They can be blocked and they can come under sniper fire; such incidents do occur, almost every day.

The United Nations General Assembly has acknowledged on several occasions the right of colonised peoples, and in particular Palestinians, to resist 'by all available means, particularly armed struggle' (UNGA 1978). The General Assembly has also said it 'strongly condemns all Governments which do not recognize the right to self-determination and independence of peoples under colonial and foreign domination and alien subjugation, notably the peoples of Africa and the Palestinian people' (UNGA 1974). This principle is understood by independently thinking Israelis. Academic Baruck Kimmerling acknowledged that 'after some 35 years of occupation, exploitation, uprooting and degradation, the Palestinian people have the right to use force to oppose the Israeli occupation which, in itself, is a brutal use of force' (Kimmerling in Bishara 2001: 25). It is less well understood by outsiders who find it easier to only contemplate passive resistance.

Who is resisting? In a 2018 survey of those in the Occupied Palestinian Territories 61% said they identified as Palestinian and 12% as Muslim (JMCC 2018). As there are Christian, Druze and Bedouin Palestinians, and as the colonial powers have always played on religious or ethnic divisions, the preferred identity remains 'Palestinian'. While most Palestinians are quite religious, only a tiny minority (2.2%) see that extremist Islamists such as ISIS/DAESH help their cause (JMCC 2016). Syrian scholar Ghada Hashem Talhami (2001) considers Palestinian nationalism as a special case of Arab nationalism. That link may help explain why there has been such a strong expectation that the neighbouring Arab nationalists of Egypt, Lebanon, Syria and Iraq, even the Gulf monarchies, would assist the Palestinian resistance.

In response, Zionists often promote the idea that Palestine 'does not exist'. The conclusion derived from this myth is that there is no occupation (Ben-Meir 2016). The late Israeli Prime Minister Golda Meir, at one time, also said 'there is no such thing as a Palestinian and Palestinians do not exist'. However as a reflective person she did not really believe it. After her death she had a message passed to her British journalist friend, Alan Hart, saying that the 'Palestine does not exist' statement was 'the silliest damn thing she ever said' (Hart 2005: 18-19). Nevertheless, such statements have been encouraged amongst Jewish communities, to help build a necessary myth of the colonial process.

Despite their appalling conditions of life, Palestinians have refused to go away. Demographic trends within Palestine/Israel demonstrate this very well. The Palestinian population is growing, relative to the Jewish population. Extreme Zionists often dismiss this 'demographic threat'. Faitelson (2009), for example, says that there is no demographic threat to the Zionist project, because of supposed declining Arab birth-rates and steady emigration, driven by extreme conditions. Similarly Yoram Ettinger, of the American-Israel Demographic Research Group, dismisses the 'demographic threat', saying that the figures are exaggerated (Eldar 2018). And Israel constantly seeks to recruit immigrant Jews.

Nevertheless, recent estimates do show a pro-Palestinian demographic shift. A report from Jerusalem in 2011 showed that the Palestinian population of that city had risen from 25.5% in 1967 to 38% in 2009. It also revealed that, while East Jerusalem comprised one third the population of the city and municipality, it received less than 10% the investment in roads, sewage, public parks, swimming pools, libraries and sports facilities, and only one percent the investment in children's playgrounds (AIC 2011: 10, 12). The colonising regime has demonstrated a consistent unwillingness to treat Palestinians with any sense of human equality.

The Jewish Virtual Library shows that the Jews of Israel / 1948 Palestine have declined from a peak of 88.9% in 1960 to 74.7% in 2017 (JVL 2017). In parallel, officials from Israel's Central Bureau of Statistics and the military-run civil administration of the Occupied Territories (COGAT) say that the Arab population of Gaza, the West Bank and Arab citizens of Israel, along with residents of the annexed East Jerusalem municipality, add up to 6.5 million, about the same number as 'Jews living between the Jordan Valley and the Mediterranean' (Heller 2018).

The Palestinian population, for its part, supports its institutions, though they have little faith in the current parties. This disillusionment comes partly from divisions between the Islamists and the secular parties. Almost all (96%) reject a Palestinian state that does not have Jerusalem as its capital; and more than half (53%) do not trust any political personality (JMCC 2018). Only 46% regarded the Palestinian National Authority's performance as good, but 66% see the need to maintain it (JMCC 2017). In July 2016 Fatah maintained the highest support at 33%, followed by Hamas at 14% and the PFLP on 3.4%. More than a third (36%) said they did not support any faction (JMCC 2016). In other words, a large majority support their nation and their institutions but, in recent times, there has been a crisis of leadership.

International support for Palestine as a nation has increased in recent years, alongside the expansion of the colonies, precisely because of the popular resistance. This is reflected in foreign opinion polls and by voting at the United Nations. Zionist repression simply helps build this international support. It is remarkable that in 2018 an Israeli journalist published details of 2,700 assassinations carried out by Zionist secret services: 'more people [murdered] than any other country in the western world' (Bergman 2018: xxii). Many Israelis probably feel some pride in this 'accomplishment'. However, the open arrogance over such 'achievements', the journalist says, blinds the leadership to its strategic failures (Bergman 2018: 629). Despite a powerful Israel lobby in Europe, for example, which tries to sanitise the occupation, 65% of Europeans believe that Israel engages in religious discrimination (Abdullah and Hewitt 2012: 41-42, 279). The Zionist argument that opposing Israel is seen as racist or 'anti-semitic' is losing ground in European popular opinion. Just over half (53%) the Europeans over 55 years of age still believe this but only 45% of 18-24 year olds (Abdullah and Hewitt 2012: 292). Of course, 'semitic peoples' refers to Arabs, North Africans and some other Middle East groups, as well as to Hebrew speakers. So the very term 'anti-semitic' (anti-Jewish in a European context) is simply another false racial construct in the Middle East.

Recognition of Palestine at the UN level has grown as that of Israel is weakening. In 1974 the UNGA recognised the Palestine Liberation Organisation (PLO) as the representative of the Palestinian people and invited it to attend plenary meetings. In 1988 the UNGA acknowledged the proclamation of the state of Palestine and began to use the name 'Palestine' in place of the PLO for the delegation. In 2011 Palestine was admitted to UNESCO (MSPUN 2013) and soon after the US stopped its membership payments to that UN body. In 2017 both Israel and the US withdrew as members of UNESCO, citing 'anti-Israel bias' (Beaumont 2017). That was an important advance for Palestine. When the UN's Human Rights Council passed several motions against Israel, including the call for an arms embargo, the Zionist state's foreign minister reacted by calling for Israel to withdraw from that body (JPost 2018).

In 2012 the UNGA accorded 'Non-member observer state' status to the delegation, 'marking the first time that the General Assembly considered Palestine to be a state' (UNGA 2012). By 2018 137 UN member states had recognised the State of Palestine (MSPUN 2018). One of the advantages of this advance has been the new capacity of the Palestinian Authority to recognise and adopt treaties such as the Statute of Rome, allowing Palestine to refer the Zionist slaughter of civilians to the International Criminal Court as 'crimes against humanity' (Morrison 2018). This was not possible before 2012.

Despite constant moves by the USA to normalise Israel and its ethnic cleansing, the international community (which the USA often pretends to represent) has held a firm line. When the Trump administration announced its plan to move its embassy to Jerusalem, in breach of numerous resolutions over the status of Jerusalem, the plan was rebuffed at the UN, with 128 states voting in favour (9 against with 35 abstentions) of the resolution declaring 'null and void' any actions to change the status of Jerusalem (UNGA 2017).

The Zionist state depends heavily on US and UK veto power at the Security Council, but often expresses fears that it may be abandoned. A 2016 motion at the Security Council to end Israeli 'settlements' in the Occupied Palestinian Territories stalled only after Israeli pressure on the incoming Trump administration to prevent it. Yet because it was not immediately rejected by the outgoing Obama administration, the Israeli government accused the US of a 'shameful move ... an abandonment of Israel, which breaks decades of US policy of protecting Israel at the UN' (Al Jazeera 2016).

At the ground level, the resistance has built some hard-won victories. The expansion options for 'Greater Israel' have been contained, to the north and the south. Over 2005-06 the Zionist colonies were withdrawn from the Gaza Strip. Soon after, in 2006, Israel was pushed back and humiliated after an adventurist incursion into Southern Lebanon.

Ariel Sharon, a brutal Zionist leader who had led repeated attacks on Gaza, the West Bank and south Lebanon, said the reason for Israeli withdrawal from Gaza was 'to grant Israeli citizens the maximum level of security' (Baker 2015). The underlying reason was unceasing resistance by the brave people of Gaza. Since that time the crowded Palestinian territory has been subject to a prison-like blockade and repeated collective punishment attacks. The apartheid state, in several operations, slaughtered thousands (Pappe 2014). Nevertheless, the retreat from Gaza set one boundary to the 'Greater Israel' project.

The following year, encouraged by Washington's

imperious project of a 'New Middle East' (Bransten 2006), Israel once again invaded south Lebanon, attempting to disarm the Lebanese resistance party, Hezbollah, created to resist earlier Israeli invasions. Although Zionist forces were able to kill many, they also suffered serious losses and were forced to withdraw, failing to meet any of their objectives (Crooke and Perry 2006). Israeli defence experts subsequently concluded that Israel could not defeat Hezbollah (Reuters 2010). In the following decade, even though some Lebanese territory (Shebaa Farms) is still annexed, Tel Aviv has been wary of adventurism on the Lebanese border. Iran's leader Ayatollah Khamenei pointed out that, since the 1980s, 'the Zionist regime has not been able to transgress against new lands, it has also begun to retreat' (Khamenei 2017). The Palestinian resistance has played the 'major and determining role' in these retreats, he said.

The mainly Shia Muslim Islamic Republic of Iran has played a major role in supporting mainly Sunni Muslim Palestine. This is non-sectarian support. The large regional power has paid money to Palestinian families of fallen resistance fighters, after they had their houses demolished in collective punishment rampages. Iran has also supported with training and weapons almost all the Palestinian militia which resist the apartheid state—even those groups linked to the anti-Shia Muslim Brotherhood (IIT 2012; 2016). Iran, Syria and Hezbollah remain valuable Palestinian allies.

But the core of resistance is on the ground. Zionist storm troops make regular raids on any part of the Palestinian territories, but particularly the 'camps': settlements created for refugees after 1948. These camps, after many decades, are now the outer suburbs of the major Palestinian cities. The Israeli troops make arrests, mostly of young men suspected of resistance activities. The raids also serve as signals of Zionist power and are sometimes even used as training exercises.

Ali, a young man in the Dehaisheh camp, now part of the southern suburbs of Bethlehem, told me his camp had been created in 1950 to house some of the hundreds of thousands of Palestinians displaced by '1948 Israel'. They did not resettle, as they imagined they would be going home soon. They kept their land title deeds and keys. A UN agency later helped them build mostly 3 x 3 metre concrete box-dwellings. After the 1967 war, when Israeli troops took control of the West Bank, the camps were heavily policed. They were seen as hotbeds of resistance and were denied access to books, as well as to normal freedoms of movement and association (Ali 2018).

For three generations people in these urban 'camps' have had 'no privacy and no property'. They had no individual titles to camp lands. In their little box houses, which could only expand upwards, those next door could hear everything. Yet these conditions also meant that camp communities maintained a strong collective spirit, with little crime and no voting, relying instead on agreements by common consensus. That spirit reinforced their resistance to the colonists (Ali 2018). Other experienced Palestinian activists, Naji (2018) and Amal (2018), who do not live in the camps, confirmed to me this special morale in the camps. That heightened sense of resistance amongst internal displaced communities may also help account for the resistance spirit of the Gaza community. Most of them are from families internally displaced from 1948 Palestine; and Gaza has the highest percentage (25%) of doubly-internally displaced people (BADIL Resource Centre 2015: 99).

While these camp communities contain various groups and political parties, in Deheisheh the community has rejected religious sectarians. Israelis were already skilfully fomenting divisions between Muslims, Christians, Druze and Bedouins (Ali 2018). For decades the colonists treated sectarian Islamist groups favourably, knowing that they would fight with the secular leadership and divide Palestinians. According to former Israeli officials Avner Cohen and David Hacham, in the 1980s Israel encouraged Hamas, seeing them as a 'counterweight' to the PLO and Fatah (Tekuma 2009). Tel Aviv observed in the 1980s that 'more violence [was] directed by ... the Muslim Brotherhood at nationalist Palestinian groups than at the Israeli occupation authorities' (Shadid 1988: 658). The result was that

Apartheid fences and 'buffer zones' divide the entire West Bank; colonies sit on the hills

the Brotherhood and the linked Islamists of Hamas were 'treated less harshly than the nationalists' (Shadid 1988: 674-675). In more recent years Raed Salah, leader of the Islamic Movement within Israel/Palestine, has been imprisoned several times, but his treatment seems much less harsh than that given to many secular activists (Lieber 2017; TOI 2018), who are often given long prison sentences or simply assassinated.

While sectarian Islamists were tolerated for 'divide and rule' reasons, the young men of the camps have been subject to savage brutality. Around 2016 a new Israeli commander ('Captain Nidal') began a wave of terror in the southern West Bank camps. He told the young men that instead of killing he would 'teach them a lesson' they would not forget (Ali 2018). From there began a wave of 'knee-capping' (shooting in the knee, to cripple), which has been widely reported (Hamayel 2016; Hass 2016; Ashly 2017). Ali told me that over 200 young men had been crippled in this way. The young man said his community wanted international support, but resented western aid agencies which come to Palestine, pretending to help but with their own ideas of 'empowerment'. He recalls a young European woman preaching to experienced Palestinian mothers about 'how to be a good mother'. Some of the women laughed, finding it hard to believe. Ali said, 'we are not helpless victims, we are people with a strong culture'.

3. Left Zionists and other False Friends

The wide popularity and legitimacy of the Palestinian cause, alongside strong western support for the Jewish colony, has created a tension which spawns a great deal of doublespeak. Even those states which supply Israel with weapons speak of their alleged support for Palestinian statehood. Yet these self-proclaimed peace-brokers, especially the governments of the USA and Britain, have repeatedly betrayed the Palestinian cause.

There are ways to identify this duplicity, which comes from many western politicians, liberals and leftists. First these false friends declare their support for Palestinian statehood. Next they make that support conditional on 'non-violent' resistance, immediately denying the colonised their full rights of resistance under international law. Finally, they denounce both the armed resistance and the key regional allies of the resistance – Hezbollah, Syria and Iran – just as fiercely as do the most extreme Zionists.

False friends also have regular recourse to 'moral equivalence' arguments, where they denounce the colonisers and the colonised in the same breath. This is a type of arrogant cynicism, with the pretence of even-handedness. Those who act in this way, while pretending to abhor colonial Israel, seem to support the idea of a nicer, kinder but still apartheid state.

Former US President Barack Obama, for example, urged Palestinians 'to pursue statehood by non-violent means'. An Arab critic says Obama failed to understand 'the true nature of the struggle, by reducing the message to a statement about the undesirability of violence on the part of an oppressed people'. He says that in all anti-colonial struggles 'there is never any question of the right of people being colonized to defend themselves' (Qumsiyeh 2011: Ch 1 and 2). Obama's eightyear regime kept arming Israel, while practising doublespeak over Palestine and waging proxy wars against Libya, Syria and Iraq.

Within Zionist culture we can see many examples of 'left Zionism'. Writing on the 70th anniversary of the creation of Israel, well known internal critic Gideon Levy was invited by Haaretz newspaper to say '70 things he loves about Israel'. Levy thought he could find only 7, but managed to find 67, many of which make him 'proud' of Israel. For example, he was proud of and 'misses' the Gaza Strip, as the Zionist state bans Israeli journalists from visiting Gaza (Levy 2018). Haaretz itself is sometimes celebrated as a critical media, but its critical content consists mostly of debates between Zionists and the left Zionists, the latter seeing themselves as temperamentally liberal, anti-racist and more humane.

Similarly, in an article which purports to advocate an end to the two-state solution and 'to stop Israeli apartheid', internal Israeli critic A.B. Yehoshua uses both the 'non-violent resistance' and 'moral equivalence' arguments over colonisation, arguing that 'it is the defective character of both the Jewish and the Palestinian national identities that is exacerbating the conflict'. He proposes 'a non-violent partnership between Israelis and Palestinians'. What does this mean? At the end of a rambling article he calls for ending new colonies ('settlements') in the West Bank but, for the most part, maintaining the status quo, with Israel continuing to control the Palestinian territories, some concessions for Arab Israeli residents but no change to the Jewish 'right of return' (Yehoshua 2018). This is simply a failure to recognise Israel's colonial reality. Within Israel, those who agonise over the injustice of the regime yet continue to enjoy its privileges are taunted by conventional Zionists as those engaged in 'shooting and crying' (Harel 2009; Benton 2015).

Repeated 'moral equivalence' claims have come from many western 'friends' of Palestine over the subject of alleged 'indiscriminate rockets' fired into Israel from Gaza. When people of the territories respond in self-defence their responses are condemned alongside calls for Israel to 'show restraint'. For example, after the Zionist attacks on Gaza in 2014, Phillip Luther from Amnesty International said:

> Palestinian armed groups, including the armed wing of Hamas, repeatedly launched unlawful attacks during the conflict killing and injuring civilians ... they displayed a flagrant disregard for international humanitarian law and for the consequences of their violations on civilians in both Israel and the Gaza Strip ... All the rockets used by Palestinian armed groups are unguided projectiles which cannot be accurately aimed at specific targets and are inherently indiscriminate; using such weapons is prohibited under international law and their use constitutes a war crime (Amnesty International 2015).

Similarly, but in a more understated way, after Israel's

2008-09 assaults on Gaza, British-Australian academic Jake Lynch, an avowed supporter of Palestine and the BDS campaign, condemned what he said was the use of 'indiscriminate weapons' by Palestinian militia:

> The home-made rockets that Hamas militiamen fired into Israel were indiscriminate weapons, and the 20 or so deaths they caused over several years are war crimes, but ... that pales into insignificance when compared with the impact of Israel's high-tech weaponry, which claimed 1300 lives (Lynch 2009).

Lynch, like Luther, repeats the popular myth that the Israeli punitive assaults were simply conflicts in which both sides committed crimes, albeit different in scale. Neither was prepared to accept that the character of colonial repression is quite different to that of anti-colonial self-defence. Many others, including the European Union (Ceren 2014) and the New York Times (Barnard and Rudoren 2014), take a similar approach. Yet repression and self-defence in this conflict are not only distinct in scale but also in character.

And have Palestinian retaliations really been indiscriminate'? If we check from independent evidence, including Israeli sources, we find that the assumptions about 'indiscriminate' Palestinian retaliation have been unfounded. For example, during the 2014 assault on Gaza, the UN said that more than 75% of the 1,088 Palestinians killed by Israeli forces were civilians (AP 2014; Ma'an 2014). That is indeed indiscriminate. From the other side, only 6% of the 51 deaths from Palestinian attacks on Israel were of civilians; 48 or 94% were IDF soldiers (UWI 2014). That is far from 'indiscriminate'. There is no moral equivalence here; either in character, nor in scale or in discriminate focus.

Table 9: The Israeli assault on Gaza, 2014

	Israeli forces	Palestinian Resistance
Deaths inflicted by	1088	51
Of which civilians	816 'at least'	3
% civilian deaths	75%	6%

Sources: AP 2014; UWI 2014, Ceren 2014; Ma'an 2014; Barnard and Rudoren 2014

Moral equivalence seems to have become a type of 'qualifying statement' in western public debate. It is thought necessary to allow the interlocutor to be able to speak. Condemn the opponents of a western or western allied regime, before any criticism is allowed. We also see this argument from Australian ethics Professor Peter Singer. He said 'I am critical of both [Hamas and Israel] ... and I think the situation is a tragic one ... clearly there are extremists on both sides ... both sides have gone to extremes ... you have to say, as far as Hamas is concerned ... they are a terrorist organisation, they are firing rockets into Israel, they are openly trying to kill Israelis where they can' (in C. Anderson 2018). This is a popular but cynical 'plague on both their houses' argument. It just helps 'qualify' the discussant. Condemn Palestinian resistance as 'criminal', after which some criticism of Israeli repression may be allowed. These 'moral equivalence' arguments, even if they point out the vast differences in scale, fail to represent the conflict in its true colors, and by that omission, aid the colonizer.

Those who pursue this type of 'left-Zionism' – pretending to be friends of the Palestinian people while condemning their resistance – seem to imagine that there is room for reform of a regime based on colonial racism. They miss the lessons of apartheid South Africa. There can be no such thing as a nicer, friendlier, apartheid state. Even former officials from conservative US administrations have recognised that there is no future for a 'two state' solution (Leverett and Leverett 2014). As Falk and Tilley (2017) have summed up very clearly, an apartheid regime is a crime against humanity, it must be dismantled and the international community has the responsibility to see that done. No amount of purely 'moral equivalence' argument will help.

Table 10: Prospects for a Democratic Palestine

Challenges	Strengths
Zionist military occupation	Ongoing Palestinian resistance
Western allies with military and media assets	Moral and international legitimacy
Fanatical Zionist mission and racial ideology	Strong and united regional allies
Disunity amongst Palestinian factions and their regional allies	Vulnerability of Israel's allies (and Jewish supporters) to exposure of apartheid crimes

4. Towards a democratic Palestine

An apartheid state must be dismantled and South Africa provides the best recent example of how to do so. A democratic Palestine would accept all its inhabitants as equal human beings. In this respect the experiment of a racialised Jewish state has failed badly. It remains an increasingly illegitimate agent of repression and a fomenter of conflict throughout the entire region. In fact, it is supported by the big foreign powers for precisely this reason: to divide the people of the region and keep them vulnerable to outside domination.

So what are the prospects for a democratic Palestine? I feel the question is best answered by considering the challenges and strengths. I outlined these in Table 10 above.

Of all the challenges, the Zionist military occupation appears to be its greatest strength. However, this is undermined by persistent resistance, exposure of the range of Israeli acts of repression and growing international illegitimacy. Whatever its main sponsor in Washington may say about Jerusalem or the occupied Golan Heights, international law has not changed in Israel's favour, over the past 50 years. The occupied peoples have not gone away and the repression and killings remain an open wound.

At the military level there has been the 'mad dog' doctrine. Israel's late Defence Minister Moshe Dayan said: 'Israel must be like a mad dog, too dangerous to bother' (Hirst 2003). Former Prime Minister Ariel Sharon similarly threatened: 'Arabs may have the oil but we have the matches' (in Avishai 2014). Discussion within Israel is often more candid than the 'soft sell' practised in other countries. It is shocking, for example, for outsiders to hear those such as Israeli Professor Arnon Soffer saying that 'if we want to remain alive, we will have to kill and kill and kill; all day every day' (Soffer in Leibowitz 2007). That genocidal affirmation was in response to the 'demographic threat' of the growing Palestinian population (JVL 2017).

The most egregious threat is known as the 'Samson option', the suggestion that, if the Zionist regime were to face military defeat, it would use its nuclear arsenal to take millions of lives with it as it went down. This idea has been around for some time. Back in the 1970s Prime Minister Golda Meir was asked: 'You are saying that if ever Israel was in danger of being defeated on the battlefield, it would be prepared to take the region and even the whole world down with it? Golda Meir: 'Yes, that's exactly what I am saying' (Hart 2005: xii). All this means that the defeat and dismantling of apartheid-Israel must be carefully managed.

Tel Aviv maintains strong western allies, who are its principal arms suppliers and diplomatic protectors. They defend Israel at the United Nations and promote its cause and ideology in various other ways. That support, alongside Jewish lobbies, helps blunt and divert international reaction to apartheid crimes, by repeating the false slogans of Israel as 'the only democracy in the region', 'opposing terrorism', and so on. But this apparent strength is vulnerable to exposure.

The ideology and fanaticism of the Zionist mission does engender a degree of solidarity and passion amongst Israelis and large parts of the international Jewish community. The extended idea of Jewish people as victims, not just of past European regimes, but of current Arab and Muslim regimes, has served well in the past. But that solidarity is weakening, and there are counter-movements. For a start, there are groups of religious Jews who reject and denounce Israel, as a distortion of and an affront to Judaism (TTJ 2018; NKI 2018). Then there is secular disillusionment. While conservative Zionists speak hopefully of Palestinians leaving the occupied territories, at the same time many European and American Israelis are taking advantage of their dual nationality and abandoning Israel. There are reports that 40% (Klingbail and Shiloh 2012), or even 59% (Walker 2014) of Israelis think of emigrating. Around 100,000 Israelis hold German passports, and a 2014 survey found that 25% of young secular Israelis 'wanted to make a life away from Israel' (Walker 2014). The Jerusalem Post reported that between 200,000 and one million Israelis, including many professionals, are already living in the USA (Sales 2017). Further undermining the sense of unified mission is the fact that the dominant European group of

Israeli-Jews does not enjoy such a harmonious cultural relationship with the Mediterranean and Oriental Jews. And the pseudo-science behind 'Second Temple Revivalism' has been undermined by more recent studies. As demonstrated above, most Jewish people have European roots.

A final obstacle to a democratic Palestine, and an asset to Zionism, is the disunity amongst Palestinian groups and parties, and divisions with its regional allies. Numerically smaller peoples can never prevail while they are divided, that is a very old and well-established lesson. Islamic sectarianism in particular has been a key divisive force and helps explain weakened support for the Palestinian leadership. More than half (53%) do not trust any party (JMCC 2018). At the regional level, the main potential Arab ally and neighbour, Egypt, has done little to help Palestine, in recent decades. The resistance has had to rely on Iran, Syria and Hezbollah. Iran's leader Ayatollah Khamenei says differences between Palestinian groups are 'natural and understandable', but 'increasing cooperation and depth' was necessary. Greater unity would build popular confidence, assist in focus and organisation and allow new steps forward (Khamenei 2016).

On the strength side, popular resistance has not gone away, despite 70 years of repression, encirclement and ethnic cleansing. Resistance remains the principal asset, and includes holding ground, building the population and the various forms of active resistance. Resistance also remains the foundation of Palestine's growing moral and international legitimacy, stronger diplomatic relations, increasing rejection of Israel and greater UN recognition of Palestine as a nation. That legitimacy is also expressed powerfully with the relative growth of the Arab-Palestinian population (Reuters 2018; JVL 2017).

The strategic importance of Palestine's regional allies can be seen in the strenuous efforts the Zionist state has made to suppress Hezbollah in Lebanon, to foment the destruction of Syria and to mount constant hysteria over a generalised threat from Iran. These three happen to be the key sources of material support for the resistance. The Gulf Arab monarchies have provided some finance (fomenting corruption) but not weapons. For these reasons Israel fears a strengthened 'Axis of Resistance' after the war on Syria. That Axis will stretch from Tehran to Beirut and will most likely take back Syria's occupied Golan Heights. That, in turn, would be a great morale boost for the Palestinian resistance.

Finally, Israel and its allies remain vulnerable to exposure of ongoing apartheid crimes. That is why Tel Aviv has moved to ban filming of its troops in the occupied territories (DW 2018). Each new crime, such as arrests and killings of civilians, does damage to the Israel 'brand' and helps isolate the regime. Open atrocities and ethnic cleansing keep weakening the old claims that criticisms of Israel are attacks on Jews as historic 'victims' or are somehow 'anti-semitic'.

At the same time the well networked Boycott, Divestment and Sanctions movement agitates against Israel, on the principle that 'Palestinians are entitled to the same rights as the rest of humanity' (BDS 2018). This may not pose a great threat to the Israeli economy in the short term, although the Rand Corporation has estimated 'potential costs at $47bn over 10 years' (White 2017). Others point out that BDS is a 'cultural, psychological battle' more than an economic one. Israel has prepared a 'black list' of those who cannot enter 'the country' (including Palestine) because of links to BDS campaigns (Bahar and Sachs 2018).

The international Jewish community, an important part of this support network, is also being alienated by Israeli crimes. That international network is relied on for financial and moral support. Yet many European and American Jews see themselves as a liberal and tolerant people and are mortified by identification with apartheid atrocities. They have reacted badly to the arrests and massacres of Palestinian protestors and civilians, both in Gaza and the West Bank (Weiss 2018). Even those who do not support the BDS movement shrink from Israel when there is bad publicity. For example, Israeli-born Hollywood actress Natalie Portman turned down $2m and the Israeli 'Genesis' prize because she was too ashamed to be seen with Prime Minister Netanyahu (Spiro 2018). Demoralisation can be seen on a wider scale with the substantial emigration, particularly amongst the large group of Israelis with dual citizenship.

Richard Falk, former UN Special Rapporteur on Occupied Palestine, said he rejected the idea of Palestine as a 'lost cause', because it was winning the legitimacy battle: 'Palestine is winning what in the end is the more important war, the struggle for legitimacy, which is most likely to determine the political outcome'. In the context of anti-colonial struggles, he continues, citing Vietnam, Algeria and Iraq, 'the side with the greater perseverance and resilience, not the side that controlled the battlefield, won in the end' (Falk 2014).

The future of Palestine is clouded with divisions, pain and sacrifice, and with fear of formidable enemies. But it is far from hopeless. There have been real gains in recent years. The Resistance has imposed limits on expansion of the colonial project, both in the north and the south. Attempts to smash and divide the 'Axis of Resistance' are failing. The key weakness has been disunity amongst the Palestinian factions and some fractures with regional allies. The key strength remains the consistent resistance of a battered but brave and resilient people.

Bibliography

Abdullah, Daud and Ibrahim Hewitt (2012) *The Battle for Public Opinion in Europe*, MEMO Publishers, London

Adalah (2017) 'The Discriminatory Laws Database', 25 September, online: https://www.adalah.org/en/content/view/7771

Adams, Jonathan and Cordelia Heß (Editors) (2018) *The Medieval Roots of Antisemitism: Continuities and Discontinuities from the Middle Ages to the Present Day*, Routledge, London

AIC (2011) 'Jerusalem: facts and figures', Alternative Information Center, December, Jerusalem and Beit Sahour, Palestine

Ali (2018) interview with this writer at Dehaisheh camp (Bethlehem), Occupied Palestine, February [*'Ali' is a pseudonym, to protect him from Israeli reprisals*]

Al Jazeera (2016) 'UN votes on ending Israeli settlements', 24 December, online: https://www.aljazeera.com/news/2016/12/set-vote-israeli-settlements-161223163243355.html

Amal (2018) interviews with this writer at Ramallah, Occupied Palestine, February

Amnesty International (2015) 'Palestinian armed groups killed civilians on both sides in attacks amounting to war crimes', 26 March, online: https://www.amnesty.org/en/latest/news/2015/03/palestinian-armed-groups-killed-civilians-on-both-sides-in-2014-gaza-conflict/

Anderson, Colin (2017) *Balfour in the Dock*, Skyscraper, Oxon

Anderson, Colin (2018) 'Another Australian Intellectual Fails the Palestine Test', Middle East Reality Check, 23 May, online: http://middleeastrealitycheck.blogspot.com/2018/05/another-australian-intellectual-fails.html

AP (2014) 'UN says three-fourths of Gaza dead are civilians; Israel says Hamas fires from homes, schools', Fox News, 23 July, online: http://www.foxnews.com/world/2014/07/23/un-says-three-fourths-gaza-dead-are-civilians-israel-says-hamas-fires-from.html

Arad Y., Y. Gutman and A. Margaliot (Editors) (2014) *Documents on the Holocaust: Selected Sources on the Destruction of the Jews of Germany and Austria, Poland, and the Soviet Union*, Pergamon Press, Oxford

Ashly, Jacyln (2017) 'How Israel is disabling Palestinian teenagers', Al Jazeera, 21 September, online: https://www.aljazeera.com/indepth/features/2017/09/israel-disabling-palestinian-teenagers-170911085127509.html

Auerbach, Yehudit (1991) 'Attitudes to an Existence Conflict: Allon and Peres on the Palestinian Issue, 1967-1987', in *Conflict Resolution*, Vol 35 Issue 3, pp. 519-54, DOI: 10.1177/0022002791035003006

Avishai, Bernard (2014) 'Ariel Sharon's Dark Greatness', *The New Yorker*, 13 January, online: https://www.newyorker.com/news/news-desk/ariel-sharons-dark-greatness

BADIL Resource Centre (2015) 'Survey of Palestinian Refugees and Internally Displaced Persons: Vol VIII 2013-2015', Bethlehem, online: https://reliefweb.int/sites/reliefweb.int/files/resources/Survey2013-2015-en.pdf

Bahar, Dany and Natan Sachs (2018) 'How much does BDS threaten Israel's economy?', Brookings Institute, 26 January, online: https://www.brookings.edu/blog/order-from-chaos/2018/01/26/how-much-does-bds-threaten-israels-economy/

Baker, Luke (2015) 'Shadow of Israel's pullout from Gaza hangs heavy 10 years on', Reuters, 11 August, online: https://www.reuters.com/article/us-israel-gaza-disengagement-insight/shadow-of-israels-pullout-from-gaza-hangs-heavy-10-years-on-idUSKCN0QF1QQ20150810

Barnard, Anne and Jodi Rudoren (2014) 'Israel Says That Hamas Uses Civilian Shields, Reviving Debate', *New York Times*, 23 July, online: https://

www.nytimes.com/2014/07/24/world/middleeast/israel-says-hamas-is-using-civilians-as-shields-in-gaza.html

BDS (2018) 'Impact', Palestinian BDS National Committee (BNC), the coalition of Palestinian organisations that leads and supports the BDS movement and by the Palestinian Campaign for Academic and Cultural Boycott of Israel (PACBI), online: https://bdsmovement.net/impact

Beaumont, Peter (2017) 'UNESCO: Israel joins US in quitting UN heritage agency over 'anti-Israel bias', *The Guardian*, 13 October, online: https://www.theguardian.com/world/2017/oct/12/us-withdraw-unesco-december-united-nations

Ben-Meir, Dovid (2016) 'The Preoccupation with an Occupation that Does Not Exist', *Jerusalem Post*, 4 Feb, online: https://www.jpost.com/Blogs/Settled-Knowledge-from-the-Hills/The-Preoccupation-with-an-Occupation-that-Does-Not-Exist-443816

Benton, Sarah (2015) 'Shooting and Crying', Jews for Justice for Palestinians, 27 May, online: http://jfjfp.com/shooting-and-crying/

Bergman, Ronan (2018) *Rise and Kill First*, Random House, New York

Bishara, Marwan (2001) *Palestine Israel: peace or apartheid*, Zed Books, New York

Bransten, Jeremy (2006) 'Middle East: Rice Calls For A 'New Middle East', Radio Free Europe/Radio Liberty, 25 July, online: https://www.rferl.org/a/1070088.html

Bridges, Tyler (2016) 'David Duke's Last Stand', Politico, 3 November, online: https://www.politico.com/magazine/story/2016/11/david-duke-louisiana-debate-214414

Brownfeld, Alan (2000) 'Non-Jewish Immigrants forcing Israel to choose between being a 'Jewish' state and a Democracy', Washington Report on the Middle East, April, online: https://www.wrmea.org/000-april/non-jewish-immigrants-forcing-israel-to-choose-between-being-a-jewish-state-and-a-democracy.html

BTSELEM (2017) 'Settlements', 'The Israeli Information Center for Human Rights in the Occupied Territories', 11 November, online: https://www.btselem.org/settlements

Ceren, Omri (2014) 'EU Blasts Hamas for "Criminal and Unjustifiable" Rocket Attacks, Calls for Disarmament', 23 July, online: http://www.thetower.org/0760oc-eu-blasts-hamas-for-criminal-and-unjustifiable-rocket-attacks-calls-for-disarmament/

Cohen, Patricia (2009) 'Book calls Jewish People an 'Invention', *New York Times*, 23 November, online: https://www.nytimes.com/2009/11/24/books/24jews.html

Costa, Marta D. Joana B. Pereira, Maria Pala, Verónica Fernandes, Anna Olivieri, Alessandro Achilli, Ugo A. Perego, Sergei Rychkov, Oksana

Naumova, Jiři Hatina, Scott R. Woodward, Ken Khong Eng, Vincent Macaulay, Martin Carr, Pedro Soares, Luísa Pereira & Martin B. Richards (2013) 'A substantial prehistoric European ancestry amongst Ashkenazi maternal lineages', *Nature Communications* 4, Article Number: 2543 (2013), 8 October, doi:10.1038/ncomms3543

Clayman, David (1995) 'The law of return reconsidered', Jerusalem Letters of Lasting Interest No. 318   18 Tamuz 5755 / 16 July 1995, Jerusalem Centre for Public Affairs, online: http://www.jcpa.org/jl/hit01.htm

Crooke, Alistair and Mark Perry (2006) 'How Hezbollah Defeated Israel', CounterPunch, 12 October, online: https://www.counterpunch.org/2006/10/12/how-hezbollah-defeated-israel/

Derfner, Larry (2012) 'The late Benzion Netanyahu's appalling views on Arabs', +972Mag, 30 April, online: https://972mag.com/the-late-benzion-netanyahus-appalling-views-on-arabs/44215/

DG EXPO (2013) 'Area C: More than 60 % of the occupied West Bank threatened by Israeli annexation', Directorate General for External Policies, European Union, April, DG EXPO/B/PolDep/Note/2013_138, online: http://www.europarl.europa.eu/RegData/etudes/briefing_note/join/2013/491495/EXPO-AFET_SP(2013)491495_EN.pdf

DW (2018) 'Israel seeks to outlaw filming of soldiers in action', 17 June, online: http://www.dw.com/en/israel-seeks-to-outlaw-filming-of-soldiers-in-action/a-44267455

Eldar, Shlomi (2018) 'Israelis, Palestinians both use demography as political tool', 27 March, online: http://www.al-monitor.com/pulse/originals/2018/03/israel-palestinians-west-bank-gaza-strip-demography-abbas.html#ixzz5GHEEjBy2

Elhaik, Eran (2016) 'How DNA traced the Ashkenazic Jews to northeastern Turkey', Aeon, online: https://aeon.co/ideas/how-dna-traced-the-ashkenazic-jews-to-northeastern-turkey

Entine, John (2013) 'Jewish researcher attacks DNA evidence linking Jews to Israel', Genetic Literacy Project, 13 May, online: https://geneticliteracyproject.org/2013/05/13/jewish-researcher-attacks-dna-evidence-linking-jews-to-israel/

Faittelson, Yakov (2009) 'The Politics of Palestinian Demography', *Middle East Quarterly*, Spring/March, Volume 16: Number 2, online: https://www.meforum.org/articles/2009/the-politics-of-palestinian-demography

Falk, Richard (2014) 'On 'Lost Causes' and the Future of Palestine', *The Nation*, 16 December, online: https://www.thenation.com/article/lost-causes-and-future-palestine/

Falk, Richard and Virginia Tilley (2017) *Palestine - Israel Journal of Politics, Economics, and Culture*; East Jerusalem Vol. 22, Issue 2/3, 191-196; also available here: https://counter-hegemonic-studies.net/israeli-apartheid/

Ghose, Tia (2013) 'Surprise: Ashkenazi Jews Are Genetically European', *Live Science*, 8 October, online: https://www.livescience.com/40247-ashkenazi-jews-have-european-genes.html

Gilbert, Martin (2014) *The Holocaust*, Rosetta Books, New York

Goldman, Nahum (1978) *The Jewish Paradox : A Personal Memoir*, Grosset & Dunlap, New York

Gutman, Yisrael and Michael Berenbaum (Editor) (1998) *Anatomy of the Auschwitz Death Camp*, Indiana University Press, Bloomington, Indiana

Hamayel, Mohammad (2016) 'Israeli military practice kneecapping against Palestinians', Press TV, 29 August, online: http://www.presstv.com/Detail/2016/08/29/482147/Israeli-military-kneecapping-Palestinians

Hammond, Jeremy (2010) 'The Myth of the U.N. Creation of Israel', *Foreign Policy Journal,* 26 October, online: https://www.foreignpolicyjournal.com/2010/10/26/the-myth-of-the-u-n-creation-of-israel/

Harel, Amos (2009) 'Shooting and Crying', Haaretz, 19 March, online: https://www.haaretz.com/1.5090830

Hart, Alan (2009) *Zionism: The Real Enemy of the Jews*, Clarity Press, Atlanta

Hass, Amira (2016) 'Is the IDF Conducting a Kneecapping Campaign in the West Bank?', *Haaretz,* 27 August, online: https://www.haaretz.com/israel-news/is-the-idf-conducting-a-kneecapping-campaign-in-the-west-bank-1.5429695

Heller, Jeffrey (2018) 'Jews, Arabs nearing population parity in Holy Land: Israeli officials', Reuters, 27 march, online: https://www.reuters.com/article/us-israel-palestinians-population/jews-arabs-nearing-population-parity-in-holy-land-israeli-officials-idUSKBN1H222T

Hertzberg, Daniel (1959) *The Zionist Idea: A Historical Analysis and Reader,* The Jewish Publication Society, Philadelphia

Herzl, Theodor (1960) *Complete Diaries,* Vol II, Hertzl Press, New York

Hever, Shir (2007) 'The separation wall in east Jerusalem: economic consequences', Alternative Information Center, January-February, Jerusalem and Beit Sahour, Palestine

Hirst, David (2003) 'The war game', *The Guardian,* 21 September, online: https://www.theguardian.com/world/2003/sep/21/israelandthepalestinians.bookextracts

Hourani, Albert (1991) *A History of the Arab Peoples*, Faber and Faber, London

IIT (2012) 'Iranian Arms Change Equation in battle between Gaza, "Israel"', 20 November, online: http://www.islamicinvitationturkey.com/2012/11/20/iranian-arms-change-equation-in-battle-between-gaza-israel/

IIT (2016) 'Iran to pay 7000 dollars for martyred Palestinian families and

30,000 dollars for demolished houses', Islamic Invitation Turkey, 27 February, online: http://www.islamicinvitationturkey.com/2016/02/27/iran-to-pay-7000-dollars-for-martyred-families-and-30000-dollars-for-demolished-houses/

Isaacs, Alick (2005) 'The destruction of the Second temple', The Jewish Agency for Israel, 23 August, online: http://www.jewishagency.org/jerusalem/content/23693

Jefferies, J.M.N. (2014) *The Palestine Deception 1915-1923*, Institute for Palestine Studies, Maryland (USA)

JMCC (2016) 'Poll No. 87 - July 2016 - Local Elections & Stalled Negotiations', Jerusalem Media & Communication Centre, 26 July, online: http://www.jmcc.org/documentsandmaps.aspx?id=872

JMCC (2017) 'Poll No. 90 - Trump, the Peace Process & Elections', Jerusalem Media and Communication Centre', 6 September, online: http://www.jmcc.org/documentsandmaps.aspx?id=875

JMCC (2018) 'Poll No. 91 - Trump's Jerusalem Decision & Freedom of Expression', Jerusalem Media & Communication Centre, 24 February, online: http://www.jmcc.org/documentsandmaps.aspx?id=878

JPost (2018) 'Lieberman: Israel must immediately withdraw from U.N. Human Rights Council', *Jerusalem Post*, 17 May, online: https://www.jpost.com/Breaking-News/Liberman-Israel-must-withdraw-immediately-from-UN-Human-Rights-Council-556701

JVL (2017) 'Demographics of Israel: Jewish & Non-Jewish Population of Israel/Palestine (1517 - Present), Jewish Virtual Library, online: http://www.jewishvirtuallibrary.org/jewish-and-non-jewish-population-of-israel-palestine-1517-present

JVL (2018) 'Israel International Relations: International Recognition of Israel', Jewish Virtual Library, online: http://www.jewishvirtuallibrary.org/international-recognition-of-israel

Khalidi, Rashid, Lisa Anderson, Muhammad Muslih and Reeva Simon (Editors) (2010) *The Origins of Arab Nationalism*, Colombia University Press, New York

Khamenei, Ayatollah (2016) 'Discord is enemy's tool to dominate Muslim nations: Ayatollah Khamenei', 17 December, Khamenei.ir, online: http://english.khamenei.ir/news/4455/Discord-is-enemy-s-tool-to-dominate-Muslim-nations-Ayatollah

Khamenei, Ayatollah (2017) 'We are with every group that is steadfast on the path of resistance: Ayatollah Khamenei', Khamenei.ir, 21 Feb, online: http://english.khamenei.ir/news/4644/We-are-with-every-group-that-is-steadfast-on-the-path-of-Resistance

Klingbail, Sivan and Shanee Shiloh (2012) 'Bye the beloved Country – why almost 40 percent of Israelis are thinking of emigrating', *Haaretz*,

15 December, online: https://www.haaretz.com/.premium-bye-the-beloved-country-1.5273011
Knesset (2014) 'Constitution for Israel: The State of Israel as a Jewish State', online: http://knesset.gov.il/constitution/ConstMJewishState.htm
Leverett, Flynt and Hilary Mann Leverett (2014) 'The Two State Solution is dead', The National Interest, online: http://nationalinterest.org/feature/the-two-state-solution-dead-10862
Levy, Gideon (2018) 'Sixty-seven Things Gideon Levy Loves About Israel', *Haaretz*, 25 April, online: https://www.haaretz.com/opinion/.premium.MAGAZINE-gideon-levy-finds-67-things-he-loves-about-israel-1.6027888
Leibowitz, Ruthie Blum (2007) 'I didn't suggest we kill Palestinians', *Jerusalem Post*, 10 October, online: https://www.jpost.com/Features/I-didnt-suggest-we-kill-Palestinians
Lieber, Dov (2017) 'The rise of Raed Salah, Israel's Islamist leader who wants Jerusalem at the heart of a caliphate', *Times of Israel*, 16 August, online: https://www.timesofisrael.com/the-rise-of-raed-salah-israels-islamist-leader-who-wants-jerusalem-at-the-heart-of-a-caliphate/
Lynch, Jake (2009) 'Politicide or politic: Gillard and the Gaza muzzle', *Sydney Morning Herald*, 10 July, online: https://www.smh.com.au/politics/federal/politicide-or-politic-gillard-and-the-gaza-muzzle-20090709-deju.html
Ma'an (2014) 'Death toll in Gaza hits 1,088 as Israel resumes bombardment', Ma'an News Agency, 29 July, online: http://www.maannews.com/Content.aspx?id=716726
Masalha, Salman (2017) 'Ashkenazi Jews are to Blame for Israel's Ethnic Rift', *Haaretz*, 3 March, online: https://www.haaretz.com/opinion/.premium-ashkenazi-jews-are-to-blame-for-israels-ethnic-rift-1.5444531
Morrison, David (2018) 'The ICC Prosecutor Warns Israel about Gaza Killings', *American Herald Tribune*, 9 June, online: https://ahtribune.com/world/north-africa-south-west-asia/palestine/2295-icc-prosecutor-gaza-killings.html
MSPUN (2013) 'Status of Palestine', Mission of the State of Palestine to the UN, 1 August, online: http://palestineun.org/status-of-palestine-at-the-united-nations/
MSPUN (2018) 'Diplomatic relations', Mission of the State of Palestine to the UN, online: http://palestineun.org/about-palestine/diplomatic-relations/
Naji (2018) interview with this writer at Bethlehem, Occupied Palestine, February
Nathan, Julie (2017a) 'Can There Be Judaism Without Zionism?', ABC Religion and Ethics, 1 August, online: http://www.abc.net.au/religion/

articles/2017/08/01/4711094.htm
Nathan, Julie (2017b) 'Antisemitism on parade', J-Wire, 24 February, online: http://www.jwire.com.au/antisemitism-on-parade/
Nirenberg, David (2013) *Anti-Judaism: The Western Tradition*, W.W. Norton, New York
NKI (2018) 'Neturei Karta International', online: http://www.nkusa.org
Ostrer, Harry (2001) 'A genetic profile of contemporary Jewish populations', *Nature Reviews: Genetics,* Vol2, November, 891-898, online: https://www.nature.com/articles/35098506.pdf
Ostrer, Harry (2010) 'Abraham's Children in the Genome Era: Major Jewish Diaspora Populations Comprise Distinct Genetic Clusters with Shared Middle Eastern Ancestry', *The American Journal of Human Genetics,* June, 43(6), DOI10.1016/j.ajhg.2010.04.015
Ostrer, Harry and Karl Skorecki (2012) 'The population genetics of the Jewish people', *Human Genetics*, 10 October, online: https://link.springer.com/article/10.1007%2Fs00439-012-1235-6
Pappe, Ilan (2006) *The Ethnic Cleansing of Palestine*, Oneworld Publications, London
Pappe, Ilan (2014) 'Israel's incremental genocide in the Gaza ghetto', Electronic Intifada, 13 July, online: https://electronicintifada.net/content/israels-incremental-genocide-gaza-ghetto/13562
Pedatzur, Reuven (2007) 'The 'Jordanian Option,' the Plan That Refuses to Die', *Haaretz*, 25 July, online: https://www.haaretz.com/1.4954947
Phillips, Laura; Arianna Lissoni and Ivor Chipkin (2014) 'Bantustans are dead - long live the Bantustans', *Mail and Guardian,* 11 July, online: https://mg.co.za/article/2014-07-10-bantustans-are-dead-long-live-the-bantustans
Provence, Michael (2005) *The Great Syrian Revolt*, University of Texas Press, Austin
Qumsiyeh, Mazin B. (2011) *Popular Resistance in Palestine: a history of hope and empowerment,* Pluto Press, London
Reeves, Philip (2013) 'On Multiple Fronts, Russian Jews Reshape Israel', NPR, 2 January, online: https://www.npr.org/2013/01/02/168457444/on-multiple-fronts-russian-jews-reshape-israel
Reinhart, Tania (2006) *The Road Map to Nowhere*, Verso, London
Reuters (2010) 'Israel can't defeat Hezbollah: Israeli expert', 16 December, online: https://www.reuters.com/article/us-israel-lebanon/israel-cant-defeat-hezbollah-israeli-expert-idUSTRE6BF20L20101216
Rubin, Rita (2013) 'Jews a Race' Genetic Theory comes under fierce attack by DNA expert', *Forward,* 7 May, online: https://forward.com/news/israel/175912/jews-a-race-genetic-theory-comes-under-fierce-atta/
Ryan, Caitlin (2015) 'Everyday resilience as resistance: Palestinian women

practicing Sumud', *International Political Sociology*, Vol 9 Issue 4, December, https://doi.org/10.1111/ips.12099

Sa'di, Ahmad H. and Lila Abu-Lughod (2007) *Nakba: Palestine, 1948, and the Claims of Memory*, Colombia University Press, New York

Sales, Ben (2017) 'Can Israel bring home its million US expats?', *Jerusalem Post*, 1 August, online: https://www.jpost.com/Diaspora/Why-more-Israelis-are-moving-to-the-US-501301

Sand, Shlomo (2010) *The Invention of the Jewish People*, Verso, London

Segev, Tom (1999) One Palestine Complete, Abacus, London

Shadid, Mohammed K. (1988) 'The Muslim Brotherhood Movement in the West Bank and Gaza', *Third World Quarterly*, Vol. 10, No. 2, Islam & Politics (Apr., 1988), pp. 658-682

Shasha, David (2010) 'Sephardim, Ashkenazim, and Ultra-Orthodox Racism in Israel', HuffPost, 21 June, online: https://www.huffingtonpost.com/david-shasha/sephardim-ashkenazim-and_b_615692.html

Shlaim, Avi (2001) *The Iron Wall*, W. W. Norton Company, New York

Singh Sarila, Narendra (2005) The Shadow of the Great Game, Harper Collins, Noida (India)

Spiro, (2018) Natalie Portman: I'm not pro-BDS, I'm anti Netanyahu', *Jerusalem Post*, 21 April, online: https://www.jpost.com/Israel-News/Culture/Natalie-Portman-Im-not-pro-BDS-Im-anti-Netanyahu-551384

Streicher, Julius (1938) Speech of 21 April 1932 in *Kampf dem Weltfeind*, Stürmer Publishing House, Nuremberg

Streicher, Julius (1945) 'Julius Streicher's Political Testament: My Affirmation', *Der Stürmer*, 3 August, online: http://der-stuermer.blogspot.com.au/2015/09/julius-streichers-political-testament.html

Talhami, Ghada Hashem (2001) *Syria and the Palestinians*, University Press of Florida, Gainesville

Tekuma, Moshav (2009) 'How Israel Helped to Spawn Hamas', *Wall Street Journal*, 24 January, online: http://web.archive.org/web/20090926212507/http:/online.wsj.com/article/SB123275572295011847.html

TOI (2016) 'Netanyahu ally: West Bank annexation would be 'a disaster', *Times of Israel*, 31 December, online: https://www.timesofisrael.com/netanyahu-ally-west-bank-annexation-would-be-a-disaster/

TOI (2018) 'Court overturns decision to free Islamist cleric accused of incitement', *Times of Israel*, 30 march, online: https://www.timesofisrael.com/court-overturns-decision-to-free-islamist-cleric-accused-of-incitement/

Trachtenberg, Joshua (2014) *The Devil and the Jews: The Medieval Conception of the Jew and Its Relation to Modern Anti-Semitism*, The Jewish Publication Society, Philadelphia

TTJ (2018) 'True Torah, Jews Against Zionism', online: http://www.

truetorahjews.org

Tuchman, Barbara (1956) B*ible and Sword: how the British came to Palestine*, Papermac, London

UNGA (1947) 'Resolution 181 (II). Future government of Palestine', United Nations General Assembly, 29 November, online: https://unispal.un.org/DPA/DPR/unispal.nsf/0/7F0AF2BD897689B785256C330061D253

UNGA (1974) 'Importance of the universal realization of the right of peoples to self-determination and of the speedy granting of independence to colonial countries and peoples for the effective guarantee and observance of human rights', A/RES/3246 (XXIX), 29 November, online: https://unispal.un.org/DPA/DPR/unispal.nsf/0/C867EE1DBF29A6E5852568C6006B2F0C

UNGA (1978) 'Resolution A/RES/33/24 'Importance of the universal realization of the right of peoples to self-determination and of the speedy granting of independence to colonial countries and peoples for the effective guarantee and observance of human rights', 29 November, online: https://unispal.un.org/DPA/DPR/unispal.nsf/0/D7340F04B82A2CB085256A9D006BA47A

UNGA (2012) 'General Assembly Votes Overwhelmingly to Accord Palestine 'Non-Member Observer State' Status in United Nations', 29 November, online: https://www.un.org/press/en/2012/ga11317.doc.htm

UNGA (2017) 'General Assembly Overwhelmingly Adopts Resolution Asking Nations Not to Locate Diplomatic Missions in Jerusalem', 21 December, online: https://www.un.org/press/en/2017/ga11995.doc.htm

UNISPAL (1967) 'Security Council: Resolution 242 (1967) of 22 November 1967, United Nations: Question of Palestine, online: https://unispal.un.org/DPA/DPR/unispal.nsf/0/7D35E1F729DF491C85256EE700686136

UN News Centre (2004) 'International Court of Justice finds Israeli barrier in Palestinian territory is illegal', UN News, 9 July, online: https://news.un.org/en/story/2004/07/108912-international-court-justice-finds-israeli-barrier-palestinian-territory-illegal

UWI (2014) 'More IDF Casualties in Gaza Operation', United With Israel', United With Israel, 28 July, online: https://unitedwithisrael.org/more-idf-casualties-in-gaza-operation/

Vidal, Dominique (1997) 'The expulsion of the Palestinians re-examined', *le Monde Diplomatique*, December, online: https://mondediplo.com/1997/12/palestine

Wadi, Ramona (2018) 'How Israel Dehumanises Palestinian Resistance', Middle East Eye, 23 April, online: http://www.middleeasteye.net/columns/

how-israel-dehumanises-palestinian-resistance-1670727322

Walker, Richard (2014) 'Tens of thousands of Jews leaving Israel for Germany', American Free Press, 26 October, online: http://americanfreepress.net/tens-of-thousands-of-jews-leaving-israel-for-germany/

Weiss, Phillip (2018) 'Israel just lost American Jews', MondoWeiss, 5 April, online: http://mondoweiss.net/2018/04/israel-just-american/

White, Ben (2017) 'BDS' effect on Israel', Middle East Monitor, 29 November, online: https://www.middleeastmonitor.com/20171129-international-day-of-solidarity-with-the-palestinian-people-2/

Yehoshua, A.B. (2018) 'Time to Say Goodbye to the Two-state Solution. Here's the Alternative', *Haaretz*, 19 April, online: https://www.haaretz.com/israel-news/.premium.MAGAZINE-time-to-nix-the-two-state-solution-and-stop-israel-s-apartheid-1.6011274

Yinon, Oded (1982) 'A Strategy for Israel in the Nineteen Eighties', Redress Online, (Originally in Hebrew in KIVUNIM (Directions), *A Journal for Judaism and Zionism,* Issue No 4, Winter 5742, February 1982), online: http://www.redressonline.com/wp-content/uploads/2016/03/A-Strategy-for-Israel-in-the-Nineteen-Eighties-Oded-Yinon.pdf

Chapter Thirteen

HEZBOLLAH AND THE REGIONAL RESISTANCE

Nasrallah: International Coalition to fight ISIS is a US cloak to re-occupy the region

2014

Axis of Resistance

Sayyed Hassan Nasrallah: "The US is not morally qualified to lead an anti-terrorism coalition because it is the mother of terrorism as it supports the terrorist entity (Israel). The US has participated in creating terrorist groups in Syria, Iraq and in other countries ... we are against ISIS and all other takfiri organizations because they constitute a threat to all the peoples of the region."

Since it expelled Israel from Lebanon, Hezbollah has enjoyed tremendous moral authority in the Arab and Muslim world

The Lebanese resistance party Hezbollah can seem a mystery. Despite its foundations as a Shi'a religious group, it has developed much wider influence in Lebanon, integrating within national structures while forming alliances across communities. Its religious foundations and close relationship with Iran lead to simple criticisms of Shi'a-Muslim 'sectarianism'. Such criticism ignores its coalition with progressive Christians and its close support for the mainly Sunni-Muslim Palestinian resistance. And while branded 'terrorist' by some western governments - mainly because of its opposition to Israel - it has proven itself a key force against the western-backed al Qaeda groups which have plagued the entire region. Hezbollah has lost well over 2,000 volunteer soldiers, defending both Lebanon and secular Syria.

Further afield, the Popular Mobilisation Forces of Iraq (PMU or Hashid al Shaabi), which led Iraq's crushing of the Saudi-backed DAESH terrorists, were modelled on Hezbollah and Iran's Basiji (volunteer forces). The PMU, like Hezbollah, harnessed religious zeal to defend and preserve a mainly 'secular' or pluralist state. Western and Israeli abuse of Hezbollah has spread confusion; but most in the region recognise it as the group which drove Israel from Lebanon. For all these reasons the Hezbollah phenomenon deserves study.

Lebanon, like many post-colonial states, was crippled by colonial design, partitioned from the rest of the Levant region and founded on a 'confessional' system designed to keep the ruling hand with an artificial majority of Maronite Christians. Partition and the creation of a weak state has often been used to enhance the options of former colonial and imperial powers. It happened in Ireland, India-Pakistan, Colombia-Panama, Iraq-Kuwait and in the fragments of the former Yugoslavia. There have been similar attempts to 'balkanise' both Iraq and Syria. Yet fragmentation is strenuously opposed in strong nations. The USA fought a bloody civil war in the 19th century, primarily to defend its union. Only weak nations acquiesce to partition.

In the case of Lebanon, essentially a state set up by the colonists to fail – with sectarian and privatised 'solutions' to all types of national challenges – it was traditional, religious mobilisation which strengthened the nation. A similar process occurred in Iraq, when popular militia were created to destroy the US-backed, Saudi-armed terrorist group DAESH. Those processes drew on important values in Arab and religious traditions. After addressing some of the popular myths about Hezbollah and the group's standing in Lebanon, this chapter sets out to explain the rise of a similar resistance movement in post-invasion Iraq.

1. Sectarian or Nationalist?

Hezbollah's religiously motivated contribution to Lebanese nationalism is not unique. Syria's nationalism also drew on traditional values. Resistance to French 'mandate rule' began early, and 'local people worked out for themselves what it meant to be part of a larger community'. This 'Syrian Arab' nationalism was not merely a function of urban modernism, as 'eventually the countryside came to lead the city', developing its own ideas 'of a larger Syrian nation' (Provence 2005: 48-49). In the case of Sultan al Atrash, a Druze Sheikh leader from Sweida, the catalysing moment was when French forces violated the sanctity of his home and hospitality by arresting Lebanese Muslim Adham Khanjar. As Provence (2005: 3-4) puts it 'according to customary law and Arab codes of honor, a guest who sought protection had to be welcomed and protected by his host.' That incident sparked attacks by Atrash on French forces. His popular theme was 'Religion is for God, the Nation is for all' (Zubaida 2011: 94; Mansour al Atrash 2018). Of course the Syrian Druze, like the Lebanese Shi'a, were minorities who favoured an independent, pluralist state. They sought neither a chauvinist religious state nor a sectarian enclave.

The Arab nationalism fomented in the early 20th century (Khalidi, Anderson, Muslih and Simon 1991) was 'secular' (almaniyya) based on its own terms and history. The Wafd Party in Egypt, for example, was called Hizb Almani, the secular party, not because it opposed religion but because it rejected a religious/ Islamic state (Najjar 1996: 2). This was distinct from secularism in Europe and Latin America, where states at times opposed religion, or reconstructed it, depending on the histories of earlier religious regimes and empires (Keddie 2004: 23, 25). Religious minorities, such as Christians, Shi'a Muslims and Druze sought refuge in the pluralist context of Syria. Syrian President Bashar al Assad (2017) has stressed that Syria's Arab nationalism does not exclude religion, though it is pluralistic and opposed to extremism.

It is not too hard to accept in principle that religious groups are not, ipso facto, sectarian. Rarely do European critics of Arab states call their own diverse Christian traditions 'sectarian'. The Christian influence is often said to have been absorbed into wider currents of western 'secular democracies', usually without reference to the colonial tradition. 'Sectarianism' is a term that has become reserved for the anti-colonial resistance. Actual sectarianism is usually associated with empires, or at least those Saudi wahhabis and other salafis who pretend to speak on behalf of the region's majority Sunni Muslims, rejecting respectful relations with other communities and insisting on dominance of their own doctrine (Allen 2007; Meijer 2009).

In the case of Hezbollah we could say that it was not Shi'a chauvinism but rather the impetus of a religious movement, which contributed to its political nationalism. In recent years the rising influence of Hezbollah within Lebanon has mainly come from its allies in other religious communities. Hezbollah had strong support from the Shi'a community long ago (Saad-Ghorayeb 2002). Yet a powerful mythology has been built around the group due to zionist and imperial frustration at its resistance role.

For their own strategic reasons, in particular to discredit the resistance, Washington-aligned sources have often predicted that indigenous Shia initiatives would be sectarian and internally destabilising (Hauslohner 2013). And sectarianism has been manufactured. The civil war in Lebanon was initially a Christian versus Muslim confrontation, aggravated by Israeli and Western interventions. Some Christian factions collaborated with Israel in the repression of Palestinian and Lebanese Muslim communities. However, after the Islamic Revolution in Iran, and the expulsion of the US from that country, a Sunni-Shia divide began to be promoted by the US military and its agents, in particular the Saudis.

In the 1980s Washington had built a new relationship with the most sectarian forms of Islam, in particular the extremist Deobandis from South Asia, trained by Saudi Arabia's wahhabis and Pakistan's ISI (Rashid 1999: 27). These in turn developed alliances with the extremist Salafis, mentored by Saudi Arabia and other Persian Gulf monarchies (Gause 2011). The administration of George W. Bush (2001-2009) used religion through the Saudis to foment violence in Iraq in attempts to keep that battered nation away from its big neighbour, Iran (Hersh 2007). A Pentagon 'Red Team' was created in 2006 'to examine a political narrative that perpetually pits Arabs and Iranians ('Persians') against each other'. Drawing on a Saudi-backed argument that 'many Arabs are fearful of Persian expansion and hegemony' the US military conclusion was that 'there does not appear to be a scenario where Arabs and Persians will join forces against the US/West' (Narwani 2011). The exercise had much to do with how to 'manage' both the Sunni Palestinian group Hamas and Lebanon's Shi'a Hezbollah. This exposed some differences in the ways the Pentagon and its key regional ally Israel saw Hezbollah. At times the Red Team 'downplayed' the Israeli suggestion that Hezbollah was a 'proxy for Iran', recognising its commitment to Lebanon (Perry 2010).

Regardless of these machinations, it is certainly true that Hezbollah's roots and foundation are as a Shi'a religious party, and also that the religious authority of Iran's leaders is recognised. However, that is not the whole story. Hezbollah has a mature political presence, as leaders of a resistance movement and defenders of Lebanon. It is insufficient to say, as does Itani (2007: 2) that Hezbollah 'is not a Lebanese nationalist movement, nor has it ever been one'; or that that it is a sectarian Shia group which wants to establish an Islamic State (Worrall, Mabon and Clubb 2016: 102). Such statements are only half true.

Itani (2007) does recognise that Hezbollah enjoys broader support within Lebanon, and that it is not a 'tool of Iran'; and he correctly points to the group's religious foundations. Sheikh

Naim Qassem, the party's deputy leader, wrote the definitive early history of the movement, beginning with Imam Mussa al Sadr's creation of predecessor groups, the 'Movement of the Oppressed' and the 'Ranks of the Lebanese Resistance' (AMAL) (Qassem 2005: 14-15). After the Iranian Revolution of 1979 and the massive Israeli invasion of 1982, a reconfiguration of groups took place, which eventually led to the birth of Hezbollah in 1985. This was a defensive Islamic movement with 'three pillars' which were and still are: Belief in Islam, Jihad (as both an internal and external struggle) and Jurisdiction of the Jurist-Theologian (al Wali al Faqih). Within these principles, notably, are commitments to an Islamic state (yet non-sectarian and based on free choice and not imposition) and valuing martyrdom for a just cause, as distinct from suicide (Qassem 2005: 21-58).

So while the party remains committed to an all-encompassing Islamic-based system, politically and in the context of Lebanon it has stressed non-sectarianism and voluntarism, using a scriptural basis to reject compulsion on questions of religious affiliation. It has adapted to social reality. As a Lebanese academic points out, a Hezbollah-led Islamic state in Lebanon 'would not only be rejected outright by Lebanese Christians, Sunnis and Druze, but even by a significant portion of the Shi'ite community'. She cites a 1992 study which said that only 13% of Shi'ites supported the idea of an Islamic republic in Lebanon (Saad-Ghorayeb 2002: 35)

The Hezbollah leadership, after the Taif Accords of 1989-90, calculated and decided to participate electorally in existing state structures. This decision was taken very seriously, as it was seen as giving legitimacy to 'a confessional system that does not represent Hizbullah's view of an ideal system' (Qassem 2005: 188). It would mean, in effect, putting aside the ideal of an Islamic state. The Hezbollah leadership group voted 10 to 2 in favour of participation, and the group's designated religious authority ('jurist-theologian'), Iran's Imam Khamenei, agreed with the move. Hezbollah then took part in the country's 1992 elections (Qassem 2005: 187-191).

While drawing on Islamic inspiration, in particular

from the Iranian Revolution, Hezbollah has principally acted to defend Lebanon. It has broadly accepted the pluralist nature of the Lebanese nation. That is why it has been described as 'a nationalist entity that defines itself primarily within the Lebanese polity, as well as an anti-imperialist party intent on countering the regional hegemony of Israel and the USA' (Husseini 2010: 803).

The relationships Hezbollah enjoys with the mostly Sunni Muslim Palestinian resistance and with secular Syria cannot be understood through sectarian ties. The Lebanese Shi'a group has even supported some anti-Shi'a Palestinian Muslim Brotherhood linked groups, such as Hamas (Husseini 2010: 811-812). Its expulsion of the Israeli invasion of 2006 earned it very broad support within Lebanon and the region. Within Lebanon it gained 87% national support for its resistance activity. That included 89% from Sunni Muslims and 80% from the Christians (BCRI 2006). Yet prior to the war on Syria, its ties with secular Syria were said to be a 'loveless marriage', merely a relationship of convenience (Husseini 2010). The more than 2,000 lives Hezbollah sacrificed in defence of Syria (Atrache 2017; Taheri 2018; Jones and Markusen 2018) suggest that this marriage was not so loveless.

2. 'Terrorist' or liberation movement?

No serious, independent analyst regards Hezbollah as simply a 'terrorist' organisation. That is merely the slogan from Washington and Tel Aviv, whose ambitions have been frustrated by the resistance group. British academics Worrall, Mabon and Clubb (2016: 18), who are critical of the group, conclude that 'Hezbollah cannot be simply dismissed as a terrorist organisation as this underplays the vast legitimacy it has within the Lebanese political system and the vast diversity of its operations and identity'. Indeed, Hezbollah has a solid and well-known geographical home base from which it has defended both Lebanon and Syria from Israel and from the extremist proxies (such as DAESH and Jabhat al Nusra) used by Washington and its allies.

Nevertheless, demonisation of the group is relentless. In November 2018 the US Treasury announced a new series of economic measures against Hezbollah and its officials, claiming the group sought to 'undermine Iraqi sovereignty and destabilise the Middle East'. In October the US Justice department called Hezbollah a top 'transnational criminal organisation' (Risk 2018). Why all the concern? Hezbollah is targeted mainly because of its operations against colonial Israel, its opposition to Israeli collaborators during the civil war, its support for the Palestinian resistance and its links to forces which drove US and French troops out of Lebanon in the early 1980s. The handful of overseas attacks on Israeli or Jewish targets attributed to Hezbollah are, for the most part, contentious and unproven.

It was not Hezbollah, formed in 1985 (Qassem 2005: 98), but rather precursor resistance groups which attacked and killed US and French troops in Beirut in late 1983, after those foreign 'peacekeepers' began partisan engagement in the civil war (Husseini 2010: 803). A little background is necessary.

In June 1982 the Israelis once again invaded Lebanon, reaching and bombing Beirut in their mission to drive the Palestine Liberation Organisation (PLO) from its bases in Lebanon. As the Lebanese Government was non-functional, due to the civil war, a UN force was organised to help Israel do this. 14,000 PLO fighters were evacuated from Beirut, many to Tunisia. In September the Phalange-led, Israeli-backed South Lebanese Army committed the Sabra and Chatila massacres in South Beirut. Between 700 and 3000 displaced persons were killed, mostly Palestinians and Lebanese Shi'a (MEMO 2017; IMEU 2018). The massacre was carried out by Lebanese fascists but was set up and organised by Israeli Defence Minister Ariel Sharon (MEMO 2017). The SLA and the Phalange Party did Israel's dirty work. Days later Phalangist leader and President-elect, Bachir Gemayel, was assassinated. He was succeeded as President by his brother Amine (IMEU 2018).

The following year the French and US 'peacekeepers', which had overseen the evacuation of PLO fighters, began to take an active and partisan role in Lebanon's civil war. They were seen by many Lebanese as backing both Israel and the Phalangist-led regime. In April 1983 the US Embassy was bombed, with

63 people killed. In October 1983 two truck bombs hit barracks holding US and French troops: 307 were killed, 241 US troops, 58 French, 6 civilians and the 2 truck bombers (Sahimi 2009; DODC 1983). In February 1984 US troops began their withdrawal from Lebanon. A US inquiry reasonably concluded that the attack was on 'US objectives' in Lebanon, not on its UN 'peacekeeper' functions. The report also said that "the 23 October 1983 bombing of the BLT Headquarters building was a terrorist act sponsored by sovereign states or organized political entities for the purpose of defeating U.S. objectives in Lebanon" (DODC 1983). The US had no legitimate objectives in Syria.

No-one was prosecuted for these attacks (Sahimi 2009) but the US pointed its finger at what were seen as predecessors or associates of Hezbollah. The resistance group, for its part, denied involvement but applauded the attacks, regarding the US and French troops as invaders who were backing both Israel and the Gemayel regime. The then Hezbollah leader Hussayn al Mussawi said it would be 'immoral' to unjustly take credit for the attack (Saad-Ghorayeb 2002: 100-101), as they had not carried it out. But they approved. This background is essential to an understanding of US hostility towards Hezbollah.

The resistance group party also denies that it participated in the kidnaping of foreigners and civilians during the 1980s. However other Lebanese Islamic groups, in particular Islamic Jihad, did so. These kidnappings were described as 'reactionary expressions against international parties ... and bargaining chips for detainees held in some foreign states' (Qassem 2005: 230-232). Hundreds of Lebanese Muslims had been kidnapped and tortured between 1982 and 1983, allegedly by Maronite militia and Israelis. Those kidnapped by the Muslim groups were used as currency in prisoner swaps. Foreigners were also targeted, since the western powers supported the Gemayel regime and Israel. Kidnapping civilians, with a high likelihood of their release, seems to have been viewed by Hezbollah with some with tolerance in the circumstances of the civil war, and seen as morally distinct from killing civilians (Saad-Ghorayeb 2002: 98-101). However,

Hezbollah deputy leader Sheikh Naim Qassem maintained that Hezbollah has always openly acknowledged its resistance activities and did not abduct any 'foreigners' in Lebanon (Qassem 2005: 228-234).

The Taif Accords of 1989-90 put an end to Lebanon's civil war and opened a new era in national politics. Hezbollah criticised the accords as 'preserving the sectarian substance' of Lebanon's political system, maintaining 'confessional' divisions with a privileged position for Maronite Christians. However, it saw the agreement's redeeming features as marking the end of the civil war and making a commitment to future abolition of political sectarianism (Saad-Ghorayeb 2002: 27). Thereafter Hezbollah assumed a role within the constraints of 'Lebanisation', or more 'normal' Lebanese political life. Hezbollah and Syria (and later the Lebanese state) came to an agreement to allow the resistance group to maintain arms to defend the country from Israel (Saad-Ghorayeb 2002: 53).

Indeed, it was the constant harassment by Hezbollah which led to Israeli withdrawal in 2000. The group launched an average of 140 attacks every month on Israeli forces (i.e. several each day) in 1999-2000, the last year of the occupation (Worrall, Mabon and Clubb 2016: 51), demonstrating their guerrilla strategy of 'winning through a thousand small victories'. By that time outside observers noted that most Lebanese also regarded the Syrian presence as a 'necessary evil', to prevent Israeli annexation of territory (Marlowe 2000). When Israel invaded again in July 2006, in an attempt to disarm the group, Hezbollah drove out the zionist forces in a humiliating retreat in just over a month (Erlanger and Oppel 2006; Sousa 2014; Worrall, Mabon and Clubb 2016: 50-57). That sealed the reputation of the resistance group in Lebanon, and in the Arab world. Hezbollah's humiliation of Israel remains at the root of the insistence by the zionist state that the resistance group is 'terrorist'.

The 'terrorist' claim against Hezbollah has been sustained by allegations of attacks on 'soft' Israeli or Jewish targets in other countries. These include attacks in Argentina in the 1990s and several between 2005 to 2014 in Azerbaijan, Egypt, Turkey, Bulgaria, Georgia, Nigeria, Thailand and Peru (Worrall, Mabon and Clubb 2016: 66-67). Most of these claims are disputed and unsubstantiated.

The Israeli embassy in the Argentine capital of Buenos Aires was bombed in 1992; that was followed by the 1994 bombing of an Israeli community centre (AMIA), where dozens were killed and hundreds injured (Brooke 1994). The Islamic Jihad organization was said to have claimed responsibility for the Embassy bombing, but both Iran and Hezbollah were accused by Israel and the USA. They claimed Islamic Jihad was a 'covername' for Hezbollah (FAS 1992); Hezbollah denies this (Qassem 2005: 232-233). The investigation and prosecutions of the AMIA bombing were long, scandal ridden and inconclusive. Two presidents of Argentina, Carlos Menem and Cristina Fernandez, were drawn into the series of scandals. Fabricated evidence was exposed and, as independent investigative journalist Gareth Porter wrote, 'it is impossible to avoid the conclusion that the case against Iran over the AMIA bombing has been driven from the beginning by US enmity towards Iran, not by a desire to find the real perpetrators' (Porter 2008).

Israel blamed Hezbollah for a bombing in Istanbul in 2011, but Turkish authorities blamed the Kurdish PKK (Haaretz 2011). Similarly, Israel blamed a 2012 attack at Bulgaria's Burgas airport on Hezbollah. That attack killed five Israelis and wounded many others. Hezbollah's armed wing was then 'placed on the European Union's blacklist, in part because of the evidence collected during the investigation into the Burgas Airport bombing' (Marcos 2018). However Bulgarian authorities made no mention of Hezbollah in their indictment and prosecution of two foreign nationals, tried in absentia, presumably because no link could be established (Marcos 2018; Bob and Weinthal 2018).

Critics of Hezbollah often display an unacceptable double standard, referring to Israeli secret service assassinations as 'professional' (Worrall, Mabon and Clubb 2016: 64), while speaking of 'The Hubris of Hezbollah' (Exum 2017). Indeed, a recent book by an Israeli journalist (Bergman 2018), using mostly Israeli sources, documents 2,700 assassinations by Israel's Mossad agents. These criminal acts by the Israeli secret service, which dwarf the list of accusations against Hezbollah, are often presented as matters of national pride.

3. The Status of Hezbollah in Lebanon

Since the expulsions of Israel in 2000 and 2006, Hezbollah's standing in Lebanon has steadily grown to the point of its assuming a leading role in government. Israeli and western labels had little impact on public opinion in the Arab and Muslim world. The group has forged political relationships across communities and is widely seen as the key defender of Lebanese sovereignty. In late 2018 even Saad Hariri, leader of the Saudi-backed Future Movement and key domestic political opponent of Hezbollah, recognised this fact. Denouncing Israeli threats and incursions into Lebanon, Hariri pointed to the futility of that aggression: "did [previous] Israeli attacks weaken Hezbollah?", he asked (Press TV 2018). For its part, the zionist state seems to have also accepted this fact, directing its threats more broadly at Lebanon. Complaining of tunnels on the northern border, Israeli minister Yoav Galant threatened that, if there were a war, "we will send Lebanon back to the Stone Age" (Benari 2018).

Hezbollah has been the main catalyst for internal changes which begin to vindicate Lebanon as a nation, after decades of sectarianism, chaos and humiliation. The group's strength in organised resistance and non-sectarian alliances is gradually changing the face of Lebanese politics. Its force is based on its commitment, organisation and unity. It has proven this time and again by defending the country from the enemy in the south and by defeating the cross- border incursions of the Saudi styled terrorist groups, Jabhat al Nusra and DAESH.

Even Al Jazeera, the Qatari-owned bastion of the anti-Shia Muslim Brotherhood, would admit in 2017 that the Hezbollah-Christian alliance had strengthened the Lebanese Government, especially in face of the clumsy Saudi kidnapping of its protégé,

Prime Minister Saad Hariri, in November 2017 (Nakhoul, Bassam and Perry 2017). That act was supposed to place some pressure on Hezbollah, but it backfired badly. The 'Islamic Resistance' [led by Hezbollah], al Jazeera acknowledged, 'was Aoun's strongest ally during this period', and Aoun was seen as 'Lebanon's first strong president since the end of civil war in 1990' (Shebaya 2017). Nevertheless, the body politic in Lebanon remains crippled with its 'confessional' system.

Modern Lebanon was founded on a 1943 pact which set up a 6:5 ratio of Christian-Muslim representation, rejecting unity with Syria (Krayem 1997). With sectarian foundations and strong pressures from the ethnic cleansing in Palestine the country erupted in a civil war which took on strong Christian versus Muslim features. In 1976, after several massacres and as the Christians were under great pressure, the Syrian Army under Hafez al Assad intervened to prevent a power vacuum that would have invited Israeli intervention and the likely annexation of south Lebanon, just after Syria had failed to reclaim the occupied Golan. Assad told Druze leader Kamal Jumblatt that he wanted to 'orient the Maronites in the direction of Syria, to gain their confidence and to convince them that their protector is neither France nor the west' (Rabil 2001: 24). Despite the collaboration of many Christian Maronite leaders with Israel, Hafez al Assad did not want to see the Christians forced out of the region. There were as many Christians in Syria as in Lebanon.

Yet the civil war, Israeli invasions and assassination of political leaders persisted throughout the 1980s. US foreign relations papers, by way of wishful thinking, suggested that Lebanon might become 'Assad's Vietnam' (Dawisha 1978); while some Maronites complained that Syria was making the country a 'quasi-colony' (Rabil 2001).

At the end of the civil war the 'confessional' state – where citizens were represented according to their religion – was reaffirmed through the 1989 'Taif Agreement', brokered by Muslim leaders Hussein el Husseini and Rafiq Hariri (Neal and Tansey 2010). The agreement also affirmed orientation of the country towards the Arab world, reasserting national institutions and equalising the Christian-Muslim representation ratio to the new population reality of 50:50 (UN 1989). There was agreement for Hezbollah in the south to maintain arms, as the group was rapidly becoming the country's main defence against zionist incursions (Saad-Ghorayeb 2002: 112-133).

Hezbollah's opposition to sectarianism in the Taif Accords was said to be 'as much an opposition to political sectarianism as it was a rejection of the Maronite monopoly of the sectarian privileges'. It also expressed opposition to the 'systematic underrepresentation of the Shi'ite community' (Saad-Ghorayeb 2002: 26). In any case Hezbollah took advantage of the internal peace process, repairing its relations with Amal, the other Shi'a Muslim party, and building a foundation in social services for its own community. Given the weakness of the Lebanese state, the group's social structures, with some justification, have been termed a 'parallel state' (Haidar 2018). It is well recognised that these social services helped build a wider popular support which "enabled the organization to transform from its social service-dominated roots to an influential political party supported by a professional guerrilla army" (Love 2010: 37).

The assassination of Lebanese Prime Minister Rafiq Hariri in February 2005 marked a turning point for Lebanon, as it catalysed the withdrawal of Syrian forces from the country and implicated Hezbollah in another internal scandal. The principal political conflict of the time was between Hariri and the Christian President Emile Lahoud, supposedly backed by Syria. However, Hariri had been in power for 10 years and had a working relationship with Syria. As a US report said at the time, Hariri "appeared to steer an even course. Unlike some of the more impetuous Lebanese clan and religious leaders, Mr. Hariri carefully avoided direct criticism of Syria's role" in Lebanon (Sachs 2005). After the assassination Hariri's son Saad took over as Prime Minister, under the 'confessional' system whereby a Maronite Christian remained President, a Shi'a Muslim President of the Assembly and a Sunni Muslim Prime Minister. So not much changed; but Syrian forces left.

The Hariri assassination was unresolved. Fingers were pointed at Syria (Khatib, Matar and AlShaer 2014: 79), and four Lebanese generals said to be linked to Syria were arrested; four years later they were released, without ever having faced charges (Black 2009). Hezbollah and Amal endorsed a National Dialogue process which began in 2006 but withdrew their support for the idea of a Special Tribunal when they saw it was aimed at them. 'Hezbollah was particularly concerned that the tribunal would be used for political purposes against them' (Worrall, Mabon and Clubb 2016: 101; Bouhabib 2010: 188). Their fears were justified. In 2009 the UN set up a Special Tribunal (based in the Netherlands) into the Hariri assassination (STL 2018). The tribunal has been criticised for having "an exceedingly narrow mandate relying solely on domestic law" and with the perception that it was set up on a "politicised" and partisan basis (Bouhabib 2010: 174, 204).

With the Syrian case set aside, a trial in absentia of several individuals linked to Hezbollah began in 2014 (STL 2018). Hezbollah denies the charges. The Resistance party and its allies regard the Tribunal as a biased outside body which forms an obstacle to normal political relations in the country (Evans 2014). While the case remains unresolved, the process serves as a basis for ongoing outside attacks on both Syria and Hezbollah (Blanford 2014).

Most likely the July 2006 Israeli invasion of south Lebanon was emboldened by Lebanon's internal conflict and the withdrawal of Syrian forces. However, it also seems to have been encouraged by US Secretary of State Condoleezza Rice's statements on Washington's vision of a 'New Middle East'. Shortly after the 2003 invasion of Iraq Rice had said that "Saddam's removal provides a new opportunity for a different kind of Middle East ... [and] a new Palestinian leadership is emerging" (Rice 2003). In the middle of her European-Middle East tour, Israel launched its invasion of Lebanon, based on the pretext of rescuing two Israeli soldiers whom Hezbollah had captured, but with the broader aiming of 'disarming Hezbollah' (Pressman 2006). The

US Secretary of State raised the stakes. US state media in Europe reported that Rice, in Jerusalem, had made it clear "that the United States is seeking major change in the Middle East, rather than a quick cease-fire ... the fight against Hizballah is a struggle that could reshape the Middle East". Rice announced, "It is time for a New Middle East", identifying as her chief villains Hezbollah, Syria and Iran (Bransten 2006).

However Israeli plans went badly wrong. In little more than a month Tel Aviv's forces withdrew, with 121 dead and 1200 wounded, having accomplished none of their goals (Pressman 2006). Former US official Andrew Exum (2017), recognised that Hezbollah had inflicted a 'humiliating defeat' on Israel but claimed that the Resistance group was causing conflict by ignoring Israel's 'red line' warnings.

The reaction in Lebanon and the Arab World was rather different. Hezbollah fighters were the new heroes of the Arab world. Not since Egypt's Nasser had there been such a defeat of European colonial powers. Western and Lebanese polling agencies confirmed that it was not only Lebanon's Shia community which saw Hezbollah as stronger after the 2006 war (92%)—that was the overall view in Lebanon (64%) with Christian (56%) and Sunni (57%) majorities (Gallup 2006). Other local polls were even stronger, showing 70% Lebanese support for Hezbollah's tactic of capturing Israeli soldiers for a prisoner exchange, 87% support for resistance confrontation with Israeli aggression and 63% confidence that Israeli could not defeat the resistance (Table 11, OROOM 2007 and Husseini 2010).

Subsequently, in line with western sectarian narratives for Arab countries, western pollsters suggested some less sanguine perspectives. Pew Global ran several polls on Hezbollah, lumping them together with Hamas and al Qaeda as 'Islamic extremists'. As Lebanese citizens are formally classified by community, unlike those in other Arab countries, there have been regular breakdowns of Lebanese opinion per community. A 2010 Pew poll found that only 52% of Lebanese Muslims had a 'favourable' view of 'Hezbollah (Pew 2010). In a 2013 poll, after Hezbollah had entered the conflict in Syria, it was said that only 41% of

Table 11:
Lebanese Opinion on Hezbollah, July 2006

	All	Sunni	Shiite	Druze	Christian
Do you support the Resistance's move to capture two Israeli soldiers for a prisoner swap? **YES**	70.1	73.1	96.3	40.1	54.7
Do you support the confrontations carried out by the Resistance against the Israeli aggression against Lebanon? **YES**	86.9	88.9	96.3	79.5	80.3
Do you believe that Israel will defeat the Resistance? **NO**	63.3	72.2	93.5	54.5	38.1
OROOM 2007 and Husseini 2010, reporting on the BCRI surveys of 24-26 July 2006					

Lebanese saw Hezbollah favourably, comprising 89% Shia, 40% Christian but only 6% Sunni (Pew 2013). Once again, in 2014, favourable Lebanese views on Hezbollah were suggested as 41%, comprising 86% Shia, 31% Christian and 9% Sunni (Pew 2014). After Hezbollah joined Damascus against the violent Salafist insurrection there was a western analytical consensus that the Resistance group was running down its credibility by supporting the Syrian 'regime' (e.g. Khatib, Matar and AlShaer 2014: 181; Worrall, Mabon and Clubb 2016: 111).

It turned out that consensus was mistaken, as was the western view (backed by billions of dollars in arms and thousands of recruited international 'jihadists') that the Syrian Army would collapse and the Syrian Government would fall. The western-backed armed groups used against Syria and Iraq also posed a threat to Lebanon; and as DAESH and Jabhat al Nusra were defeated, the standing of Hezbollah in Lebanon grew stronger. Michel Aoun, the fiercest anti-Syrian Maronite general of the 1980s (Krayem 1997), became a close ally of both Hezbollah and Syria and then became President (JPost 2016). The Resistance party, far from working for sectarian advantage, built its cross-community alliances, first with progressive Christians in the south and then with all communities. That cooperation was increasingly recognised by the Lebanese public.

When Saudi Prince Mohammed Bin Salman foolishly kidnapped Prime Minister Saad Hariri (Barnard and Abi-Habib 2017), both President Aoun and Hezbollah defended Hariri and the integrity of the Lebanese system. None of them tried to score cheap political points over Hariri's humiliating 'resignation' message, sent from Riyadh. It was well understood in Lebanon (despite Hariri's role as Prime Minister) that the ruling coalition was led by Hezbollah and Aoun's Christian Free Patriotic Movement. When an IPSOS poll asked, "Did Michel Aoun do a good job in handling the [Hariri kidnap] crisis?", 79% of the Lebanese people said yes. Within that poll 67% of Sunni Muslims and 81% of Christians agreed (Shebaya 2017).

Building on this episode, in the country's May 2018 elections, Hezbollah built an even stronger position within government, though not by increasing the Shi'a or Hezbollah vote. In Lebanon's 'confessional' system 64 seats are allocated to Muslims and 64 to Christians. Hezbollah increased its numbers through associated Resistance candidates from all religious communities. Most of the seats lost by the Saudi-backed and Saad Hariri-led Future Movement (from 34 to 21) were picked up by Hezbollah allies. The main Shia parties Hezbollah and Amal won 29 seats; their main Christian partner, the Michel Aoun-led Free Patriotic Movement (FPM), gained 17 and Resistance allies at least another 11 (Ajroudi 2018). That put the FPM-Hezbollah-Amal coalition in the strongest position. Hezbollah remained with just 12 seats but, with 'resistance' allies across all communities, the coalition held 74 seats, a clear majority in the 128 seat parliament (Rizk 2018). Even many enemies were forced to conclude that Hezbollah was vindicated politically as a national force (Ajroudi 2018). The renewed US aggression against Iran and Hezbollah by the Trump administration, with considerable Israeli instigation, seems not to be shared fully by the Europeans, who 'continue to distinguish between the group's political and military wings' (Rizk 2018). They seem more inclined to keep open their channels of communication with Lebanon.

4. The Iraqi Resistance

It is well known that a range of civilian militia (under the umbrella name Hashid al Shaabi or Popular Mobilisation Units) were created in Iraq, during the threat from the US-instigated, Saudi-styled terrorist group, DAESH. Many of these PMUs drew inspiration from Iran's volunteer corp (Basij) and from Lebanon's Hezbollah; many also had direct support from Iran's military. But they were not a monolithic group (Gurbuz 2017). These forces were necessary and central to the defeat of sectarian terrorism in Iraq, and were fairly quickly absorbed into Iraqi state structures (Abbas 2017; McDonald 2016). They compensated for the critical failure of the Iraqi military, under the tutelage and constraints of US occupation forces. To some extent they kept links with the Iraqi resistance to the US invasion of 2003 (ICG 2006), but in other respects they were a new development.

In June 2014, after DAESH took the city of Mosul, the Iraqi government appealed for help against DAESH to the United Nations (Zebari 2014). Washington then prepared a coalition of forces which re-entered Iraq in August 2014 under the guise of fighting that terrorist group (Nicks 2014). But they did not fight DAESH. Multiple local reports, for example from the first three months of 2015, showed that US forces were aiding DAESH (Table 12). Foreign 'protection' failed rapidly. An indigenous mobilisation was needed to save the country.

Table 12
Reports of US forces aiding DAESH in Iraq, early 2015

Iraqi Source	Report	Citation
Nahlah al Hababi MP	US 'not serious' about fighting DAESH and tries to stop popular forces doing so	Islam Times 2015
Salahuddin Security Commission	Unknown planes dropped arms to DAESH in Tikrit	FNA 2015a
Majid al Gharawi MP	US planes supplied DAESH with arms	Al Watan 2015
Hakem al-Zameli MP	US coalition dropping cargo to DAESH terrorists	FNA 2015b
Commander of Iraq's Ali Akbar Battalion	Wiretaps show links between US air drops and DAESH	Islam Times 2015
Hakem al-Zameli MP	US and British planes are dropping supplies to DAESH, two British planes shot down	FNA 2015b/c/d
Khalef Tarmouz, head of al Anbar Provincial Council	Weapons made in the USA, Europe and Israel discovered in areas liberated from DAESH	FNA 2015c

Western duplicity and aggression towards Iraq has been consistent and long term. The British set up a colonial regime in Iraq after the First World War, putting down national resistance with aerial bombing, machine gunning and mustard gas (Omissi 1990; GPF 2018). British sources have tried to deny Britain's use of chemical weapons (Douglas 2009; Heydon 2015); however, Winston Churchill had no such scruples, saying, "I am strongly in favour of using poisoned gas against uncivilised tribes" (Churchill 1919). Germany, France and Britain all used poison gas during the First World War (Richter 1992); subsequently, Britain carried out the first aerial chemical bombing of Bolshevik troops in Russia in 1919 (Jones 1999). In 1921 Britain tried to set up a monarchy in Iraq, suggesting popular consent from a bogus referendum; that monarchy last a few months (Tripp 2000).

After the Iranian revolution of 1979 expelled and humiliated the US Government, Washington urged Iraqi attacks on Iran, and backed Iraqi President Saddam Hussein's use of chemical weapons. Between 1983 and 1988 Saddam's forces used about 100,000 chemical munitions against both Iranian troops and the Kurds of Halabja (Hiro 2002). CIA documents show that the US knew early in that war of Saddam's use of mustard gas against Iran's 'human wave' troop tactics. Later, under a direction from President Reagan that 'an Iranian victory is unacceptable', the US military helped Saddam with satellite intelligence on Iranian troop movements east of Basrah and on the Yao peninsula. That intelligence assisted Saddam's 'Blessed Ramadan Offensive', where most of his sarin nerve gas was used on Iranian troops (Harris and Aid 2013). Saddam Hussein would not tolerate the sectarian Muslim Brotherhood in Iraq, but he joined with the US and Saudis in backing its insurrection in Hama, Syria, against the government of Hafez al Assad in the early 1980s (Seale 1988: 336; Fuller 2003: 11).

Finally the US turned against Saddam Hussein and launched its brutal and illegal invasion of Iraq in March 2003, a war of aggression which destroyed people, infrastructure and the state itself. Using totally cynical and false pretexts (CIA 2004; CICUSRWMD 2005; CNN 2005; Chilcott 2016) the US destroyed Iraq, seeking its own direct strategic advantage in the region, in furtherance of what came to be known as the plan for a 'New Middle East'.

A new Iraqi nation slowly grew from the ashes of the invasion, but crippled by a foreign occupation which kept its hands on the oil industry, the defence forces and strategic relations. Washington moved to divide the country and block re-alignment with its neighbours, and particularly with Iran. Veteran US journalist Seymour Hersh (2007) called this plan to foment sectarian division and violence a 'redirection'. Through the agency of its client state Saudi Arabia, al Qaeda in Iraq (AQI, later ISI), emerged in early 2006, at first committing a terrible massacre by bombing a large Shia mosque (Knickmeyer and Ibrahim 2006). Inciting sectarian conflict was an important part of this mission.

The 'jihadist' insurgency needed and acquired foreign mercenaries. Documents uncovered on Iraq's borders showed that the international recruits for this 'Iraqi' al Qaeda came mainly from Saudi Arabia (41%) and North Africa (37%) (Felter and Fishman 2007: 7-8). However, AQI/ISI remained a hit and run terrorist group until 2012, when it was weaponised to join in the attacks on the Syrian Government. US intelligence reported in August 2012 that "the Salafist, the Muslim Brotherhood and AQI are the major forces driving the insurgency in Syria ... [building a] Salafist principality in eastern Syria ... exactly what the [US and allies] want, in order to isolate the Syrian regime" (DIA 2012). From about that time onward the Islamic State in Iraq and Syria (ISIS) or in Iraq and the Levant (ISIL), DAESH became the preferred vehicle for foreign 'jihadist' terrorists and gained sufficient force to occupy towns and even cities in both Iraq and Syria. The peak of its influence was in 2014-2015, when it occupied Mosul in Iraq and Raqqa and a large part of Deir Ezzor in Syria. The US American 'liberators' once again betrayed Iraq, delivering only 4 of 36 purchased F-16 fighter planes in June 2014, just as DAESH was taking over Mosul (Shalal 2014). The US 'anti-ISIS coalition' in Iraq, beginning September 2014 (Nicks 2014) did little to contain the advance of the terrorist group, because the USA and its allies were covertly arming them (see Table 2). So much was admitted by senior US officials in late 2014, when General Martin Dempsey admitted that "major Arab allies" fund ISIS (Dempsey 2014), while Vice President Joe Biden admitted that Turkey, the Saudis and the Emiratis had "poured hundreds of millions of dollars and tens, thousands of tons of weapons into anyone who would fight against Assad", including al Qaeda and ISIS (Biden in Dickey 2014). It is fair to conclude that DAESH/ISIS was mostly a western proxy and one which, according to a British monitoring group, "used chemical weapons at least 52 times in Syria and Iraq" (Schmitt 2016).

However, after the September 2015 entry of Russian air power into the anti-DAESH campaign, Syrian and Iraqi forces were able to reclaim their major towns and cities (RT 2017; Mneimneh 2018). By late 2017 both Syria and Iraq were declared liberated from DAESH/ISIS, even though pockets of the group persisted in desert areas (Bassam and McDowall 2017; Sharman

PMU leader addresses the media at an anti-terrorism conference in Baghdad, October 2017. Hashid al Shaabi gets the credit from Iraqis for defeating DAESH.

2017) and hundreds were set free (CBC 2017) or absorbed into another US proxy, the formerly Kurdish-led 'Syrian Democratic Forces' (SDF) (Abed 2017). The US military has played down the Kurdish component of the SDF (in March 2017 it was said to be "40% Kurdish YPG forces, and 60% Syrian Arab Coalition") in part because the SDF was being used in mainly Arab cities like Manbij and Raqqa, in part because it was absorbing the remnants of other US proxies, defeated in other parts of Syria (Humud, Blanchard and Nikitin 2017: 12). Direct US military occupation of eastern and southern Syria was imposed, to prevent complete defeat of the proxy armies (Gowans 2018).

In Iraq the popular militias led the resistance, given the failure of the US-mentored Iraqi military to contain DAESH. These militia were formed after a fatwa from Iraqi Muslim leader Grand Ayatollah Ali al-Sistani on 13 June 2014. The Imam called on all Iraqi citizens to defend the country, its people, the honour of its citizens and its sacred sites. It was not a sectarian call. 'Tens of thousands' joined the Iraqi Security Forces, while another 65,000 volunteers 'including 17,000 Sunni tribesman' joined militia under the command of Prime Minister Haidar al Abadi (al Khateeb 2015). Many but not all the Iraqi popular militia were backed by Iran, and in particular by the external Quds Force wing, led by the legendary General Qassem Soleimani, a man hated and described as a 'terrorist' by Washington (Esfandiari 2015). Unlike in Lebanon, this fairly diverse grouping of popular militia were immediately incorporated into the Iraqi state; and many were assisted by Iranian forces, outside the realm of US military tutelage. Further, the Iraqi Government readily agreed to host a Russian-led anti-DAESH intelligence centre in Baghdad (Dehghanpisheh 2015; Boyer and Scarborough 2015). Rivalry between Washington, Moscow and Tehran was thus played out in Baghdad, as the emerging Iraqi state, fighting for its life, began to assert some independent political will.

Substantial energy has been put into creating the myth that Hashid al Shaabi in Iraq was a sectarian force, an 'Iranian proxy', an 'exclusively Shia faction' even a 'Shi'a DAESH' or a group that collaborated with DAESH (MEMO 2018). This Washington inspired propaganda is far from the truth. It is true that some former DAESH members were recruited into the Iraqi security forces, just as has happened in Syria, under reconciliation processes. Analyst Fanar Haddad criticises the Washington caricatures, saying that 'outside of Iraq, few things are as misrepresented as the PMU'. He recognises that Iraq's popular militia are quite diverse, have strong popular support and do not oppose the Iraqi state; indeed they are a function, if not a product of the dysfunctional post-2003 Iraqi state (Haddad 2018). Contrary to the anti Hashid propaganda, Sunni leaders and communities both participate in and praise their country's popular militia. A variety of outside reports recognised Sunnis and Shi'a fighting together to retake Iraqi towns from DAESH (Bradley 2015; Kittleson 2016). Even US State Department spokesman Mark Toner admitted that the PMUs were 'an assortment of militias that includes of course Shi'a, but also Turkomen, Christian and Sunnis; and ... not all Shi'a militia are Iranian-supported or funded'(ARA News 2017).

In March 2015 Iraqi Sunni cleric Sheikh Adnan al Ani confronted Egypt's Mufti at al Azar Mosque, condemning sectarian myths over the PMUs in these terms:

> Were it not for the popular mobilisation units, the army would never have made it this far. It was the strength of the PMU ... who liberated Diyala my dear brothers? Who liberated it? Did you not witness Salah al Din welcome PMU forces? They [Iraqi Sunnis] welcomed the PMU, or is the Mufti of Azar blind? How did they welcome them and dance with them, their brothers, but in joy! Where was al Tayab [Egyptian Sunni cleric] when ISIS was killing us? And where was Egypt? Occupied with the House of Saud. God damn them!" (IEPLus 2015).

Despite the diversity of the militia it is true that their

creation has enabled stronger friendly coordination with Iran as also with Syria. The Axis of Resistance countries, plus Russia, are thus building a new partner in Iraq, much to the dismay of Washington and Tel Aviv, and while the US pretended to claim credit for the defeat of DAESH (Superville 2017), the matter was better understood within the region. Iran's Quds Force leader General Qassem Soleimani, reporting to his leader Ayatollah Khamenei in late 2017, announced the "termination of the rule of this vicious cursed entity [DAESH] ... by the resistance of the Iraqi and Syrian governments and the perseverance of [their] armies" (Iranwire 2017). General Soleimani's personal supervision of operations across four allied countries shows why Iran is feared by both Tel Aviv and Washington. This was the message of a regional resistance leader, a key strategist, who had fought the enemy from Saddam Hussein's assaults on Iran, through defense of south Lebanon from Israel's incursions, to defeats of al-Nusra in the towns of the Qalamoun, to the liberations of Aleppo and Tikrit, and the series of victories over DAESH (ISIS), culminating in those at Deir Ezzor and al-Bukamal.

A notable achievement, during the rout of DAESH in Iraq, was the role of Hashid al Shaabi in the rapid retaking of the northern city of Kirkuk from Kurdish separatists (France24 2017; Chmaytelli and Mahmoud 2017). Barzani-led Kurdish forces were driven out with barely a shot fired. That helped Iraqi forces to follow on and take control of the country's northwestern borders for the first time in decades—a matter of national pride. We must also recognise that Hashid forces have played an important role in assisting Syria, with the integration of a number of PMU forces with the Syrian Arab Army across Syria's eastern desert, as also along the Syria-Iraq border, from 2016 onwards (Watling 2016; Rudaw 2018). This writer saw PMU flags at checkpoints in the east Syria desert, over 2016-2017.

The PMU role in liberating Iraq from DAESH, and in rebuilding an independent political will in the country, was also reflected in the national elections of 2018. Groups led by Shia Iraqi nationalist Muqtada al Sadr and PMU leader Hadi al Ameri came ahead of the others (Xinhua 2018), "because they were perceived to be outside the system", a system seen as weak and corrupt (Mansour and van Den Toorn 2018). Iraq's resistance forces are spread more across parties than the Hezbollah-led bloc in Lebanon, but their indigenous mobilisation has introduced a new 'backbone' to the body politic.

It is precisely Hashid al Shaabi groups which are behind the 2018-2019 agitation to expel US forces from Iraq, after 15 years of military occupation. After a June 2018 missile attack on PMU units at the Syria-Iraq border, Kata'ib Hizbullah, one of the PMU groups, blamed their key enemies Israel and "the evil and destructive" USA, vowing retaliation. Fifty PMU fighters were killed (MEMRI 2018). Sheikh Qais al-Khazali, leader of Asaib Ahl al-Haq (League of the Righteous), called for US military withdrawal in 2017 (Press TV 2017), and repeated that in 2019. He said there was no longer any justification for the presence of US forces, asserting his belief that more than half the new National Assembly "reject the presence" of US troops. "If the United States wants to impose its presence by force, and to bypass the Iraqi constitution and parliament, Iraq can treat it the same way and drive it out by force... But the first phase is political," al-Khazali said (Abdul-Zahra and Karam 2019). PMU units were said to be monitoring and intercepting US patrols in eastern Mosul (MECRA 2019).

Colonial forces smear both Hezbollah and Hashid al Shaabi, with lies that they are extreme sectarians who do not care about their own people. Coming from the sponsors of al Qaeda, al Nusra and DAESH, that criticism carries neither good faith nor credibility. The sectarian accusation, from western and Zionist sources, has more to do with the frustration of their 'divide and rule' strategies, as well as their dismay in seeing a revival of political will amongst their opponents. Sectarian accusations can never explain Iranian support for pluralist Syria and Sunni Muslim Palestine; nor the Hezbollah-Christian alliance in Lebanon; nor the powerful Shia-Sunni alliance within Hashd al Shaabi. It is true that important resistance initiatives have come from the

Shi'a communities of Lebanon and Iraq. There are historical reasons for this, to do with centuries of oppression, martyrdom and resistance. However, those accounts of an alliance of the downtrodden (mustadafin), have helped engage communities with their neighbours. Mature leadership has succeeded in building wider alliances.

Bibliography

Abbas, Hassan (2017) 'The Myth and Reality of Iraq's al-Hashd al-Shaabi (Popular Mobilization Forces): A Way Forward', Friedrich-Ebert-Stiftung, Amman, September, online: http://library.fes.de/pdf-files/bueros/amman/13689.pdf

Abdul-Zahra, Qassim and Zeina Karam (2019) 'Iraqi militia leader wants US troops to leave', Associated Press, 29 January, online: https://apnews.com/109a9aabe987430cbe63e4a668711833

Abed, Sarah (2017) 'Syria: Kurdish SDF and ISIS-Daesh, An Unholy Alliance Consecrated by the U.S.', Global Research, 4 October, online: https://www.globalresearch.ca/syria-kurdish-sdf-and-isis-daesh-an-unholy-alliance-consecrated-by-the-u-s/5611970

Ajroudi, Asma (2018) 'Hezbollah, Amal and allies biggest winners in Lebanon elections', Al Jazeera, 8 May, online: https://www.aljazeera.com/news/2018/05/hezbollah-amal-allies-claim-lebanon-election-sweep-180507160524402.html

Al Assad, Bashar (2017) 'President al-Assad: Main goal of war on Syria is undermining pan-Arabism and affiliation', SANA, 14 November, online: https://sana.sy/en/?p=118174

Al Khateeb, Luay (2015) 'Sistani's Jihad Fatwa One Year On: the man who pulled Iraq from the brink with a single statement', Huffington Post, 14 June, online: https://www.huffingtonpost.com/luay-al-khatteeb/sistanis-jihad-fatwa-one_b_7579322.html

Al Watan, Donia (2015) 'Iraqi MP: Israel, Western Powers Continue Supplying ISIL with Weapons', 10 March, online: https://english.alwatanvoice.com/news/2015/03/10/676274.html

Allen, Charles (2007) *God Terrorists: the Wahhabi Cult and the hidden roots of modern jihad*, Abacus, London

ARA News (2017) 'US: Iraq trying to control Shi'a militias, Kurds fear future clashes', 24 March, online: https://avim.org.tr/en/Bulten/US-IRAQ-TRYING-TO-CONTROL-SHIA-MILITIAS-KURDS-FEAR-FUTURE-CLASHES

Atrache, Susan (2017) 'Hizbollah's Pyrrhic Victories in Syria', Crisis group,

3 July, online: https://www.crisisgroup.org/middle-east-north-africa/eastern-mediterranean/syria/las-victorias-pirricas-de-hezbola-en-siria

Barnard, Anne and Maria Abi-Habib (2017) 'Why Saad Hariri Had That Strange Sojourn in Saudi Arabia', *New York Times*, 24 December, online: https://www.nytimes.com/2017/12/24/world/middleeast/saudi-arabia-saad-hariri-mohammed-bin-salman-lebanon.html

Bassam, Laila and Angus McDowall (2017) 'Syrian army, allies, take last IS stronghold in Syria: commander', Reuters, 8 November, online: https://www.reuters.com/article/us-mideast-crisis-islamic-state/syrian-army-allies-take-last-is-stronghold-in-syria-commander-idUSKBN1D81NM

BCRI (2006) 'Briefing: Lebanese public opinion', Beirut Center for Research and Information, Mideast Monitor, 1(32), in Oroom (2007) 'Lebanese public opinion during and after July war', 14 November, online: https://www.oroom.org/forum/threads/lebanese-public-opinion-during-and-after-july-war.30269/

Benari, Elad (2018) "We will send Lebanon to the Stone Age', Arutz Sheva, 9 December, online: http://www.israelnationalnews.com/News/News.aspx/255881

Bergman, Ronen (2018) *Rise and Kill First,* Random House, New York

Black, Ian (2009) 'Lebanese generals held over Rafiq al-Hariri killing to be released', *The Guardian*, 29 April, online: https://www.theguardian.com/world/2009/apr/29/rafiq-hariri-suspects-release

Blanford, Nicholas (2014) 'Was Syria behind Hariri assassination? Special tribunal takes another look', *Christian Science Monitor,* 17 November, online: https://www.csmonitor.com/World/Middle-East/2014/1117/Was-Syria-behind-Hariri-assassination-Special-tribunal-takes-another-look

Bob, Yonah Jeremy and Benjamin Weinthal (2018) 'Hezbollah Role unmentioned in charges for 2012 Bulgaria terrorist attack', *Jerusalem Post*, 31 January, online: https://www.jpost.com/Middle-East/Hezbollah-role-unmentioned-in-charges-for-2012-Bulgaria-terrorist-attack-540367

Bouhabib, Melia (2010) 'Power and Perception: The Special Tribunal for Lebanon', *Berkeley Journal of Middle Eastern & Islamic Law*, Vol 3 Article 4, 173-205, online: https://scholarship.law.berkeley.edu/cgi/viewcontent.cgi?article=1015&context=jmeil

Boyer, Dave and Rowan Scarborough (2015) 'White House alarmed as Iraq uses intelligence center operated by Russia, Iran, Syria', *Washington Times,* 13 October, online: https://www.washingtontimes.com/news/2015/oct/13/iraq-uses-intelligence-center-operated-by-russia-i/

Bradley, Matt (2015) 'Iraqi Sunnis, Shiites Find Some Common Ground Against Islamic State', *Wall Street Journal,* 13 April, online: https://www.wsj.

com/articles/iraqi-sunnis-shiites-find-some-common-ground-against-islamic-state-1428959064

Bransten, Jeremy (2006) 'Middle East: Rice Calls For A "New Middle East"', Radio Free Europe Radio Liberty, 25 July, online: https://www.rferl.org/a/1070088.html

Brooke, James (1994) 'Argentina's Jews Cry for Their Torn Heart', *New York Times,* 21 July, online: https://www.nytimes.com/1994/07/21/world/argentina-s-jews-cry-for-their-torn-heart.html

CBC (2017) 'U.S. quietly let hundreds of ISIS fighters flee Raqqa', 14 November, online: https://www.cbsnews.com/news/report-us-allowed-isis-fighters-escape-raqqa-sdf-deal/

Chilcott, John et al (2016) 'The Report of the Iraq Inquiry: Executive Summary', Report of a Committee of Privy Counsellors, HC264, online: http://www.iraqinquiry.org.uk/media/247921/the-report-of-the-iraq-inquiry_executive-summary.pdf

Chmaytelli, Maher and Mustafa Mahmoud (2017) 'Iraqi forces seize oil city Kirkuk from Kurds in bold advance', 16 October, Reuters, online: https://www.reuters.com/article/us-mideast-crisis-iraq-kurds-kirkuk/iraqi-forces-seize-oil-city-kirkuk-from-kurds-in-bold-advance-idUSKBN1CK0XL

Churchill, Winston (1919) 'Churchill's 1919 War Office Memorandum', in National Churchill Museum, 12 May, online: https://www.nationalchurchillmuseum.org/churchills-1919-war-office-memorandum.html

CIA (2004) 'Regime Strategic Intent', in DCI Special Advisor Report on Iraq's WMD, updated to 2013, online: https://www.cia.gov/library/reports/general-reports-1/iraq_wmd_2004/Comp_Report_Key_Findings.pdf

CICUSRWMD (2005) 'Report to the President of the United States', The Commission on the Intelligence Capabilities of the United States Regarding Weapons of Mass Destruction, 31 March, online: http://www.nytimes.com/packages/pdf/politics/20050331_wmd_report.pdf

CNN (2005) Report: Iraq intelligence 'dead wrong': Bush says fundamental changes needed in spy agencies, 1 April, online: http://edition.cnn.com/2005/POLITICS/03/31/intel.report/index.html?iref=mpstoryview

Dawisha, Adeed I. (1978) 'Syria in Lebanon: Assad's Vietnam?', *Foreign Policy,* 15 December, online: http://foreignpolicy.com/1978/12/15/syria-in-lebanon-assads-vietnam/

Dempsey, Martin (2014) 'General Dempsey acknowledges U.S. Arab allies funding ISIS', C-Span, online: https://www.c-span.org/video/?c4718678/general-dempsey-acknowledges-us-arab-allies-funding-isis

Dehghanpisheh, Babak (2015) 'Iraq using info from new intelligence center to bomb Islamic State: official', Reuters, 13 October, online: https://www.reuters.com/article/us-mideast-crisis-iraq-russia-iran/iraq-using-info-from-new-intelligence-center-to-bomb-islamic-state-official-idUSKCN0S71JC20151013

DIA (2012) 'Pgs. 287-293 (291) JW v DOD and State 14-812', DIA via Judicial Watch, 12 August, online: http://www.judicialwatch.org/wp-content/uploads/2015/05/Pg.-291-Pgs.-287-293-JW-v-DOD-and-State-14-812-DOD-Release-2015-04-10-final-version11.pdf

Dickey, Christopher (2014) 'VP Biden Apologizes for Telling Truth About Turkey, Saudi and ISIS', The Daily Beast, 5 October, online: https://www.thedailybeast.com/vp-biden-apologizes-for-telling-truth-about-turkey-saudi-and-isis

DODC (1983) 'Report of the DoD Commission on Beirut International Airport Terrorist Act', October 23', 20 December, online: https://web.archive.org/web/20071014031852/http://ibiblio.org:80/hyperwar/AMH/XX/MidEast/Lebanon-1982-1984/DOD-Report/index.html#toc

Douglas, R.M. (2009) 'Did Britain Use Chemical Weapons in Mandatory Iraq?', *The Journal of Modern History*, Vol. 81, No. 4 (December), pp. 859-887

Erelanger, Steven and Richard A. Oppel Jr. (2006) 'A Disciplined Hezbollah Surprises Israel With Its Training, Tactics and Weapons', *New York Times*, 7 August, online: https://www.nytimes.com/2006/08/07/world/middleeast/07hezbollah.html

Esfandiari, Golnaz (2015) 'Wanted For Terrorism, Commander Of Iran's Quds Force Is Actually Kind And Emotional, Brother Says', Radio Free Europe / Radio Liberty, 25 August, online: https://www.rferl.org/a/persian-letters-soleimani-brother-interview/27207883.html

Evans (2014) 'Justice elusive as Lebanon's Hariri trial opens without accused', Reuters, 15 January, online: https://www.reuters.com/article/us-lebanon-tribunal/justice-elusive-as-lebanons-hariri-trial-opens-without-accused-idUSBREA0E0Q320140115

Exum, Andrew (2017) 'The Hubris of Hezbollah', *The Atlantic*, 18 September, online: https://www.theatlantic.com/international/archive/2017/09/hezbollah-israel-lebanon-isis-syria-iran/540105/

FAS (1992) 'Patterns of Global Terrorism: 1992. The Year in Review', Federation of American Scientists, online: https://fas.org/irp/threat/terror_92/review.html

Felter, Joseph and Brian Fishman (2007) 'al Qa`ida's Foreign Fighters in Iraq: A First Look at the Sinjar Records', Combating Terrorism Center, West Point New York, online: https://www.files.ethz.ch/isn/45910/CTCForeignFighter.19.Dec07.pdf

FNA (2015a) 'Iraqi Hezbollah: Unidentified Planes Supplying ISIL with Arms from Saudi Arabia', Fars News Agency, 10 January, online: http://en.farsnews.com/newstext.aspx?nn=13931020001065

FNA (2015b) 'Iraqi MP: Evidence Shows US-Led Coalition Helping ISIL to Survive', 24 Jan, online: http://en.farsnews.com/newstext.aspx?nn=13931104000575

FNA (2015c) 'Iraq's Popular Forces Release Photo of Downed US Chopper Carrying Arms for ISIL', Fares News Agency, 28 February, online: http://en.farsnews.com/newstext.aspx?nn=13931209001345

FNA (2015d) 'Iraqi Army Downs 2 UK Planes Carrying Weapons for ISIL', Fars News Agency, 23 February, online: http://en.farsnews.com/newstext.aspx?nn=13931204001534

France24 (2017) 'Iraqi capture of Kirkuk changes calculation for Kurds', 17 October, online: https://www.france24.com/en/20171017-iraq-haider-al-abadi-seisure-kirkuk-changes-calculation-kurds-masoud-barzani

Fuller, Graham E. (2003) 'Islamist Politics in Iraq after Saddam Hussein', United States Institute of Peace, Special report 108, August, online: https://www.usip.org/publications/2003/08/islamist-politics-iraq-after-saddam-hussein

Gallup (2006) 'Lebanese see Hezbollah as politically stronger after conflict with Israel', Gallup Polls, 17 November, online: http://news.gallup.com/poll/25489/lebanese-see-hezbollah-politically-stronger-after-conflict-israel.aspx

Gause, F. Gregory (2011) *Saudi Arabia in the New Middle East*, Council on Foreign Relations Press, Washington

Gowans (2018) 'The (Largely Unrecognized) US Occupation of Syria', What's Left, 11 march, online: https://gowans.wordpress.com/2018/03/11/the-largely-unrecognized-us-occupation-of-syria/

GPF (2018) 'British Colonialism and Repression in Iraq', Global Policy Forum, online:https://www.globalpolicy.org/iraq-conflict-the-historical-background-/british-colonialism-and-repression-in-iraq.html

Gurbuz, Mustafa (2017) 'The Popular Mobilization Forces and Iraq's Next Elections', Arab Centre Washington, 6 September, online: http://arabcenterdc.org/policy_analyses/the-popular-mobilization-forces-and-iraqs-next-elections/

Haaretz (2011) 'Report: Istanbul Attack Was Attempted Hezbollah Strike on Israeli Envoy', 18 July, online: https://www.haaretz.com/1.5030272

Haddad, Fanar (2018) 'Understanding Iraq's Hashd al-Sha'bi', The Century Foundation, 5 March, online: https://tcf.org/content/report/understanding-iraqs-hashd-al-shabi/?agreed=1

Haidar, Nasser (2018) 'The Parallel State: Hezbollah And Its Replicas', 24 July, online: http://natoassociation.ca/the-parallel-state-hezbollah-and-its-replicas/

Hauslohner, Abigail (2013) 'Hezbollah's role in Syrian civil war drives sectarian tension in Lebanon', *Washington Post,* 27 April, online: https://www.washingtonpost.com/world/middle_east/hezbollahs-role-in-syrian-war-drives-sectarian-tension-in-lebanon/2013/04/27/942ae1ac-ae5c-11e2-a986-eec837b1888b_story.html

Harris, Shane and Matthew Aid (2013) 'CIA Files Prove America Helped Saddam as He Gassed Iran', *Foreign Policy,* 26 August, online: http://foreignpolicy.com/2013/08/26/exclusive-cia-files-prove-america-helped-saddam-as-he-gassed-iran/

Hersh, Seymour (2007) 'The Redirection', *The New Yorker,* 5 March, online: https://www.newyorker.com/magazine/2007/03/05/the-redirection

Heydon, Tom (2015) 'The 10 greatest controversies of Winston Churchill's career', BBC, 26 January, online: https://www.bbc.com/news/magazine-29701767

Hiro, Dilip (2002) 'Iraq and Poison gas', *The Nation,* 28 August, online: https://www.thenation.com/article/iraq-and-poison-gas/

Humud, Carla E., Christopher M. Blanchard and Mary Beth D. Nikitin (2017) 'Armed Conflict in Syria: Overview and U.S. Response', Congressional Research Service, 26 April, online: https://www.refworld.org/pdfid/591c08bc4.pdf

Husseini, Rola el (2010) 'Hezbollah and the Axis of Refusal: Hamas, Iran and Syria', *Third World Quarterly,* Vol 31, No 5, pp 803-815

ICG (2006) 'In their own words: reading the Iraqi insurgency', International Crisis Group, Middle East Report N°50, 15 February, online: https://www.globalpolicy.org/images/pdfs/0215ownwords.pdf

IEPLus (2015) 'Iraqi Sunni Cleric Slams Media, Egypt's Azhar', YouTube, 20 March, online: https://www.youtube.com/watch?v=lXJny1oXbKU&list=PLujxCZ2NjjytaeZe3W5mpAQQILr5hSIDW&index=45&t=0s

IMEU (2018) 'Israeli Crimes Against Humanity: Remembering the Sabra and Shatila Massacre', Institute for Middle East Understanding, Global Research, 31 August, online: https://www.globalresearch.ca/israeli-crimes-against-humanity-remembering-the-sabra-and-shatila-massacre/5545969

Iranwire (2017) 'Ghasem Soleimani: ISIS is Finished', 22 November, online: https://iranwire.com/en/features/4986

Islam Times (2015) 'Iraqi Commander: Tapped Communications Confirms US Aids to ISIL', 19 March, online: https://www.islamtimes.org/en/article/448544/iraqi-commander-tapped-communications-confirms-us-aids-to-isil

Itani, Faysal (2007) 'Hizbullah and Lebanese Nationalism', SAIS Europe Journal, 1 April, online: http://www.saisjournal.org/posts/hizbullah-

and-lebanese-nationalism
Jones, Simon (1999) ' "The Right Medicine for the Bolshevist": British airdropped chemical weapons in North Russia, 1919', *Imperial War Museum Review,* No. 12
Jones, Seth G. and Maxwell B. Markusen (2018) 'The Escalating Conflict with Hezbollah in Syria', Centre for Strategic and International Studies, 20 June online: https://www.csis.org/analysis/escalating-conflict-hezbollah-syria
JPost (2016) 'Lebanon's new pro-Hezbollah President vows to retake 'Israeli-occupied' land', *Jerusalem Post,* 31 October, online: https://www.jpost.com/Middle-East/Hezbollah-ally-Michel-Aoun-elected-President-of-Lebanon-471301
Keddie, Nikki (2004) 'Trajectories of Secularism in the West and the Middle East', *Global Dialogue,* Winter Spring, 23-33
Khalidi, Rashid; Lisa Anderson, Muhammad Muslih and Reeva S. Simon (1991) *The Origins of Arab Nationalism,* Colombia University Press
Khatib, Lina; Dina Matar and Atef AlShaer (2014) *The Hizbullah Phenomenon: politics and communication,* Hurst and Company, London
Kittleson, Shelley (2016) 'Sunni town, Shiite PMU join forces in fight against IS', al Monitor, 26 November, online: https://www.al-monitor.com/pulse/originals/2016/11/iraq-hawija-mosul-al-alam.html
Knickmeyer, Ellen and K.I. Ibrahim (2006) 'Bombing Shatters Mosque In Iraq', 23 February, online: http://www.washingtonpost.com/wp-dyn/content/article/2006/02/22/AR2006022200454.html
Krayem, Hassan (1997) 'The Lebanese War and the Taif Agreement', American University of Beirut, online: http://ddc.aub.edu.lb/projects/pspa/conflict-resolution.html
Love, James (2010) 'Hezbollah: Social Services as a Source of Power', JSOU Report 10-5, Joint Special Operations University, Florida, June, online: https://www.globalsecurity.org/military/library/report/2010/1006_jsou-report-10-5.pdf
Mansour al Atrash, Rim (2018) Résumé of the autobiography of Sultan Pasha Al-Atrash, online: http://sultanalattrache.org/bio.php?type=9
Mansour, Renad and Christine van Den Toorn (2018) 'The 2018 Iraqi Federal Elections: A Population in Transition?', LSE Middle East Centre Report, July, online: http://eprints.lse.ac.uk/89698/7/MEC_Iraqi-elections_Report_2018.pdf
Marcos, Immanuel (2018) 'Bourgas Airport bombing trial: Prosecution leaves Hezbollah and terrorism out of the case', *The Sofia Globe,* 1 February, online: https://sofiaglobe.com/2018/02/01/bourgas-airport-bombing-prosecution-leaves-hezbollah-and-terrorism-out-of-the-case-2/
Marlowe, Lara (2000) 'Most Lebanese see Syrian presence as necessary evil',

The Irish Times, 21 June, online: https://www.irishtimes.com/news/most-lebanese-see-syrian-presence-as-necessary-evil-1.284200

McDonald, Alex (2016) 'Iraqi militias to be given official army status, says prime minister', Middle East Eye, 27 July, online: https://www.middleeasteye.net/news/new-apolitical-pmu-grouping-be-created-iraqi-government-1271520919

Meijer, Roel (Ed) (2009) *Global Salafism: Islam's new religious movement*, Colombia University Press, New York

MECRA (2019) 'Tensions rise in Mosul as Hashd al-Shaabi (PMU) warns US forces against "provocative" patrols', Middle East Centre for Reporting and Analysis, MECRA Research Blog, 3 February, online: https://www.mideastcenter.org/research-blog/tensions-rise-in-mosul-as-hashd-al-shaabi-pmu-warns-us-forces-against-provocative-patrols

MEMO (2017) 'Survivors recall Lebanon's 1982 Sabra and Shatila massacre', Middle East Monitor, 17 September, online: https://www.middleeastmonitor.com/20170917-survivors-recall-lebanons-1982-sabra-and-shatila-massacre/

MEMO (2018) 'Report: Iraq's Shia militias partnering with Daesh militants', Middle East Monitor, 17 October, online: https://www.middleeastmonitor.com/20181017-report-iraqs-shia-militias-partnering-with-daesh-militants/

MEMRI (2018) 'Popular Mobilization Units (PMU) Threaten To Respond To Attack On Their Forces At Iraq-Syria Border: We Can Fire Missiles At The U.S. Embassy, U.S. Forces In Iraq', Middle East Media Research Institute, 28 June, online: https://www.memri.org/reports/popular-mobilization-units-pmu-threaten-respond-attack-their-forces-iraq-syria-border-we-can

Mneimneh, Hassan (2018) 'Washington Should Recognize the Russian Strategic Achievement in Syria', The Washington Institute, 29 may, online: https://www.washingtoninstitute.org/fikraforum/view/washington-should-recognize-the-russian-strategic-achievement-in-syria

Nakhoul, Samia; Laila Bassam and Tom Perry (2017) 'How Saudi Arabia turned on Lebanon's Hariri', 12 November, Reuters, online: https://www.reuters.com/article/us-lebanon-politics-hariri-exclusive/exclusive-how-saudi-arabia-turned-on-lebanons-hariri-idUSKBN1DB0QL

Najjar, Fauzi M. (1996) 'The debate on Islam and Secularism in Egypt', *Arab Studies Quarterly*, Vol 18 No 2, Spring, 1-21

Narwani, Sharmine (2011) 'Pentagon game to divide Iranians and Arabs', Salon, 26 October, online: http://www.salon.com/2011/10/26/pentagon_game_to_divide_iranians_and_arabs/

Neal, Mark W and Richard Tansey (2010) 'The dynamics of effective corrupt leadership: Lessons from Rafik Hariri's political career in Lebanon',

The Leadership Quarterly. 21: 33–49, online: https://www.sciencedirect.com/science/article/pii/S1048984309001970

Nicks, (2014) 'U.S. Forms Anti-ISIS Coalition at NATO Summit', Time, 5 September, online: http://time.com/3273185/isis-us-nato/

Omissi, David (1990) *Air Power and Colonial Control: The Royal Air Force 1919-1939*, Manchester University Press, Manchester

OROOM (2007) 'Lebanese public opinion during and after July war', The Orange Room, 14 November, online: https://www.oroom.org/forum/threads/lebanese-public-opinion-during-and-after-july-war.30269/

Perry, Mark (2010) *Talking to Terrorists: Why America Must Engage with its Enemies,* Basic Books, New York

Pew (2010) 'Muslim publics divided on Hamas and Hezbollah', Pew Research Centre, 2 December, online: http://www.pewglobal.org/2010/12/02/muslims-around-the-world-divided-on-hamas-and-hezbollah/

Pew (2013) 'As it fights in Syria, Hezbollah seen unfavourably in the region', Pew Research Centre, 7 June, online: http://www.pewresearch.org/fact-tank/2013/06/07/as-it-fights-in-syria-hezbollah-seen-unfavorably-in-region/

Pew (2014) 'Concerns about Islamic extremism on the rise in Middle East', Pew Research Centre, 1 July, online: http://www.pewglobal.org/2015/07/16/extremism-concerns-growing-in-west-and-predominantly-muslim-countries/extremism-concerns-02/

Porter, Gareth (2008) 'Bush's Iran/Argentina Terror Frame-Up', *The Nation,* 19 January, online: https://www.thenation.com/article/bushs-iranargentina-terror-frame/

Press TV (2017) 'Hashd al-Sha'abi commander calls for US forces withdrawal from Iraq', 24 October, online: https://www.presstv.com/Detail/2017/10/24/539730/Iraq-Hashd-alShaabi-US

Press TV (2018) 'Israel won't succeed if it launches another war on Lebanon, says Hariri', 13 December, online: https://www.presstv.com/Detail/2018/12/13/582843/Israel-wont-succeed-if-it-launches-another-war-on-Lebanon-says-Hariri

Pressman, Jeremy (2006) 'The United States and the Israel-Hezbollah War', Crown Centre for Middle East Studies, November, online: https://www.brandeis.edu/crown/publications/meb/MEB13.pdf

Provence, Michael (2005) The Great Syrian Revolt, University of Texas Press, Austin

Qassem, Naim (2005) *Hizbullah: the story from within,* SAQI, London

Rabil, Robert G (2001) 'The Maronites and Syria Withdrawal: from 'isolationists' to 'traitors'? *Middle East Policy,* September, 8,3 pp.23-43

Rashid, Ahmed (1999) 'The Taliban: Exporting Extremism', *Foreign Affairs,* Vol 78, No 6, (Nov-Dec) 22-35

Rice, Condoleezza (2003) 'Dr. Condoleezza Rice Discusses Foreign Policy', The White House, 7 August, online: https://georgewbush-whitehouse.archives.gov/news/releases/2003/08/20030807-1.html

Richter, Donald (1992) *Chemical Soldiers: British Gas Warfare in World War I*, University Press of Kansas, Lawrence

Rizk, Ali (2018) 'U.S. Escalates Against Hezbollah: Israel Happy, EU Not', LobeLog, 27 November, online: https://lobelog.com/u-s-escalates-against-hezbollah-israel-happy-eu-not/

RT (2017) 'Russia's Syria op: Key points of campaign that helped crush ISIS & gave peace a chance', 12 December, online: https://www.rt.com/news/412873-russian-syria-op-key-points/

Rudaw (2018) 'Hashd deploys 20,000 fighters to fortify Iraq-Syria border', 31 October, online: http://www.rudaw.net/english/middleeast/iraq/311020181

Saad-Ghorayeb, Amal (2002) *Hizbu'llah*, Pluto Press, London

Sachs, Susan (2005) 'Rafik Hariri, Ex-Premier of Lebanon, Dies at 60', *New York Times,* 15 February, online: https://www.nytimes.com/2005/02/15/world/middleeast/rafik-hariri-expremier-of-lebanon-dies-at-60.html

Sahimi, Muhammad (2009) 'The Fog over the 1983 Beirut Attacks', Frontline, PBS, 24 October, online: https://www.pbs.org/wgbh/pages/frontline/tehranbureau/2009/10/the-1983-beirut-bombing-attack.html

Schmitt, Eric (2016) 'ISIS Used Chemical Arms at Least 52 Times in Syria and Iraq, Report Says', *New York Times*, 21 November, online: https://www.nytimes.com/2016/11/21/world/middleeast/isis-chemical-weapons-syria-iraq-mosul.html

Seale, Patrick (1988) *Asad: the Struggle for the Middle East*, University of California Press, Los Angeles

Shalal, Andrea (2014) 'Lockheed to deliver first of 36 F-16s to Iraq this week', Reuters, 4 June, online: https://www.reuters.com/article/us-usa-lockheed-martin-iraq/lockheed-to-deliver-first-of-36-f-16s-to-iraq-this-week-idUSKBN0EE2HZ20140603

Sharman, Jon (2017) 'Iraq 'totally liberated' from Isis, country's armed forces claim', *The Independent,* 9 December, online: https://www.independent.co.uk/news/world/middle-east/iraq-liberated-isis-islamic-state-latest-war-armed-forces-free-a8100896.html

Shebaya, Halim (2017) 'Where do Lebanon's Christians stand on Hezbollah?', 30 November, Al Jazeera, online: http://www.aljazeera.com/indepth/opinion/lebanon-christians-stand-hezbollah-171128102446572.html

Sousa, David (2014) 'Three Phases of Resistance: How Hezbollah Pushed Israel Out of Lebanon', E-IR, 28 April, online: https://www.e-ir.info/2014/04/28/three-phases-of-resistance-how-hezbollah-pushed-israel-out-of-lebanon/

STL (2018) 'Special Tribunal for Lebanon', online: https://www.stl-tsl.org/en/

Superville, Darlene (2017) 'Trump says 'America is being respected again' by defeating ISIS, street gangs at home and abroad', *Washington Post*, 8 December, online: https://www.pbs.org/newshour/politics/watch-live-trump-to-speak-at-rally-in-florida-ahead-of-alabama-election

Takeri, Amir (2018) 'Why Iran's Intervention in Syria Proved so Costly', Asharq al Awsat, 14 March, online: https://aawsat.com/english/home/article/1204601/exclusive-why-iran's-intervention-syria-proved-so-costly

Tripp, Charles (2000) *A History of Iraq*, Cambridge University Press, New York

UN (1989) 'Taif Accords', 22 October, online: https://peacemaker.un.org/lebanon-taifaccords89

Watling, Jack (2016) 'The Shia Militias of Iraq', *The Atlantic*, 22 December, online: https://www.theatlantic.com/international/archive/2016/12/shia-militias-iraq-isis/510938/

Worrall, James, Simon Mabon and Gordon Clubb (2016) *Hezbollah: from Islamic Resistance to Government,* Praeger, Santa Barbara California

Xinhua (2018) 'Iraq announces final results of parliamentary elections after manual recount', 10 August, online: http://www.xinhuanet.com/english/2018-08/10/c_137379859.htm

Zebari, Hoshyar (2014) 'Letter dated 25 June 2014 from the Permanent Representative of Iraq to the United Nations addressed to the Secretary-General', United Nations Security Council, 25 June, online: https://www.securitycouncilreport.org/wp-content/uploads/s_2014_440.pdf

Zubaida, Sami (2011) *Beyond Islam: a new understanding of the Middle East*, Library of Modern Middle East Studies, I B Tauris, London, online: https://epdf.tips/beyond-islam-a-new-understanding-of-the-middle-east-library-of-modern-middle-eas.html

Chapter Fourteen

WHY IRAN MATTERS

Armenian museum, Isfahan, Iran, August 2017. Iran's diverse cultures are treasured and protected.

Both the friends and enemies of Iran agree, this nation is uniquely important and central to the region. Of course, their reasoning differs. Iran's enemies claim it represents a huge danger, while for its allies Iran is the great counterweight and guarantor of an independent region.

The shrillest denunciations of Iran come from Apartheid Israel. In 1993 Zionist leader Benjamin Netanyahu wrote: "the most dangerous threat to Israel's existence is not in the Arab world, but rather in Iran" (Stoffel 2018). Twenty-five years later he told Europeans that Iran was "the world's greatest threat" (Agius 2018). Netanyahu's fear is based on Iran's commitment, since 1979, to dismantling the racist colony in Palestine. Matching words with deeds, Iran supports the armed Palestinian resistance. Zionists often falsely portray demands to dismantle their racist state as a 'genocidal' threat to Jewish people. Yet Iran has one of the most secure Jewish communities in the region (Sengupta 2016; Hjelmgaard 2018).

Washington also regularly expresses deep fears over Iran. In this case the fear, and associated threats, stem from concern for its own role and influence in the region. A democratic Palestine and good neighbourly relations between the Arab states would threaten Washington's 'protection' racket. The main US rationale for having troops in the region has become 'protection' from the terrorist proxies it has itself created, to divide and weaken the independent states. In face of this aggression and deception, Iran remains the main obstacle. The Islamic Republic has a voice, capacity and consistency. US General Stanley McChrystal, speaking of Iran's Quds Force General Qassem Suleimani (but he might as well have been speaking of Iran as a whole) said that Suleimani was "driven by the fervent nationalism that is the lifeblood of Iran's citizens and leadership", acknowledging that Suleimani and the state he serves are "singularly positioned to shape the future of the Middle East" (McChrystal 2019). That shows a US-American jealous realism towards the large, independent nation.

The US drove a coup against the democratically elected government of Iran back in 1953, imposing a dictatorial and brutal monarchy that lasted for the next 25 years (Ruehsen 1993; Halliday 1979). When that regime was suddenly overthrown and its US sponsors expelled in the 1979 revolution, Washington experienced a trauma from which it has not yet recovered. It launched a semi-permanent war against independent Iran. President Jimmy Carter declared the Persian Gulf part of the "vital interests" of the USA, to be defended with force (Davis 2017). President Ronald Reagan backed Iraq under Saddam Hussein in a long war against the new Islamic Republic, to weaken both countries. During that war the Reagan administration also covertly sold missiles to Iran, to help fund mercenaries for another war in Central America (PBS 2019). After President George W. Bush invaded Iraq in 2003, he targeted Iran with unilateral disarmament demands, claiming Iran "threatens to put a region already known for instability and violence under the shadow of a nuclear holocaust" (Shipman 2007). For forty years the US has obsessively threatened Iran.

These threats were part of a new campaign to control Iran's nuclear energy technology under the pretext of preventing its nuclear weapons program, a matter discussed below. Aggressive rhetoric continued. Democrat Hillary Clinton, running for president in 2008, declared she would "attack Iran" to protect Israel. If they "foolishly consider launching an attack on Israel, we would be able to totally obliterate them," she exclaimed (Morgan 2008). The Obama administration led a sanctions regime against Iran before it finally agreed to a nuclear energy control deal, in exchange for the removal of sanctions (JCPOA) in 2015. This was torn up the following year by the incoming Trump administration. Imposing extreme economic siege measures, which affected third parties and lacked a specific rationale, Donald Trump echoed Israel's cry that "Iran is a great threat" (Fabian 2019).

The US-Israeli claim that Iran sponsors terrorist groups does not stand up to scrutiny. Even most of those in the Middle East on the official US classification of terrorist groups (USDOS 2019) are extremist Sunni groups, closely linked to US ally Saudi Arabia (Weinstein 2017). Of those on the US list which are linked to Iran, virtually all are Palestinian or Shi'a resistance groups, opposed to Israeli ethnic cleansing and to the various foreign interventions in Lebanon, Syria and Iraq (USDOS 2019).

On the ally side, the Islamic Republic of Iran has enjoyed a strong relationship with the Syrian Arab Republic since 1979. Although Syria is ideologically a secular, pan-Arab state, its relations with the Islamic Republic of Iran have been better than those with many other Arab countries (Tibi 1986). The reason for this alliance was spelt out by Goodarzi (2009: 3, 294). The Iran-Syria alliance has been:

> essentially defensive and emerged in response to acts of aggression orchestrated by [Saddam Hussein's] Iraq (1980) and Israel (1982), in both cases with the prior knowledge and tacit support of the USA ... Hafez Assad, Ruhollah Khomeini and their successors have viewed the region as a strategic whole and regarded their alliance as a vital tool with which to further Arab-Islamic interests and increase regional autonomy.

It has been, in other words, an anti-imperial alliance of independent states.

Iran's relations with the small but powerful Shi'a resistance group in Lebanon, Hezbollah, makes clear use of religious bonds. Indeed, Iran's supreme religious leader acts as the arbitral authority for Hezbollah (Qassem 2005: 50-58). Iran also backs many of the Popular Mobilisation Units (PMUs) of Iraq, through Shi'a networks. However, with close allies in secular Syria and largely Sunni Muslim Palestine, Iran's regional network cannot properly be regarded as sectarian.

Iran's leading role in the region keeps both Washington and Tel Aviv on the verge of panic. It repeatedly reminds the US why it cannot dominate the entire region. Apart from its own independence, Iran actively supports the other independent peoples of the region, those in Palestine, Lebanon, Syria, Iraq, Bahrain and Yemen. It is a 'threat' mainly to the ambitions of outside hegemonic powers, and to the destructive role of Apartheid Israel.

Despite constant aggression, at the 40th anniversary of the Islamic Republic in 2019, Iran presents as a much stronger nation-state than four decades earlier. It has consolidated its state institutions and independence. Its industrial capacity has developed substantially. The internal political factions, 'principalists' (those said to adhere more firmly to Islamic principles – often called 'hardliners' in the west) versus liberals, are well entrenched.

There are independent opinion polls in Iran, and they give little comfort to the country's external critics. The UNDP reports that 71% trust their national government, compared to the 39% in the USA (UNDP 2018b: Table 14). After protests at economic conditions in early 2018 a joint US-Canada-Iran study group polled Iran's social and political opinion. They found that 81% saw the country's top problem as economic (unemployment, inflation and low income). 77% did not agree that 'Iran's political system needs ... fundamental change' (15% agreed). There was overwhelming support for the country's defence missile program (95%) and for its nuclear program (86%). Nevertheless, 73% felt the (Rouhani-led liberal) government should do more 'to help the poor'. A strong majority of 86% supported Iran's regional campaigns against terrorism and 55% wanted to increase them. Of the 2018 protests, 66% thought the police handled them well (24% said 'badly') but 65% felt the arrested protestors should be released. Yet most also thought that those who had burned the flag (63%) or had damaged public property (60%) should be 'punished harshly' (Gallagher, Mohseni and Ramsay 2018). These responses suggest a fairly stable democracy, whatever any outsider may think about hybrid theocracy-democracies.

Importantly, the country's human development indicators advanced strongly. Between 1980 and 2017, average life expectancy in Iran rose a remarkable 22 years: from 54.1 to 76.2 years. Average years of schooling more than quadrupled, from 2.2 to 9.8 years, and almost at gender equity (UNDP 2016; UNDP 2018a). Inequality and poverty fell substantially (UNDP 1999; World Bank 2019). These are extrordinary achievements. Iran moved ahead while its enemies carried out dreadful and futile wars. A US military study into the invasion of Iraq ('the Iraq war') found that "an emboldened and expansionist Iran appears to be the only victor" (South 2019). This was not the first time that a would-be empire 'shot itself in the foot'.

However, Iran was and still is subject to an extraordinary political-economic assault, which at one stage included all the big powers. The nation was forced to open its nuclear and strategic energy technology to foreign supervision and control. Since the JCPOA agreement, and the subsequent reversal by Washington on its agreement, a new economic aggression has begun. For Iran, this necessarily means more restructuring of the country's financial, trade and strategic relations.

With that background, this chapter begins by explaining the Iranian origins of the revolution, and of Iran's particular version of 'political Islam'. It then recognises Iran's human development achievements and challenges, before documenting key elements of the permanent aggression waged against the country, including the deceptive nuclear deal. Finally, the chapter returns to Iran's role in the region, as leader of the Axis of Resistance.

1. The 1979 Revolution

This section has its focus on the 1979 revolution, as this marks the definitive beginning of the modern independent state of Iran; although there are important antecedents including the 1890 Tobacco Revolt and the 1905-1911 constitutional revolution. Iran endured its own emperor, imposed by the US after a CIA-backed coup in 1953. Democratically elected Prime Minister Mohammed Mossadegh was overthrown as a result of imperial reactions to his attempts to nationalise assets controlled by British Petroleum. Prime Minister Mossadegh was trying to assert legitimate national claims over the country's natural resources. However, 'Operation Ajax', run by the US and backed by Britain, arrested and jailed Mossadegh, installing Shah Reza Pahlavi as absolute monarch (Ruehsen 1993). Under Pahlavi a US-led consortium, which excluded Iranian partners, assumed control of the country's oil resources. Political repression under SAVAK, the Shah's hated secret police, was severe. Many thousands were killed, to protect the puppet monarchy (Halliday 1979).

An important consequence of that repression was that the secular political opposition was crushed and dismantled. The coup not only destroyed the Mossadegh-led government, it dismantled 'trade unions, professional associations and all independent political parties'. The Pahlavi regime had claimed modernisation and advances for women (Halliday 1979), but this showcased a tiny elite. It was a regime of mass exclusion. The remaining power base left to mobilise against this dictatorship was a well organised clergy of over 90,000 (Abrahamian 1990: 22, 24). Structural explanations of the Iranian Revolution have stressed the tension between a rigid, elitist state and strong social solidarity networks, notably urban migrants, a large small merchant class and the strong religious class (Parsa 1989).

It was clear that Pahlavi, for all his imperial pretensions, was a US puppet, and that opposition to this puppet king meant opposition to US control of Iran. The New York Times recognised that cries for 'liberty' and 'independence', while aimed at the Shah, 'could only' have meant independence 'from the US and its western allies', as they had propped up the Shah for decades (Cohen 2014). Huge mobilisations, holding up the exiled Ayatollah Khomeini as their moral leader, eventually drove the Shah into exile. The collapse of this US-backed dictatorship was notable for the failure of royalists to mount any real counter-offensive. A regime with the fifth largest army on earth, well-armed and well-funded, went down without much of a fight (Abrahamian 1990: 21), exposing the near absence of domestic support.

For these historical reasons, the leadership of the revolution became Islamic and the character of the new system remained Islamic. A quite original version of political Islam was developed by Imam Khomeini, distinct from the western dependent Islamist movements, the sectarian Muslim Brotherhood and the sectarian Salafism of the Saudis. This was a political difference, more than a sectarian or 'Shi'a versus Sunni' divide. Khomeini's vision has been termed 'a coalition based on nationalism, anti-imperialism and Islamism' (Panah 2007: ch.3).

In North America there was an entirely different discussion about the Iranian revolution. This had to do with supposed 'anti-Americanism', the fate of US embassy staff held prisoner by revolutionary students, generalised attacks on theocracy and the new 'Carter doctrine' that claimed a US 'national interest' in the Persian Gulf (Wolf 2006; Klare 2006; Davis 2017). This mostly self-referential debate has little to do with Iran or this discussion.

The vision of Imam Khomeini shared the common idea of a great Islamic community (Ummah), a supra-national Muslim Society. However, unlike the Salafi version, it included all sects and necessarily rejected the Salafist 'takfiri' doctrine, where those of other faiths or sects were open to attack. One could say that Khomeini's synthesis drew on the historical minority and persecuted status of Shi'a Muslims in much of the region. In any case, this Great Community was officially non-sectarian. Khomeini's vision contrasted a 'Pure Muhammadan Islam' of the downtrodden and humble with 'American Islam', a religion of the arrogant, luxurious and opportunists. He described 'American Islam' as 'the Islam of comfort and luxury ... of compromise and ignominy, the Islam of the indolent'. By contrast, 'pure Mohammedan Islam' was seen as 'the Islam of the barefooted ... the scourge of the despised ones of the bitter and disgraceful history of deprivation, the annihilator of modern capitalism and bloodthirsty communism' (ITF 2014). This was a vision linking Islamic principle to ideas of popular emancipation from the recent neo-colonial experience.

While its key values have remained constant, Iran's political culture seems more adaptive. The Republic developed democratic structures, albeit under religious guidance, and an evolving policy and practice under a strong state. With an overwhelming majority (around 90%) of Shia Muslims, chauvinism was always a possibility. Yet there has been particular protection of Iran's Jewish community, reinforced by a decree from Imam Khomeini (Demick 2014). Whatever disadvantage they might face, it has been pointed out that Iranian Jews are much better off than Palestinians in the territories occupied by Israel (Cook 2007). There are also special protections for the Christian and Zoroastrian minorities. The Baha'i group, on the other hand, was branded a political 'fifth column' for Israel and has indeed suffered discrimination (MacEoin 1987; Astani 2010). Baha'i attempts to convert Muslims and their base in Tel Aviv help sustain this strong prejudice. This has recently been subject to internal criticism, with a senior Iranian cleric criticising 'violations against the rights of these children of God' (Masoumi-Tehrani 2014).

The Islamic Republic of Iran does maintain sensitivity to the position of Shi'a communities (mostly minorities) in regional countries such as Pakistan, Afghanistan, Lebanon, Syria and Egypt. Yet most of its strategic relationships are with non-Muslim countries. Even Hezbollah in Lebanon has given up its idea of an Islamic state and cooperates with other communities, defining its wider community as an anti-Zionist and anti-imperial 'Resistance' (El Husseini 2010). War, economic sanctions and regular threats from Israel and the US (especially over its arming the Palestinian resistance) have helped build self-reliance in Iran. The close relationships formed with Russia and Venezuela are clearly to do with anti-imperialism, unencumbered by sectarian religion.

Links to the late Venezuelan President Hugo Chávez, a Christian socialist, are a case in point. Chávez made many trips to Iran, as did former President Ahmadinejad to Venezuela. Political figures in the US made ludicrous claims that those links were to do with terrorism and nuclear weapons (Golinger 2012), missing the point that this was part of the creation of an anti-imperial network. Over several years the two countries developed literally hundreds of agreements, ranging from energy to telecommunications, biotechnology and housing (Primera 2009). Chávez defended the Islamic Republic, stressing the solidarity developed between nations under attack from the great power. 'They will never be able to restrict the Islamic revolution in whatever way ... we will always stand together', he said. For his part Ahmadinejad said that Iran and Venezuela were part of a wider revolutionary front stretching through East Asia to Latin America (Miller Llana 2010). The relationship survived the death of Chávez and a change of presidents in Iran. In August 2014 Venezuelan Foreign Minister Elias Jaua met President Hassan Rohani in Tehran, where they discussed regional conflicts and the maintenance of their various economic agreements (AVN 2014).

The current Supreme Leader, Ayatollah Ali Khamenei, reinforces the independent and anti-imperial themes of Iran's political Islam, in a thinly veiled attack on collaborative Salafism. He is talking about the Brotherhood and the Islam of the Gulf monarchies when he says that 'American Islam ... despite its Islamic appearance and label, is in compliance with despotism and Zionism, yields to the supremacy of arrogant powers and entirely serves the goals of despotism and the US' (ABNA 2014). 'American Islam' is thus seen as an imperial collaborator, seeking to divide the region and standing in the way of genuine Islamic enlightenment. Khamenei says 'the enemy is investing in civil wars in the region and pins hope on a Shi'a-Sunni war to relieve itself of the concern of Islamic Awakening'. He pointed to the 'evil hand of the enemy's intelligence services' in staging upheavals in some Islamic communities, including Iraq (ABNA 2014).

When we factor in the anti-imperial element, the claims of a natural 'Sunni-Shi'a' divide in the Middle East look quite different. The Iran-Syria-Hezbollah-Palestine 'Axis of Resistance' is quite explicitly anti-sectarian. On the other hand, the sectarianism promoted by most of the Gulf monarchies – and supported by the imperial powers – seeks to accentuate divisions. This should not be surprising. Most claims of natural communities or religious divides obscure the role of power politics. History is important and formative. The political Islam of Iran developed as a popular anti-imperial force (Ayoob 1979: 543). This is different from the Muslim Brotherhood, which for most of its history has looked for foreign assistance in its attempts to depose Arab or secular nationalism (Curtis 2012: 24).

2. Human development achievements and challenges

On the 40th anniversary of the Iranian revolution US President Donald Trump published a series of propaganda graphics suggesting Iran had experienced '40 years of failure' (AFP 2019). Such claims from a dedicated enemy cannot be taken at face value. Yet in any such controversy it makes sense to look for independent evidence. We have just that, from the United Nations Development Programme (UNDP), whose human development measures have been collected from most countries since 1990. Key indicators have been combined into a Human Development Index (HDI), which measures three elements: "a long and healthy life, being knowledgeable and having a decent standard of living" (UNDP 2019b). Other more specific UNDP indicators show areas of strength and weakness, or challenge.

The human development evidence on Iran in recent decades is not just good, it is outstanding. The UNDP lists the Islamic Republic as second only to the Peoples' Republic of China in its growth in human development – amongst the world's top 100 nations – from 1990 to 2017. Iran's HDI grew on average 1.21% per year over those 27 years, and China's 1.51% (UNDP 2018b: Table 2). In the case of China this was due to exceptional and sustained per capita economic growth; in the case of Iran it was due to exceptional and sustained improvements in life expectancy – mainly due to health care improvements and child survival – and to improvements in education (UNDP 1999; UNDP 2018a).

Table 13 shows Iran's progress compared to the average 'high human development' group, and to comparable regional countries, Turkey and Lebanon. The data shows strong achievements in education, at almost gender equality, as well as in maternal health and child nutrition. Social cohesion is also strong, in the sense of trust in the national government. The challenges appear in unemployment and women's political representation and, as later data will show, in regional disparities and women's economic independence.

Table 13
Iran: key human development data, 2017

	I.R. of IRAN	High Human Development	Turkey	Lebanon
HDI rank (2017)	60	[60-112]	64	80
Av life expectancy, years	76.2	76.0	76.0	79.8
Mean years of schooling	9.8	8.2	8.0	8.7
MYS male	9.9	8.6	8.8	8.9
MYS female	9.7	8.0	7.1	8.5
Maternal mortality rate (per 100,000 pregnancies)	25	38	16	15
Infant mortality (per 1,000 live births)	13	11.2	10.9	6.9
Child malnutrition (mod. to severe stunting)	6.8	9.5	9.5	na
Female MPs %	5.9	22.3	14.6	3.1
Inequality (Gini co-eff)	38.8	na	41.9	31.8
Unemployment (2017)	13.1	6.3	11.3	6.3
Trust in national government (2012-2017)	71	na	59	22

All data from UNDP 2018b (Tables 1, 3, 4, 5, 8, 11, 14)

Iran's problems of unemployment and economic development generally must be seen in the context of four decades of economic aggression. Unemployment in 2017 was 13.1%, with youth unemployment at 30.3% (UNDP 2018b). That this has not translated into high poverty measures is due to strong social security practices.

When considering the data on poverty we must again be wary of partisan sources. The US state media, for example, often runs extravagant reports. One of these suggested that "due to the failure of the Iranian regime, its people have become increasingly poorer over the past 40 years". An Iranian exile is quoted as saying, without supporting evidence, that he "believes close to two thirds of the Iranian population lives below the poverty line" (Mohammad 2017). Any emerging poor data is seized on for political purposes. For example, research for Iran's parliament showed a rise in inflation and poverty (over 2016-2017) and, in response, one US writer suggested this poor outcome (combined with domestic protests over the cost of living) might raise "an opportunity" for the US to criticise "the regime" (Ghasseminejad 2018). There is a constant effort to discredit a perceived enemy.

Fortunately, we have some more sober data from the Washington based and US-dominated World Bank, which cannot be accused of pro-Iran bias. The World Bank noted that both poverty and inequality in Iran fell strongly between 1990 and 2015. The more than 3 million in poverty in 1990 fell to 300,000 in 2005, rising again to 700,000 in 2009 before falling again strongly through to 2013, before rising again under the pressure of inflation (Table 14).

Table 14: Poverty in Iran, 1990-2014

	1990	1994	1998	2005	2009	2013	2014
In poverty (million)	3.2	1.9	1.6	0.3	0.7	0.1	0.2
Source: World Bank 2019 (at $1.90 a day, 2011 PPP)							

Translating that raw data into percentages, the fall in poverty between 2009 and 2013 was from 13.1% to 8.1% and, according to the World Bank, "likely due to a universal cash transfer program in late 2010, which preceded the elimination of subsidies on energy and bread ... However poverty increased in 2014, which may have been associated with a declining social assistance in real terms due to inflation" and to depreciation of the currency (World Bank 2018). That cash transfer program, under President Ahmadinejad, provided household subsidies of as much as 29% of median household income. A US study found that, except for youth, there was "no evidence that [these] cash transfers reduced labour supply" (Salehi-Isfahani and Mostafavi-Dehzooei 2017). Youth had other options, not least free tertiary education. Yet multiple and long-term sanctions led by the USA have been a major contributor, not just in squeezing exports and making imports more expensive, but in weakening the currency and helping drive price inflation.

Iran's human development challenges–alongside stabilising the currency and prices, and lowering unemployment – can be seen in the need to address regional disparities and the deficits of women's political and economic participation. Regional variation in poverty can be high. When in Tehran the poverty rate was put at 12%, in the most neglected region of Sistan and Balouchistan it was put at 38% (Ghasseminejad 2018; also Sabermahani et al 2013).

Although there have been great advances for Iran's women and girls in education, there are relatively few women members of parliament (see Table 1) and economic independence seems low. The World Bank and the UNDP cite women's labour force participation at only 17% (MEI 2009) and women's independent income at only 20% that of men (UNDP 2018a: Table 4 & 5). However, there is serious controversy over these figures.

It is often said (outside Iran) that women's access to the formal labour market was undermined by the religious expectations of women; yet their educational status improved strongly and they continued to play key roles in many professions as well as in the agricultural and services sectors (Kian 2014: 338). They are over-represented at universities. Women freely access both informal and formal labour markets (Bahramitash 2003; Rostami-Povey 2010, Honarbin-Holliday 2013), running businesses and working in the financial sector (Simon 2015; Solomon 2015). An MEI study notes differing estimates of women's labour participation, from 18.5% to 24.6%; and an even 'higher figure in the Socio-Economic Characteristics of Households panel data' (MEI 2009). A study by Fatemeh Etemad Moghadam (2009), Professor of Economics at Hofstra University in New York, goes further, saying that "women's labour force participation is undercounted in Iran ... An examination of a large body of field research on the subject ... suggests a much higher participation rate, about 40% of the total agricultural labor". That same study shows that "a large number of educated upper and middle class women were active in the informal market ... in sharp contrast to the studies in other developing countries in which informal participants are generally poor and unskilled and are unable to join the modern formal economy". In Iran there are a large number of "middle and upper income educated women in the informal economy" (Moghadam 2009).

People at craft market, Isfahan, Iran

Bahramitash and Esfahani (2011) support Moghadam (2009), saying that the higher levels of education for women

> have fundamentally transformed the nature of female LFP [labour force participation] and employment in the country ... an increasingly larger proportion of educated women aged 20-50 years are employed in the private sector in professional positions in urban areas. This is quite different from the expansion of female employment before the Revolution, which predominantly consisted of jobs for very young, uneducated women in rural areas mostly as unpaid family workers in producing carpets and handicraft.

Mehran (2003) concludes that the Islamic Republic of Iran has deliberately used formal schooling to close educational and income opportunity gaps. She says this can only be understood if one analyses how women "have made the best use of the opportunities created by the interplay of tradition and modernity to become active participants in educational endeavours" (Mehran 2003: 286). We can conclude that the World Bank figures on women's economic participation do not tell the full story.

Polemics against Iran often come from US sources, yet Iran compares favourably with the USA in several areas. According to the World Bank (2019b), Iran reduced its inequality (as measured by the Gini index) from 47.40 in 1986 to 38.80 in 2014. Inequality in the US remains significantly higher, at 41.5 (Gini). Despite the rhetoric of 'freedom', the US imprisonment rate (the highest on earth at 698 per 100,000 population) was more than double that of Iran (at 287); and far more Iranians trust their national government (71%) than is the case in the USA (39%) (UNDP 2018b: Tables 3, 12 & 14).

3. The permanent war

Just a few hundred metres from Tehran's famous Tabiat

Bridge (the Nature Bridge) lies the Museum of Holy Defence, a powerful reminder of the horror and patriotic sacrifice of hundreds of thousands of Iranians during the Iraq-Iran war (1980-88). Three decades after the end of that war, visitors can walk through a reconstruction of the besieged city of Khorramshahr, experience the extreme heat and cold of the defenders' bunkers, walk across replicas of mine-laden wetlands and gaze up at a glittering ceiling which holds thousands of name tags of the fallen. That terrible war lives in Iranian imagination, and in the tradition of the volunteer defenders, the Basiji (Haines and Fox 2014: 105), whose legacy can be seen today, not just in Iran's militia, but also in the Lebanese Resistance and in Iraq's Hashid al Shaabi.

The Islamic view of patriotic defence, combined with the theme of righteous martyrdom for a great cause, built a strong Iranian belief that resistance to aggression from Saddam's Iraq was a 'sacred' duty. It was a battle for justice (edālat) and truth (haq) against injustice (zolm) and vanity (bātel) (Khosronejad 2011). One commentator observes: "even the most disparate groups in Iran were brought together through mutual anger and frustration towards American imperialism" (Swerdlow 2017). Despite subsequent internal divisions over economic policy, many point to the links between that wartime strategic unity and a range of self-sufficient developments (satellite, defence and industrial technologies) achieved as a result of constant outside attacks (Bangash 2019; Smith 2015). This virtually permanent war has included incessant propaganda, terrorism and economic siege.

Saddam Hussein's September 1980 invasion of Iran was encouraged by the USA. Humiliated by its expulsion from Iran and fearing less than favourable access to the energy resources of the region, the US under President Jimmy Carter in 1980 declared the "Persian Gulf region" to be essential to "the vital interests of the United States of America". Those interests would be guarded "by any means necessary" including by "military force" (Davis 2017). US agencies were at work to weaken the fledgling Islamic Republic. Prior to September 1980 there had been "a few border clashes" between Iraq and Iran, but it was in

September that Saddam Hussein scrapped Iraq's 1975 treaty with Iran and made his move (Tripp 2000: 232-3). Western accounts of the war play down western backing for Saddam Hussein, whom Washington would later depose. The Iraqi invasion of southwest Iran in September 1980 did have a particular declared motive, to resolve a longstanding territorial dispute over control of a southern waterway, the Shatt al-Arab river. However, Saddam chose his moment, knowing that Washington had been humiliated by Iran, that its new government was not yet strong and with the belief that Shi'a uprisings in the entire region, including in Iraq, had been inflamed by revolutionary Iran (Wright 1980). Saddam correctly guessed that Washington would back him as he tried (but failed) to take all of Khuzestan province, the southwestern, oil-rich and Arab speaking part of Iran (Swerdlow 2017).

The USA was not alone in backing Saddam. Jeremy Salt points out that "all five permanent members of the Security Council" provided weapons to Iraq. France alone sold Iraq $4 billion in weapons between 1977 and 1980, and another $12 billion during the war, between 1981 and 1988 (Salt 2008: 283-4). Saddam's western backers also helped with his chemical weapons attacks. The US and the UK, which had signed and ratified conventions banning chemical and biological weapons, made statements against Saddam's 'Project 922' chemical weapons program, but in secret they helped him with it (Salt 2008: 292-3). For example, US satellite information was provided to help Saddam target massed Iranian troops (Harris and Aid 2013). Iraq began chemical attacks "on all battlefronts" in 1983, using mustard gas against Kurdish Peshmerga and Iranian troops. These attacks continued in every subsequent year until 1988, and later included the use of the nerve agents tabun and sarin. With US President Reagan directing that the US should do "whatever is necessary" to ensure that Iran did not prevail, USA agencies helped Saddam both with supply and satellite intelligence for the attacks (Hersh 1992). Much of the evidence on supply came out at 1992 US Senate Committee hearings, which covered the Export Administration Act (Salt 2008: 294-8). The Iraqi military carried out two major chemical weapons attacks on urban areas, at

Sardasht in 1987 (western Iran) and Halabja in 1988 (eastern Iraq). Thousands died and thousands more were injured (Haines and Fox 2014: 105-106). When a UN brokered ceasefire was finally signed in August 1988, Saddam had achieved none of his original territorial objectives (Tripp 2000: 247-8).

Since Washington and its satellites later overthrew Saddam Hussein after their 2003 invasion, on false 'self-defence' pretexts (CIA 2004; CICUSRWMD 2005; Chilcott 2016), western revisionist historians have been at work. Saddam was tried and executed for his crimes against the Kurds, including his use of chemical weapons in Halabja. Yet, not only had the US helped Saddam gas Iranians and Kurds, the British had used chemical weapons against an anti-colonial uprising in Iraq, back in the 1920s. Winston Churchill openly boasted about his wish to use chemical weapons. That gave later revisionist historians (even with assistance from the BBC and Wikipedia) a more difficult task. They tried to say Churchill was only speaking about tear gas, or of chemicals which just made people "sneeze". Richard Langworth of the International Churchill Society, for example, wrote that "Churchill confused the matter when he used the general term 'poison gas'", citing his approval for its use. A further problem for the revisionists was that Churchill, the next year, urged "fullest use" of chemical weapons against Bolsheviks in Russia, during British support for counter-revolutionary attacks (Langworth 2013). Despite that sordid history, after the 2003 invasion, with Saddam condemned for using Churchill's tactics, British historians have sought to distance Britain from that unsavoury aspect of warfare.

During the Iraq-Iran war both Washington and Saddam made use of a formerly left Iranian group, which had fallen out with Tehran. The Mojahedin-e Khalq (MEK) was categorised as a terrorist group by both Iran and the USA for many years. It had opposed the Shah's regime and participated in the 1979 Revolution, but quickly turned on the new government and its supporters. After the MEK was driven out of the country it was adopted by the Iraq-Saudi-CIA bloc, helping Saddam Hussein in his aggression against Iran. With Saddam's support the MEK created a 'National Liberation Army' (NLA) of Iran, based in Baghdad, and used this to destroy Iranian villages, even during a UN brokered ceasefire. But their role in the slaughter of Iranian patriots destroyed the MEK's reputation within Iran (Carey 2018). Very quickly the group's hybrid anti-imperialist, socialist and Islamic philosophy was abandoned as it became an opportunistic cult (Merat 2018). In the 1990s they continued as mercenaries for Saddam Hussein, helping suppress Iraqi Shi'a and Kurd resistance in Iraq (USDOS 2007; Merat 2018). Then after the 2003 invasion of Iraq they were protected by US forces at the 'Camp Ashraf' base, precisely because they were seen as a tool which could be used against Iran (Cartalucci 2018).

The US Brookings Institute admitted that the MEK was "undemocratic and enjoys little popularity in Iran itself". Nevertheless, the think tank recognised that the MEK might be used as a proxy force. However, to do so openly "Washington would need to remove it from the list of foreign terrorist organizations" (Pollack et al 2009). The US kept the MEK on this list until 2012, noting that it had killed "several US military personnel and civilians in the 1970s" while maintaining centres in Europe and carrying out "terrorist operations against the Iranian [government] for nearly three decades, from European and Iraqi bases" (USDOS 2007). Yet after the proxy wars of the Arab Spring – when the US backed a range of al Qaeda affiliates in Iraq, Libya and Syria – the MEK was gradually brought in from the cold. The Obama administration removed them from the 'foreign terrorist' list in 2012.

The claim made for removal was that the MEK had publicly renounced violence, had not carried out terror attacks for 'more than a decade' and had cooperated with US occupation forces at Camp Ashraf (USDOS 2012). This was a deceptive rationale. That same year US officials linked the MEK to the assassination of two Iranian nuclear scientists. Iranian officials believed the MEK was collaborating with and trained by Israel's secret service, Mossad (Marizad 2012). The utility of the group was not for 'renouncing violence' but rather because they were committed to ruthless violence against Iran and had proven themselves pliable opportunists (Cartalucci 2018). The MEK has been adopted by Washington as a proxy force, like the al Qaeda groups used against Iraq and Syria, but with a distinct ideology. They are a nominal 'alternative', like the other exile bodies set up by Washington for Iraq, Libya and Syria. Their tiny support within Iran is not considered that important. They are useful to denounce, destabilise and attack (Parsi 2018; Carey 2018). They also help confuse gullible people in the organised misinformation campaigns against Iran.

Between 2013 and 2016 Washington moved the 2,900 Camp Ashraf MEK members to Albania, where they had also moved some former DAESH / ISIS fighters (Spahiu 2018; Khodabandeh and Khodabandeh 2018). The USA and NATO appear to be using Albania as a home for these terrorist 'assets'; and the Albanian government seems to expect some leverage with the US for performing this hosting service. The MEK in Albania runs social media campaigns, attacking Tehran and promoting its leader, Maryam Rajavi (Merat 2018). NATO has been 'normalising' the MEK among the European states, as various European figures have endorsed or attended their 'Free Iran' rallies, in recent years. For example, Trump advisor John Bolton is reported to have been paid large sums of money to advocate for the MEK (Merat 2018), while Trump legal advisor Rudy Giuliani has also visited the MEK in Albania, on the invitation of Maryam Rajavi (Jazexhi 2018). It seems highly likely the group is still backed by Saudi money and Israeli advisers. In September 2018 the MEK was linked to an attack on a military parade in the southwest Iranian city of Ahvaz (MNA 2018). Saudi sponsorship of the MEK-linked 'al Ahwazia' group was strongly suspected by Iranian authorities (Osman 2018). DAESH may also have been involved. With common sponsors and a common safe haven in Albania, the two terrorist groups might be working together.

The economic war against Iran has run in parallel with the other regional aggressions, as part of a hybrid war against the Islamic Republic. Washington's aim has been to cripple the Iranian economy, regardless of the cost to the people, so as to weaken the capacity of this independent state. A hope behind these measures is "to make the economy scream", forcing political upheaval, as was said of similar measures against Chile in the early 1970s (Kornbluh 2017).

US economic sanctions against Iran began in 1979, when Iran's imports were banned and $12 billion in Iranian assets were 'frozen' (Sen 2018). Throughout the Iraq-Iran war, the US designated Iran a 'state sponsor of terrorism', because of its support for Lebanese and Palestinian resistance groups. Under Bush (the son) and Obama administrations Washington managed to get Iran sanctions passed in UN Security Council resolutions of 2007 (UNSC 1747), 2008 (UNSC 1803) and 2010 (UNSC 1929); the pretexts for all were to control the supposed threat from Iran's nuclear energy program (Sen 2018). Resolution 1803 called on member states "to exercise vigilance over the activities of financial institutions in their territories with all banks domiciled in Iran, and their branches and subsidiaries abroad" (UNSC 2008; McGlynn 2008). This was a significant diplomatic victory for the US, as they were joined not just by the European Union but also by Russia and China. That added weight to the sanctions which forced Iran into the 2012-2015 negotiations which led to the JCPOA ('Joint Plan of Action') 'nuclear deal'.

The question of why Iran was singled out for treatment deserves study. Unilateral disarmament has become a key feature of the contemporary uneven application of international law, and bears little relation to actual international threats. One US commentator has even argued that the interests of a stable region might have been better served if Iran had acquired nuclear weapons, to balance Israel's monopoly, because 'nuclear balancing would mean stability (Waltz 2012: 2)'. However, it seems that Israel's allies, including Russia, wanted to maintain the Zionist state's monopoly. The only benefit for Iran, in opening up its nuclear energy sector to international supervision, was relief from economic sanctions. As it turned out, Iran had no demonstrable nuclear weapons program. The International

Atomic Energy Agency (IAEA), which had expressed concerns about prior enrichment activity and disclosure, has certified from 2014 through to 2019 that Iran is not developing nuclear weapons (Sen 2018; VOA 2019).

The 'nuclear deal' was announced with much fanfare. In July 2015 representatives of the EU and of Iran said they had 'delivered on what the world was hoping for: a shared commitment to peace and to join hands in order to make our world safer'. The agreement would "ensure that Iran's nuclear programme will be exclusively peaceful" and anticipated that there would be a "comprehensive lifting of all UN Security Council sanctions as well as multilateral and national sanctions" (Mogherini and Zarif 2015).

Yet the JCPOA was denounced by incoming President Donald Trump, who raised questions about the value of the entire process. Within a short time the US had imposed even harsher sanctions on Iran, including third party sanctions. Section 1245 of the National Defense Authorization Act (NDAA) targeted Iranian oil sales (Ritter 2019: 293). Trump had no support from the EU, nor from Russia nor China. Instead, he threatened to impose sanctions on any country doing business with Iran. The rationale claimed was for 'the safety of the American people', of the Saudis in Riyadh and of the Israelis illegally occupying the Syrian Golan (Pompeo 2018). Contrary to the IAEA, Washington claimed an Iranian nuclear threat was still alive. The renewed US sanctions would target Iran's energy sector, its financial system, trade and foreign investors (White House 2018; Pompeo 2018). The actual rationale was US frustration at Iran's ongoing role in the region. Without a hint of irony, Secretary of State Mike Pompeo cited Iran's alleged 'terrorism' and 'proxy wars', through its support for independent nationalist forces in Yemen, Afghanistan, Iraq, Syria, Lebanon and Palestine. For good measure he tried to blame Iran for providing "sanctuary for al Qaeda", the terrorist network sponsored by the US and its allies (Pompeo 2018). Yet al Qaeda and its affiliates have always expressed a Saudi-styled sectarian hatred for Iran and for all Shi'a Muslims.

US weapons inspector and analyst Scott Ritter wrote that Donald Trump's denunciation of the JCPOA agreement 'threatens to return the world to that precipice' of large scale war (Ritter 2019). Of course, this US backflip over an agreement which it initiated and brokered over several years would also destroy Iranian interest in attempting any similar agreement for years to come. Ritter (2019: 312) pointed out "there is no compelling narrative than can be crafted that would compel Iran to walk away from the JCPOA in favor of renegotiating its nuclear rights".

Decades of mainly US sanctions have certainly damaged Iran's economy, especially exports and the currency. While cloaked in other language, damaging state capacity has helped ensure that the primary impact of sanctions has been, predictably, to "harm ordinary Iranians" (Waltz 2012: 5). Sanctions arbitrarily linked to the country's nuclear program have helped aggravate unemployment, damage finance, trade and the currency, and raise prices for many goods. The main compensation for ordinary Iranian people has been through state social security measures.

Yet Iran's economy is large, diverse and resilient, and far from the collapse which is often suggested by the country's enemies. Adaptation to aggression is producing some advantages. Tehran has been organising non-dollar trade, including oil sales with big customers China and India. Links within the Eurasian bloc are developing, especially through mega-infrastructure projects, like the northern trade corridor to Russia. Steel production has risen strongly. In late 2018 the US-based International Trade Administration recognised that between 2015 and 2018, Iran had moved from a net importer of steel into one of the world's top 20 steel exporters (ITA 2018). Iran no longer exports crude oil and imports fuel, because its expanded refinery capacity has ensured national fuel self-sufficiency (Paraskova 2019). And the country's motor vehicle industry, which employs about 4% of the national workforce, has export markets and/or joint ventures in Algeria, Azerbaijan, Cameroon, Ghana, Egypt, Iraq, Pakistan, Senegal, Syria, Sudan and Venezuela (Iran Daily 2017). The industry's success has led to more specific targeting measures by the US 'sanctions' regime (Dudley 2018). In other words, this large and resource rich country, which has strongly invested in its own people, has been able to adapt and grow in capacity, despite being subject to four decades of aggression.

4. Iran and the Resistance

The shrill cries of its enemies tell us that Iran matters, but why is it so important? It is certainly not because of any threats to peaceful nations, nor from 'terrorism'. Those are all false pretexts. Iran has not invaded another country in centuries. It is attacked because it remains the largest independent nation of the region, with both the capacity and the will to resist and frustrate outside imperial powers, and to organise a regional resistance. The only nations of comparable size in the Middle East are Turkey, with its own imperial legacy and still embedded in NATO, and Egypt, which saw a collapse in both political will and economic capacity in the 1970s. Iran can and does organise the defence of other independent nations in the region. That is the 'threat', to those with imperial ambitions.

In secular terms it is the anti-imperial character of Iran which conditions its strategic role in the region, and in the world. Further, we should not ignore the role of what might be called the 'secular' development of the Islamic Republic. It has been said that there is a long-standing 'secular tradition of government' in the region going back many centuries, including within older 'Islamic' states (Salt 2008: 29). Iran is now engaged with a wider group of international partners, none of which share its religious traditions but many of whom coincide in a number of social values. On this basis there is collaborative policy and practice. Most of Iran's strategic partners (Russia, China, Syria and Venezuela) are secular-pluralist or non-Islamic states. The strategic relationship with Russia is strong (Tarock 1997; Khajehpour 2014). Iran enthusiastically engages in industrial, infrastructure, and financial collaboration with Christian-socialist Venezuela and is strongly committed to defence of the secular, Pan-Arab Socialist Republic of Syria (Goodarzi 2009: 2-3). It also arms the Palestinian resistance, a combination of secular, Sunni Muslim and socialist forces. Such partnerships are built on common concerns, in the case of Iran and Syria to counter aggression and strengthen regional autonomy (Goodarzi 2009: 294).

Iran has helped Palestine resist ethnic cleansing; it has helped the Lebanese resistance expel Israeli occupation; and it has backed both Iraq and Syria in their victories over a sectarian terrorism generated by the Gulf monarchies, Israel and NATO. Iran has the biggest multi-lingual media network in the region and has done more than any other to expose the forgotten Saudi war against independent and revolutionary Yemen. It has engaged with wider anti-imperial forces to help build counter-hegemonic ideas and media, a new financial architecture and a multi-polar world (YVKE Mundial 2009; Hiro 2014). It promises to build a transport corridor between Tehran and Beirut (Silk Road Briefing 2018), a move which would contribute greatly to regional development; but which is feared and opposed by Israel (Lappin 2018; Mojon 2018). Iran's enemies have done all they can to fragment and divide the peoples of the region. They do not want that integration and independent prosperity. So it is the capacity, consistency and political will of the Islamic Republic of Iran that matters, and that is why Iran leads the independent people of the region.

Bibliography

ABNA (2014) 'Iran Supreme Leader urges vigilance against 'American Islam', Zionism', Ahlul Bayt News Agency, 30 June, online: http://www.abna.ir/english/service/important/archive/2014/06/30/620182/story.html

Abrahamian, Ervand (1980) 'Structural Causes of the Iranian revolution', MERIP Reports, No 87, Iran's Revolution: the rural dimension, May, 21-26

AFP (2019) 'US slams Iranian revolution for 40 years of failure as Rouhani threatens military expansion', *Arab News*, 11 February, online: http://www.arabnews.com/node/1450261/middle-east

Agius, Connie (2018) 'PM Netanyahu says Iran still the world's greatest threat', ABC Radio, 19 February, online: https://www.abc.net.au/radio/programs/am/pm-netanyahu-says-iran-still-the-worlds-greatest-threat/9460562

Astani, Sina (2010) 'The Bahai Question: A Case of Religious Discrimination in Post-Revolutionary Iran', Baha'i Library online, online: http://bahai-library.com/astani_discrimination_post-revolutionary_iran

AVN (2014) 'Jaua sostuvo encuentro bilateral en Irán con president Rouhani', Agencia Venezolana de Noticias, 04 agosto, online: http://www.avn.info.ve/contenido/jaua-sostuvo-encuentro-bilateral-ir%C3%A1n-presidente-rohan%C3%AD

Ayoob, Mohammed (1979) 'Two faces of Political Islam: Iran and Pakistan Compared', *Asian Survey*, Vol. 19, No. 6, June, 535-546

Bahramitash, Roksana (2003) 'Revolution, Islamization, and Women's Employment in Iran' *The Brown Journal of World Affairs* (9:2) 229-241

Bahramitash, Roksana and Hadi Salehi Esfahani (eds) (2011) *Veiled Employment: Islamism and the Political Economy of Women's Employment in Iran* Syracuse University Press: Syracuse USA

Bangash, Zafar (2019) 'Islamic Iran: 40 years of valiant resistance', *Crescent International*, ICIT, online: http://parstoday.com/en/radio/iran-i99959-islamic_iran_40_years_of_valiant_resistance

Carey, James (2018) 'The MEK: from revolutionary group to imperialist asset', Mint Press, 24 January, online: https://www.mintpressnews.com/mek-revolutionary-group-imperialist-asset/236653/

Cartalucci, Tony (2018) 'The US has delisted anti-Iranian MEK terrorists still openly committed to violence', Global Research, 2 October, online: https://www.globalresearch.ca/the-us-has-delisted-anti-iranian-mek-terrorists-still-openly-committed-to-violence/5655808

Chilcott, John et al (2016) 'The Report of the Iraq Inquiry: Executive Summary', Report of a Committee of Privy Counsellors, HC264, online: http://www.iraqinquiry.org.uk/media/247921/the-report-of-the-iraq-inquiry_executive-summary.pdf

CIA (2004) 'Regime Strategic Intent', in DCI Special Advisor Report on Iraq's WMD, updated to 2013, online: https://www.cia.gov/library/reports/general-reports-1/iraq_wmd_2004/Comp_Report_Key_Findings.pdf

CICUSRWMD (2005) 'Report to the President of the United States', The Commission on the Intelligence Capabilities of the United States Regarding Weapons of Mass Destruction, 31 March, online: http://www.nytimes.com/packages/pdf/politics/20050331_wmd_report.pdf

Cohen, Roger (2014) '1979: Iran's Islamic Revolution', Upfront, *New York Times*, online: http://teacher.scholastic.com/scholasticnews/indepth/upfront/features/index.asp?article=f091806_TP_Iran

Cook, Jonathan (2007) 'Israel's Jewish Problem in Tehran', Counterpunch, August 3, online: http://www.counterpunch.org/2007/08/03/israel-s-jewish-problem-in-tehran/

Curtis, Mark (2012) *Secret Affairs: Britain's collusion with radical Islam*, Serpent's Tail, London

Davis, Daniel L. (2017) 'Don't Take the Oil: Time to Ditch the Carter Doctrine', *The National Interest*, 3 February, online: https://nationalinterest.org/feature/dont-take-the-oil-time-ditch-the-carter-doctrine-19310

Demick, Barbara (2014) 'Iran: Life of Jews Living in Iran', Foundation for the Advancement of Sephardic Studies and Culture, online: http://www.sephardicstudies.org/iran.html

Dudley, (2018) 'How US Sanctions Could Cause Turmoil For The Iranian Auto Market' Forbes, 1 June, online: https://www.forbes.com/sites/dominicdudley/2018/06/01/how-us-sanctions-could-cause-turmoil-for-the-iranian-auto-market/#1212d06567b4

El Husseini, Rola (2010) 'Hezbollah and the Axis of Refusal: Hamas, Iran and Syria', *Third World Quarterly*, Vol 31, issue 5, pp. 803-815

Fabian, Jordan (2019) 'Trump: 'Time will prove' I am right in fight with intel chiefs', *The Hill*, 31 January, online: https://thehill.com/homenews/administration/427883-trump-time-wil-prove-i-am-right-in-fight-with-intel-chiefs

Gallagher, Nancy; Ebrahim Mohseni and Ray Ramsay (2018) 'Iranian Public Opinion after the protests', Centre for International Security Studies at Maryland, July, online: https://www.cissm.umd.edu/publications/iranian-public-opinion-after-protests-0

Ghasseminejad, Saeed (2018) 'New Report Shows Increased Poverty in Iran', Foundation for Defence of Democracies, 18 December, online: https://www.fdd.org/analysis/2018/12/18/new-report-shows-increased-poverty-in-iran/

Golinger, Eva (2012) 'Venezuela: the threat of a good example?' Postcards from the Revolution, Jan 12, online: http://www.chavezcode.com/2012/01/venezuela-threat-of-good-example.html

Goodarzi, Jubin M. (2009) *Syria and Iran: diplomatic alliance and power politics in the Middle East*, I.B. Tauris, London

Haines, D.D. and S.C. Fox (2014) 'Acute and long-term impact of chemical weapons: lessons from the Iran-Iraq war', *Forensic Science Review*, Vol 26 No 2, July

Halliday, Fred (1979) *Iran: Dictatorship and Development*, Penguin, London

Harris, Shane and Matthew M. Aid (2013) 'CIA Files Prove America Helped Saddam as He Gassed Iran', *Foreign Policy*, 26 August, online: https://foreignpolicy.com/2013/08/26/exclusive-cia-files-prove-america-helped-saddam-as-he-gassed-iran/

Hersh, Seymour (1992) U.S. Secretly Gave Aid to Iraq Early in Its War Against Iran', *New York Times*, Jan 26, online: http://www.nytimes.com/1992/01/26/world/us-secretly-gave-aid-to-iraq-early-in-its-war-against-iran.html

Hiro, Dilip (2010) *After Empire: the birth of a multipolar world order*, Nation Books, New York

Hjelmgaard, Kim (2018) 'Iran's Jewish community is the largest in the Mideast outside Israel – and feels safe and respected', *USA Today*, 1 September, online:https://www.usatoday.com/in-depth/news/world/inside-iran/2018/08/29/iran-jewish-population-islamic-state/886790002/

Honarbin-Holliday, Mehri (2013) *Becoming Visible in Iran: Women in Contemporary Iranian Society*, IB Tauris: London UK

Iran Daily (2017) 'Production surges in Iran's car industry', 27 January, online: http://www.iran-daily.com/News/176525.html?catid=3&title=Production-surges-in-Iran-s-car-industry

ITA (2018) 'Steel Exports Report: Iran', International Trade Administration, Washington, September, online: https://www.trade.gov/steel/countries/pdfs/2018/q2/exports-iran.pdf

ITF (2014) 'Imam Khomeini, and the Idea of Grand Islamic State and Free and Independent Republics', Islamic Thought Foundation, online: http://www.imam-khomeini.com/web1/english/showitem.aspx?cid=2021&pid=2355

Jazexhi, Olsi (2018) 'Is Albania a Partner of the US In Supporting International Terrorism?', Global Research, 27 March, online: https://www.globalresearch.ca/is-albania-a-partner-of-the-us-in-supporting-international-terrorism/5633671

Khajehpour, Bijan (2014) Iran opens new chapter in relations with Russia', Al Monitor, Feb 7, online: http://www.al-monitor.com/pulse/originals/2014/02/iran-russia-relations-new-chapter.html#ixzz3FYDqVLhl

Khodabandeh, Anne and Massoud Khodabandeh (2018) 'US Forces Albania To Take IS Fighters After Hosting MEK', LobeLog, 8 June, online: https://lobelog.com/trump-forces-albania-to-host-islamic-state/

Khosronejad, Pedram (2011) 'Remembering the sacred defence', *Anthropology News*, September, p.15, online: https://www.academia.edu/33447008/Remembering_the_Sacred_Defence

Kian, Azadeh (2014) 'Gender Social Relations and the Challenge of Women's Employment', Middle East Critique (23:3) 333-347

Kornbluh, Peter (2017) 'Chile and the United States: Declassified Documents Relating to the Military Coup, September 11, 1973', National Security Archive Electronic Briefing Book No. 8, online: https://nsarchive2.gwu.edu/NSAEBB/NSAEBB8/nsaebb8i.htm

Klare, Michael T. (2006) 'Oil, Iraq, and American Foreign Policy: The Continuing Salience of the Carter Doctrine', *International Journal*, Vol. 62, No. 1, Winter, pp. 31-42

Langworth, Richard M (2013) 'Leading Myths: "Churchill Advocated the First Use of Lethal Gas"', International Churchill Society, Autumn, online:

https://winstonchurchill.org/publications/finest-hour/finest-hour-160/leading-myths-churchill-advocated-the-first-use-of-lethal-gas/

Lappin, Yaakov (2018) 'The Danger of a Widening Iranian Corridor Through Syria', Begin-Sadat Center for Strategic Studies, 24 December, online: https://besacenter.org/perspectives-papers/iranian-corridor-syria/

MacEoin, Denis (1987) 'The Baha'is of Iran: The Roots of Controversy', *Bulletin*, British Society for Middle Eastern Studies, Vol. 14, No. 1 (1987), pp. 75-83

Marizad, Mehdi (2012) 'Israel teams with terror group to kill Iran's nuclear scientists, U.S. officials tell NBC News', 9 February, online: http://rockcenter.nbcnews.com/_news/2012/02/08/10354553-israel-teams-with-terror-group-to-kill-irans-nuclear-scientists-us-officials-tell-nbc-news

Masoumi-Tehrani, Ayatollah Abdol-Hamid (2014) 'We Must Defend the Rights of Baha'is: An Interview With Ayatollah Abdol-Hamid Masoumi-Tehrani', Iran Press Watch, May 4, online: http://iranpresswatch.org/post/9840/

McChrystal, Stanley (2019) 'Iran's deadly Puppet Master', *Foreign Policy*, https://foreignpolicy.com/gt-essay/irans-deadly-puppet-master-qassem-suleimani/

Mehran, Golnar (2003) The Paradox of Tradition and Modernity in Female Education in the Islamic Republic of Iran, *Comparative Education Review*, Vol. 47, No. 3 (August 2003), pp. 269-286

MEI (2009) 'Where Are Iran's Working Women?', Middle East Institute, 29 January, online: http://www.mei.edu/content/where-are-irans-working-women

Merat, Arron (2018) 'Terrorists, cultists – or champions of democracy?' The wild story of the MEK', *The Guardian*, 9 November, online: https://www.theguardian.com/news/2018/nov/09/mek-iran-revolution-regime-trump-rajavi

Miller Llana, Sara (2010) 'Hugo Chávez embraces Iran and Syria, wins Russian support for nuclear program', *Christian Science Monitor*, October 22, online: http://www.csmonitor.com/World/Americas/2010/1022/Hugo-Chavez-embraces-Iran-and-Syria-wins-Russian-support-for-nuclear-program

MNA (2018) 'Iran: US masters responsible for today terror attack in Ahvaz (joint "al-Ahwaz" and "MEK" terror attack)', Mehr News Agency, 22 September, online: https://iran-interlink.org/wordpress/iran-us-masters-responsible-for-today-terror-attack-in-ahvaz-joint-al-ahwaz-and-mek-terror-attack/

Moghadam, Fatemeh Etemad (2009) 'Undercounting Women's Work in Iran', *Iranian Studies*, volume 42, number 1, February, online: http://www.persiangendernetwork.org/Publications/UndercountingWomen%20

WorkinIran.pdf

Mogherini, Federica and Javad Zarif (2015) 'Joint Statement by EU High Representative Federica Mogherini and Iranian Foreign Minister Javad Zarif', European Union External Action, 14 July, online: https://www.auswaertiges-amt.de/blob/202518/56221bd6e0f78df2d1a7ebe3615823a6/150714-irn-deal-erklaerung-hvin-zarif-data.pdf

Mohammad, Majid (2017) 'Iran's Freefall Into Poverty', Radio Free Europe/Radio Liberty, 6 August, online: https://en.radiofarda.com/a/iran-population-sliding-into-more-poverty/28661812.html

Mojon, Jean-Marc (2018) 'US pullout strengthens Iran 'land bridge' to the Mediterranean', *Times of Israel*, 21 December, online: https://www.timesofisrael.com/us-pullout-strengthens-iran-land-bridge-to-the-mediterranean/

Morgan, David (2008) 'Clinton says U.S. could "totally obliterate" Iran', Reuters, 22 April, online: https://www.reuters.com/article/us-usa-politics-iran/clinton-says-u-s-could-totally-obliterate-iran-idUSN2224332720080422

Osman, Marwa (2018) 'Ahvaz Terrorist Attack Exposes US's New Chapter of Regime Change Wars', Al Ahed, September, online: https://english.alahednews.com.lb/44667/269#.W6j0R5NKhbU

Panah, Maryam (2007) *The Islamic Republic and the World: global dimensions of the Iranian Revolution*, Pluto Press, London

Paraskova, Tsvetana (2019) 'Iran Says It's Now Self-Sufficient In Gasoline', Oil Price, 18 February, online: https://oilprice.com/Latest-Energy-News/World-News/Iran-Says-Its-Now-Self-Sufficient-In-Gasoline.html

Parsa, Misagh (1989) *Social Origins of the Iranian Revolution*, Rutgers University Press, New Brunswick (NJ)

Parsi, Trita (2018) 'Why Trump's hawks back the MEK terrorist cult', *The New York Review of Books*, 20 July, online: https://www.nybooks.com/daily/2018/07/20/why-trumps-hawks-back-the-mek-terrorist-cult/

PBS (2019) 'The Iran-Contra Affair', online: https://www.pbs.org/wgbh/americanexperience/features/reagan-iran/

Pollack, Kenneth, Daniel Byman, Martin Indyk, Suzanne Maloney, Michael O'Hanlon and Bruce Riedel (2009) 'Which Path to Persia? Options for a New American Strategy toward Iran', The Saban Center for Middle East Policy at the Brookings Institute, Analysis paper No 20, June, online: https://www.brookings.edu/wp-content/uploads/2016/06/06_iran_strategy.pdf

Pompeo, Mike (2018) 'After the Deal: A New Iran Strategy', US Dept of State, 21 May, online: https://www.state.gov/secretary/remarks/2018/05/282301.htm

Primera, Maye (2009) 'Hugo Chávez refuerza su alianza con Irán', *El País*, 26 Nov, online: http://elpais.com/diario/2009/11/26/

internacional/1259190001_850215.html
Qassem, Naim (2005) *Hizbullah: the story from within*, SAQI, London
Ritter, Scott (2019) *Dealbreaker: Donald Trump and the Unmaking of the Iran Nuclear Agreement*, Clarity Press, Atlanta GA
Rostami-Povey, Elaheh (2010) *Women, Work & Islamism* Zed Books: London UK
Ruehsen, Moyara de Moraes (1993) 'Operation 'Ajax' Revisited: Iran, 1953', *Middle Eastern Studies*, Vol. 29, No. 3 (Jul., 1993), pp. 467-486
Sabermahani, Asma & Barouni, Mohsen & Seyedin, Hesam & Aryankhesal, Aidin. (2013). 'Provincial Human Development Index, a Guide for Efficiency Level Analysis: The Case of Iran', *Iranian journal of public health*. 42. 149-57.
Salehi-Isfahani, Djavad and Mohammad H. Mostafavi-Dehzooei (2017) 'Cash transfers and labour supply: evidence from a large scale program in Iran', The Economic Research Forum (ERF), Giza (Egypt), Working Paper 1090, May, online: http://erf.org.eg/wp-content/uploads/2017/05/1090.pdf
Salt, Jeremy (2008) *The Unmaking of the Middle East*, University of California Press, Berkeley
Sen, Ashish Kumar (2018) 'A Brief History of Sanctions on Iran', Atlantic Council, 8 May, online: https://www.atlanticcouncil.org/blogs/new-atlanticist/a-brief-history-of-sanctions-on-iran
Sengupta, Kim (2016) 'Iran's Jews on life inside Israel's 'enemy state': 'We feel secure and happy'', *The Independent*, 16 March, online: https://www.independent.co.uk/news/world/middle-east/irans-jews-on-life-inside-israels-enemy-state-we-feel-secure-and-happy-a6934931.html
Shipman, Tim (2007) 'Will President Bush bomb Iran?', *Telegraph*, 2 September, online: https://www.telegraph.co.uk/news/worldnews/1561974/Will-President-Bush-bomb-Iran.html
Silk Road Briefing (2018) 'Iran Planning Super-Highway to Connect with Mediterranean', 11 April, online: https://www.silkroadbriefing.com/news/2018/04/11/iran-planning-super-highway-connect-mediterranean/
Simon, Dick (2015) 'The biggest myths about doing business with Iran' CNBC, online: http://www.cnbc.com/2015/07/14/the-biggest-myths-about-doing-business-with-iran.html
Smith, Wright (2015) 'Our Defence is a Holy Defence! – The Iran-Iraq War and its Legacy in Contemporary Iranian Factional Politics', Journal of Georgetown University-Qatar Middle Eastern Studies Student Association, online: http://www.qscience.com/doi/pdf/10.5339/messa.2015.3
Solomon, Chris (2015) 'Women rise up in the Middle East' Global Risk Insights, 19 August, online: http://globalriskinsights.com/2015/08/women-rise-

up-in-the-middle-east/
South, Todd (2019) 'Army's long-awaited Iraq war study finds Iran was the only winner in a conflict that holds many lessons for future wars', *Military Times*, 18 January, online: https://www.militarytimes.com/news/your-army/2019/01/18/armys-long-awaited-iraq-war-study-finds-iran-was-the-only-winner-in-a-conflict-that-holds-many-lessons-for-future-wars/
Spahiu, Ebi (2018) 'MEK in Albania—Potential Implications and Security Concerns for Albania', *Terrorism Monitor*, Volume: 16 Issue: 19, The Jamestown Foundation, 12 October, online: https://jamestown.org/program/mek-in-albania-potential-implications-and-security-concerns-for-albania/
Stoffel, Derek (2018) 'Trump's Iran decision is victory for Netanyahu — but now come the risks', CBC News, 9 May, online: https://www.cbc.ca/news/world/israel-iran-decision-netanyahu-stoffel-1.4654817
Swerdlow, Leora (2017) 'American Imperialism in Iran and Iraq: 1979-1988', Oberlin College, 13 December, online: https://languages.oberlin.edu/blogs/relg270/leora-swerdlow-american-imperialism-in-iraq-and-iran/
Tarock, Adam (1997) 'Iran and Russia in 'Strategic Alliance'', *Third World Quarterly*, Vol. 18, No. 2 (Jun., 1997), pp. 207-223
Tibi, Bassam (1986) 'The Iranian revolution and the Arabs: the quest for Islamic identity and the search for an Islamic system of government', *Arab Studies Quarterly*, Vol. 8 No 1, Winter, 29-44
Tripp, Charles (2000) *A History of Iraq*, Cambridge University Press, New York
UNDP (1999) 'Human Development Report of the Islamic Republic of Iran, 1999', United Nations development programme, Tehran, online: http://hdr.undp.org/sites/default/files/iran_1999_en.pdf
UNDP (2016) Human Development Report, Table 2 'Human Development Index Trends, 1990-2015, online: http://hdr.undp.org/sites/default/files/2016_human_development_report.pdf
UNDP (2018a) 'Briefing note for countries on the 2018 Statistical Update, Iran (Islamic Republic of), online: http://hdr.undp.org/sites/all/themes/hdr_theme/country-notes/IRN.pdf
UNDP (2018b) 'Human Development Indices and Indicators, 2018 Statistical Update', United Nations Development Programme, online: http://hdr.undp.org/sites/default/files/2018_human_development_statistical_update.pdf
UNDP (2019) 'Human development report: Iran (Islamic Republic of)', online: http://hdr.undp.org/en/countries/profiles/IRN
UNDP (2019b) 'Human Development Index (HDI)', United Nations Development Programme, online: http://hdr.undp.org/en/content/

human-development-index-hdi

UNSC (2008) 'Resolution 1803 (2008)', 'Adopted by the Security Council at its 5848th meeting, on 3 March 2008', United Nations Security Council, 3 March, online: https://undocs.org/en/S/RES/1803%20(2008)

USDOS (2007) 'Mujahedin-e Khalq Organization (MEK)', Foreign Terrorist Organizations', US State Department, 30 April, online: https://www.state.gov/j/ct/rls/crt/2006/82738.htm

USDOS (2012) 'Delisting of the Mujahedin-e Khalq', US Department of State, Bureau of Counterterrorism and countering violent extremism, 28 September, online: https://www.state.gov/j/ct/rls/other/des/266607.htm

USDOS (2019) 'Foreign Terrorist Organizations', US Department of State, online: https://www.state.gov/j/ct/rls/other/des/123085.htm

VOA (2019) 'UN Nuclear Watchdog Says Iran Still Complying With Deal Terms', Voice of America, 22 February, online: https://www.voanews.com/a/un-nuclear-watchdog-says-iran-still-complying-with-deal-terms-/4800052.html

Waltz, Kenneth (2012) 'Why Iran Should Get the Bomb', *Foreign Affairs*, New York, July-August, pp. 2-5

Weinstein, Adam (2017) 'The Real Largest State Sponsor Of Terrorism', *Huffington Post*, 16 March, online: https://www.huffingtonpost.com/entry/the-real-largest-state-sponsor-of-terrorism_us_58cafc26e4b00705db4da8aa

White House (2018) 'Statement from the President on the Reimposition of United States Sanctions with Respect to Iran', 6 August, online: https://www.whitehouse.gov/briefings-statements/statement-president-reimposition-united-states-sanctions-respect-iran/

World Bank (2018) 'Islamic Republic of Iran: overview', 11 October, online: http://www.worldbank.org/en/country/iran/overview

World Bank (2019) 'Poverty & Equity Data Portal: Islamic Republic of Iran', online: http://povertydata.worldbank.org/poverty/country/IRN

World Bank (2019b) 'GINI index (World Bank estimate), Iran, Islamic Rep. online: https://data.worldbank.org/indicator/SI.POV.GINI?locations=IR

Wolf, Lawrence A. (2006) 'America Held Hostage: The Iran Hostage Crisis of 1979-1981 and U.S.-Iranian Relations', *OAH Magazine of History*, Vol. 20, No. 3, May, pp. 27-30

Wright, Claudia (1980) 'Implications of the Iraq-Iran War', *Foreign Affairs*, Winter 1980-81 Issue, online: https://www.foreignaffairs.com/articles/iran/1980-12-01/implications-iraq-iran-war

YVKE Mundial (2009) 'The Iran-Venezuela Bi-national Bank Launched', MRZine, March 4, online: http://mrzine.monthlyreview.org/2009/veniran030409.html

Girls go back to school in Douma (September 2018), after the Syrian Arab Army drove out the Saudi-backed 'Islamist' gangs, Jaysh al Islam and Jabhat al Nusra. There were no real schools under al Qaeda gangs, just religious classes.

Chapter Fifteen

TOWARDS WEST ASIA

An independent 'Middle East' would most likely bear another name, one not determined by Eurocentric views of the world. That is why many observers already refer to the region as 'West Asia' or the 'Arab and Muslim' world. But what would such a region look like, and what is required for its independence?

This is difficult concept for western audiences, whose ignorance is underwritten by a consensus between 'realist' and 'liberal' elites. Both believe in interventionist wars. The former group justifies them on crude self-interest, the latter on a 'civilising' mission, a fantasy that they are saving other peoples from their own states. But their audiences have been deceived and liberal imperialism, in particular, has contributed to a collapse in western internationalism.

Responding to the western confusion I have argued that understandings must be guided by the historic right of peoples to self-determination, the founding principle and achievement of the International Bill of Rights. That is the basis for all other human rights and serves as the foundation for defending national sovereignty and laws of non-intervention. The recent invention of a 'responsibility to protect' is little more than a colonial device to normalise intervention and wars of aggression. It has not changed international law. Without a grasp of the principle of self-determination and its legal consequences, there can be no proper perspective on this century's endless wars.

The multiple wars of the Middle East region, I have argued, are really distinct theatres of a single greater war, directed by Washington, to dominate and control access to the entire resource-rich region. Yet the US project for a 'New Middle East' hit a rock in

Syria, and the failure of that war began to unravel the 'gains' of all other neighbouring wars. The extraordinary pretexts for the recent interventions should be studied, but they cannot be understood separately. Nor can resistance be understood in an idealised sense. It has a common character but contingent personalities. Many believe that big power determines all; but coordinated resistance has proven to be the key factor in the defeat of imperialism in this region.

The countries of the region, fragmented from colonial restructuring a century ago, must regain coherence, though not as the add-on of some new empire. Regional unity is necessary to defeat the ambitions of the imperial and colonial powers. Small countries, divided within and amongst each other, simply do not have the capacity to resist alone. So much was said several times throughout two centuries of 'second independence' struggles in Latin America.

It is clear that Iran must lead and is leading this regional union, as it is the only nation with the capacity, firm principle and proven will for the task. This independent nation is already the guarantor of resistance forces in Palestine, Lebanon, Syria and Iraq; if not yet in Yemen. That does not mean that the allied independent countries will share the political or religious system of the Islamic Republic of Iran; indeed they cannot. While Lebanon's Hezbollah has a firm religious link to Iran, within Lebanon the resistance group has built strong cross-community bonds. The Axis itself has been pluralist from the beginning, combining different religious and secular traditions, as I have pointed out several times throughout this book.

While many features of a West Asian alliance will only become clear in the making, there must be closer security, economic and cultural ties, whether through stronger bilateral or regional agreements and practice, or through some form of federation. The express fears of the imperial power and its regional collaborators – of increased Iranian influence, of a 'Shi'a crescent', of a regional 'Iranian land bridge', of Palestinian 'terrorism' against Zionist ethnic cleansing, and of an Iranian presence 'at Israel's border' – simply indicate, albeit in pejorative terms, the necessary development of the Resistance.

The future of an independent and prosperous region must include even closer military integration, deep economic and logistic bonds, shared cultural projects and integrated information technologies. A rail, road and communications super highway between Tehran and Beirut – and beyond that linked to Chinese 'belt and road' networks – is essential to lift the peoples of the region out of their current under-development. And close cooperation between Iran, Iraq, Syria and Lebanon is also needed to bring to bear sufficient pressure to force democratic change in colonised Palestine.

Such a regional bloc can easily include an independent Yemen, currently under terrible siege. It could even include the petro-states of the Persian Gulf, if they went through sufficient transformation as to be able to cut their ties with Wahhabism and their imperial patrons.

However, there is no legitimate place in the region for the former colonial powers, France and Britain, nor for the imperial power in Washington. They have proven their inability to contemplate respectful relations with independent countries. Neighbouring Turkey, on the other hand, with its own imperial history in the region, might have more constructive relations if the regime in Ankara were to abandon its hegemonic ambitions. Russia has proven itself a great ally, however its relations with the Axis countries are limited by its historical ties with Israel.

I believe my chapter on Palestine made it clear that there is no place for Zionist apartheid in the future of an independent region. The peoples of the region cannot afford another 70 years of ethnic cleansing and colonial warfare. None of that negates a legitimate place for Jewish people in a democratic Palestine.

A tremendous future for the peoples of the region is possible, including in war-torn Palestine, Yemen, Syria and Iraq – but the foreign bodies must be removed and regional cooperation must be consolidated. The Resistance already knows this.

Part IV:

Postscript

Reme Sakr and I talk to the Syrian media after visiting wounded soldiers in a hospital in Latakia, December 2013. We were both abused by the Australian media for this visit, in which we also met the Syrian President. Photo by Sana.

Chapter Sixteen

WAR, SOLIDARITY AND ABUSE

Why support other peoples, especially during conflict? Some explanation seems necessary because wartime debates often degenerate into simplistic clichés, personal abuse and confusion. I am one of many who have been subject to this abuse. In western cultures, even the sanity of the critics of war is attacked, in attempts to disqualify opposing voices. Confusion is sown through the extreme nature of war propaganda, and its invented pretexts.

In the most recent half-dozen Middle East wars, all driven by Washington and its minions, it has become common to dismiss dissenters as 'apologists' for this or that enemy. In reality, whatever the virtues or flaws of these 'regimes', they are all independent, and targeted precisely for their independence. For this same reason they are branded 'dictatorships', in attempts to legitimise neo-colonial aggression. Consequently, the loyal western corporate and state media, on a war footing, replaces reasonable discussion with abuse and shows little interest in or respect for other peoples under attack.

The clichés and abuse replicate the aggression of war mentality. Many abandon their normal rules of verbal engagement, reducing discussion to combative point scoring. Having been subject to some of these attacks in recent years, mainly for my defence of Syria, I feel it appropriate to give some personal account of my motives and some of that abuse.

As I see it, human society is founded on cooperation and reinforced by communities determining their own affairs and building their own social structures. We are social beings and our natural human urge is to help others. Social dysfunction comes after social cooperation, and the most toxic of all such dysfunctions is imperialism. Outside interventions are always disastrous, destructive and tainted with the ambitions of the interveners. That is why uninvited interventions are rightly banned, these days under international law. However, law is rarely applied to the great powers.

I believe that support for popular self-determination, and the defence of peoples under attack, is an essentially human urge. In my opinion this comes before the pathological drive to dominate. The natural sense of support for other human communities must especially include support for formerly colonised peoples and those under attack. That is consistent with human values such as respect for others, and not putting one's voice in the place of others.

At any rate, that is the thinking behind my support for independent peoples under threat or attack. In my experience of recent decades this has included support for the peoples of Cuba, Venezuela, Papua New Guinea, East Timor, Palestine, Iraq, Iran and Syria. However I have refused to become part of the multi-billion dollar 'development cooperation' industry, remaining an independent writer, academic and volunteer.

Solidarity activity is not simply altruism. Engaging with other peoples is a rewarding learning experience, indeed a privilege. I believe in and remain open to learning from other cultures.

Yet imperial pathology is also a reality. Its demands, pronouncing what others 'must do', the refusal to listen, domineering, interventions and outright war represent a fundamentally anti-social mentality. From that perspective I came to see the wars of the 21st century – propaganda, economic and real wars – as a continuation of the older politics of imperialism, while often adopting the contemporary language of 'human rights'. Largely for this reason I began teaching university courses on the political economy of human rights, and then of 'human rights in development'.

I spent years defending Cuba and Venezuela from a barrage of fake human rights propaganda, including from supposedly independent agencies such as Human Rights Watch and Amnesty International (Anderson 2005; Anderson 2010, Anderson 2013).

Amnesty International, for example, attacked Cuba in 2003 for arresting several dozen US-paid agents (dubbed 'dissidents' in the US media), just as Havana anticipated that the mad emperor George W. Bush, having just invaded Iraq, was about to invade Cuba (Amnesty 2003). In fact, Cuba had documented US payments to these people as part of a Washington program to overthrow the Cuban government and its constitution (Elizalde and Baez 2003). There is virtually no state in the world that would not criminalise such activity.

Yet these agents became the 'Cuban dissidents' of Amnesty, which used 'human rights' as the pretext to back US aggression against its island neighbour (Barahona 2005; Anderson 2008; Lamrani 2014). That same human rights group took several years to say anything about the torture prison President Bush established at Guantanamo Bay, an illegally occupied part of Cuba (Anderson 2009). The prisoners there (unlike the US agents in Cuba) were held without charges or trial, abuses that used to be the substance of Amnesty International's activity.

Human Rights Watch (HRW), for its part, made repeated savage political attacks on Venezuela and Cuba, while saying next to nothing about the appalling human rights violations by Washington and its close allies. Many western liberals went along for the ride, but the partisan nature of HRW was obvious to any serious observer. A group of academics and writers assailed HRW over its heavily politicised reports on Venezuela (NACLA 2009). Later several Nobel Prize winners condemned HRW for its refusal to cut ties with the US Government (Alternet 2014).

I saw such abuses in my own country's intervention in neighbouring East Timor in 2006. There, an internal conflict attracted Australian intervention, largely on false pretexts. Australian state media gave prominence to claims that East Timor's then Prime Minister, Mari Alkatiri, had killed dozens of political opponents (Jackson 2006). The Prime Minister was deposed, the journalists involved were given awards; but the claims turned out to be quite false (Anderson 2006).

So when this human rights industry turned on Libya and Syria I was half-prepared. I had already written on my own country's shameful involvement in the aggressions against Afghanistan and Iraq, detailing Australian involvement in war crimes in both countries (Anderson 2005b; Kampmark 2008; Doran and Anderson 2011). I would go on to document Australian war crimes against Syria.

However, in early 2011 I did not have detailed knowledge about Libya or Syria. In March 2011 I had to look on a map to find Daraa, the border town where the violence in Syria began (Anderson 2013a). Further, I did not then know that the petro-monarchy Qatar -- owner of the successful Al Jazeera media network -- was funding and arming sectarian Islamist terrorists in both Benghazi (Libya) and Daraa (Syria) (Khalaf and Smith 2013; Dickinson 2014).

Once Libyan leader Gaddafi was murdered and the state was destroyed, Amnesty International (France) would admit that most of the claims they had made against the Libyan leader were baseless (Cockburn 2011). US analysts confirmed the fakery (Kuperman 2015).

The violence in Libya and Syria deserved scrutiny, especially when Washington, the main aggressor in the world, was urging regime change, and most independent countries were urging caution. I wrote a dozen articles against the war on Libya, over the NATO double speak, regime change motives and NATO's 'humanitarian' missile attacks (Anderson 2011a, 2011b). Tragically, indeed criminally, that little country, with the highest living standards in Africa, was rapidly destroyed.

My first article on Syria in May 2011, 'Understanding the Syrian Violence', simply urged people to read more widely. The conflict was clearly not just 'demonstrators v. police' (Anderson

2011). After that I researched a wider range of sources including, of course, Syrian sources. I began to document the propaganda war, the deceptive doctrine of humanitarian intervention, the failures of the western 'left', and the lies that fuel regime change. I shared a detailed list of sources for 'Reading Syria' and began to explore several false flag massacres (Anderson 2011c, 2012, 2012a, 2012b, 2012c).

There was very little western critical discussion of the conflict in Syria so, in 2012, a number of us, mainly Syrian-Australians, formed the group 'Hands Off Syria'. Later that year I wrote of a 'malignant consensus' which had been created over Syria, one which supported a foreign-backed insurgency and a drive to wider war (Anderson 2012d). It was clear to me that a campaign of lies was afoot, just as there had been with the attacks on Afghanistan, Iraq, Cuba, Venezuela and Libya.

The official war narrative – directed from Washington – was that 'peaceful protestors' were being slaughtered by the forces of a 'brutal dictator' intent on 'killing his own people'. This was said to be a 'civil war', with no foreign aggression (see Anderson 2016: Chapter 3). It was an extraordinary claim, with little reason, but reliance on jihadist-linked sources and repetition of the claims made it effective, at least amongst western populations.

Yet sectarian Islamist insurrections, linked to the banned Muslim Brotherhood, had a long history in Syria. Since the 1950s such violence had always been backed by Syria's enemies, particularly Washington and Israel. There was virtually no recognition of this in the loyal western media. Almost all western governments demanded an extreme, fabricated story which could serve as a basis for humanitarian intervention.

However, the 'peaceful protestor' lie was contradicted by independent witnesses and fatally undermined by multiple admissions by US Government officials. The witnesses spoke of sectarian violence from the beginning, which drove political reform rallies off the streets. The leaked documents showed that Washington knew, from the beginning, that extremists were fomenting the violence, with the aim of imposing a religious state.

Washington, Israel and the former colonial powers Britain and France armed these extremists, both directly and indirectly, through allies such as Saudi Arabia and Qatar (Anderson 2016: Chapters 2, 4, 6 and 12). The 'peaceful protestors v regime' fiction served as the basis for arming terrorists, while imposing a cruel economic blockade on the entire Syrian nation.

In late 2013 I helped organise an Australian delegation to Syria, to meet with government and non-government people to find out more about Syria and to express solidarity with a people under attack. Most of us stayed on after the official tour to meet new friends, exploring Damascus. On our return we were attacked by the Australian state and corporate media, in particular for a meeting we had with President Bashar al Assad, the principal target of western demonization (Worthington 2013). I had expected criticism from those who backed the war, but the Murdoch media made some special efforts.

In January 2014 Christian Kerr from The Australian newspaper rang me up for a very brief interview about the trip. It lasted less than one minute. The next day Kerr published a 1,600 front page article 'Academic with a murky past stirs fresh controversy with trip to Damascus' (Kerr 2014). This was mainly a personal attack, with little reference to the actual visit. The reporter dishonestly claimed that I was on "a pilgrimage to honour a dictator". The hit piece called me an 'extremist' for supporting Cuba, Venezuela and Palestine, for opposing Aboriginal deaths in custody and the destructive role of the World Bank in the Pacific.

The Murdoch paper called on the then Education Minister, Christopher Pyne, to "remind" universities that they "should be partners" to the government with a view to "build revenue ... by growing the international student market ... and ensure that their reputations support rather than hinder that ambition". This meant that universities should distance themselves from controversy. Pyne presented a nice summary of the commercial imperatives placed by successive Australian governments on universities. These days that same commercialisation is regarded by an overwhelming majority (84%) of academics as at the root of a decline in the quality of Australian tertiary education (Evans 2017).

Soon after that the Channel Seven television program Today Tonight invited me into their studio for an interview with presenter Nick Etchells. However, once there, the Channel Seven people placed me in a separate room of the same building, so that I could not hear Etchells' introduction, which was a vicious personal attack. They had only pretended an interest in the Syria visit. They cut out any answers they did not like. These personal attacks show how closed the Australian corporate media was to hearing another side to the war on Syria.

Over 2014-2015 I wrote *The Dirty War on Syria* (Anderson 2016), to address the western myths and to begin a documented history of the conflict. The book was published in Canada in January 2016 and, over the next two years, was translated into and published in ten languages (English, Arabic, German, Greek, Italian, Spanish, Bosnian, Swedish, Farsi and Icelandic). Over 2016-2018 I did an average of 4 or 5 interviews per week, from media in Iran, Lebanon, Syria, Iraq, Korea, Italy, China, Canada, Germany, Russia and the USA. I was invited to speak at conferences in Greece, Iraq and Germany. There was less interest in my own country.

After September 2015, when Russia and Iran began a more direct involvement in the conflict, in defence of Syria, the tide of the war began to turn in the government's favour. But the propaganda war remained strong. Personal attacks against prominent defenders of Syria became more organised. Dissident voices were seen as a threat to the war's legitimacy.

Independent journalists Eva Bartlett (Canada) and Vanessa Beeley (England), for example, attracted hostile attention for helping expose the grossly distorted western media coverage of the liberation of the city of Aleppo, in late 2016. The UK Guardian – a strong backer of the 'humanitarian war' against Syria – commissioned a long hit piece from a San Francisco based journalist with no experience in the Middle East (Solon 2017). Britain's Channel 4 (Worrall 2016) and self-appointed 'fact checkers' of the US Snopes family business pretended to debunk the critical reports from Bartlett and Beeley. These would-be gatekeepers backed the Washington-led humanitarian war story on Syria, claiming it was a 'civil war' in which 'we' had to help the people of Syria overthrow their 'brutal dictator'.

In early 2017 the new US President Donald Trump ordered a missile attack on Syria's Shayrat airbase, after a chemical weapon provocation had been carried out by terrorist groups in Khan Sheikhoun (Idlib). This happened just as we were preparing an academic conference on the Syrian conflict at the University of Sydney (CCHS 2017). On social media I called Trump, Obama and Bush as 'the masterminds of terrorism in the Middle East' (Anderson 2017).

The Murdoch media responded with another personal attack, running front page smears against myself and a colleague. This abuse began with a Daily Telegraph article by Kylar Loussikian (2017), titled 'Sarin Gasbag: academic claims Trump a terrorist and tyrant Assad didn't launch chemical attack', next to a picture of me in Syria. This was a response to my assertions - based on detailed research - that chemical weapons claims against the Syrian Army were baseless (Anderson 2016: Chapter 9). There was not the slightest corporate media interest in evidence over the chemical weapons allegations. When we criticised journalist Loussikian on social media, he ran to university authorities, complaining that he was the victim of a 'personal attack'.

Underlining the absurdity of Trump's 2017 attack, in 2018 the US Secretary of Defence admitted that, while 'others' were saying it, 'we do not have evidence' of Syria's use of sarin gas (Wilkie 2018; see adjacent graphic). This had been one of the key pretexts for US aggression against Syria, over several years. But war propaganda was never concerned with evidence.

A similar media attack occurred after I visited North Korea, in July 2017, as the drums of war were beating. By this time I had been studying several countries subject to Washington-led 'sanctions'. These included Cuba, Lebanon, Syria, Iran, Venezuela and North Korea (DPRK). Not that the loyal western media was interested in any such study.

THE AUSTRALIAN

Extremist boffins 'risk' to uni repute

CHRISTIAN KERR THE AUSTRALIAN JANUARY 04, 2014 12:00AM

THE AUSTRALIAN

Academic with a murky past stirs fresh controversy with trip to Damascus

CHRISTIAN KERR THE AUSTRALIAN JANUARY 04, 2014 12:00AM

The Daily Telegraph

Fake: I have said precisely nothing, so far, about the North Korean leader

SYDNEY UNIVERSITY'S TIM ANDERSON PRAISES NORTH KOREAN LEADER KIM JONG-UN DURING 'SOLIDARITY VISIT'

Media attacks followed our 2013 visit to Syria

In 2018 US Defence Secretary Mattis admitted what I was smeared for saying

NOW MATTIS ADMITS THERE WAS NO EVIDENCE ASSAD USED POISON GAS ON HIS PEOPLE

The Daily Telegraph
SYDNEY UNI SHOCKER
SARIN GASBAG
Academic claims Trump a terrorist and tyrant Assad didn't launch chemical attack

Multiple personal attacks by the Murdoch media (News Corp)

On seeing some social media photos, Murdoch reporter Loussikian penned another smear story, titled 'Sydney University's Tim Anderson praises North Korean leader Kim Jong Un during a solidarity visit'. An introductory paragraph read:

> A controversial Sydney University lecturer who backed Syria's murderous al Assad regime has travelled to Pyongyang and pledged "solidarity with the North Korean dictatorship against "aggression" from the west (Loussikian 2017a).

It certainly was a solidarity visit, but the lie behind the headline and its sub-head should have been obvious. There was no quote in Loussikian's article to justify that claim that I had praised any North Korean leader. I did not even mention them. Nor had I mentioned solidarity with the government ('dictatorship'). In principle, solidarity is always with peoples.

The night before the article this journalist had asked me, by email: "It was unclear whether you were expressing concern about warfare ... or whether you had a view in supporting the North Korean Government". Because of his previous dishonesty over Syria I did not reply.

Similar abuse, mostly focused on my defence of Syria, also came from some of the western 'left'; or rather what many of us now call 'the imperial left'. These are small groups of Trotskyists and Anarchists who swallowed the Washington line that the conflicts in Libya and Syria were popular 'revolutions'. They repeated the western state and corporate media clichés that the highly internationalised conflict in Syria was a civil war, and that the fanatical jihadist-terrorists were revolutionaries (e.g. Karadjis 2014; and in Norton 2014).

Some of these people – having observed that some extreme right wing figures also questioned the war on Syria, or supported Russia, or opposed Israel – decided to smear me with the lie that I 'work with' or am 'friends' with fascists. The evidence they show for this is that some extremist and right figures attended some of my public talks; and that those figures also attended a funeral wake for the murdered Russian Ambassador to Turkey, at the Russian consulate in Sydney. On that basis I was said to 'work with Nazis'.

Such attacks do not mean much from tiny groups, barely relevant except when they oppose imperial wars. Yet many western liberal-leftists today join with Washington, NATO, the Saudis, Israel -- and their fanatical, reactionary mercenaries -- against the remaining independent states of the Middle East.

In fact, the new fascism in the world – militarised-corporate, racial, neo-colonial aggression – can be seen precisely in that chain of wars aimed at destroying independent African, Arab, West Asian and Latin American states. Western cheerleading squads for these wars have served to minimise opposition and protect the mission of humanitarian war.

This century's military, economic and propaganda wars against Palestine, Afghanistan, Iraq, Iran, Lebanon, Libya and Syria have successfully conscripted western liberals, leftists, NGOs and of course the corporate and state media. Very few question the war narratives; and those who do are abused.

But that is not the future. The world is changing. BRICS and other regional groupings and states, especially in Africa, Asia and Latin America, are on the rise. In my opinion, support and respect is due to all independent peoples. It is not about whether we agree with everything they do. It is about respect for other peoples. Commitment to support their self-determination is our human responsibility.

Bibliography

Alternet (2014) 'Nobel Peace Laureates Slam Human Rights Watch's Refusal to Cut Ties to U.S. Government', 8 July, online: https://www.alternet.org/world/nobel-peace-laureates-slam-human-rights-watchs-refusal-cut-ties-us-government

Amnesty International (2003) 'Cuba: Massive crackdown on dissent', April, AMR 25/008/2003, online: https://www.amnesty.org/download/Documents/104000/amr250082003en.pdf

Anderson, Tim (2005) 'Contesting 'Transition': the US plan for a Free Cuba',

Latin American Perspectives, Vol 32, No 6, November, pp.28-46

Anderson, Tim (2005a) 'Cuba: the propaganda offensive', Online Opinion, 15 March, online: http://www.onlineopinion.com.au/view.asp?article=3243&page=0

Anderson, Tim (2005b) 'Indictment and prosecution of John Winston Howard', *The Guardian*, Sydney, 17 August, p.2, online: http://www.cpa.org.au/guardian-pdf/2005/Guardian1241_17-08-2005_screen.pdf

Anderson, Tim (2006) 'Timor Leste: the second Australian intervention', *Journal of Australian Political Economy*, December, pp.62-93

Anderson, Tim (2008) 'Cuba and the 'independent journalists', *Green Left Weekly*, 24 May, online: https://www.greenleft.org.au/content/cuba-and-independent-journalists

Anderson, Tim (2009) 'Hypocrisy over Cuba's 'political prisoners', *Green Left Weekly*, 19 September, online: https://www.greenleft.org.au/content/hypocrisy-over-cubas-political-prisoners

Anderson, Tim (2010) 'How Credible Is Human Rights Watch on Cuba?', MRonline, 16 February, online: https://mronline.org/2010/02/16/how-credible-is-human-rights-watch-on-cuba/

Anderson, Tim (2011) 'Understanding the Syrian violence - check your sources', 7 May, Facebook, online: https://www.facebook.com/notes/tim-anderson/understanding-the-syrian-violence-check-your-sources/10150186018711234

Anderson, Tim (2011a) 'The Double Speak on Libya: conflict resolution or regime change?', Facebook, March 19, online: https://www.facebook.com/notes/tim-anderson/the-double-speak-on-libya-conflict-resolution-or-regime-change/10150125374666234

Anderson, Tim (2011b) 'Humanitarian attack on Libya - first volley, 112 tomahawk missiles hit two cities', Facebook, 20 March, online: https://www.facebook.com/notes/tim-anderson/humanitarian-attack-on-libya-first-volley-112-tomahawk-misiles-hit-two-cities/10150126117161234

Anderson, Tim (2011c) 'Propaganda war rages over Syrian violence', Facebook, 8 August, online: https://www.facebook.com/notes/tim-anderson/propaganda-war-rages-over-syrian-violence/10150273915031234

Anderson, Tim (2012) 'Humanitarian Intervention and the Left in Imperial Cultures', Facebook, 1 March, online: https://www.facebook.com/notes/tim-anderson/humanitarian-intervention-and-the-left-in-imperial-cultures/10150603967576234

Anderson, Tim (2012a) 'The lies that fuel intervention and 'regime change' – Iraq, Timor Leste, Libya, Syria', Facebook, 8 May, online: https://www.facebook.com/notes/tim-anderson/the-lies-that-fuel-intervention-and-regime-change-iraq-timor-leste-libya-syria-/10150806025926234

Anderson, Tim (2012b) 'Reading Syria', Facebook, 24 May, online: https://www.

facebook.com/notes/tim-anderson/reading-syria/10150862173381234

Anderson, Tim (2012c) 'Massacres in Syria: the awful truth', Facebook, online: https://www.facebook.com/notes/tim-anderson/massacres-in-syria-the-awful-truth/10150895942696234

Anderson, Tim (2012d) 'The malignant consensus on Syria', The Conversation, 19 September, online: https://theconversation.com/the-malignant-consensus-on-syria-9565

Anderson, Tim (2013) 'Hugo Chávez, Venezuela and the Corporate Media', Online Opinion, 9 April, online: http://onlineopinion.com.au/view.asp?article=14882&page=0

Anderson, Tim (2013a) 'Syria: how the violence began, in Daraa', OpEd Opinion, 13 May, online: https://www.opednews.com/articles/Syria-how-the-violence-be-by-Tim-Anderson-130513-875.html

Anderson, Tim (2016) *The Dirty War on Syria*, Global Research, Montreal

Anderson, Tim (2017) 'Masterminds of terrorism in the Middle East.', Twitter, 7 April, online: https://twitter.com/timand2037/status/850516689036861440

Barahona, Diana (2005) 'Reporters Without Borders Unmasked', Counterpunch, 17 May, online: https://www.counterpunch.org/2005/05/17/reporters-without-borders-unmasked/

CCHS (2017) 'Syria Conference 2017', online: https://counter-hegemonic-studies.net/category/conf/sc-2017/

Cockburn, Patrick (2011) 'Amnesty questions claim that Gaddafi ordered rape as weapon of war', *The Independent*, 23 June, online: https://www.independent.co.uk/news/world/africa/amnesty-questions-claim-that-gaddafi-ordered-rape-as-weapon-of-war-2302037.html

Dickinson, Elizabeth (2014) 'The Case Against Qatar', *Foreign Policy*, 30 September, online: http://foreignpolicy.com/2014/09/30/the-case-against-qatar/

Doran, Chris and Tim Anderson (2011) 'Iraq and the case for Australian war crimes trials', *Crime, Law and Social Change: An Interdisciplinary Journal*, 23 August, online: http://www.mapw.org.au/files/downloads/doran-anderson-war-crimes-2011%20%282%29.pdf

Elizalde, Rosa Miriam and Luis Baez (2003) *The Dissidents*, Editora Política, La Habana; partially online here: http://www.redandgreen.org/Cuba/Disidents/index.html

Evans, Michael (2017) 'State of the Uni Survey: Thousands of uni staff have their say', NTEU Advocate, online: https://www.nteu.org.au/article/State-of-the-Uni-Survey%3A-Thousands-of-uni-staff-have-their-say-%28Advocate-24-03%29-20157

Jackson, Elizabeth (2006b) 'E Timor Prime Minister denies new 'hit squad' claims', ABC Radio, AM, 10 June, online: http://www.abc.net.au/am/

content/2006/s1660023.htm

Kampmark, Binoy (2008) 'John Howard and War Crimes', CounterPunch, 26 June, online: https://www.counterpunch.org/2008/06/26/john-howard-and-war-crimes-2/

Karadjis, Michael (2014) 'Why the Syrian rebels oppose U.S. air strikes', *Socialist Worker*, 6 October, online: https://web.archive.org/web/20161105044008/https://socialistworker.org/2014/10/06/why-syrian-rebels-oppose-us-air-strikes

Kerr, Christian (2014) 'Academic with a murky past stirs fresh controversy with trip to Damascus', *The Australian*, 4 Jan 2014

Khalaf, Roula and Abigail Fielding Smith (2013) 'Qatar bankrolls Syrian revolt with cash and arms', *FT*, 16 May, online: http://ig-legacy.ft.com/content/86e3f28e-be3a-11e2-bb35-00144feab7de#axzz5BBZYAcu2

Kuperman, Alan J. (2015) 'Obama's Libya Debacle', *Foreign Affairs*, March/April, online: https://www.foreignaffairs.com/articles/libya/obamas-libya-debacle

Lamrani, Salim (2014) *Cuba, the Media, and the Challenge of Impartiality*, Monthly Review Press, New York

Loussikian, Kylar (2017) 'Sarin Gasbag: academic claims Trump a terrorist and tyrant Assad didn't launch chemical attack', *Daily Telegraph*, Sydney, 10 April

Loussikian, Kylar (2017a) 'Sydney University's Tim Anderson praises North Korean leader Kim Jong Un during a solidarity visit', *Daily Telegraph*, 4 September

NACLA (2009) 'Critics Respond to Human Rights Watch's Defense of Venezuela Report', North American Congress on Latin America, 13 January, online: https://nacla.org/news/critics-respond-human-rights-watchs-defense-venezuela-report

Norton, Ben (2017) 'Michael Karadjis whitewashes Syrian al-Qaeda as "decent revolutionaries"', 10 May, online: https://bennorton.com/michael-karadjis-syrian-al-qaeda-jabhat-al-nusra/

Solon, Olivia (2017) 'How Syria's White Helmets became victims of an online propaganda machine', *The Guardian*, 18 September, online: https://www.theguardian.com/world/2017/dec/18/syria-white-helmets-conspiracy-theories

Wilkie, Ian (2018) 'Now Mattis admits there was no evidence Assad used poison gas on his people', *Newsweek*, 8 February, online: http://www.newsweek.com/now-mattis-admits-there-was-no-evidence-assad-using-poison-gas-his-people-801542

Worrall, Patrick (2016) 'Eva Bartlett's claims about Syrian children', 20 December, 4 News, online: https://www.channel4.com/news/factcheck/factcheck-eva-bartletts-claims-about-syrian-children

Worthington, Kerri (2013) 'Australian delegation condemned for Syria visit', SBS, 2 January, online: https://www.sbs.com.au/news/australian-delegation-condemned-for-syria-visit

INDEX

Abbas, Hadiya Khalaf 123
Abdul Ghani, Fadel 161-2
Abdul Rahman, Rami (SOHR) 160-2, 173
Abu Jandal (ISIS) 75
Adalah group (Palestine) 236
Afghanistan 11-12, 22, 41, 56, 75, 85, 137, 155, 174, 214, 219-221, 226, 230, 324, 338, 360, 361, 367
Ahmadinejad, Mahmoud 324, 329
Ahvaz, Iran 336, 345-6
Al Abadi, Haidar 301, 309
Al Abeid, Abd al Najem 125, 129
al Ahwazia group 336
Al Ameri, Hadi 303
Al Ani, Adnan 302
al Ashkar, Maytham 97
Al Assad, Bashar 54, 82, 90, 119, 134, 160, 178, 192, 196, 202, 207, 209, 281, 305, 362
Al Assad, Hafez 68, 202, 204, 290, 298, 319
Al Atrash, Sultan Pashar 280, 311
Al Bukamal 126, 303
Al Dabbit hospital (Aleppo) 91, 96, 101
Al Gharawi, Majid 122, 297
Al Habib, Farouq 182
Al Hababi, Nahlah 122, 297
Al Hassan, Suheil 89
Al Jaafari, Bashar 123, 132
Al Jazeera 33, 67, 84, 131, 176, 253, 267, 268, 289, 290, 305, 314, 360
Al Ka'abi, Sheikh Akram 126
al-Khazali, Sheikh Qais 304
Al Maghrebi, Abu Mansour 77
Al Mussawi, Hussayn 286
Al Okaidi, Abdul 75
Al Qaeda 16, 54, 66, 69-74, 85, 88-89, 93, 97-98, 104, 138-142, 146-7, 150, 159-160, 165, 182-3, 185, 188, 198, 200, 204-213, 279, 293, 299-300, 304, 335-8, 350, 370
AQI / ISI 69-72, 206, 299
Al Quds (Jerusalem) 234, 236-8, 245-7, 250-1, 253, 263-4, 267, 269-276, 293, 306, 311
Al Quds hospital (Aleppo) 91-96
Al Razi hospital (Aleppo) 91, 95-6
Al Sadra, Mussa 283
Al Sadr, Muqtada 303
Al Sheikh, Abu Jaber 183
Al Sistani, Ayatollah Ali 301, 305
Al Tallawai, Abdo Khodr 166
Al Tanf 122, 131
Al Turk, Riyad 204, 208, 210-211
Al Zameli, Hakem 122, 297
Al Zarzour hospital (Aleppo) 99-100
Al Zaatari camp (Jordan) 221, 225
Alawi / Alawite 69, 85, 204, 207, 215
Alawis to the grave, Christians to Beirut (salafi slogan) 207
Albania 219, 336, 344, 348
Aleppo / Halab 16, 66, 69, 87-106, 121, 131, 133, 137-8, 159-160, 168-172, 180, 183-189, 191, 195, 197, 199, 204, 207, 209-210, 213, 219, 223, 224, 227-9, 303, 363
Aleppo Media Centre (AMC) 137, 183-4, 187
Aleppo Medical Association (AMA) 91-2, 102
Aleppo's last paediatrician 91, 94, 104
Alexander the Great 26, 32
Alkatiri, Mari (East Timor) 360
Alkhateb, Khaled 97
Allende, Salvador 15, 38
Allon Plan (1967) 245, 268

Index

Amal party (Lebanon)   283, 291-2, 296, 305
American century   154-5, 195
American Islam   323, 325, 341
AMIA, Israeli community centre (Argentina)   288
Amnesty International   17, 42, 52, 58, 137, 151, 153, 156-7, 161-3, 171-177, 185-199, 259, 268, 359-360, 367, 369
Annan, Kofi   172, 193
Antaki, Nabil   91-94, 102, 104
Anti-Americanism   323
Anti-colonial struggles   21, 56, 235, 258, 260, 267, 281, 334
Aoun, Michel   290, 295, 296, 311
Apartheid   17, 37, 39, 52, 56, 234, 236, 245-9, 253-8, 262-6, 269, 271, 277, 317, 320, 353
Arab Spring   335
Arab state in Palestine   235-8
Army of Conquest (Jaysh al Fatah)   88, 221
Army of Islam (Jaysh al Islam)   142-3, 206, 209, 350
Asaib Ahl al-Haq (League of the Righteous)   304
Ashrafieh Sahnaya   139
Astana talks   79, 102, 177
Australian delegation to Syria   356, 362, 371
Australian military in Syria   109-120, 128-9, 132, 134
Avaaz   176, 178, 180, 194, 215
Axis of Resistance / Resistance   11-18, 67, 77-81, 85-6, 266-7, 279, 310, 321, 325, 343, 352-3
Ayn al Arab / Kobane   108, 169

Baghdad   38, 300-1, 335
Baha'i   324, 342, 345
Balanche, Fabrice   113
Balfour Declaration (1917)   237, 268

Ban, Ki-Moon   97
Barrel bombs   94, 142, 168-171, 180-3, 192-3, 196
Bartlett, Eva   97, 363, 370
Barzani, Masoud   303, 309
Basiji (Iran)   279, 296, 332
BCRI survey   284, 294, 306
Beeley, Vanessa   92, 97-8, 103, 105, 140, 146, 151, 182-188, 363
Beirut   12, 45, 48, 69, 207, 215, 266, 285, 306, 308, 311, 314, 341, 353
Ben Gurion, David   239-241
Bellingcat   137, 142, 161, 163, 185, 191
Biden, Joe   73, 86-7, 98, 105, 109, 116, 133-4, 208, 300, 308
Bin Jassim, Hamad   208, 211
Bin Salman, Mohammad   295, 306
Binskin, Mark   118
black mercenaries (Libya)   157, 176
Bolívar, Simón   26
Bolshevik   298, 334
Bolton, John   336
Boycott Divestment and Sanctions (BDS)   37, 159, 260, 266-269, 275, 277
Boyle, Francis   174, 188, 213, 229
Bricmont, Jean   151, 172, 188
British Broadcasting Corporation (BBC)   80, 82, 86-7, 96, 101, 103-4, 134, 142, 144, 147, 151, 160, 187, 310, 334
British forces in Syria   109, 123, 128
British Raj (British Empire)   21-25, 33
Brookings Institute, USA   49-50, 268, 335, 346
BTselem (Jerusalem)   246, 269
Burgas airport attack (Bulgaria)   288
Bush, George W   13, 156, 174, 189, 282, 307, 313-4, 318, 337, 347, 359, 364
Burkhalter, Holly   155
Burma   41, 43

373

Camp Ashref (Iraq)   335
Caesar (Syrian defector)   167, 197
Canada   43, 214, 230, 320, 363
Cancer hospital (Aleppo)   99, 101
Carter doctrine (USA)   323, 343-4
Chávez, Hugo   164, 191, 324-5, 343, 345-6, 369
Chile   15, 18, 38-9, 50, 337, 344
China   13, 24, 41, 46-50, 53, 158-9, 242, 326, 337-340, 363
Christians   14, 69, 82-3, 170-1, 188, 190, 195, 207, 210, 215, 228, 237, 242, 249, 255, 279, 281, 283-4, 287
Christian-socialist   340
Christians to Beirut, Alawis to the grave (salafi slogan)   207
Churchill, Winston   298, 307, 310, 334, 344-5
Churkin, Vitaly   119, 131
Chemical weapons   61, 71, 135-149, 152, 169, 185, 187, 195, 298, 300, 308, 311, 333-4, 343, 364
CIA   44, 108, 147, 165, 298-9, 307, 310, 321, 334, 343, 364
Colonisation   22, 23, 28, 78, 235, 246, 249, 258
constitutional revolution (1905-1911, Iran)   321
Clinton, Hillary   73-4, 83, 156-7, 190, 318, 346
Coe, Richard   112-118, 130
COGAT (Israel: Coordinator of Government Activities in the Territories)   251
Cold war   49, 18, 128, 134, 245
Consensus, elite/western/malignant   15, 295, 351, 361, 369
Creative destruction   155
Cuba / Cuban Revolution   35-53, 154, 164, 187, 202, 239, 358-364, 367-370

DAESH / ISIS / ISIL   16, 45, 61, 65-6, 71-79, 82, 84-6, 89-90, 107-128, 130, 132-4, 202, 206-9, 212, 218, 221, 250, 279-80, 284, 289, 295-7, 299, 300-305, 309-10, 312, 336
Damascus   11, 54, 65-71, 74, 76, 80, 85-6, 89, 92, 109, 119, 133, 138, 142-3, 147, 162, 166-7, 180-1, 208, 210, 213, 217-9, 221, 225, 228-9, 295, 362, 370
Damascus Center for Human Rights Studies (DCHRS)   162
Damascus Declaration (2005)   208, 210, 218, 228
Danish forces in the ME and Syria   109, 120, 182, 219
Daraa   66, 68, 86, 166, 185, 187, 204, 221, 225, 360, 369
Daraya   70, 83
Dayan, Moshe   263
Deir Ezzor   66, 107-109, 113, 119-126, 128-134, 180, 212, 299, 303
Deir Yassin   240
Del Ponte, Carla   138, 187
Dempsey, Martin   73, 86, 109, 116, 133, 208, 300, 307
De Zayas, Alfred   43
Diab, Hassan   143
Diab, Khaled   182
Dirty War on Syria   12, 14, 16, 18, 59, 67, 70-1, 81-2, 102, 136, 146, 150, 187, 206, 210, 363, 369
Divan, Jome   22
Douma 54, 137, 142-9, 206, 350
Druze   14, 249, 255, 280-1, 283, 290, 294
Duke, David   243
Dwella / Duella (Damascus suburb)   80

East Ghouta   66, 71, 84, 136-140, 142-3, 152, 180, 202, 206
East Timor   30, 358-9, 368-9
Economic sanctions – see sanctions

374

Egypt   26, 33, 41, 67, 245, 250, 265, 280, 288, 302, 312, 324, 339-40, 347
Elhaik, Eric   242, 270
Empire   13, 21, 23-26, 30-33, 194, 197, 236, 238, 242, 321, 344, 352
Erdoğan, Bilal   77
Erdoğan, Recep Tayyip   77, 79, 81-2, 212-13, 222, 224, 228, 231
Etchells, Nick   363
Ettinger, Yoram   250
Exceptionalism   55, 154, 156
Euphrates   75, 122, 125-6, 245
European Jews   236, 238, 241-4, 266, 268, 270-1, 273-7
Exum, Andrew   288
Eye Hospital (Aleppo)   99

Falk, Richard   236, 262, 267, 270
False flag violence   70-1, 99, 140, 148, 153, 361
Fanon, Franz   29, 31
Farouq Brigade   70, 159, 207
Fatah (Palestine)   251, 255
Filipov, Roman   79
Fisk, Robert   70, 76, 83-4
Flynn, Michael   72-3, 84
Ford, Peter (UK)   177
Ford, Robert (USA)   75
Forensic principles   58-60, 136-7, 139, 144, 152
Foua and Kefraya (Idlib)   98-99, 105
France / French   26, 28, 50, 58, 66, 91, 99, 104, 113, 121, 137, 145, 157, 159, 169, 173, 176, 183-4, 187, 202, 219, 236-7, 280, 285-6, 290, 298, 333, 353, 360, 362
Free Patriotic Movement (Lebanon)   295-6
Free Syrian Army   70, 73, 75, 99, 101, 104, 131, 159-60, 176, 180-1, 207, 215-16, 221

French hospital (Aleppo)   99
Full Spectrum Dominance   156, 190
Future Movement (Lebanon)   289, 296

Gaddafi   58, 137, 157-8, 176, 189, 360, 369
Galant, Yoav   289
Garrigos, Genevieve   157, 176
Gaul   25
Gaza   168-170, 235, 246, 251, 253, 255, 258-261, 266, 268-271, 273-6
Gaza casualties 2014   260-1
Gazdiev, Murad   97
Gemayel, Bashir   285-6
Genesis Prize   266
Geneva   91, 104, 159, 246
Geneva Convention   246
Georges, Abu Khazen   96, 102
Ghouta Media Centre   142-3
Gini index   327, 331, 349
Giuliani, Rudy   336
Golan   78, 263, 266, 290, 338
Goldmann, Nahum   240
Graham, Lindsey   73
Greater Israel (Eretz Yisrael)   245, 253
Guerra Cabrera, Angel   27, 32
Gulf War, First   38, 137, 171, 174, 197

Haidar, Ali   225
Halabja   137, 298, 334
Halwi, Shadi   97
Hama   68, 84, 204-5, 211, 221, 225, 230, 298
Hamas (Palestine)   251, 255, 257, 259-261, 268-9, 275, 283-4, 293, 310, 313, 343
Harfoush, Iyad Kamel   166
Hart, Alan   250, 264, 271

375

Hariri, Rafiq 208, 290-2, 308, 314
Hariri, Saad 289-90, 295-6, 306, 312-13
Hashid al Shaabi (Iraqi PMU) 279, 296, 300-304, 311-12, 332
Hassoun, Mufti Ahmed Badreddin Acknowledgements 213, 228
Hayat Tahrir al Sham (HTS) 65, 71, 213
Hayward, Tim 173, 191, 193
Helms Burton Law (re Cuba) 40, 44, 50
Hersh, Seymour 139, 147, 282, 299, 310, 333, 343
Hezbollah / Hizbollah 17-18, 45, 48-9, 66, 78, 85, 97, 130, 254, 258, 265, 270, 274, 278-315, 319, 324-5, 343, 352
Higgins, Elliot 161, 163, 191
Hill and Knowlton 174
Hizb Almani 280
Homs 69, 87, 89, 159, 165-6, 182, 198, 205, 207, 215, 221, 225
Holy Roman Empire 238
Hospitals 45, 89-96, 99-105, 142-4, 167, 174, 280, 356
Houla (Syrian town) 70, 159
Human development 17, 320-1, 325-7, 329, 347-9,
Human rights 15, 17, 21, 27-30, 39-40, 51-2, 57-8, 67, 70, 80, 84, 97, 126, 137, 140-1, 146-7, 150-199, 229, 252, 269, 272, 276, 351, 358-60, 367-70
Human Rights Data Analysis Group (HRDAG) 161-2, 191, 195
Human rights industry 150-199
Human Rights Watch (HRW) 17, 67, 84, 137, 140-1, 147, 149-151, 153, 155-6, 163, 167, 172, 176, 185-8, 191-6, 359, 367-8, 370,
Humanitarian war 150-199
Hussein, Muhammad Awad 126
Hussein, Saddam 39, 68, 137, 147, 205, 298, 303, 309-10, 318-19

Ibn Rushd hospital (Aleppo) 91, 96, 101-2
Imperial left 366
Indigenous peoples 11, 29-32
Idlib 65-66, 69, 79, 84, 97-99, 105, 139-140, 148, 166, 185, 213, 221, 364
Imperialism / Imperial 11-16, 19, 21-33, 48, 55-57, 59, 80, 153-156, 172, 186, 188, 193, 195, 197, 201, 203, 211, 279, 281, 284, 311, 319, 321-5, 332
Incubator babies (Kuwait) 137, 174, 195
Internally Displaced Peoples (IDPs) 99, 101, 212-213, 219-221, 224, 225-7, 229-30, 255, 268
International Atomic Energy Agency (IAEA) 338
International Organization for Migration (IOM) 101, 104, 214, 223, 225, 229
International Socialist Organization (ISO) 203, 211
Iraq 11-12, 16-17, 31, 38-9, 41, 45, 48, 56-7, 59, 61, 66-7, 69, 71-3, 76, 78, 83-5, 108-110, 117-18, 120, 122-3, 129, 134, 136-7, 141, 155-6, 172, 174, 191, 193, 200, 206, 214, 219, 220, 226, 229, 230, 250, 258, 267, 278-282, 292, 295, 296-315, 318-19, 321, 325, 332-9, 341-4, 347-9, 352-3, 358-61, 363, 367-9
Iraq invasion (2003) 17, 31, 38, 57, 59, 141, 156, 172, 219-21, 280, 292, 296, 298, 299, 321, 334-5
Iran-Contra scandal 346
Iran, Islamic Republic of 11-12, 17-18, 26, 35, 39-41, 43-46, 49-50, 52, 56, 65-67, 75-79, 85-86, 98, 102, 108, 129, 137, 140, 147, 148, 155, 239, 242, 254, 258, 265, 271-2, 279, 281-2, 288, 293, 296, 298-9, 301, 303, 306, 308, 310, 313, 316-349, 352-3, 358, 363-4, 367

376

Index

Iranian land bridge 12, 18, 346, 352
Iranian Revolution 17, 27, 155, 281, 283-4, 298, 318, 321-326, 331, 334, 341-8
Isfahan (Iran) 316, 330
ISIS / ISIL / DAESH 16, 45, 61, 65-6, 71-79, 82, 84-6, 89-90, 107-128, 130, 132-4, 202, 206-9, 212, 218, 221, 250, 279-80, 284, 289, 295-7, 299, 300-305, 309-10, 312, 336
Islamic Jihad 286, 288
Islamic Movement (Israel/Palestine) 257
Islamic Resistance (Lebanon) 290, 315
Israel 11-12, 56, 66-7, 71, 74, 77-9, 81-2, 84-6, 121-2, 136-7, 171-2, 188, 234-277, 279, 281-2, 284-94, 297, 304-5, 308-9, 313-14, 317-320, 324, 341-8, 353, 361-2, 366-7
Israel's prime ministers 240-1, 250, 263, 264, 266
Israeli-West Bank 'Separation Barrier' 246-7, 271, 275
Issa, Abdullah 96

Jabal al Tharda (Deir Ezzor) 16, 76, 83, 107-134
Jaber, Hala 69-70, 166, 192
Jabhat al Nusra / Nusra 65, 71, 73, 75, 77-9, 83-4, 91-3, 96, 99, 101, 104, 121, 124, 133, 138-140, 142-3, 150-1, 165, 181, 185, 193, 206-7, 216, 221, 284, 289, 295, 303-4, 350, 370
Jazairy, Idriss 40, 43
Jericho 236
Jerusalem 234, 236-8, 245-7, 250-1, 253, 263-4, 267, 269-276, 293, 306, 311
Jerusalem Media & Communication Centre (JMCC) 249-51, 275, 272

Jewish community in Iran 317, 323, 342, 344
Jewish Virtual Library (JVL) 239, 263, 265, 272
Jews, European 236, 238, 241-4, 266, 268, 270-1, 273-7
Jews, Sephardic 241, 243, 343
Jihad / Jihadist 45, 65, 71, 76, 87, 89, 108, 121, 136, 150, 157, 160, 162, 166-7, 169, 173, 176-9, 182-4, 203, 206, 208, 213, 217-19, 224-7, 283, 299, 305, 361, 366
Jobar 139
Johnston, David 111-12, 116, 119-120, 131
Joint Comprehensive Plan of Action (JCPOA 45-46, 50, 318, 321, 337-9
Juche (DPRK) 47, 50
Judaism 237, 242, 244-5, 264, 273-4, 277
Jumblatt, Kamal 290

Kanaan, Nihad 107,109-110, 112-114, 116, 124-5, 131
Kata'ib Hizbullah 304
Kelechi, Moustafa 96
Kerr, Christian 362, 370
Kerry, John 74, 87
KhAB-250 bomb 141
Khamenei, Ayatollah Ali 46, 254, 265, 272, 283, 303, 325
Khanjar, Adham 280
Khomeini, Imam Ruhollah 319, 322, 323, 344
Khadour, Mohammad Abdo 166
Khan Sheikhoun 140-1, 147-8, 185, 193, 364
Khan al Asal 137-9
Khatab, Asser 97
Khatib, Khaled 178, 180, 190, 192
Khazaei, Mohsen 97
Khorramshahr, Iran 332
King of Jordan 205

377

Kirkuk 303, 307, 309
Knee capping (Israeli) 257
Kobane / Ayn al Arab 108, 167, 169
Koning AbuZayd, Karen 159
Korea, North (DPRK) 35, 41, 46-8, 50-1, 364
Kuperman, Alan 58, 157-8, 173, 176, 192, 360, 370
Kurds / Kurdish 65-7, 86, 137, 148, 208, 221, 298, 305, 307, 309, 334
Kuwait 72, 113, 174, 279

Labour hospital (Aleppo) 101
Langworth, Richard 334, 344
Latakia 181, 217, 356
Lavrov, Sergei 66, 84
Law of Return 240, 270
League of Nations 238
Lebanisation 287
Lebanon / Lebanese 11, 17, 39, 41, 45, 48-9, 56, 66, 69, 76, 78, 83, 121, 126, 129, 208, 210, 214-15, 221, 225, 228, 235, 237, 246, 250, 253-4, 265, 274, 278-296, 301, 303-315, 319, 324, 326-7, 332, 337-8, 341, 352-3, 363-4, 367
Lefèvre, Raphaël 68, 84, 204, 211
Left Zionism 235, 257-8, 262
Le Mesurier, James 106, 182, 198
Lesvos 212
Levant 71, 83, 130, 210, 236-7, 241-3, 279, 299
Levy, Gideon 258, 273
Liberalism 22-23, 33, 153, 197
Libya 11-12, 16, 41, 43, 56, 58-59, 67, 136, 157-8, 163, 173, 176, 186, 188, 190, 192-3, 197-8, 202, 214, 258, 335-6, 360-1, 366-8, 370
Lloyd, Richard 139, 147
Lloyd George, David 237
Local Coordinating Committees (LCCs) 205-6
Loussikian, Kylar 364

Luck, Edward 156-7, 193
Luther, Phillip 259-260

Ma'arrat al Numan (Idlib) 69
Maes, Daniel 166, 187
Magnier, Elijah 133
Majlis al Shaab (Peoples Congress/ Assembly, Syria) 208, 211
Manbij 301
Maronite Christians 279, 286-7, 290-1, 295
Martí, José (Cuba) 13-14, 18
Mar Yakub monastery 166
Martyr 80-1, 271-2, 283, 305, 332
Mattis, James 144, 147-8, 370
McChrystal, Stanley 317, 345
McKeigue, Paul 185, 193
Médecins Sans Frontières (MSF) 92, 94, 105
Meir, Golda 250, 264, 269
Mill, John Stuart 23, 153-4, 193
Moderate rebels 69, 71-5, 85, 93, 98, 102, 121, 133, 182
Moghadam, Fatemeh Etemad 330-1, 345
Mojahedin-e Khalq (MEK) 334-6, 342, 344-6, 348-9
Mood, Robert 159
Mossad (Israel) 289, 335
Mossadegh, Mohammed 321-2
Mosul (Iraq) 122, 228, 297, 299, 304, 311-314
MIT (Turkish intel) 77
Musawi, Ali 97
Museum of Holy Defence, Tehran 332, 347
Muslim Brotherhood (Ikhwan) 67-69, 72, 82-84, 160, 200, 202-206, 208-211, 254-5, 257, 275, 284, 289, 298-9, 322, 325, 361
Mustadafin (downtrodden) 305

Index

North Atlantic Treaty Organization (NATO) 22, 58-8, 89, 97, 105, 136-7, 139, 155, 157-8, 165, 174, 176, 194, 197, 214-15, 219, 226-7, 313, 336, 340-1, 360, 367
Naqqash, Anees 12, 18, 77, 78, 85
Narwani, Sharmine 69, 85, 166, 194, 282, 312
Nasrallah, Hassan 78-9, 85, 278
Nasser, Gamal Abdel 293
Nathan, Julie 244-5, 273-4
National Defense Authorization Act (NDAA), USA 338
National Defence Forces (NDF) 80
National Dialogue (Lebanon) 292
National Endowment for Democracy (NED) 161-4, 191
Nazi Holocaust 237-8, 240, 268, 271, 318
Neo-Marxist / Marxist 22, 24-5, 209
Netanyahu, Benzion 243, 244, 270
Netanyahu, Benyamin 266, 275, 317, 341, 348
New Middle East (NME) 11, 13, 15, 17-18, 65, 155-6, 186, 194, 254, 269, 292-3, 299, 307, 309, 351
New World Order (NWO) 23
Nixon, Richard 38
Nossel, Suzanne 156, 172, 174, 191, 194
Nurse Nayirah 174
Nusra – see Jabhat al Nusra

Obama, Barrack 13, 18, 40, 47, 72-4, 85, 102, 139, 164-5, 190, 192, 208, 253, 258, 318, 335, 337, 364, 370
Obeidat, Mosab (White Helmets) 182, 193
Oberg, Jan 97-8, 105, 155, 194
Occupied Palestinian Territories (OPTs) 235, 245-7, 249, 251, 253, 263-4, 266-70, 273, 290, 324
OFAC (US Treasury Department) 40, 42, 44, 51
O'Neill, James 113, 120, 128
Operation Ajax 321, 347
ORB polls 218, 229
Organisation for the Prohibition of Chemical Weapons (OPCW) 140-1, 143-4, 148, 185
OROOM poll 293-4, 306, 313
Ortiz, Carla 97
Oslo Accords (1993, 1995) 246
Ottoman Empire 236

Pahlavi, Reza 321, 322
Papua New Guinea 358
Palestine 17, 27, 39, 56, 78, 86, 196, 203, 234-277, 285, 290, 304, 317, 319, 325, 338, 341, 352-3, 358, 362, 367
Palestine demographics 247-251, 271-2
Palestinian ID cards 247
Palestinian National Authority (PNA) 247, 252
Palestinian nation-state, recognition of 251-3
Palmyra 65-6, 79, 81, 89, 109, 119, 1217, 131, 221
Pan Arabism / Pan Arab 27, 81-2, 305, 319, 340
Pappe, Ilan (historian) 239-40, 253, 274
Payne, Marise 109, 111-112, 118, 132
Peaceful protest 67, 69, 153, 165-6, 176, 202, 235, 338, 340, 361, 362
Pentagon 155-6, 185, 282, 312
Persian Gulf 155, 197, 282, 318, 323, 332, 353
Pew Global poll 293, 295, 313
Phalange /Phalangist 285
Phelan, Lizzie 97-8, 105
Pinheiro, Paolo 159
PKK, Kurdish (Kurdistan Workers

379

Party: Turkey) 67, 288
Plan Dalett 239
Pluralism 27, 57, 80
Pompeo, Mike 39, 49, 338, 346
Popular front for the Liberation of Palestine (PFLP) 251
Popular Mobilisation Units (PMU, Iraq = Hashid al Shaabi) 279, 296, 300-304, 311-12, 332
Porter, Gareth 113, 115, 132, 160, 195, 288, 313
Portman, Natalie 266, 275
Post-colonial 27, 31, 55, 58, 154, 279
Postol, Ted (Theodore) 139-40, 147-8, 185, 195
Press TV 84, 99, 105, 125-6, 132, 177, 195, 271, 289, 304, 313
Project 922, Iraq 333
Prokhorenko, Alexander 79
Propaganda / propaganda for war 13-14, 35, 67, 80, 90-1, 105, 110, 121, 128, 136, 141, 144, 151-4, 183, 186, 189-90, 198, 200, 212, 215, 302, 326, 332, 357-9, 361, 363-4, 367-8, 370
Pure Muhammadan Islam 323
Purpose (US NGO) 178, 194, 215
Putin, Vladimir 74, 76, 79, 84-5, 123, 133, 147
Pyne, Christopher 129, 362

Qalamoun mountains 66, 303
Qara (countryside Damascus) 166
Qatar 67, 71-3, 121, 137, 167, 169, 176, 190, 196, 208, 239, 347, 360, 362, 369-70
Qassem, Naim 283, 285-8, 301, 303, 313, 317, 319, 347
Quds Force 301, 303, 308, 317
Quneitra 66
Qusayr 89

Racial ideology 25, 55, 235-6, 240-4, 247, 252, 262, 367
Rajavi, Maryam 336, 345
Ramallah 236, 248, 268
Rand Corporation 266
Raqqa 75, 82-3, 99, 109, 126, 132, 202, 206, 299, 301, 307
Rashidin 98
Reagan, Ronald 298, 318, 333, 346
Realism / realist 15, 55, 153-6, 165, 317, 351
Red Cross / Red Crescent 93, 104, 182, 220-1
Red Team (Pentagon) 282
Refugees 17, 101, 103, 178, 180-1, 187, 198, 212-230, 240, 254, 268
Refugee poll (Germany) 180-2, 187, 212-13, 215-18, 229
Resistance 11-18, 67, 77-81, 85-6, 266-7, 279, 310, 321, 325, 343, 352-3
Responsibility to protect (R2P) 58-60, 156-8
Rice, Condoleezza 13, 18, 269, 292-3, 307, 314
Ritter, Scott 141, 148, 185, 196, 338, 339, 347
Roth, Kenneth 141, 164-5, 169-71, 182, 193-4, 196
Roman Empire 22, 25, 237-8, 242
Rouhani/Rohani, Hassan 464, 86, 320, 325, 341-2
Rovera, Donatella 173
Russia 12-13, 41, 46, 48, 65-7, 76-80, 82, 84-7, 93, 96, 98, 102-3, 111, 114-15, 119, 129, 131-3, 139-40, 143, 147, 149, 158-9, 185, 187, 190-1, 195, 213, 243, 298, 303, 306, 308, 311, 324, 334, 337-40, 344, 348, 353, 363, 366
Rwanda 138, 155, 195

380

Index

Sabra and Chatila massacres (Lebanon) 285, 310, 312
Sakr, Reme 356
Salafi / salafist 56, 65, 68-72, 81, 111, 176, 200, 203, 206-7, 281, 282, 295, 299, 312, 322-3, 325
Salah, Raed 257, 273
Saleh, Yassin al Haj 200-211
Salt, Jeremy 68, 86, 166, 196, 333, 340, 347
Sammonds, Neil 173
Sanctions / economic sanctions 13, 16, 34-53, 70, 266, 318, 324, 329, 337-40, 343, 347, 349, 364
Sand, Shlomo 241, 275
Saraqueb /Saraqib (Idlib) 139
Sarin gas 138-144, 147-8, 151-2, 185, 187, 190, 196, 298, 333, 364, 370
Saudi Arabia 11, 13, 68-9, 73, 79, 91, 93, 96-7, 121, 129-130, 137,166, 169, 208, 221, 279-82, 289, 295-6, 299, 306, 308-9, 312, 318, 334, 336, 338, 341, 350, 362
SAVAK (Persian secret police, pre-1979) 322
Saviour complex 16
Saydnaya 176-7, 186
Seale, Patrick 68, 86, 204, 211, 298, 314
Second Israel (Kurdistan) 66-7, 84-5
Sectarian 13, 67-70, 136, 155, 160, 176, 200, 202-4, 206-7, 209, 235, 254-5, 257, 279-84, 287, 289-91, 295-6298-9, 301-2, 304, 310, 319, 322-5, 338, 341, 360-1
Self-determination 14, 16, 19, 21, 23, 25, 27-33, 56, 58, 60, 152, 154, 198, 249, 276, 351, 358, 367
Shaw, Jonathan 145
Sharon, Ariel 253, 263, 285
Shayrat airbase 121, 140, 364
Shehabi, Fares 99
Shetty, Salil 173, 196
Shi'a Muslim 14, 98-99, 279, 281-2, 284-5, 291, 296, 301-2, 305, 318-19, 322-4, 333, 335, 338, 352
Shi'a crescent 352
Singer, Peter 261
Sistan and Balouchistan (Iran) 329
Smart power 40, 49, 156, 158, 163, 172, 191, 194
Smith, Ashley 203, 205, 208, 211
Soffer, Arnon 263
Soleimani, Qassem 301, 303, 308, 310
Solidarity 15, 40, 102, 264, 277, 322, 324, 357-9, 361-3, 365-7, 370
Solmazturk, Haldun 213
Soros, George 161-4, 172, 176, 178, 197
South Africa 28, 37, 39, 52, 247, 362-3
South African Bantustans 247, 274
Special Apparatus (Muslim Brotherhood) 205
Sumud (steadfastness) 235, 247, 275
Sunni Muslim 14, 73, 85, 208, 254, 279, 281-2, 284, 291, 293-5, 301-2, 304, 310-11, 318-19, 322, 325, 341
Streicher, Julius 243-4, 275
Swedish Doctors for Human Rights (SDHR) 183, 190
Syria 11-12, 14, 16-18, 27, 34-35, 39, 41, 44, 46, 51, 54, 56, 59, 61, 64-88, 89-106, 107-134, 135-149, 150-2, 155, 158-163, 165-173, 176-198, 200-211, 212-231, 250, 254, 258, 265-6, 274-5, 278-281, 284, 286-7, 290-3, 295, 298-315, 319, 324-5, 335-6, 338-341, 343, 345, 350, 352-3, 356-8, 360-4, 366-371
Syrian American Medical Association (US NGO, SAMA) 142
Syria Campaign, The (TSC: US NGO) 153, 176, 178-9, 186-7, 198, 215-16, 218, 230
Syrian Arab Army / Syrian Army (SAA) 16, 66, 68, 70, 73, 76, 80-1, 85-6, 90-1, 98-99, 105, 109,

381

112-14, 122, 124-6, 128, 130-1, 133, 135-6, 138-40, 142-3, 146, 148, 152-3, 160, 162, 173, 176, 178, 180-2, 188, 191, 195, 203, 207, 211, 215-18, 220, 290, 295, 303, 306, 350, 364
Syrian arrivals in Europe (asylum seekers) 221-213
Syrian Center for Statistics and Research (CSR-SY) 162
Syrian Communist Parties 202-4, 208-9
Syrian Democratic Forces (SDF) 66, 75, 83, 109, 126, 301, 305, 307
Syrian Network for Human Rights (SNHR) 161-2, 173, 177-8, 196-7
Syrian Observatory for Human Rights (British agency, SOHR) 160-2, 173, 175, 178, 197

Tabiat Bridge (Nature Bridge), Tehran,,,331-2
Tabqa (Raqqa) 121
Taif Accords (Lebanon) 283, 287, 290-1, 311, 315
Takfiri (sectarian doctrine) 97, 278, 323
Talhami, Ghada Hashem 250, 275
Tarmouz, Khalef 122, 297
Tehran 12, 266, 301, 314, 324-5, 329, 331, 334, 336, 339, 341-2, 345, 348, 353
Tel Aviv 12, 67, 77, 246, 254, 255, 264, 266, 284, 293, 303, 319, 324
Terrorism /terrorists 13, 16-17, 35, 40, 49, 56, 65-67, 71-2, 74, 76-7, 79, 84, 87, 91, 93, 97, 102-5, 108-9, 111, 116-118, 121-3, 126, 131, 133-4, 142, 151-2, 155, 172, 181-2, 187-90, 200, 204-5, 215, 218, 226, 235, 246, 261, 264, 296-7, 299, 300-1, 305-6, 308, 311, 313, 317-18, 320, 324, 332, 334-8, 340-2, 344-6, 348-9, 352, 360, 362, 364, 366, 369-70
TESEV pollsters (Turkey) 203, 211, 218, 230
Tiger Forces 89
Tilley, Virginia 236, 262, 270
Tobacco Revolt (1890, Iran) 321
Toner, Mark 302
Trump, Donald 33, 40, 44-5, 67, 85, 139, 140, 147-8, 162, 165, 194, 196, 253, 272, 296, 315, 318, 326, 336, 338-9, 343-8, 364, 370
Tunisia 41, 203, 239, 285
Turkey / Turkish 65-7, 69, 71-3, 76-9, 82, 85-6, 96, 98, 101-2, 121, 137-8, 177, 185, 203, 208, 211-12, 217-18, 221-31, 241-2, 270-2, 288, 300, 308, 326-7, 340, 353, 367
Turkomen 302
Turnbull, Malcolm 117-118

Ummah (great community) 323
United Nations 27-28, 31-33, 39-41, 43, 47, 50, 52, 58, 87, 106, 129, 134-5, 148, 154, 159, 172, 186, 230, 236, 239, 249, 251, 264, 269, 273, 276, 297, 315, 326, 348-9
United Nations Charter (1945) 28, 58
United Nations Development Programme (UNDP) 320, 326-9, 331, 348
United Nations High Commissioner for Refugees (UNHCR) 148, 216-17, 219, 222, 228, 230-1
United Nations Humanitarian Affairs Office (UNOCHA) 183, 185, 198
UN General Assembly 28, 30, 32-33, 37, 47, 50, 52, 249, 252, 276
UN Security Council 30, 44-5, 58-9, 78, 86-7, 97, 102, 106, 118, 129,

382

Index

134, 138, 156-8, 176, 246, 253, 276, 315, 333, 337-9

Van der Lugt, Frans 68, 165-6, 198
Venezuela 20, 26, 33, 41, 43-4, 51-2, 56, 164-5, 186, 191, 196, 324-5, 339-40, 343, 349, 358-9, 361-2, 264, 369-70
Violations Documentation Center (VDC) 162
Vivanco, José Miguel 165

Wafd Party (Egypt) 280
Wahhabi 281-2, 305, 353
Washington 11-12, 23, 35-40, 43-6, 48, 50-1, 56, 65-9, 71-4, 79, 81, 84, 87, 93, 97, 102, 107-11, 117, 151, 155-6, 158, 160, 163-5, 169, 171, 174, 183, 189, 191, 194-5, 200, 205-6, 209, 230, 253, 263, 269, 281-2, 284, 292, 297-9, 301-3, 306, 309-12, 315, 317-19, 321, 328, 333-8, 344, 351, 353, 357, 359-62, 364, 366-7
Weizmann, Chaim 241
West Asia 11-12, 14, 17, 273, 351-3, 367
Weapons of Mass Destruction (WMD) 16, 61, 71, 135-7, 139, 141, 144, 146, 299, 307, 334, 342
West, Alan 145-7
West Asian Alliance 17, 352
West Bank (Palestine) 236, 245-7, 251, 253, 255-7, 259, 266, 270-1, 275
White Helmets, The (TWH) 92, 101, 103-6, 140-1, 145-8, 150-1, 153, 160, 175, 178, 180, 182-90, 193-4, 196-8, 215, 370
Women 22, 26, 37, 142, 145, 158, 174, 178, 181, 187, 189, 206, 216, 247, 257, 274, 322, 329-31, 344-5, 347
World Health Organization (WHO) 34

Yalon, Moshe 74
Yarmouk 66
Yavuz, Celalettin 213
Yehoshua, A.B. 258-9, 277
Yemen 11, 39, 41, 78, 85, 129, 242, 319, 338, 341, 352-3
Yinon Plan (1982) 245, 277
YPG (Kurdish) 181, 216, 301
Yugoslavia 138, 155, 194, 279

Zabadani 99
Zakharova, Maria 123, 177, 195
Zionism / zionist 12, 17, 234-41, 243-5, 247, 249-54, 257-9, 262-5, 271, 273, 275, 277, 281, 287, 289, 291, 304, 317, 324-5, 337, 341, 352-3

383